The Globetrotter

THE GLOBETROTTER

Victorian Excursions in India, China and Japan

Amy Miller

First published in 2019 by
The British Library
96 Euston Road
London NW1 2DB

Text © Amy Miller 2019
All images © British Library Board
and other named copyright holders 2019

ISBN: 978 0 7123 5258 1

Cataloguing in Publication Data
A catalogue record for this publication
is available from the British Library

Designed by Chris Benfield
Picture research by Sally Nicholls
Printed and bound by Bell & Bain, Scotland

BACK COVER: from Frank Morris Jonas,
Netsuké, 1928.
ENDPAPERS: adapted from Christopher Dresser,
Studies in Design, 1874–6.
FRONTISPIECE: Agra, inside the fort.
Photography by Samuel Bourne, 1863–5.

CONTENTS

INTRODUCTION

In 1872, Thomas Cook (1808–92) offered an 'Around the World Tour'. It was a timely offer, as access to new tourist destinations in the East came at a time when the Franco-Prussian War (1870–1) curtailed travel to parts of the Continent. This was part of a wider, long-standing aspiration to extend leisure travel beyond the European Continent and the Grand Tour, which was undertaken from the mid-seventeenth century, originally focusing on Italy but later comprising Italy, France, Switzerland and the Rhine. In January 1859, *The London Times* reviewer of John Murray's *A Handbook for India* noted that 'after conducting travellers and tourists over the whole of Europe, Mr. Murray has extended his valuable guide to the East ... a tour in India need scarcely occupy much more time than one in Russia'. The author proposed that a return trip, including sightseeing, might be achieved in just nine weeks, making it clear that the East, as represented by India, was now just as close as more exotic parts of Europe. This ambition came to fruition a decade later, when the Suez Canal officially opened in November 1869. The new route provided access to the East and became part of the network of railways and shipping lines.

This influx of new leisure tourists at Eastern ports, dubbed 'globe-trotters', did not go unnoticed: Maria Hay Murray Mitchell (1820–1907), wife of missionary John Murray Mitchell (1815–1904), wrote of her encounter in Madras with 'three young-looking lords, who are "doing" the East, they say; India, China and Japan being now quite included in the "grand tour"'.[1]

These three countries are what is generally signified by the 'East' in the context of the globetrotters. Globetrotting began in earnest in the 1870s; by the early 1880s, however, the identity of the globetrotter increasingly changed from the groups of wealthy young men, for example the 'young-looking lords' encountered by Mitchell, to women and family parties. Travelling around the world became available to anyone with the means to afford it. Globetrotters were a cultural phenomenon; they

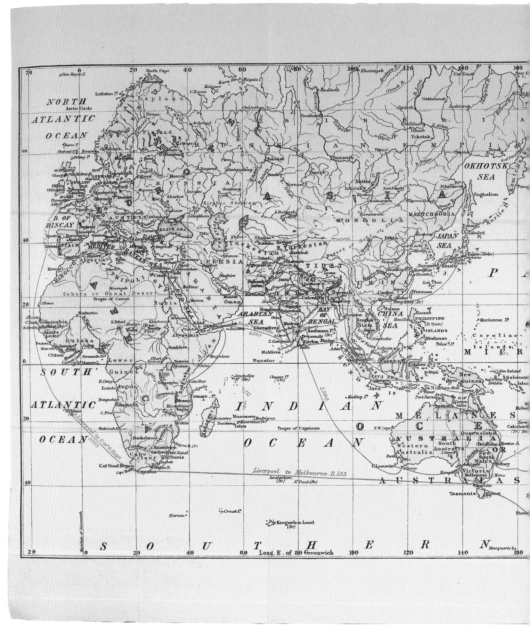

◄ PAGE 8: The Suez Canal at Port Said, deemed the first Eastern port
for those travelling on to India via the old Overland Route, c.1890–1910.

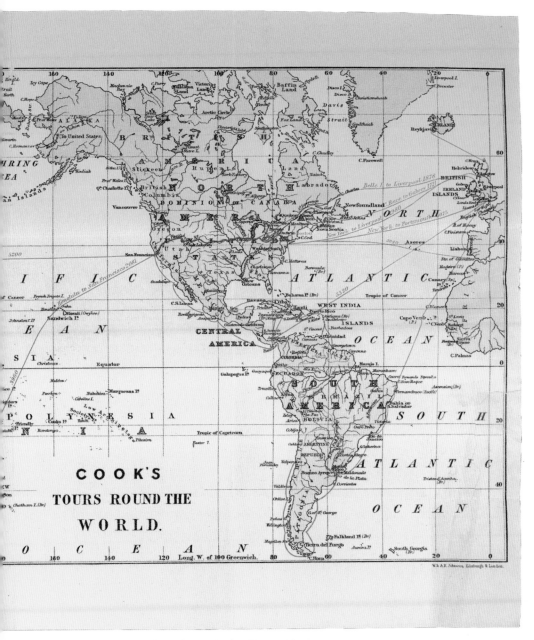

▲ ABOVE: Map from *Cook's Indian Tours*, 1881. The number of routes to India indicates the popularity of the Eastern tour.

held a unique place on the edges of politics and trade but at the centre of technological change and globalisation, adeptly exploiting these networks to access cultural encounters. Their published accounts, the photographs with which they illustrated them and the objects they collected shaped Victorian perceptions about the East and forged an enduring set of tropes still used by the media today.

WHO WERE THE GLOBETROTTERS?

The globetrotters were, above all, a type of traveller formed as a result of the technological advances of steampower and engineering that allowed for a network of railways and shipping to connect the world. As Jules Verne noted in his 1873 novel, *Around the World in 80 Days*, 'the world is smaller, because we can now travel around it ten times faster than a hundred years ago'.[2] The development of routes eastwards – such as the Overland Route, which was expanded in the 1830s – sent travellers east via Suez instead of the Cape of Good Hope, reducing the journey from six months to nine weeks, but it was expensive. In 1869, the Suez Canal opened, further cutting time spent traversing between Britain and the Indian Ocean. One of the early globetrotters to go through the Suez Canal, Arthur Drummond Carlisle (1847–1929), reported only a month's travel between Southampton and the Ceylonese port of Galle in 1870. The new ease of access that the expansion of these technologies engendered meant that not only were the British colonies, with their mercantile and military concerns, effectively nearer to home, but also the world itself might be circled in a matter of months.

Carlisle (travelled 1870–1) had graduated from Trinity College, Cambridge, shortly before his World Tour. His account, *Round the World in 1870*, was published in 1872, the same year he took up the post as Assistant Master at Repton School. Later that year he began teaching at Haileybury College, long associated with the education of British imperial officials. His journey was merely the beginning of what would become a trend; just as Carlisle returned home in 1871, Egerton Laird (1848–1912) set out from Birkenhead. Laird completed his World Tour in 1874, and was the first to use the term globetrotter in his account, *The Rambles of a Globe Trotter* (1875). Laird's self-designation as a globetrotter, like his choice of the term 'rambles' to describe his journey, was knowingly self-deprecating. It indicated a traveller who was, at best, amateur, and at worst, shallow. Laird clearly displayed his awareness of the connotation of the term when he wrote: 'I am afraid that if I were asked what my

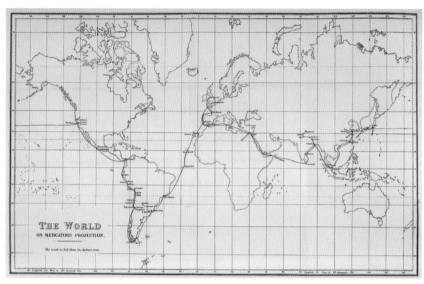

Map of Arthur Drummond Carlisle's 1870 World Tour, which followed the Overland Route, through the Suez Canal, to India.

occupation was, I could only say, a "Globe Trotter" in search of "the Elixir of Life" ... or any other visionary article'.[3] Laird epitomised what would become the caricature of the globetrotter: he was the son of a wealthy shipbuilder from Birkenhead, who would inherit £20,000 three years after he embarked on his World Tour, which financed his further travels. Yet, beneath his knowing self-satire, Laird's narrative was among the most insightful, indicating an understanding of political and social tropes and attempting, as far as was possible, to engage with other cultures. Despite popular perceptions of globetrotters as superficial travellers, Laird demonstrated that they were, in fact, active social agents.

Unlike Laird, most globetrotters sought to distance themselves from the much despised 'Cook's' tourists who had, it was felt, flooded the European Continent and tarnished the social exclusivity of the Grand Tour. Cook & Son opened the European Continent to the package tour, characterised by herds of lower-class tourists with little cultural sensibility, the slaves of timetables and guidebooks, who were unable to fully appreciate the finer points of travel. One of the draws of globetrotting was the social prestige that was potentially conferred from a World Tour, particularly an Eastern tour that gave travellers access to the colonial elite in India, maharajahs, mandarins and the Meiji Emperor's (r.1867–1912) court in Japan. The majority of nineteenth-century globetrotters were

financially elite, possessing the funds required for a global journey that
took, at the very least, up to a year, but often lasted several.* Very few
actual globetrotters were formally part of aristocratic circles, however,
thus the World Tour was a means of gaining unofficial ennoblement. Both
Carew Davies Gilbert (travelled 1877–8) and Charles James Lucas (travelled 1877–9, hereafter referred to as Charles Lucas) were young men
whose families occupied the ranks of the upper middle class in Britain.
Lucas (1853–1928) was the son of the builder and engineer, Charles
Thomas Lucas (1820–95), whose firm built such landmarks as the Royal
Albert Hall (1871) and Alexandra Palace (1873). Gilbert (1852–1913) was
an only child of landed gentry, who owned properties in Sussex and Corn-
wall, and sought to socially distinguish himself on this global tour. He also
noted in a letter to his mother, written in Hong Kong in 1877, the increasing ubiquity of these new travellers: 'we have met several pleasant Globe
Trotters, but it is a very common occupation now'.[4]

As groups of wealthy young men gave way to couples and family parties
in the 1880s, the number and type of travellers increased, and so too did
their cultural reach. Annie and Merton Russell-Cotes (travelled 1884–6)
were engaged in the hotel trade. They owned and operated the Royal Bath
Hotel in Bournemouth and Merton (1835–1921) was given the mayoralty of
the town in 1894. Their near contemporary in travel, Percy Powell-Cotton
(travelled 1889–91), was the eldest son in a family that had a long association with the East India Company. He was born in Margate and divided his
time between London and, as a teenager, Quex Park, the estate his father
purchased in Birchington, Kent. Both the Russell-Coteses and Powell-Cotton would create their own museums with objects gathered on their World
Tours forming part of the founding collections.

Frederick Diodati Thompson (travelled 1891–3) was a wealthy American
globetrotter. An elite member of New York society, he also belonged to
the Knickerbocker and Union Clubs, the Sons of the Revolution, and the
Society of Colonial Wars, and was a trustee of the New York Genealogical
Society. Thompson's published account of his World Tour, *In the Track
of the Sun: Readings from the Diary of a Globe Trotter* (1893), was used by
the novelist James Joyce as an additional feature in his own work, *Ulysses*
(first serialised 1918–20). While structured around the themes in Homer's

---

* Arthur Drummond Carlisle travelled for just over twelve months, Egerton Laird
spent just under two years on his travels and Annie and Merton Russell-Cotes
travelled from 1884–6.

Colonel Elphinstone and the author on the Maharajah's elephant.

Photograph from *In the Track of the Sun,* 1893. The Maharajah of Jaipur cooperated with Thomas Cook to offer tourists elephant rides to the Amber Fort, allowing them to aspire to the elite society of the Raj.

epic poem the *Odyssey*, Joyce brought the idea of wandering the globe up to date by including references to Thompson's memoir of his travels as Leopold Bloom navigates Dublin, comparing it to Thompson's circumnavigation of the world.

Nancy Dearmer (travelled 1916–19) had financial resources other than family wealth that allowed her global travel. She visited India in 1916 on her wedding trip. Her new husband (she was his second wife), Percy Dearmer, was a renowned vicar later known for working with composer Ralph Vaughan Williams on the hymnal *Songs of Praise* (1926) and for broadcasting a programme of the same name on BBC radio from 1933–6. The Dearmers were able to afford a lavish wedding trip because Percy arranged a lecture tour with the YMCA, which paid for all travel expenses and accommodation as long as he had a lecture scheduled. For globetrotters like the Dearmers, new ways beyond family wealth were employed as a means to experience the World Tour.

CONJURING THE EAST

The published narratives and collections of globetrotters literally presented the East (as India, China and Japan) to their readership. There

Illustration by Edward Corbould (1815–1905) from an 1842 edition of *Lalla Rookh*. Thomas Moore's Romantic epic poem gave a Byronic dimension to a tour of the East.

Kinkaku-ji (the Golden Pavilion), Kyoto, from Charles Lucas's album. This was originally the residence of the Shogun Ashikaga Yoshimitsu (1358–1408) and became a temple after his death.

were three key elements to the vision of the East they created: Romantic Orientalism, the authentic, and cosmopolitanism. Romantic Orientalism drew on the Romantic sublime, a way of seeing that was part of the early nineteenth-century European Grand Tour. Initially defined by Edmund Burke in his *Philosophical Enquiry* (1757), the Romantic sublime excited feelings of awe and terror, conveyed through the experience of nature. In the late eighteenth and early nineteenth century, the Grand Tour to Europe was extended beyond the ancient, medieval and Renaissance glories of Rome, Venice and Florence, to take in the sublime spectacle of the Alps and the Rhine River. The Romantic poets Lord Byron and Percy Bysshe Shelley, among others, captured the awe-inducing power of these landscapes as well as the historical beauties of Italy.

British Grand Tourists to the European Continent during the long eighteenth century designated the Italian cities of Florence, Rome, Naples and Venice with certain identities that were characterised by specific sites and experiences. Globetrotting leisure tourists then used the language and imagery of the European Grand Tour to communicate the significance of their own experiences and create identities for Eastern sites. For instance, while sailing through the Indian Ocean, Laird not only mused on the peaceful scene but also quoted Byron's *The Siege of Corinth* (1816), referencing the 'shining isles of light'. In so doing, Laird conveyed a more modern version of a culturally elite global tour. Sometimes, this view was combined with an imperialist outlook that reinforced the way in which world travel was buttressed by the infrastructure of the British Empire. In India, for example, Thomas Cook's 1885 *Indian Tours* recommended a boat trip on the Brahmaputra River, designated the 'Rhine of India', which would take in the plantations of Assam, cultivated to produce tea for a British market.

This gaze, entrenched in the Romantic sublime – and its darker side, the Gothic – while linked to the Grand Tour, was also tied to Orientalism. It was a way of seeing that characterised the East as a place of lush exoticism imbued with a degree of the supernatural, as conveyed in the opiate dreams of Samuel Taylor Coleridge's *Kubla Khan* (1816). Thomas Moore's epic poem *Lalla Rookh* (1817) cast Persian and Kashmiri landscapes in a Byronic style, creating a sense of place charged with Romantic sensibility. Globetrotters were aware of these associations and employed them in their own travel accounts. For example, Robert Nicholas Fowler quoted a verse from *Lalla Rookh* to describe his own moonlight walk through the Japanese city of Kyoto in 1877.[5] The application of a poetic description of

Kashmir to Kyoto, two very different cultures, highlights the question of what exactly Romantic Orientalism signified for globetrotters. This use of older imagery applied across Eastern cultures further contributed to the trope that globetrotters were superficial travellers, who were unable to differentiate between India, China and Japan, seeing them instead as interchangeable.

Edward Said reconceptualised Orientalism in his 1978 publication of the same name. Rather than the Romantic sublime, he proposed a more contentious way of looking at the East, in which Western travellers defined the East and Eastern residents. Globetrotters drew on older definitions and images of the East (as India, China and Japan) to inform the early stages of their travels. But their tour was not about them defining other cultures and creating an identity for them. Instead, through their travels and encounters, globetrotters challenged many of the prevalent images that circulated at home. They replaced these images with what they believed was an authentic (non-Westernised) representation of these cultures, created through social engagement and immersive cultural experiences. What made their global tour so important was not just how they observed local customs and habits in mosques, temples, markets and bazaars, but also how social interaction with individuals transformed a merely touristic experience into what they felt was an authentic one.

This happened in a number of ways: through social networks, dining in local restaurants and shopping in the markets and bazaars. However, there were often unexpected encounters as well. Laird wrote of his hotel room being overrun by a group of local Japanese 'swells', or fashionable men, eager to make his acquaintance. What he first thought would be a visit of perhaps half an hour extended to more than two hours. He noted in a letter to his sister that they 'watched us intently eating our dinners, and when I began to write, looked over me so closely that all mistakes in writing must be forgiven'.[6]

These experiences were represented in globetrotters' collections: the objects that they purchased abroad were a way of documenting, visually and materially, what was ultimately an ephemeral experience. Much of what they brought back – Kashmiri shawls from India, porcelains and carved ivories from China, and Japanese novelties – was already available in the British markets because of Britain's extensive trading networks. However, the difference between purchasing a Kashmir shawl at Liberty in London and buying one in India was, as Laird noted in a letter to his

'Shanghai. A Public Conveyance', from Egerton Laird's *The Rambles of a Globe Trotter*, 1875. The 'wheelbarrow', a common sight in Chinese cities, was also a popular souvenir. Percy Powell-Cotton collected carved wooden figurines of the wheelbarrow.

sister on his first impressions of Delhi: 'the barbaric splendour imparted to it by the native swells ... enveloped in the most lovely cashmere shawls'.[7] Such shawls were something of which his sister would most certainly have been aware, since they were a trading staple between Britain and India from the late eighteenth century. In Britain, the shawl was a luxury object indicative of social status and gentility. However, Laird stripped the shawl of its genteel identity and included it as part of the display of 'barbaric splendour' that he witnessed and that, for him, defined India. He also made what was a well-known object, with an exotic history, exotic again, by noting that it was the fashionable Indian men who wore the shawls not, as in Britain, the women. In this way, globetrotters took what was familiar and, by placing it back into its more exotic, Eastern context for their readers, used it to represent not only their personal experiences, but also turned these objects into emblems of cultural encounter.

This consumption of cultural difference was at the heart of globetrotting experiences, which represented a growing sense of cosmopolitanism. Like the technological innovations and networks that dominated the

Stereographic photographs by Underwood and Underwood, *c.*1900, showing the Bund and Nankow Roads in Shanghai, a city of cosmopolitan encounters.

latter part of the nineteenth century, cosmopolitanism was a defining element of the globetrotter. It was about the pleasure gained from consuming things that were different, such as unusual cuisine, or interacting with people from different cultures. However, many of the globetrotters' encounters took place in cosmopolitan port cities, for example Shanghai, which were a complex mix of cultures that almost threatened to render them as 'non-places', as there was not a single clear-cut cultural identity.[8] For globetrotters, the latest Western amenities in hotels and restaurants were counterbalanced by a desire to seek and experience what they felt to be authentic local culture. For example, Laird wrote of a train journey from Yokohama to Tokyo in 1872 that 'it seems curious going with the iron horse to the capital of the Mikado'.[9] That same Western technology that allowed him to 'trot' around the world with such ease was not entirely welcome when it threatened his experience of an authentic Japan.

Cosmopolitanism was also underpinned politically by British Liberalism, with its emphasis on the ideas of individual liberty and the economics of free trade: the free market and unrestricted competition. John Stuart Mill's essay *On Liberty* (1859) advocated the freedom of individual choice. At home in Britain, this was put into practice in the domestic interior, where the display of Eastern objects was part of the popular Aesthetic Movement (1868–1914). Liberalism and cosmopolitanism also informed much of British economic engagement with the East, especially Japan. A key component of Aesthetic interiors were 'Oriental' designs and art objects that included Indian textiles, Chinese porcelains and Japanese ivories. However, objects incorporated into these interiors, such as the Kashmir shawl, often evoked conflicting views of the East. The shawl was both a means of showing the genius of Indian craftsmanship and its degradation as it was increasingly diluted through Western influences, in which globetrotters themselves played a role. The relationship between politics, trade and culture is crucial in considering the East that globetrotters conjured through their own personal experiences.

THE EAST OF INDIA, CHINA AND JAPAN

Globetrotters' expectations were shaped before they set off on their travels. One of the defining cultural events at home, the industrial exhibitions, presented a global vision of imperial expansion that influenced travellers' ideas of the world they would encounter. The inaugural event was the Great Exhibition of the Works of Industry of All Nations, which opened in 1851. It was the brainchild of Queen Victoria's husband, Prince Albert, and was staged in London's Hyde Park, in Joseph Paxton's specially-designed glass and iron structure known as the Crystal Palace.

Front cover to the song score for 'The High-Art Maiden', 1881. The elements of the East are incorporated into the Aesthetic interior: Indian peacock feathers, Japanese fans and Chinese blue and white porcelain.

The aim of the Exhibition was to promote British industrial might and technological innovation on an international stage. The displays of the Indian Court, organised by the East India Company, included Indian products and Kashmir shawls, as well as the trappings of princely splendour embodied in the centrepiece of the Court. This took the form of an elaborate tent, in which stood an ivory throne encrusted with precious stones, presented to Queen Victoria by the Maharajah of Travancore. By contrast, China was represented by a much smaller display of the commodities of trade, although, like the Indian exhibits, many of the items were submitted by British merchants, in this case those resident in the Chinese treaty ports. The first dedicated display of Japanese objects came in the International Exhibition of 1862 in London. Like the Chinese displays of 1851, it belonged to a Westerner, the British diplomat Sir Rutherford Alcock (1809–97). The Japanese government only began actively engaging in international exhibitions in the dying years of the Tokugawa Shogunate, in the late 1860s. These earlier displays were significant, however; the Alcock collection, for example, influenced the work of designer Christopher Dresser (1834–1904) who travelled to Japan in 1876–7 at the invitation of the Meiji government to advise on art manufactures. They also served to familiarise British audiences with the

The first International Exhibition, 1862, in which Japan participated. The displays were organised by Sir Rutherford Alcock and featured his own collections. From *The Illustrated London News*, 1862.

The ivory throne, presented by the Maharajah of Travancore to Queen Victoria, was a centrepiece of princely splendour at the Great Exhibition. From *Dickinson's Comprehensive Pictures of the Great Exhibition of 1851*, 1854.

The Chinese displays at the Great Exhibition were largely put together by Western merchants resident in China. From *Dickinson's Comprehensive Pictures of the Great Exhibition of 1851*, 1854.

material culture of India, China and Japan, and visually reinforce ideas of cultural and political difference between them: India was located as part of the Empire, while China and Japan occupied places on the edges of British imperialism.

Although the Crystal Palace showcased Britain's global reach, particularly with regard to India, all was not as secure as the displays implied. Six years later, the 1857 Rebellion, or the Indian Mutiny, which ultimately brought parts of India under Crown rule, created a new construction of India in the British imagination: a country that was both imperially dominated and innately untrustworthy. Although the Mutiny occurred just over a decade before the first globetrotters sailed through the Suez Canal, bound for Bombay, its events cast a long shadow and influenced tourists' expectations and itineraries. For example, the Mutiny sites of Cawnpore and Lucknow were among the most visited in India, made notorious through news reports and lurid popular novels. The experiences that globetrotters had of viewing these sites, and being told by their guides the narrative of the events that unfolded there, had an impact on how they perceived India and engaged with local populations.

Just as India was defined for nineteenth-century travellers by the events of 1857, so too was China defined by the Qing government's opposition to British demands for greater trade access, which led to the Opium Wars (1839–42; 1856–60). The Opium Wars, or First and Second China Wars, were the outcome of the British smuggling opium into China in exchange for silver to pay for Chinese trade goods. While addiction to the drug pre-dated British trade, numbers rose alarmingly due to the sheer volume flooding the country. A high-ranking Chinese official, Commissioner Lin, famously confiscated and destroyed one cargo of opium, creating a situation that escalated tensions, which in turn led to the military action of the First Opium War. The outcome, a British victory, demonstrated British military strength, and the Treaty of Nanking (1842) gave Britain greater access to Chinese ports and the lease of Hong Kong. For China, the defeat exposed military weaknesses and political vulnerabilities, making the country susceptible to imperial demands from other Western powers. In the period between the First and Second Opium Wars, the liberal politician Mill noted that China had visibly declined from its once illustrious past, and if it were to be 'further improved ... it must be by foreigners'.[10]

The Second Opium War culminated in the destruction of the Old Summer Palace or Yuanmingyuan. The burning and looting of the

Suttee Chowra Ghat, where Nana Sahib placed his victims in boats and then shot at them as the boats floated down the river.

We brought an aloe from these steps and now have several off-shoots from it.

◄ PREVIOUS PAGE: The Japanese displays at the International Exhibition of 1862 had a long-standing impact. Christopher Dresser's own design work was influenced by the exhibits. From *Studies in Design*, 1874–6. ▲ ABOVE: The 'Massacre Ghat' in Cawnpore, a site of the Indian Mutiny where travellers could reflect on the events that brought India under Crown rule. From Merton Russell-Cotes's *Home and Abroad*, 1921.

building, ordered by Lord Elgin in response to the kidnapping and torture of British envoys and their escort (two of whom subsequently died), was meant to demonstrate to the Chinese what European powers could do. The event itself led not only to the end of the Second Opium War, but also to the establishment of legations in Peking and the opening of further treaty ports. It had an irrevocable impact on British perceptions of China at home as the country went from being regarded as a celestial empire to one that was backward. As with India, cultural encounters were imbued with a degree of distrust. Similarly, both countries were respected for their illustrious pasts, seen in places such as the abandoned Mughal palace of Fatehpur Sikri or the Ming Tombs complex of Chinese emperors. At the same time, it was noted that these ancient, albeit authentic sites were in a state of decay indicative of the inefficiency of native rule.

These parallels notwithstanding, we must also consider the differences in the way that globetrotters experienced India and China, as their encounter would have been comparative.

Late nineteenth-century travellers to Japan still viewed the country as a cultural novelty, despite it having been open to British trade since the late 1850s. This made it a particularly desirable destination. Japan was going through a period of political and social upheaval triggered by the opening of the country to Western trade by the American Commodore Matthew Perry in 1854. Known retrospectively as the Bakumatsu period (1854–68), it was a time of decline for the military government of the Tokugawa Shogunate that had been in power since the early seventeenth century. The Bakumatsu period would culminate in the restoration of the Emperor as the head of government. The period was characterised by both anti- and pro-Western factionalism within the government, as the political clout of the shogun decreased and the influence of the Emperor and his court rose. This was spurred on by the 'unequal treaties' imposed

▲ ABOVE: The ruined palace and city of Fatehpur Sikri, founded in the mid-sixteenth century by the Mughal Emperor Akbar and abandoned in the early seventeenth century. From Charles Lucas's albums. ▶ OVERLEAF: Hand-tinted photograph created by a Japanese photographer. This was an expensive souvenir of Japan that also communicated an idealised vision of the experience of the country. From the studio of Kusakabe Kimbei, c.1870s–1890s.

on Japan by the West, as first the Americans and, in 1856, the British, opened specific Japanese ports to Western trade and occupation. At this time, these included Tokyo, Kobe, Nagasaki, Niigata and Yokohama. In terms of a political relationship with the West, Japan, like China, only had treaty ports and enclaves of British residents, thus making it part of an informal empire unlike the formal Empire of the Raj experienced in India. The Boshin War (1868–9) marked the definitive end of the Bakumatsu with the restoration of the Emperor, who took the name Meiji, meaning 'Enlightened Rule'.

The newly restored Emperor and his government instituted sweeping reforms of what was essentially a feudal system, promoting technological development in the form of an expanding railway, while at the same time establishing a cohesive national identity based on traditional culture. For example, the tea ceremony, previously the preserve of elite court culture, was promoted as a means for all classes to express their 'Japanese-ness'.[11] This joining of tradition and technology found its outlet in places like Kusakabe Kimbei's (1841–1934) photography studio in Yokohama. This was a cosmopolitan space where globetrotters and locals could mix, considering and purchasing Kimbei's images of traditional geisha captured on a new technology. These images would come to represent a new Japan, created by the Japanese and consumed by globetrotters. Travellers, however, went in search of a Japan that was untouched by Western influences. This was the ideal of 'Old Japan', represented by the samurai and valorised in diplomat and writer A. B. Mitford's (1837–1916) bestselling *Tales of Old Japan* (1871). It was a Japan that, as the Meiji government adopted Western customs and technology, was felt to be disappearing almost overnight. Instead of Old Japan, globetrotters who arrived in the treaty ports encountered a juxtaposition of old and new that defined Meiji Japan.

This book explores certain themes of the globetrotting experience that work together not only to create an idea of the World Tour, but also to give a sense of how culturally significant it was for those at home. The first chapter, 'Guidebooks and Networks', considers how globetrotters exploited the technological infrastructure, created through political expansion, of railways, steamships and the post, to 'trot' around the globe. The travellers' handbooks published by John Murray and Thomas Cook, among others, helped globetrotters to connect these web-like schedules of shipping and railway networks. The handbooks, which were published in separate volumes for each country of the East – India, China

and Japan – offered a means not only of navigating the world, but of accessing significant local experiences that defined each country.

'Authentic Spaces' contemplates how globetrotters accessed what they deemed to be authentic. This included a series of encounters with what they believed to be the unchanged landscape as well as ancient temples and iconic cultural sites. These spaces and experiences were unique to each country: for example, the holy city of Benares on the sacred Ganges, with its gilded Hindu temples and burning ghats, was an enduring image of India. The quasi-domestic spaces of Chinese inns and Japanese teahouses provided a degree of immersion in daily life. This chapter also considers the darker side of tourism and how that played out in key locations, such as the floating brothels of Canton, which were the ultimate in immersion and cultural confrontation.

'Consuming the East' examines how India, China and Japan were defined and differentiated through food and culinary encounters. Dining, and its accompanying modes and manners, played a key role in the quest for the authentic. To eat curry in India, or view the infamous cat and dog restaurants in Canton, was a means of literally consuming the East; in some cases, breaking Western food taboos was part of the lure. What imbued food with such significance was not simply that tourists consumed local food, but that they did so with local populations, as part of social engagement. These shared meals were important in initiating social bonds and placed tourists in the roles of active social agents, who presented more nuanced experiences in their accounts.

The bazaars, markets and curio shops of India, China and Japan were a social experience, and the objects for which tourists negotiated and then purchased provided them with a material representation of their travels. 'Collecting the East' looks at how the objects that globetrotters collected were a means of distinguishing themselves from the mere role of common tourists, as discerning connoisseurs. In some cases, special commissions from local craftsman presented a refined version of the Eastern experience. Beyond the excitement of the bazaar, souvenirs were also acquired in photographers' studios. These provided a cosmopolitan, multicultural space in which to exchange news and recommend sites and encounters.

The conclusion, 'Coming Home', considers how the collections and accounts of a World Tour were presented to the public, and how they brought something new to readers: a global East that, notwithstanding its Orientalist lens, distinguished between Asian cultures. Globetrotters noted the differences between India, China and Japan, and chronicled a journey of distinct cultures and customs that both challenged and confirmed public perceptions of what constituted an authentic East. In addition to conjuring their own version through their experiences and the objects that they brought home, globetrotters also charted a journey of self-transformation through travel.

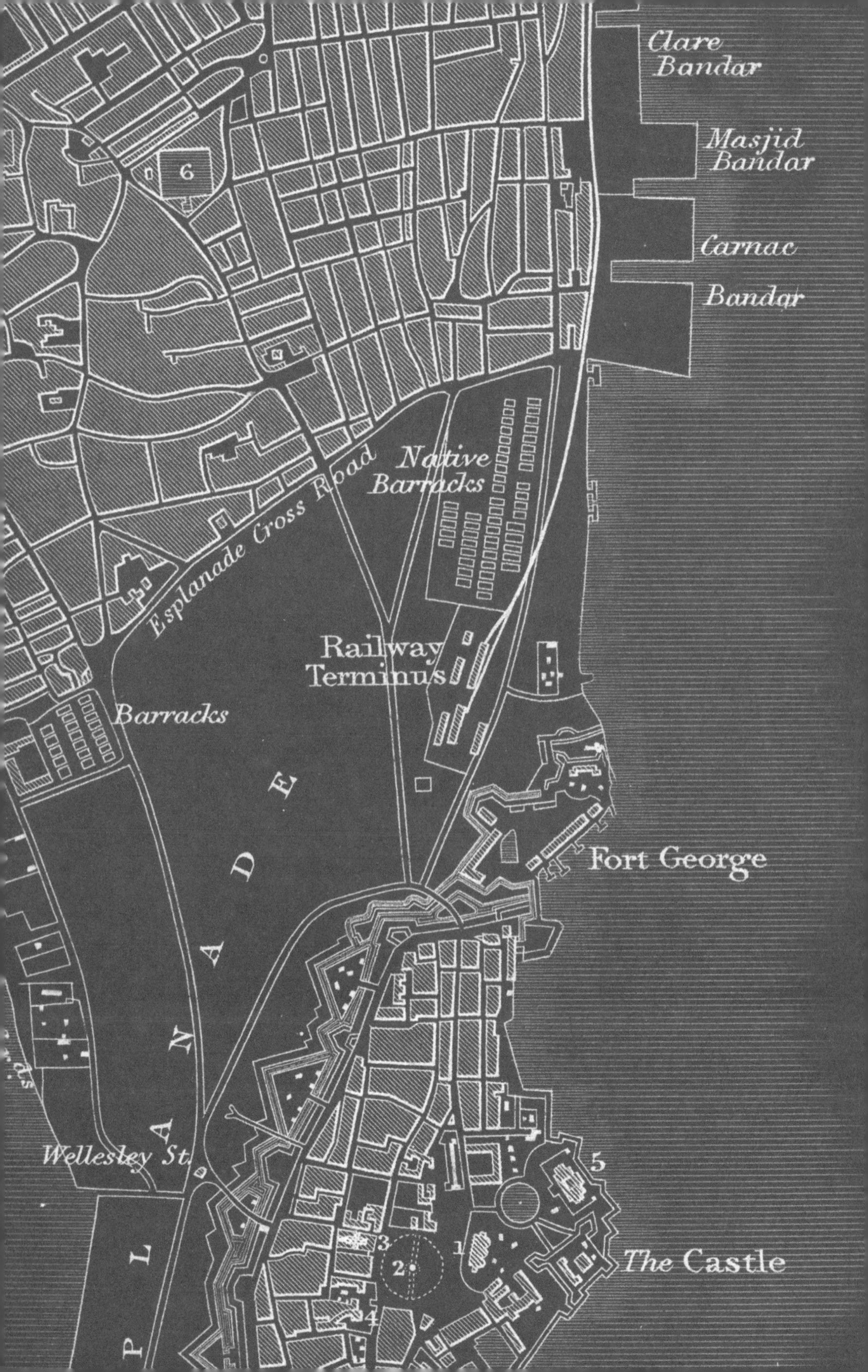

Clare
Bandar

Masjid
Bandar

Carnac

Bandar

6

Native
Barracks

Esplanade Cross Road

Railway
Terminus

Barracks

E

S

P

L

A

N

A

D

E

Fort George

5

Wellesley St.

The Castle

3

2

1

4

P

L

A

N

A

D

E

1 GUIDEBOOKS AND NETWORKS

In January 1890, twenty-four-year-old Percy Powell-Cotton (1866–1940) recorded a day spent in the Indian city of Agra in his travel journal. Not only was Agra the location of the Taj Mahal, among the most visited sites in India, but it was also home to both maharajahs and upper-class colonial society. Powell-Cotton's journal shows that he attempted to experience it all within a short space of time:

> 8.30 coffee, hair cut, break, round to Club ... called on Woodburn, wrote, tiff[in], looked up trains, out with Smith to the Sta[tion] bought marble work, down to Taj back, wrote, din[ner], pack, dress, dropped Aku [local servant employed by Powell-Cotton] and lug[gage] at Sta[tion] drove to ... Ball given by Maharajah of Bhurtpore [Bharat-pur] ... late, so stopped at 1 gate but managed tother [*sic*], grounds illum[inated] hundreds pop lanterns, about 200 guests, 2 dancing rooms ... A.1. show. Drove to Sta[tion] 3am train to Delhi changing at Tundlu, got some sleep.[1]

Taken together, Powell-Cotton's pursuits over just one day create a specific identity for India, fashioned from the activities of sightseeing and shopping that took in the iconic Taj Mahal and the inlaid marble souvenirs that copied its decorations. He hobnobbed with the society of the Raj, calling at the local club, and ended his evening with the splendour of a ball, confirming his social status by participating in a princely version of local culture. Given that his time spent in India was short, an indispensable part of Powell-Cotton's day was the use of travellers' handbooks. He consulted these to structure his time, cramming as many activities as possible into a compressed period. Produced by John Murray and Thomas Cook, these guides offered the key to experiences like those that Powell-Cotton enjoyed in India. Through suggested itineraries and railway and shipping timetables, travel guides not only helped travellers

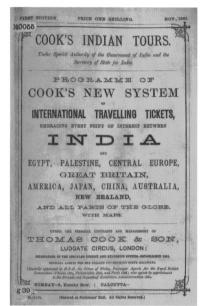
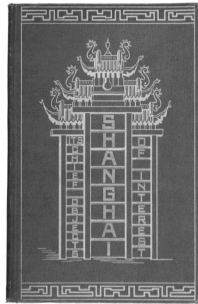

◂ PAGE 34: The Taj Mahal was an iconic experience in the sublime. Photograph by John Murray, *c.*1858. ▴ ABOVE, LEFT: Front cover of *Cook's Indian Tours*, November 1881. Thomas Cook offered tours for both residents of India touring Europe on their furloughs and globetrotters coming from Britain.
▴ ABOVE, RIGHT: Front cover of Revd C. E. Darwent's handbook, *Shanghai*, 1912. The publisher, Kelly & Walsh, was based in Shanghai and published guidebooks as well as distributing photographs from local studios.

to trot globally, but also offered them access to important social, political and historical local experiences.

A reviewer of one of Murray's many publications noted in *The Spectator* that 'two books may be said without exaggeration to form the Englishman's library – the Peerage when he is at home, Murray when he travels'.[2] This reflected a preoccupation with class but also confirmed that travel – particularly farther afield than the European Continent – enhanced status. Although Murray's *Handbooks* were stalwart publications among British travellers, the firm faced increasing competition in the latter half of the nineteenth century as rival companies published guidebooks catering for the growing numbers of travellers to the European Continent and the newly emergent market of globetrotters.[3] A separate guidebook was published for the individual countries that were encountered on the global tour and, as such, each guide constructed a very specific identity for India, China and Japan, through the sites and experiences they recommended. Further, just as globetrotters were created through rapidly

developing political and technological networks, so too were travellers'
handbooks. These books were part of the expanding print culture of
the late 1800s and brought together different strands of technological
developments that defined the century itself: they tracked the growing
networks of railways and global shipping lines. In the first half of the
nineteenth century John Murray published the majority of travel guides
to the European Continent. Thomas Cook, whose guides were part
of the tours his firm organised, later challenged him. In the East, the
supremacy of Cook and Murray as guidebook publishers was ousted by
publisher-booksellers, such as Kelly & Walsh in Shanghai, who offered
high-quality guides written by resident experts.

Not only did guidebooks shape itineraries, but they also shaped
perceptions of the East and the way in which globetrotters, rather than
being blind followers, built on these to create their own versions of the
East that were in turn brought home. Certain experiences and encounters challenged pre-existing impressions both of the East and of Britain's

Victoria Terminus Railway Station, Bombay. The railway was a means of
connecting global tourists with local experiences across India.

global role there. For example, the sites recommended in guidebooks used by British travellers were, in addition to being of cultural significance, often central to British imperial interactions. In India, both Murray's *A Handbook for India* and *Cook's Indian Tours* focused on places that represented British mercantile and political activity, such as Bombay, Madras, Calcutta and New Delhi, all large cities. These were presented in conjunction with Cawnpore and Lucknow, memorials to the 1857 Indian Mutiny that led to the imposition of Crown rule.

That guidebooks were a key to deciphering the technological networks that moved globetrotters around the East was apparent in travellers' own narratives. In November 1916, Nancy Dearmer (1889–1979) wrote to her mother noting that despite spending only a few days in Bombay, she and her new husband Percy (1867–1936) were moving on to Madurai. She described their visit to the railway station to 'book a comp't on Madras Express for Monday night and to wire … there to expect us … we bought a Murray's Guide and another little guide book'.[4] In Dearmer's letter the railway marked a point of physical access for India – its key significance for most travellers – while the guidebook offered an intellectual decoding of what she was about to see and experience.

The railway project in India began before the advent of the Raj, but its designation by Sir Rowland Macdonald Stephenson as 'Our Indian Railway' in the 1847 *Calcutta Review* made clear that it was an imperial enterprise.* The development of railways was not limited to colonial India, but occurred throughout the East at this time, albeit that China was slower than Japan to exploit the technology. In China, defeat in the Opium Wars forced the Qing government and ailing Xianfeng Emperor (r.1850–61) to grant concessions to Britain that led to the development of Hong Kong and the expansion of British enclaves in treaty ports. However, the Qing government was resistant to further attempts by British mercantile firms to build railways, regarding them as a 'foreign imposition' redolent of national humiliation at the hands of Western powers during the Opium Wars.[5] Like China, Japan also experienced treaty ports being granted to Western trade and residence as the country was 'opened', initially by American forces in 1854. For Japan, however, rapid industrialisation – particularly through the construction of railways

---

* R. M. Stephenson was an engineer and later a politician and colleague of Isambard Kingdom Brunel. He was involved in the development of a third of railways and bridges across Britain.

Dapoorie Viaduct, Bombay. The railways across the East were the most visible aspect of a web of technological expansion.

that connected the country – not only literally engineered an infrastructure, but also created a country that was stronger both economically and politically. Japan was therefore able to assert itself on a global stage and avoid the indignity suffered by China. These political and industrial changes across the East meant an increased flow of people, an established Western presence and, as a result, an expansion of English-language print culture that included colonial newspapers in India and treaty port publications in China and Japan, many of which, such as the *China Mail* and *Japan Gazette*, published their own travellers' handbooks. It was not solely under Western influence that guidebooks developed; Japanese publishers also began producing English-language handbooks for sites in China in the wake of the Second Opium War.

The choice of guidebook had a lot to say about where travellers saw themselves on the social ladder. Murray's *Handbooks*, for example, were seen by consumers as erudite volumes produced by experts for discerning travellers. Cook's tourist guides were deemed representative of the crowds of solidly middle-class tourists who spoilt the exclusivity

Palace of the Winds, Jaipur, photograph by Lala Deen Dayal, 1890s. Jaipur was a destination that elite globetrotters felt had been overrun with Cook's tourists, spoiling their own pursuit of an exclusive experience.

of the European Grand Tour. In the 1880s and 1890s, Cook's tourists increasingly encroached on the elite social circles enjoyed by wealthy globetrotters; their presence in India prompted Nora Beatrice Gardner's (1866–1944) tart comment that the city of Jaipur was 'on the route of Cook's tours, and Amber one of the happy hunting grounds of the "personally conducted" ... I have come to the conclusion that I hate compulsory sight-seeing and loathe my fellow sight-seers'.[6]

Although globetrotters were dependent on guidebooks, they did not blindly follow the advice. Much of what they wrote questioned the wisdom of *Murray's* and *Cook's* writers. Personal annotations, as well as the introduction of other texts into travellers' accounts, revealed opposing views and allowed them to connect with a number of different audiences. While guidebooks told them what to see and how to get there, globetrotters were independent visitors. They often challenged the received ideas about the meanings of the sites they visited and expressed viewpoints that disputed the idea of the East created in the guidebooks.

INDIA: RAILWAYS AND THE RAJ

In the preface to Murray's 1859 *A Handbook for India*, the author, Edward Backhouse Eastwick (1814–83), wrote of how, through the expansion of technology and steam, India and Britain were brought closer together despite their geographical distance. He noted that beyond this there existed a 'sympathy' between them that even 'the recent abortive effort to dissever the two countries' – by which he meant the Indian Mutiny (1857) – had failed to undermine.[7] From the very beginning of his *Handbook*, Eastwick clearly acknowledged the imperial relationship and the need to support it in the wake of recent events, signifying what sort of experience travellers should expect in the following pages. That Murray, renowned for his selection of experts to author his handbooks, should have chosen Eastwick was indicative of an overarching national and political need in the wake of the Indian Mutiny to create an image of a securely governed colonial possession. Eastwick himself had a long-standing connection with India: his family was involved in the British East India Company and he served in the Bombay Infantry. As a talented linguist, he translated a number of texts from Persian and Sindhi. Ill health cut his career in India short, forcing a return to Britain. In 1845, he took up the post of Professor of Hindustani at Haileybury College in Hertfordshire, an institution that was the cradle of administrators for the British Empire. During his time there he wrote *A Handbook for India*, which, like Murray's *Handbooks* for Europe, contained all the information that a traveller might require: a vocabulary of local dialects, itineraries of sites of historical interest, and shipping and railway schedules. However, one key difference between guidebooks for Europe and those that Eastwick produced for India was that he incorporated details clearly aimed at an audience of British residents of India. These included the pay scales for civil servants as well as the revenues collected in the Madras and Bombay presidencies. Although a reviewer in *The Times* suggested that *A Handbook for India* would be useful for tourists, the material provided was more relevant for a readership ready to take up long-term residence in India than for nascent globetrotters. Indicating the adaptability of travel guides when used in a colonial context, this also showed that globetrotting was not yet as established as it would become in the latter part of the century.

This confusion about for whom the guide was actually meant can also be seen in the reviews that the book received in the popular press. *The Times* felt that the guide would open the subcontinent for adventurous travellers in the same way that Murray's *Handbooks* made Europe accessible. *The Spectator* was far more critical, skewering the very knowledge that made Eastwick such an ideal author: his skill and familiarity with Eastern languages.[8] Eastwick did not use the spellings for towns and cities in India that were already familiar from the British press: for example, the

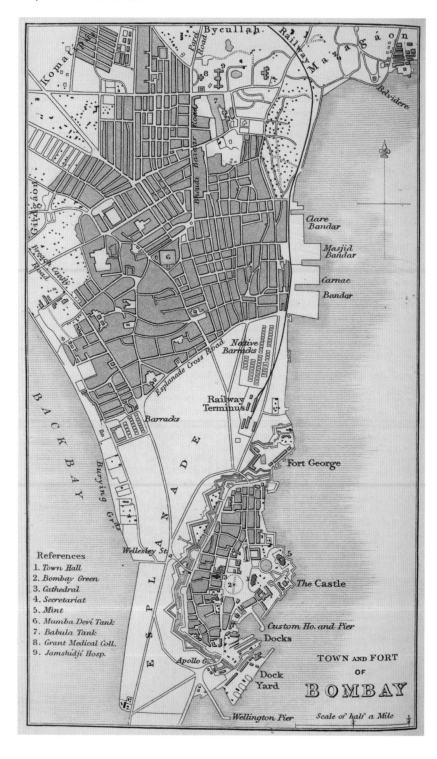

References
1. Town Hall
2. Bombay Green
3. Cathedral
4. Secretariat
5. Mint
6. Mumba Devi Tank
7. Babula Tank
8. Grant Medical Coll.
9. Jamshidji Hosp.

TOWN AND FORT
OF
BOMBAY

Scale of half a Mile

town of Cawnpore, known throughout Britain as a site of massacre in
the Indian Mutiny, was transformed to Kahnpur. Deemed more accurate
by Eastwick, this 'renaming' led *The Spectator's* reviewer to note that the
publication was produced by 'some "scholar" double-dyed in pedantry'.[9]
This gap between what was viewed as accurate knowledge and its acces-
sibility for a general readership continued, despite Eastwick's revisions to
the handbooks that included *Madras* (1879), *Bombay* (1881), *Bengal* (1882)
and *Punjab* (1883). Lord Ronald Gower (1845–1916), who made his World
Tour between 1883 and 1884, wrote of his exasperation with *A Handbook
for India*, particularly in regard to Cawnpore:

> One feels when travelling in India the want of a good guide to these
> historic scenes: the one published by Murray and written by Eastwick
> is most unsatisfactory; one is not told what is worth seeing, but only
> confused by a wearisome and endless list of places, of which the spell-
> ing alone is enough to bewilder the reader.[10]

What globetrotters wanted, according to Gower, was a guide that aligned
the experience of India with the picturesque landscapes of the European
Grand Tour, not the details of colonial administration. Gower himself
aimed to replace the hated *A Handbook for India* with his own book, *Notes
of a tour from Brindisi to Yokohama* (1885), which he requested be printed

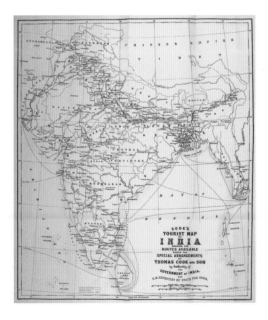

◄ OPPOSITE: Map of Bombay
from Murray's *A Handbook
for India*, 1859. Sites of
colonial administration were
prioritised in Murray's map
including the 'Town Hall',
'Secretariat' and 'Mint'.

◄ LEFT: 'Cook's Tourist Map
of India', from *Cook's Indian
Tours*, 1881, makes clear the
number of circuits and tours
available for globetrotters as
India increased in popularity
as a winter destination.

in 'pocket size' so that it would be of use to other travellers.[11] His book may have fulfilled a Romantic expectation, but it failed to inform travellers of important details such as the location of the post office, hotels and how to engage a guide.

Eastwick died in 1883, just as Murray's competitor, Thomas Cook & Son, began publishing its own guidebooks to India, *Cook's Indian Tours*, which served a tourist market that Cook himself had helped to create. Thomas Cook was brought up as a Baptist and was active in the temperance movement. His first organised excursion in July 1841 escorted 500 people from Leicester to a temperance rally in Loughborough via the Midland Counties Railway. In 1851 he arranged excursions to London to view the Great Exhibition in Hyde Park. As the decade progressed he expanded his services to excursions abroad including a circular tour of Belgium, Germany and France, followed by further expansion in the 1860s to Switzerland, Italy, Egypt and the United States. He was present, with a group of 'personally escorted' tourists, at the celebrations for the opening of the Suez Canal in 1869.[12] In 1872, he launched the first 'Round the World Tour', a 222-day trip that crossed North America via the transcontinental railway, sailed from San Francisco to Yokohama in Japan, continued by steamer to China, Singapore, Ceylon and India, reached Cairo via the Red Sea and then returned to London. Cook excited public

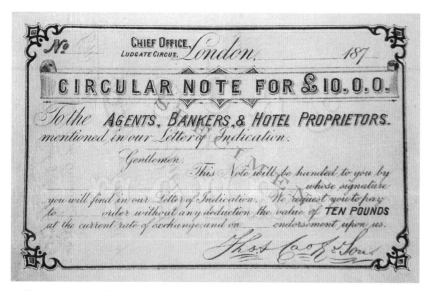

Example of the circular note. This could be used in exchange for currency and was, if not an innovation of Cook's, certainly something that the firm developed.

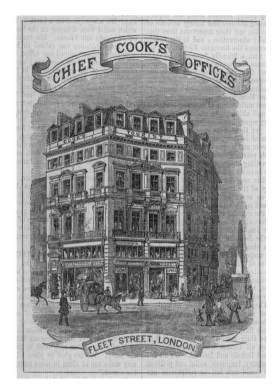

Cook's offices across the globe were not only a means of booking a tour, but they also fulfilled an important function in globetrotting networks, receiving and forwarding letters from globetrotters' families.

interest in the tour by sending regular dispatches to the newspapers in Britain, and in 1873 he published these collected letters co-authored with Dr Jabez Burns (1805–76), a fellow non-conformist, in *Letters from the Sea and from Foreign Lands*.

Adept at business, Cook aimed his World Tours not only at those interested in travelling out from London, moving east, but also at those residents in India who might wish to make a World Tour while on furlough from civil or military service and who would travel west. The impetus for this last innovation came from the Italian government, which, shortly after the Suez Canal opened, suggested to Cook that he include the Italian port Brindisi as a stopping point for travellers setting out for or returning from India rather than going directly through Suez. Cook in turn approached the British government in India offering a circular ticket that required travellers to leave from and return to the same port, progressing onwards through a series of destinations. He also issued circular notes, which allowed travellers to exchange a paper note from Thomas Cook & Son for local currency. In addition to organising Indian Tours, Thomas Cook & Son published a guidebook for residents of India

A Bombay bazaar, from Charles Lucas's album. The bazaars, markets and curio shops were places where globetrotters could engage with locals and acquire the souvenirs that documented their travels.

that presented a range of tour options to the United States and Europe based on the length of furlough. In Thomas Cook's hands the World Tour, and all its possibilities, expanded beyond simply buying a ticket at the company's Cornhill Offices in London. He created and exploited a global web of travel that meant travellers could start their World Tour from multiple locations across the globe.

The earliest edition of *Cook's Indian Tours*, from 1881, further collapsed the vast spaces of India to ten points of interest that were easily accessed by the railways. Among the ten cities and towns mentioned was Bombay, which it described as 'the head of Indian ports so far as interchange of trade with Europe is concerned'.[13] It was also generally the point of arrival in India for travellers coming through the Suez Canal. On the east coast, Calcutta was, according to *Cook's Indian Tours*, 'retained as the seat of the Vice-Regal Government of India ... the port for interchange of commerce as between Hindustan, Burmah, China and Australasia'.[14] It was the departure point for those moving on to China and the port of arrival for those travelling, as Annie Russell-Cotes (1835–1920) did in 1886, westward from San Francisco. Between these two cities, the rest of India could be accessed, including the two most visited sites in India in the latter part of the nineteenth century, Cawnpore and Lucknow, known for their roles in the Indian Mutiny of 1857.

The 'Massacre Ghat' at Cawnpore, from Charles Lucas's album. Images of the 'Massacre Ghat' were in heavy circulation among globetrotters, as they were a means of both experiencing the local and connecting it with Britain.

Lucknow, also from Charles Lucas's album. In contrast to Cawnpore, tours of the ruined Residency at Lucknow provided a more uplifting narrative of rescue.

There were a number of contributing social and political factors that led to the outbreak of the Mutiny, including the annexation of Oudh by the East India Company, civilian disquiet over taxes and the Company's misunderstanding of religious and social concerns. Of the towns involved in the uprising, Cawnpore and Lucknow were given particular focus in the British press. The cantonment at Cawnpore was under an extended siege in June 1857 for which it was unprepared. Suffering casualties and running low on supplies, the garrison surrendered to Indian leader Nana Sahib (1824–1859) on the understanding that the troops would be given safe conduct from Cawnpore. According to histories published after the event, the decision to surrender was taken by Major General Hugh Wheeler (1789–1857), who was in command of the cantonment. It was unpopular with his officers, but as he was married to an Indian woman he believed that he had a greater understanding of local culture. After boarding boats at the Satichura Ghat, the men were fired on by Nana Sahib's troops, and the women and children were taken into captivity at the nearby Bibighar (house of the women). On 15 July, with news of British forces approaching under the command of Major General Henry Havelock

Carlo Marochetti's marble angel was synonymous with Cawnpore. This photograph from Samuel Bourne's *Indian Views*, 1864, was a popular one in globetrotters' collections.

The bridge of boats was the entry point to the city of Cawnpore. Photograph by Felice Beato, 1858–1862.

(1795–1857), the women and children were killed and their bodies were thrown down a dry well near to the site. Cawnpore was captured by British troops a day later. Expecting to free captives, they discovered instead the blood-stained Bibighar and the gruesome contents of the well. Cawnpore became one of the infamous names of the Indian Mutiny; it was the subject of novels, paintings and plays, and the site of the well, with Carlo Marochetti's mourning marble angel on top, became one of the memorials to the sacrifices of Empire made by those who died at Cawnpore, specifically the women and children of the cantonment. The well was completed in 1865 and attracted immediate pilgrimages in the aftermath. By comparison, Lucknow was besieged for a longer period and relieved twice by British troops (Havelock died from dysentery during the second siege) before the Residency was finally evacuated. Lives were lost, disease was rife and supplies were low. However, because Lucknow did not experience the same terrible fate as Cawnpore, travellers were encouraged to visit Cawnpore first, followed by Lucknow, so that they might finish their tour on the more uplifting narrative of British victory.

Early globetrotter Arthur Drummond Carlisle noted as he journeyed onwards from Cawnpore to Lucknow in 1870 that it was 'only a distance of forty-seven miles, which we traverse by rail in two hours and a half, after crossing the Ganges by the Cawnpore bridge of boats. Would that in

1857 the transit between the two places had been as easy!'[15] The impact of the Mutiny in British minds engendered anxieties that found an outlet in a number of ways, including vital railway building projects as a means of connecting India. The railways brought isolated areas closer to centres of colonial administration. By criss-crossing the country, the railways also bound the states of India together and through these new connections made British India a political entity.

That the Mutiny loomed large in the British imagination was also reflected in the guidebooks, which in turn contributed to the ongoing public fascination with the sites. The entry for Cawnpore in the first edition of *Cook's Indian Tours*, which incidentally remained unaltered for the next twenty years, shows how certain sites were used to define India and its relationship to Britain. Its importance as a site of memorial was undisputed, but its significance went beyond this, as Cawnpore was given one of the longest entries of the ten key sites of interest. Further, it was the only site where a specific guide was recommended to personally escort travellers around the relatively recent ruins. On arrival in Cawnpore, the guidebook suggested that 'for the subsequent incidents and the retribution afterwards inflicted, the visitor cannot do better than ask Mr. Lee, of the Railway Hotel, to drive over the ground, and with him "fight the battle o'er again"'.[16] Joe Lee was the proprietor of the Railway Hotel, located directly next to the station; he claimed to have been a retired sergeant major and the last eyewitness to the massacres at Cawnpore. Acting in a similar capacity to Cook himself, by personally escorting visitors around the key Mutiny sites, his audiences included globetrotters and residents alike. A retired lieutenant-colonel in the Royal Army Medical Corps reminisced of Christmas spent in Cawnpore in 1882: 'at the time of our visit, the proprietor of the Railway Hotel was a Mr. Lee ... [who] accompanied us throughout the entire day, so that we had full descriptions of the horrors from a reliable eye-witness'.[17]

Lee himself wrote *The Indian Mutiny: and in Particular a Narrative of Events at Cawnpore, June and July 1857* (1893), which served as a local guidebook. Among the testimonials Lee featured in the book were those from tourists who made winter tours of India, including the writer and politician William Edward Baxter (1825–90) who travelled with his family in 1877. Baxter described his encounter with Lee in his own account, *A Winter in India* (1882): 'a very remarkable man ... was in nearly all the great battles in Scinde'.[18] In 1891, the American globetrotter Frederick Diodati Thompson (1850–1906) wrote in his diary that he was greeted at the Cawnpore railway station by 'Joseph Lee a former soldier ... one of that heroic band that entered Cawnpore with Havelock – unfortunately, two hours after the last of the English prisoners was killed by mutineers under that barbarous murderer, Nana Sahib'.[19] Joseph Lee not only presented a dramatic retelling of events, thus satisfying in part a macabre fascination with the site, but also allowed travellers to make emotional connections with the events of Cawnpore. This joining of the political and the personal meant that for many travellers Cawnpore offered the promise of a defining experience of India.

The narrative of Cawnpore that Cook's and Murray's guidebooks presented was one of British sacrifice and heroism; globetrotters themselves did not leave this view unchallenged. Most globetrotters used other writers' opinions in conjunction with their own words to convey the importance of a site, its emotional resonances or their own critical view. For example, Egerton Laird regularly referred to the account of

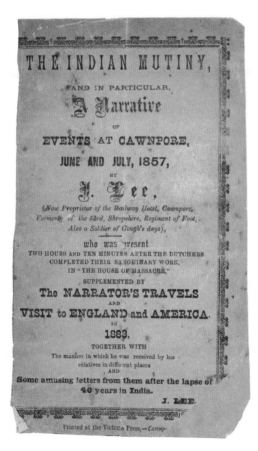

Cover of J. Lee's *The Indian Mutiny*, 1893. Joe Lee was a popular guide for the Mutiny sites of Cawnpore and his published eyewitness accounts gave travellers the chance to relive their experiences once they returned home.

aristocratic diplomat Ludovic de Beauvoir (1846–1929), *A Voyage Round the World* (1870), to corroborate his own experiences.[20] Twenty years later, Thompson quoted at length from a description of the Taj Mahal by poet, journalist and renowned Orientalist Edwin Arnold (1832–1904) to express his own emotional transports on encountering architectural perfection.[21] By using the words of others, often those who were seen as authorities on the subject, globetrotters were able to confirm and validate their own thoughts. Laird consistently incorporated other texts that couched his own reaction to iconic sites, like Cawnpore, in opposition to the expected, conventional narrative presented in travellers' handbooks. On his visit to Cawnpore, instead of merely recounting the horrors and subsequent solemn memorialisation of the site, Laird introduced another text that suggested a far more controversial interpretation of his experience. After touring the site, taking in Marochetti's marble angel over the well and noting the recently constructed foundations of the memorial church, Laird commented: 'I suppose, however, the mutineers thought they were fighting for release from a foreign power. I have not read a full account of the Mutiny, but believe a book by Trevelyan is well worth reading'.[22] Sir George Otto Trevelyan's (1838–1928) publication *Cawnpore* (1865) offered a more sympathetic view of the role of Indians in the Mutiny that, in turn, provoked outrage in the popular press. A reviewer in *The Spectator* denounced the book in a piece that was published in newspapers across Britain. Pronouncing it 'utterly valueless' he stated that Trevelyan undertook 'to represent the whole of his countrymen there, civilians excepted, as brutal oppressors of the native soil'.[23] The *Shields Daily Gazette* reprinted the review with additional commentary noting that the publication was like the political stances taken by Trevelyan as a Member of Parliament, the result of 'juvenile vanity and conceit'.[24] That Laird relied on his readership's knowledge of the contentious text allowed him to put forward what was an unpopular political opinion through another authorial voice, thereby deflecting censure. This placed his personal experience of Cawnpore outside of the expected formula of memorialisation and challenged a popular perception that globetrotters' accounts were merely cursory obvervations of a country through which they travelled at speed.

CHINESE GUIDEBOOKS: OPENING A CLOSED COUNTRY

Murray and Cook published the majority of guidebooks for India, but the Chinese market was distinctly different, and many publications for globe-

'Arrival of the first locomotive in China'. The railways in China were slower to develop than those in India and Japan, but started out under the auspices of Western merchants.

trotters were produced in Shanghai and Hong Kong, both significant port cities. This reflected a burgeoning English-language publishing industry in China that linked to shipping lines. That there was not the same type of publishing inland indicated the absence of a developed railway. Cook & Son, in particular, was dependent on the railways for its tours. The Chinese government did not strategically develop the railways until after the First Sino-Japanese War (1894–5). Fought between China and Japan for influence in Korea, it not only saw Japan go nearly undefeated, but it also marked a new challenge to China, which had been the dominant power. The humiliating loss served to spur on a number of political reforms in China, which had been resistant to adopting Western technology, specifically railways; technological reforms largely took place under the auspices of Western powers. British firms such as Jardine, Matheson & Co. – the pre-eminent trading company in the East and heavily involved in the opium trade – built the first commercial railway in China in 1876, which ran between Shanghai and Woosung. It was dismantled a year later because they had not sought government approval. In the wake of the First Sino-Japanese war, railway building accelerated as the government

The dock front in Hong Kong by John Thomson, 1870–71. The view on arrival
in Hong Kong encapsulated Britain's mercantile networks; the firm of Jardine,
Matheson & Co. on the right-hand side dominates the image.

granted concessions to Western powers and to Japan to construct rail
routes. In 1904, in the face of popular criticism that the Qing government
had conceded railway development, and more importantly the financial
dividends this generated for foreigners, it allowed the provinces to establish their own railway companies, thus stimulating local economies.

Although Britain and other Western powers clearly exerted political
influence, China was never directly governed in the way that India was.
Further, the Chinese largely curtailed British encroachments to treaty
ports, the presence of diplomatic legations in Peking and the ceding of
Hong Kong Island. Murray never produced a Chinese handbook, most
likely because the firm sold its handbook concession in 1901, too late to
take advantage of the developing Chinese railways. Cook did not publish
one until 1910, and the company's first tour to China was via the Overland Route where, instead of going East by way of Suez, travellers passed
through Russia and Central Asia on the railways.

One of the earliest guidebooks to China and Japan came not from
Britain, but from a United States shipping line, the Pacific Mail Steamship

Company. Their shipping networks facilitated the rapid development of English-language newspapers in Eastern ports that covered local political, financial and transport news, disseminating them to a global audience. The newspapers were invaluable for investors; they provided a sense of insider knowledge that in turn supported burgeoning international financial networks in this period. The guides produced by English-language newspapers in China, such as the *Guide for Tourists to Peking and its Environs* (1876) written by Nicholas Dennys (1839–1900), editor of the *China Mail* in Hong Kong, were a means of communicating the first-hand knowledge and experiences of those who were resident. They also drew on the language and images used in older sources on China, with which readers would have already been familiar. One example was Sir John Barrow's (1764–1848) *Travels in China* (1804), which gave an account of the country at the time of the failed Macartney embassy (1793). Sent to China to gain trade concessions for Britain, the embassy was unsuccessful but the publications by its members, including the artist William Alexander (1767–1816), proved culturally influential in Britain for the next fifty years.

◄ LEFT: Front cover of *Pacific Tours, and 'Round the World*, 1900.

► OVERLEAF: William Alexander accompanied the 1793 Macartney mission. His watercolours of Chinese landscapes and costumes conjured the country for readers at home and also set the formula for later photographers.

Just as Cawnpore received overwhelming attention as a symbol of Britain's relationship with India in the second half of the nineteenth century, so too did Peking, specifically the Yuanmingyuan or Old Summer Palace located just outside the north-west walls of the imperial city. Laid out as a 'perfect world' of eternal beauty, the Yuanmingyuan was a retreat for the Emperor.[25] The palace also housed a rich collection of art and artefacts. Its looting and destruction by British and French forces at the end of the Second Opium War opened Peking and marked a shift in the balance of power between China and the West. Where China could once reject Britain's overtures for trade with the Macartney embassy, it was now Britain that was in a position to dictate trading concessions. The site of the Yuanmingyuan figured prominently in travellers' handbooks and presented a view of China that reflected the resistance of the Qing government towards Britain, which was at once both historical and contemporary to globetrotters.

Political interactions informed globetrotters' views of China before they even left home, yet they were also expecting another Chinese experience that was shaped by ideas of the Romantic sublime. Just outside of Peking was the Great Wall, which not only invoked ideas of the sublime, but also the 'stupendous': a version of the sublime that inspired wonder, astonishment and disappointment (the last because the mind was unable to fully process the significance of the encounter).[26] Barrow mentioned

The ruined Yuanmingyuan was viewed by some travellers as both a demonstration of British power and a reproach on its potential misuse. Photograph by John Thomson, from *Illustrations of China and Its People*, 1873-1874.

his awe and disillusionment with the Great Wall, as well as with Chinese court culture as a whole. He wrote that China was a country that despite its fabled wealth left its citizens filthy and poorly ruled by a 'haughty court' that still had the power to refuse Britain a trade agreement in order to 'feed its pride'.[27] Barrow himself was allocated what he described as a 'hovel' in the Yuanmingyuan in order to oversee the unpacking and display of British gifts for the Chinese emperor.[28] Barrow wrote that, when unobserved, he took the opportunity to explore the Yuanmingyuan in a series of 'little excursions I made by stealth' venturing 'from our lodging in the evening in order to take a stolen glance at these celebrated gardens'.[29] Although the Macartney embassy may have been unsuccessful, Barrow found a way, in his account, to secretly defy the Qing Emperor.

Barrow's *Travels in China* was published sixty-five years before the advent of globetrotting and it enjoyed a longevity among the British public. This was in part due to a scathing rebuttal of the book published by William Jardine Proudfoot (*c*.1804–87) in 1861. Proudfoot was the grandson of astronomer and member of the Macartney embassy, James Dinwiddie (1746–1815). Feeling that Dinwiddie had been belittled by Barrow's representation of him, Proudfoot specifically contested Barrow's description of how he illicitly accessed the gardens and buildings of the Yuanmingyuan, noting that it simply would not have been possible to elude their Chinese guards. Proudfoot published a second volume in 1868 that was a biography of Dinwiddie, in which he reiterated the strictures placed on Dinwiddie and Barrow during their residence in the Yuan-mingyuan.[30] In addition to Proudfoot's publications, Barrow's account was used as a guide by the British military during the Second Opium War, which allowed the expeditionary forces to locate the palace in the outskirts of Peking. The text gave an idea of the treasures that the palace held, which were then looted by the joint French and British forces. Therefore, Barrow's account, which praised the beauty of the gardens and pavilions of the Yuanmingyuan, also facilitated the destruction of the site in 1860. The Emperor and court were forced to flee to Chengde, an imperial complex to the north of Peking. There, from a position of political and military weakness, the Emperor agreed to the ratification of the Treaty of Tianjin (1860), which ultimately set in place an infrastructure that was exploited by globetrotters.

Peking emptied of foreigners in the build-up to the Second Opium War, but after the cessation of hostilities and the creation of diplomatic legations in the city, they returned in even greater numbers. One of the first handbooks to China for globetrotters, Dennys's 1876 *Guide for Tourists to Peking and its Environs*, commented on the increased presence of tourists in the city, which 'has of late attracted more visitors as the facilities of travelling progress, and the want of a practical guide book has been more and more felt'.[31] One of the sites Dennys advised travellers to visit was the Yuanmingyuan, although he warned that access was difficult.[32] In 1874 the Qing government closed the site to deter souvenir hunters and begin ambitious plans to rebuild. In the 1880s the Empress Dowager Cixi (1835–1908) improved the nearby site, the New Summer Palace or Yiheyuan, for her own residence. Building works were sporadic, due to depleted governmental resources, and lasted into the 1890s. As a result, the Yuanmingyuan remained closed for most of this period. In an echo of Barrow, Dennys encouraged tourists not to be deterred by the lack of access to the ruins:

> Yüan-ming-yüan is strictly closed … entrance is, however, possible, only one should try a little wicket on the northern side, but none of the large gates on the south, east or west. Even should the trial prove a success, one should not proceed too far into the park, where foreign visitors had some disagreeable meetings with soldiers, but be contented with taking a view of the buildings in the northern and north-eastern part of the park.[33]

Just as Cawnpore was a site where globetrotters accessed the local experience that connected them to the British Empire, the Yuanmingyuan was one where globetrotters overcame Chinese resistance to Britain by re-enacting Barrow's stealth.

Egerton Laird's reaction on his visit to the ruins of the Yuanmingyuan tested the sense of moral supremacy that most British texts expressed in regard to China at this time. Laird, as a tourist, experienced other cultures from the viewpoint of his own cultural superiority, yet seeing the Yuanmingyuan clearly challenged that position, moving Laird to muse:

> Is it a wonder that the Chinese hate us? No marvel they think us barbarians. I wonder whether it was necessary to have destroyed the most beautiful palaces and grounds in the world. Some people say it was, as it made the Chinese feel our power; but I must say I think they might have done so without pillage; however, it will always remain a sad and blackened memorial of what the Allies did in China, and I am

sorry such a one exists, as it will not tend to increase the admiration of Celestials for Europeans, however much it may hold them in terror of our armies.[34]

In condemning what had happened at the site, Laird cast his own countrymen in the role of, as he termed it, 'the destroyer'.[35] However, his overall view of China was largely negative and pithily summed up through the off-hand comment: 'from what I have seen of the Celestials, there is a remarkable want of appreciation of springs about them, as proved by their carts, water, and beds'.[36]

Laird's sense of innate superiority was challenged and potentially undermined when he was confronted with a sight that brought into question the moral position of the British in China. His equilibrium appeared recovered a few pages later:

> When I mentioned the other day what a sin the destruction of the Summer Palace appeared to be, I did not know anything about the cause, &c., but I have since read Lord Elgin's Second Embassy by Loch; and as the Emperor had offended by killing and torturing some Europeans, Sir Hope Grant thought it best to retaliate by burning the Summer Palace, as it was only the Emperor that felt the loss, and not the people. Anyhow, judging from the other buildings, it would have gone to ruin sooner or later.[37]

In essence, Laird absolved the British by adopting the official narrative that laid blame for the destruction of the Yuanmingyuan not with the Chinese people, but their government. This idea of China would become an enduring trope throughout the nineteenth and early twentieth centuries. It suggested that the country was being led by an ineffectual and corrupt government, and that this was ultimately the source of Chinese troubles both at home and abroad. The destruction of the Yuanmingyuan was depicted as an inevitability, since the 'haughty court' that Barrow condemned seventy years earlier could neither wage war to protect its cultural treasures, nor could it govern effectively in peacetime to preserve them.

Laird's use of this trope was not unusual; what was different was that he kept his opposing viewpoints in his narrative, which potentially encouraged his readers to question whether the destruction of the Yuanmingyuan was unavoidable. Although his sympathies were not as

Illustration from *Meeting the Sun: a journey all round the world* by William Simpson, 1874. The avenue of colossal statues that led to the Ming Tombs was seen as a relic of China's past glories.

clear-cut as those he expressed at Cawnpore, he did not entirely condemn the Chinese nor did he express unquestioning approbation for the British forces. Travellers like Laird show that, although sites such as Cawnpore and the Yuanmingyuan were meant to be regarded by Britons as evidence of British power globally, they were viewed critically.

The ruins of the Yuanmingyuan were viewed as a cypher for bad government. They were also part of the trope of forcing open or illicitly accessing closed sites, which had a wider application in globetrotters' narratives. Laird wrote of his visit to the Temple of Heaven in Peking: 'it is against all rules and regulations for anybody to go in, so we had to get in by stealth ... we managed to slip in by a small postern; and when your [*sic*] are once in the porters do not interfere with you'.[38] Percy Powell-Cotton enacted a similar transgression in 1891 at the Ming Tombs when he 'got rid of guardian climbed a tree and got a yellow dragon facing tile off a wall'.[39] Traveller and author Eliza Scidmore (1856–1928), who was commissioned to write the 1892 China guidebook for The Canadian Pacific Railway Company, noted: 'the sights of Peking are lessening in number each year because of the authorities closing show places to foreigners' and recommended bribery to breach defences.[40] By entering areas that were forbidden, globetrotters not only forced open what was closed, but they also forced their way 'behind the scenes'.[41] Guidebooks and globetrotters alike recommended transgression as a means of visiting what was identified as an authentic cultural site, such as the Temple of Heaven or the Ming Tombs. Such recommendations further indicated that, unlike India, which as a British possession was accessible, China was still able to dictate space that could not be accessed and therefore must be transgressed.

By the late nineteenth century the Qing dynasty, if not in decline, was ill-equipped to deal with China's changing social and political landscape. Officials were vulnerable to corruption as private interests trumped those of public service. A Chinese population boom, combined with a reduction in local administrators and the growth of mass civil disobedience, weakened the role of the government, which was unable to institute much-needed reforms or to defend the borders of its Empire. Government forces were unable to stop the Wuchang Uprising (1911) in the Yangtze Valley, which began in part because the government mishandled its plan to nationalise China's railways. After granting the oversight of railway development to individual provinces, the government moved to nationalise railways in order to use the proceeds to relieve debt incurred during the Boxer Rebellion (1901). The Railway Protection Movement began a programme of civil disobedience and revolutionaries in Wuchang saw this as an opportunity and began their uprising. Unable to bring the situation under control, the child Emperor Pu Yi (r.1908–1912) was forced to abdicate in 1912, effectively ending the reign of the Qing dynasty (1644–1912). In its place was a new central Republican government. The instability in China did not deter travellers, but Cook's 1910 guide acknowledged that globetrotters might face a more dangerous visit due to the political and social volatility. The first site mentioned was the British legation, which was 'surrounded by a high and fairly substantial wall', and 'has from time to time served as a place of general rendez-vous in times of impending trouble'.[42]

The firm's 1917 guide to China marked the changes of the early Republican period, presenting a new outlook on China as a modern, forward-looking country, no longer tied to the crumbling past represented by its outmoded imperial government. The reality was that during this time, China was in political turmoil marked by factional struggles, civil war and famine. Chinese industries, though, were expanding, creating a tumultuous and unsettled state of affairs. Interestingly, Cook's guide turned a blind eye to these issues, instead presenting a new China that was underscored by the way that the guide connected modern technologies with the potential for rediscovering the country. The guide specifically highlighted the importance of the railways in accessing the country and noted that their development within 'the last few years has opened the eyes of the tourist to the possibilities of finding something new'.[43] The novelty afforded by Chinese sites reflected the absence of the Qing government with their ever-increasing strictures on which places foreigners could actually visit. However, it also reflected the idea of a China, led by a new Republican government, that was more closely in line with governments in the West, which meant that the country was no longer held back by the restrictions of the Emperor and court. These viewpoints, as voiced in the guidebooks, implied that the natural outcome of having a Westernised government was that it recognised and implemented the need for technological modernisation of the railways. At odds with the Chinese experience, the guidebooks' authors were also quick to point out that, with the advent of the Republican period, prosperity would return to China. Cook's 1917 guide noted that Peking had once been a 'network of filthy streets ... that contrasted strongly with the magnificence of the marble ways and granite courts' under the old imperial regime, but now 'there is certainly no city in China under purely Chinese administration with better streets and a more wholesome atmosphere'.[44]

The author placed responsibility for the previously deplorable state of China on the Empress Dowager Cixi. As it had so often in the past been a symbol for the failure of the Qing, the Yuanmingyuan was again cited as emblematic of Cixi's political shortcomings. Travellers were advised to visit the park, which was now completely open, and to begin by viewing the Yiheyuan, a retreat built by Cixi at the expense of the government purse. The first point of interest was one of the architectural relics of her long rule: a marble junk from an earlier period that she had restored and which was 'badly painted ... scarcely in keeping with the other build-ings'.[45] Visitors were encouraged to move on from this display of Cixi's poor taste, commensurate with her lack of political judgement, to the ruins of the Yuanmingyuan, which was 'destroyed by the British and French in 1860 as a demonstration against the procrastinating diplomacy of the Chinese and as a punishment for the imprisonment and torture of emissaries ... little is left of the pavilions, but a survey of the grounds gives some idea of the former beauty and is well worth making'.[46] While governments changed and access was improved, an iconic site like the

Stereographic photographs by Underwood and Underwood, c.1900, showing the British Legation in Peking, which was a British site of refuge during the Boxer Rebellion, and the marble bridge leading to the destroyed Yuanmingyuan.

Yuangmingyuan was, in the guidebooks, implicitly figured as a physical remnant of the failures and excesses of Chinese imperial rule that ultimately allowed for British interventions.

JAPAN: NETWORKS OF MODERNITY

Japan, unlike India and China, was only formally opened to wider Western trade in 1854. This relatively new interaction with Britain, which negotiated treaties with Japan in 1856, meant that there was no key site, like Cawnpore or the Yuanmingyuan, that symbolised Anglo-Japanese relations. In addition, this idea of novelty was enhanced within Japanese sites themselves as the newly restored Emperor moved his seat of government from the traditional location of Kyoto to Tokyo, creating a new capital. Guidebooks focused on cultural engagement rather than overtly political information. When Japan was considered in comparison to China, the guidebook writers expressed a mix of concern and approbation for the country's embrace of Western industrial modernity. For the Japanese, railway building was a priority of the Meiji government: developing a strong infrastructure was Japan's first step to successfully asserting itself on the world stage.

One of the earliest English-language guidebooks for visitors to Japan, *A Guide Book to Nikkô* (1875), was written by the British diplomat Ernest Mason Satow (1843–1929). It was published in Yokohama by the *Japan Mail*, a bi-weekly English-language newspaper that included shipping timetables, political analysis and local gossip. Satow's guide offered

The temples at Nikko were an important site for globetrotters, bringing together the history and beauty of Old Japan. The red lacquer bridge was crossed only by the imperial family. Annie Russell-Cotes reported that it was dilapidated when she saw it in 1886. From Charles Lucas's abum.

the traveller the opportunity to connect with Japanese history and the picturesque in the site of the temple complex that was 'the resting place of the founder of the Tokugawa dynasty and his illustrious grandson'.[47] In 1875, the Tokugawa Shogunate represented relatively recent history, and Satow recommended travelling to Nikko along the Oshiu Kaido, which he described as 'the route taken by the Shoguns when they went to pay their respects to the founders of the family'.[48] Nikko was a site of architectural beauty for Westerners, and an evocation of an idealised Old Japan, in this case epitomised by the vanished world of the shogun and samurai. The site encapsulated the experience of history, politics and the picturesque that globetrotters actively sought.

This idea of Old Japan, a country that globetrotters idealised as having remained unchanged for centuries, was so attractive partly because it offered an antidote to their own constant movement. As globetrotters travelled from one country to another by steam and rail, their interaction with a Japan untouched by Western modernity provided a welcome degree of stillness. It was also a means of connecting with what they believed was the older, and thereby more authentic, culture of Japan. What they encountered, however, was a rapidly industrialising country, which in turn led them to write about the Japanese experience in

heightened elegiac terms. In his account of his time in Japan, Egerton
Laird referred not to historical or political texts, as he had done in India
and China, but to seventeenth-century poet John Milton's (1608–74)
epic *Paradise Lost* (1667), as he gazed on the Japanese landscape of
the Tokaido:

> Sweet is the breath of morn – her rising sweet,
> With charm of earliest birds; pleasant the sun
> When first on this delightful land he spreads
> His orient beams, on herb, tree, fruit, and flower,
> Glistering with dew; fragrant the fertile earth
> After soft showers; and sweet the coming on
> Of grateful evening mild.[49]

Laird selected a stanza from Milton's poem describing the idyll of the
Garden of Eden just as Satan entered it. He located Japan as a paradise
in its own right, assuring his readers that the country was as close to
Edenic perfection as possible: a combination of English climate and
azure 'Australian sky'.[50] Laird's choice of text alludes to the fact that he,
or rather Western encroachments, are the serpent within the paradise
that was Japan, and that it would shortly be lost through industrialisation. However, this was almost too clear-cut; Laird used a section of the
poem describing paradise before the effects of Satan are felt, but Satan
as Milton created him was a sympathetic anti-hero. In his own narrative,
Laird cast himself as a more sympathetic globetrotter who, like Milton's
Satan, was an unlikely and troubling protagonist. Although his travels
and presence had an impact on the cultures that he sought out, Laird
preferred to view himself as a purveyor of the cosmopolitan who was
mostly appreciative of cultural difference.

This consumption of cultural difference was shaped and guided by
Satow's early guides, which reflected both his knowledge and cultural
sensitivity. Although Satow left Japan in 1883, his guides were, as Basil
Hall Chamberlain (1850–1935) noted in his entry on guidebooks in *Things
Japanese* (1890), still considered indispensable for translating the culture:

> By far the fullest and best is Murray's *Handbook for Central and Northern
> Japan*, by Satow and Hawes ... unfortunately this work, which is a
> mine of information, not only on the topography, but on the history,
> traditions, art, etc. of Japan, is now out of print, and second-hand

G24   TOKAIDO, NEAR HATA

copies command high prices. There is a smaller *Tourists' Guide* by W.
E. L. Keeling; a *Handy Guidebook to Japan Island*, by W. H. Seton Kerr,
and an *Official Railway and Steamboat Traveller's Guide*, of which new
editions appear every few months. All these small guide-books are
more or less compilations from Messrs. Satow and Hawes work.[51]

This astute assessment of the keen competition between publishers for
the tourist market was hardly disinterested. Chamberlain himself edited
the 1891 edition of Murray's *A Handbook for Travellers in Japan*, reusing
much of what had been written by Satow and Albert George Sydney
Hawes (1842–97; a retired lieutenant in the Royal Marines) in their 1884
edition. This was an example of how Murray attempted to penetrate
what was a volatile market using the pre-existing network of publishers
and publications. *A Handbook for Travellers in Central and Northern Japan*
(1884) by Satow and Hawes was a reprint of the authors' 1881 handbook
of the same title published by Kelly & Walsh in Yokohama, a publishing partnership that was formed in 1876 between Shanghai booksellers
Kelly & Company and F. C. Walsh. In the 1880s, the firm expanded its

◄ OPPOSITE: The landscape of the Tokaido, from a Japanese photograph
album, 1895. ▲ ABOVE: 'Japan. A Public Conveyance', from Egerton Laird's *The
Rambles of a Globe Trotter*, 1875. Although they were viewed as quintessentially
Eastern, jinrikshaws were created for Western travellers, first in Japan and then
spreading throughout the East to centres of imperial administration.

offices first to Hong Kong and then to Yokohama. With Murray as their publisher, the authors were able to expand their audiences beyond Yokohama and Shanghai, to Britain. The influence of Murray's *Handbooks* was acknowledged by Hawes and Satow themselves, when they noted in their introduction to the 1881 guide that they modelled it on the *Handbooks*, which they 'followed as far as was practicable'.[52] Murray brought together a collection of scholars and travellers to create a unique travel library. These included Basil Hall Chamberlain and the intrepid traveller and writer Isabella Bird (1831–1904). Bird's own account, *Unbeaten Tracks in Japan*, was published by Murray in 1880. The publication history of Japanese guides shows how the images of Japan that globetrotters would come to expect were produced through a network of writers, travellers and publications.

Despite this, handbooks for Japan should not be seen as an exercise in which Western writers defined the country for Western travellers. Japan was incredibly proactive in creating and controlling its own image. As was the case in China, a number of handbooks were published under the

In addition to travellers' handbooks, Murray published the accounts of intrepid travellers like Isabella Bird.

auspices of English-language newspapers. For example, an 1890 edition of *The Official Railway and Steamboat Traveller's Guide* published by the *Japan Gazette* survives in Percy Powell-Cotton's collection from his World Trip at Quex Park. Editor John Reddie Black (1826–80) launched the newspaper in 1867. Black started his career at the *Japan Herald*, the first English-language newspaper in Japan, launched in 1861. For his new paper, the *Japan Gazette*, Black sought to move beyond the shipping news and port gossip to devise a newspaper that encouraged wider debate and engaged the Western enclaves in Yokohama and Tokyo, as well as the Japanese communities. For example, his early issues featured extensive coverage of the Bakumatsu reforms.

Black further expanded his publications with an illustrated fortnightly newspaper, *The Far East*, introduced in 1870, which included the work of Western photographers William Saunders (1832–92), Michael Moser (1853–1912) and Black himself, as well as notable Japanese photographers such as Uchida Kuichi (1844–75) and Suzuki Shin'ichi (1835–1918). In 1872, Black launched a third publication, the Japanese-language news-paper *Nisshin Shinjishi*, which published articles calling for reform in Japanese politics. By creating a Japanese-language newspaper, Black extended his reach beyond the English-speaking populations of the treaty ports and had the potential to influence Japanese readers. The Meiji government recognised this, and in 1874, it offered Black an advisory position to the Daijo-kan (Council of State), which in effect controlled the press, on the condition that he resigned the editorship of *Nisshin Shinjishi*. He accepted, and the following year laws were introduced prohibiting foreigners from holding editorships of Japanese-language newspapers. Shortly after this, Black was transferred to a lesser position in the Translation Bureau before being dismissed entirely from govern-ment. The Meiji government maintained its influence over what was deemed a foreign press, not only controlling information but also creating a specific image of Japan.

This creation and control of image also extended to travellers' guidebooks. In 1893, Japanese entrepreneurs founded the Welcome Society of Japan, the country's first tourist board that also had full government backing. Operating out of the Tokyo Chamber of Commerce, the Welcome Society published its own English-language travellers' guidebooks. There were no key differences in the sites and experiences the publications recommended compared with those published by Murray or the *Japan Gazette*. However, the Welcome Society's guidebooks

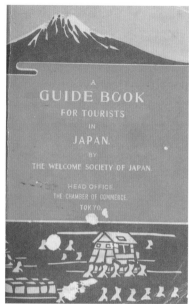

▲ ABOVE, LEFT: Edited by John Reddie Black, *The Far East* featured the work of Western and Eastern photographers. ▲ ABOVE, RIGHT: Front cover to the Welcome Society of Japan's *Guide Book for Tourists*, 1910. The Japanese began to publish their own travellers' handbooks, thus directing the gaze of Western tourists.

represented Japan's continued and active control over the creation and propagation of its own image. Through the images in the guidebooks, the Meiji government exploited Western travellers' desire for what they perceived as culturally authentic experiences of Old Japan, while at the same time promoting a new, technologically advanced Japan.

Guidebooks shaped perceptions of the country to be encountered. They offered globetrotters a means of bridging global travel and local experiences. Often written by resident 'experts', like Eastwick, Dennys or Satow, they reflected to a certain extent the individuality of the writer. For example, Eastwick's publications focused on his linguistic interests, to the dissatisfaction of some of his readership. As much as the handbooks were the work of an individual writer, the text was also borrowed and adapted by other guidebook writers in what was a competitive market. For example, the guides produced by the Japan Gazette took complete sections of text from Satow's original guides with little amendment. In this publishing atmosphere, texts were often distorted from their original meanings. Finally, they also reflected political ideas of the East that were formed at home, rather than being an accurate reflection of the state of Indian, Chinese or Japanese politics themselves. Cook's guides, for example, continued to give voice to the trope of China being ruined by poor imperial leadership, even when the country was enduring hardship during the Republican period.

The guidebooks defined a sense of place by emphasising certain sites of cultural and political significance. In the case of India and China, they also represented the imperial nature of British interaction by encouraging, either through local guides or transgressive behaviours, globetrotters to insert themselves into historical events, almost as a type of ritual sightseeing. Although the handbook industry burgeoned in the late nineteenth century, the authors often drew on older sources and as a result maintained and perpetuated attitudes and prejudices.

However, the Japanese experience was markedly different from that of India and China and illustrated how British imperialism could be controlled and directed. In India and China, travellers located themselves in landscapes such as those of Cawnpore or the Yuanmingyuan, which were shaped by political events, but this was not enough to foster a more direct personal and potentially transformative encounter with place. For this, globetrotters moved beyond their guidebooks to exploit personal networks and to access what they felt were authentic spaces. These experiences challenged the views put forward in Murray's and Cook's handbooks and created an alternative geography of experience.

2   AUTHENTIC SPACES

Although globetrotting was still relatively new in 1877, the increasing numbers that Carew Davies Gilbert remarked upon when he described it as 'a very common occupation' were indicative of the search for novel experiences beyond Europe.[1] The range of sites open to globetrotters – temples and shrines in India, Chinese gatherings in private spaces and Japanese teahouses – represented specific types of engagement and encounter. The nature of the activity that globetrotters designated for each space, whether social, cultural or transgressive, contributed to the identities that they relayed of the differentiated East. The activities performed by globetrotters and locals in these spaces played an important role in the travellers' transformation of self. Globetrotters were representative of international connections, accessing countries via trade routes made possible through political interventions, whether colonial or part of the informal empire of the treaty ports in China and Japan. Travellers turned their gaze upon what they believed was the authentic experience of these countries and conveyed it homeward through their letters, objects and photographs. The significance of their experiences in sites such as temples and teahouses was built on pre-existing frameworks of travelogues written by Grand Tourists. Earlier tourists to the European Continent used sites such as the Basilica of St Peter in Rome to achieve a connection between Roman history and the city's present day inhabitants. St Peter's was built over a Roman necropolis, tying it with the antique landscape. It was also linked to early Christians and was believed to have been the burial place of St Peter (c.1 AD – c.64 AD), the first pope. The Basilica was a trove of painting and sculpture by notable Renaissance and Baroque artists in a stunning architectural setting. The site was a draw for tourists, offering views of art, architecture and the locals. Further, it was a space of performance where travellers were observed by fellow tourists, as they engaged in cultural pursuits. Here travellers created an identity of place connected with authentic culture and confirmed their social status.

PAGE 76 AND ABOVE: The Yomeimon Gate (above) and Tosho-gu, the Shinto shrine, dedicated to the founder of the Tokugawa Shogunate, Tokugawa Ieyasu. These were built in the seventeenth century, during the Edo period (1603–1868). From Charles Lucas's album.

Like the churches and cathedrals of the Grand Tour, a constant on generations of globetrotters' itineraries were temples or shrines. A feature of both urban and rural settings, they were often built on promontories above a city or town, offering a panoramic, picturesque experience of the landscape from a site that itself enhanced those qualities. These locations were often used for observation rather than engagement. Just as Catholic ritual at St Peter's was observed but not enacted, Hindu, Buddhist and Shinto practices observed in the East were treated as a type of theatre, where local populations were watched while making meaningful connections with these sites.

Although temple sites connected to an older, ancient iteration of culture, globetrotters also sought out contemporary and ostensibly authentic experiences, through active social interaction with locals. This was important because they tied the identity of place, in part, to the nature of these interactions. If temples were sites where cultural practice was observed, but not engaged with, then where were the sites of engagement? Genuine culture was often found in the small everyday acts that took place behind the scenes, where globetrotters could immerse themselves away from other tourists.

Spaces of accommodation, such as hotels, inns and teahouses, were sites where globetrotters and locals met on an equal social footing, as even Western-style hotel rooms were used by locals. Egerton Laird discovered this when a group of Japanese men came to gaze on him and his fellow travellers while they were writing letters and performing other everyday tasks. This exposure not only meant that globetrotters had to culturally engage with the 'other' (a term that for them indicated any non-Western citizen) but also, as travellers, globetrotters themselves had become the 'other'. Additionally, spaces of accommodation also provided a means of conveying social status and creating a wider network of globetrotting companions. Clubs, to which travellers only had access if their names had been written down in advance by another member, were places in which globetrotters could display and strengthen their social connections. They also constituted a British space in a foreign land.

Interior of a temple in Canton, titled 'Joss House, Canton', by Lai Afong, from Charles Lucas's album. Laird wrote that, in his experience, Chinese joss houses were 'rather tumble down affairs, and the dust of ages is scattered all around'. Globetrotters emphasised the decay of ancient sites when presenting China in their narratives.

April 21ˢᵗ – 24ᵗʰ
May 22ⁿᵈ – 23ʳᵈ

The hotel in Hakone in which Charles Lucas stayed. Lucas's notation at the bottom of the photograph states that he made two trips, roughly a month apart. On his second trip, with a new set of travelling companions from Yokohama, he displayed what he felt was his growing expertise in Japanese customs.

Through the course of their travels, globetrotters maintained ties with home through letters, which created a bridge between familiar spaces and their sites of travel. In 1916, in the early days of her wedding trip through India, Nancy Dearmer instructed her mother to follow her progress, suggesting: 'if you have a good map look up our route. Poona, we passed about 3 a.m. Sholapur 8 a.m., Gulbarga about 11.30, Riachur 3.15 and Sooth just now about 8 p.m.'[2] Dearmer defined her movements against what she perceived to be the stationary position of home, but also included her mother as her virtual travelling companion. Throughout the duration of her travels in the East, Dearmer used her letters to maintain a connection to one place, noting to her mother that 'it is fearfully difficult to keep abreast with things, but if I don't, it looks as if I should spend my first year at home merely in picking up threads. Your letters and comments are the greatest help to keeping in touch.'[3] Nevertheless, Dearmer's letters also charted the new connections and ties she created with places and people in the East. They recorded the changing nature of her own identity as she not only experienced the other, but gradually became a version of the other herself to friends and family as a result of her travels.

Part of the documentation of this transformation of self were the photographs that Dearmer and other travellers regularly sent home. Studios run by both local and Western photographers proliferated in Eastern ports in the second half of the nineteenth century. Following in the wake of imperial and technological expansions, Western photographers, including Felice Beato (1832–1909), John Thomson (1837–1921), Samuel Bourne (1834–1912) and Raimund von Stillfried (1839–1911), set up studios across the East. They provided a photographic record not only of individuals but also of events, such as the Indian Mutiny, the Opium Wars and the British military expedition to Shimonoseki in 1864. The studios of Bourne & Shepherd in India, for example, photographed landscapes that both evoked the idiom of the Romantic picturesque and communicated strategic geographical features that were of importance to the British and held military or political significance. John Thomson's work, capturing Chinese 'types' in his four-volume publication, *Illustrations of China and its People* (1873–4), was a means of ethnographically cataloguing the Chinese population for readers in Britain.[4] However, there was also an increase in the number of studios that were owned and operated by local photographers. For example, Lala Deen Dayal (1844–1910) and Pestonjee Dosabhoy (*fl.*1877) sold their prints of maharajahs to Western travellers in India. Hong Kong

Photograph by Bourne & Shepherd of the Indian landscape around Ootacamund, from Charles Lucas's album. The hill station of Ootacamund, or Ooty, was a haven for the elite of the British Raj; its exclusive reputation led to the nickname 'Snooty Ooty'.

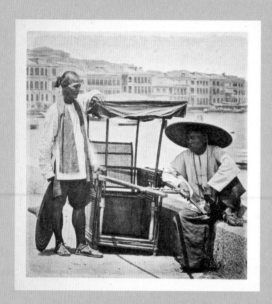

and Shanghai teemed with studios run by Chinese photographers, including Lai Afong (*c*.1839–90, known as Afong) and Gong Tai (*fl*.1860–1890). In Japan, Uchida Kuichi was the first photographer allowed a sitting by the Emperor (*r*.1867–1912) and Empress Haruko (*r*.1869–1912) in 1873.

Photographers' studios represented new spaces of cosmopolitan encounter and exchange. Here, photographers and their clientele could interact and share their local and global knowledge, respectively. Photographs and letters also played a role in globetrotters' construction of self. The epistolary self was an unstable creation, an image that evolved and adapted throughout the course of travel. Letters were a means of conveying engagements in behind-the-scenes spaces that, due in part to their transgressive nature, were omitted from published accounts. These included approximating Kashmiri life, opium smoking in China or adopting a Japanese lifestyle.

Photographs and letters were enshrined at home: they were the physical documentation of the ephemeral experiences of authentic engagement.

◄ OPPOSITE: John Thomson's 'Chinese types', from *Illustrations of China and its People*, 1873–4. Thomson's photographs of China are one of the most extensive visual records of the region in this period. They also served as a catalogue of ethnographic types for British readers.

◄ LEFT: 'Raja Nurinder Parsad Peshkar Narain Prasad', by Pestonjee Dosabhoy, *c*.1875. Dosabhoy was one of a number of local photographers working in India. His images captured the Indian elite.

► OVERLEAF: Photographs by Uchida Kuichi of Emperor and Empress Haruko. Until Uchida's photograph of Emperor Meiji, no Japanese emperor had ever been officially photographed. Uchida was the only artist permitted to photograph him, in 1871 and 1873.

The quality of letters – difference in paper, printed headings and ink, for example – further documented exotic locations. As such, these letters can be treated as both object and narrative, reflecting the desire voiced by globetrotters themselves. Gilbert urged his mother to 'keep these letters, as I have not kept a Diary of my journey in Java'.[5] Charles Lucas's letters were transcribed by his mother and bound into a presentation album of his journey. The originals were also preserved in a separate, specially bound album. Nancy Dearmer requested that her mother might have their correspondence bound as a diary that represented her experiences.

Letters were essential in charting changing mobilities and the meanings that globetrotters ascribed to spaces of encounter with other cultures. There are commonalities in their letters that highlight the changing nature of travel, while presenting a consistent sense of its drawbacks. In a letter from Kobe written in May 1877, Gilbert expressed his frustration as letters arrived late or went astray: 'it realy [sic] is hard to make a long letter, I have not heard from you since the date of October so cannot chat at all'.[6] Similarly, writing from Madras in 1916, Dearmer noted: 'I am longing to hear home news – a month seems a long time to wait for it, but after this I shall get letters regularly if we are not moving about very much'.[7] Incorrect timetables and missed connections featured in both Gilbert's and Dearmer's letters, which were separated by a span of forty years.

TEMPLES

The presence of tourists in India, China or Japan in the nineteenth century meant that they were themselves representative of a world in flux, through both technological and political change. Across these three countries, temple sites featured in globetrotters' narratives as a means of connecting with an older, authentic iteration of the cultural East. In both letters and published accounts, these sites were situated within the natural landscape, often literally connecting with it. For example, Gilbert paused, en route to China, to explore the Indonesian island of Java. He noted in a letter from Samarang, in February 1877, a visit to the ninth-century temples of Borobudur:

> The Temple is of Budhist [sic] origin, & of very Ancient Date, it is in a considerably dilapideated [sic] condition, but its solid form prevents it falling to pieces, as it otherwise would do. … there was a small sort of out post Temple about ½ mile from the main ruins, thro [sic] which an

enormous tree was growing, the tree was evidently an old tree therefore the Temple must have been in ruins centuries ago.[8]

Current scholarship places the date of abandonment in the fourteenth
century. Ruins featured in eighteenth- and nineteenth-century discourse
concerning the Romantic as a means of musing on the fleeting aspects
of time and age. The temple complex, long disused, was a site in which
to meditate on the passing of the Eastern empires, as powers rose and
fell, leaving behind magnificent ruins. That the temple itself was literally
anchored to the landscape by a tree enhanced its Romantic and picturesque possibilities. Its redundancy as an active site of religious practice
meant that this was also an undisturbed space where Gilbert could reflect
on the past and connect with ancient culture.

In 1891, Powell-Cotton described his experience of a ruined temple in
Burma: 'walked ½ way up bad path originally covered with pent roofing,
carved, now falling down, here is a huge carved teak figure some 35' high,
gilt, R. hand pointing to Mandalay'.[9] His description was of the Shweyat-
taw Buddha on Mandalay Hill. Built in 1857 by King Mindon (r.1853–78),
Mandalay was the last royal capital in Burma. The temples on Mandalay
Hill were an extension of the city complex, and the gesturing Buddha
was commissioned to indicate that Mindon had succeeded in fulfilling a
prophecy made by Gautama Buddha that, 2,400 years after his death, a
city devoted to the study of Buddhism would be built on the site to which
he pointed. Powell-Cotton recorded a version of this account in his diary:
'King dreamed he saw Buddha pointing to site of city from this hill – city
built – fig placed accordingly'.[10] While the ruined site connected directly
to the history of a specific place, it was also a space in which to experience
both landscape and culture.[11]

This narrative thread remained consistent, as nearly thirty years later
Dearmer described her experience at the Vandiyur Mariamman Temple in
Madurai, situated in the middle of a temple pond or Teppakulam. Built in
the mid-seventeenth century for the worship of incarnations of Shiva and
the goddess Parvati, the site in the centre of the pond consisted of a large
complex, which included several smaller temples and a pipal tree. It was
the tree that drew Dearmer's attention, and she noted its role in Hindu
ritual in a slightly confused passage:

Women pray when they want a child. I am not sure if it is to the tree
or if the tree is an emblem of the goddess, but I know you have to walk

This view was taken from Mandalay Hill, a site that Beato advised globetrotters to visit. Later, they could buy the souvenir of their experience from his studio. Photograph by Felice Beato.

Charles Lucas's souvenir from his visit to the Teppakulam, Madurai, in the late 1870s. This site was still firmly on globetrotters' itineraries in 1916, when Nancy Dearmer described it as both beautiful and sinister.

round this tree and I think you have to eat a leaf. This particular tree was hung with tiny wooden cradles put there by anxious would-be mothers.[12]

Not only were these sites linked to the past through their histories and the centuries of ritual enacted there, but they also made up the social fabric and identity of place. This is not to say that temples across the East were encountered without regard to cultural differentiation, but rather that these were sites through which to access what was considered to be ancient and thereby representative of authentic culture. This remained true even if, in cases such as the Mandalay temple, the site was not yet thirty years old.

Globetrotters' experiences of temple sites, however, appear to have been confined to observation rather interaction with local populations. One of the earliest globetrotters, Arthur Drummond Carlisle, recoiled from Hindu religious practice in Benares, noting that, in relation to the suffocating smells in the temples, 'if cleanliness is next to godliness, filthiness is very near idolatry'.[13] Britta Martens identified a similar attitude voiced by British travellers to Italy in their nineteenth-century travelogues. In addition to sites and artefacts of Roman antiquity, Italian Catholic churches were a significant draw for tourists. Similar to temples in the East, these were spaces in which British travellers viewed religious rituals and ceremonies, both observing cultural difference and confirming their own superiority with regard to the other, in this case non-Protestant, southern Europeans.

Remarks on the cultural differences between the British and the Italians were also a means of political commentary. Italians were characterised as 'degraded' due in part to living under political and religious oppression.[14] British writers contrasted Italian poverty and adherence to 'popish superstition' with their own prosperity at home, born of a well-regulated parliamentary democracy and supported by a hardworking Protestant population.[15] Charles Dickens's (1812–70) popular account of his tour of the country, *Pictures from Italy* (1846), which was continuously in print throughout the nineteenth and twentieth centuries, described Rome as a city whose sites merged into a 'dream of churches', their shared similarities a broad characterisation of Italian Catholicism:

A vast wilderness of consecrated buildings of all shapes and fancies, blending one with another; of battered pillars of old Pagan temples …

'Vishnu Pud' and other temples near the Burning Ghat, Benares. Arthur Drummond Carlisle described the approach to Benares as an almost uninterrupted succession of broad flights of stone steps – called 'ghats' in India – that were 'extending here for the length of nearly a mile'. Photograph by Samuel Bourne, 1860s.

of pictures, bad, and wonderful, and impious, and ridiculous; of kneeling people, curling incense, tinkling bells ... of Madonne, with the breasts struck full of swords ... of actual skeletons of dead saints, hideously attired in gaudy satins, silks and velvets trimmed with gold: their withered crust of skull adorned with precious jewels, or with chaplets of crushed flowers; sometimes of people gathered round the pulpit, and a monk within it stretching out the crucifix, and preaching fiercely...[16]

In his description, Dickens's connection of Catholic shrines with earlier pagan temples implied that these supposedly Christian sites were inherently imbued with paganism, not least due to the theatricality of Catholic religious spectacle with its veneration of relics that verged on idolatry.

The clear parallels in the language used in globetrotters' accounts and letters indicated that they employed this already extant popular framework to convey their impressions of the East and the inhabitants of India, China and Japan through their different religious practices. Carlisle wrote in 1870 of his visit to Benares, the 'holy city of the Hindus', noting that, like Dickens's Roman 'dream of churches', the city was 'full of idols ... every passage-corner, every nook, contains a shrine to some god whose attributes and symbols are more or less loathsome'.[17] There were further commonalities between the two writers and their descriptions of the other. Dickens observed the Pope blessing a line of supplicants in St Peter's:

> as they carried him along, he blessed the people with the mystic sign ... when he had made the round of the church, he was brought back again ... There was, certainly, nothing solemn or effective in it; and certainly very much that was droll or tawdry.[18]

The blessing that Carlisle observed in Benares was carried out under a canopy – similar to that used in St Peter's – and by a high priest who made 'with his forefinger a red mark of some paint or dye of each worshipper who chose to pass in front of him'.[19] Nor would the priest object to rupees in exchange for his blessing. In both cases it was about the empty theatrical qualities of what Dickens and Carlisle observed was a corrupt religion. This, both authors felt, was one of the influences that kept the inhabitants of Italy and India in a perpetual state of ignorance.

This element of the Grand Tour perspective was applied, in Carlisle's case, to India, but it was also applied more widely to the East. Carlisle's observations were couched in a touristic script already set out in travelogues that specifically focused on religious practice and the temple site, equating them with the negative aspects of Catholicism. At the Honan Temple in Canton, Carlisle recounted the priests holding 'strings of beads, their chanting in procession, and the genuflexions, we can not help being struck with the similarity, in the form of service, to a Roman Catholic one'.[20] This was included in a narrative that portrayed the Chinese, like the Italians, as 'degraded' from a glorious past. Even Japan, a country that fared well in globetrotters' opinions and was often regarded as an earthly paradise, did not escape these comparisons. Carlisle likened the Buddhist Sensoji temple in Asakusa, a district of Tokyo, to St Peter's in Rome. The temple, founded in 645 AD, was one of the oldest in Tokyo. It was enlarged under the Tokugawa Shogunate, and was an important site of pilgrimage. In Carlisle's description of the temple interior, thronged with pilgrims,

◄ OPPOSITE: Chinese priests, photographed by John Thomson. Globetrotters placed the shrines and temples of India, China and Japan within the context of the Roman Catholicism they had experienced in Italy. They used this to communicate the pageantry of ceremony and to compare it with what they deemed the more rational aspects of Protestantism. ▲ ABOVE: Asakusa Temple, from *The Far East: An Illustrated Fortnightly Newspaper*, 1870. In globetrotters' narratives, acts of devotion at the Asakusa Temple in Japan were likened to religious practice at the Vatican in Rome.

he recorded that 'in one corner is an old wooden image of a god, whose features are quite rubbed away, like the great toe of the bronze statue of St Peter in Rome, by the constant stream of people who come to rub it with their hands'.[21] Travelling just a year after Carlisle, Laird repeated the analysis of the Sensoji: 'the image, like St Peter's toe in St Peter's at Rome, is rather the worse for wear. I suppose the people believe they have only to touch [it] to be healed'.[22] This was a long-standing trope, as Frederick Diodati Thompson noted of the site in 1891 that 'the priests remain near the altar, which is lighted with small candles, and their dress and mitres reminded me of their Roman Catholic brethren'.[23]

Other aspects of the touristic script of the Grand Tour were applied only to the Eastern leg of the World Tour For, example, Carlisle compared hiring a guide in Benares with the same activity in Italy: 'Shiva Datta Pundit speaks English very well and is well up in all the lore necessary to a cicerone'.[24] The importance of the cicerone on the Grand Tour was not only as a tour guide, but also as an individual who interpreted the sites for travellers, possessing both academic knowledge and the folkloric information that was the key to connecting with a sense of place. In 1883, Lord Ronald Gower (1845–1916) likened the sites of India with those of the Roman Campagna, noting that Delhi was a city where the Mughals 'built temple on temple, mosque upon mosque, palace upon palace. A circumference of twenty miles encircles the ruins of this Indian Rome'.[25] By 1891, Thompson had extended his reference points beyond Rome, including other Italian cities but also taking in the sites of the expanded, Romantic iteration of the Grand Tour. He equated Japanese craft in Yokohama with Venetian gondolas, and Indian rivers with the Rhine.[26] This last comparison also appeared in Thomas Cook's Indian guides of the same period, which solidified this idea of the East as a new Grand Tour. This knowing invocation of the Grand Tour was something that only featured in published accounts. It was an additional layer of interpretation, situating global travel within an elite narrative and highlighting Western tourists' knowledge of references to well-known, long-standing travel discourse.

'Beam view of a junk at anchor', from Charles Lucas's album. Globetrotters used the language of the European Grand Tour to communicate their own experiences in India, China and Japan. Frederick Diodati Thompson equated Japanese boats with Venetian gondolas.

The significance of temple sites in travelogues lay not in their means of social connection with other cultures, but as spaces in which to observe the other and perform one's own social distinction. Since this was communicated in published accounts, the common image of globetrotters was that they confined their activities to observation and did not necessarily interact with local populations. However, the spaces of encounter revealed in globetrotters' letters indicated a departure from the well-known touristic script. This was driven by a desire for meaningful interaction with the other that was found not in the public temple sites, but in the behind-the-scenes spaces of the World Tour.

BEHIND-THE-SCENES ENCOUNTERS

Ideas of agency were constantly shifting as travellers moved through the East, from the colonial spaces of India to the treaty ports of China and Japan. As these spaces of encounter changed, so too did the balance in power between the local inhabitant and the globetrotter.

The behind-the-scenes spaces of encounter and exchange were often located outside of what globetrotters (not always correctly) designated

The Nizam of Hyderabad, from Charles Lucas's album. Lucas restyled Hyderabad as outside of British reach to give the impression that he and his brother travelled intrepidly off the beaten track. He wrote to his mother that they rode through the city on a elephant.

Photographs of Kashmir, by Bourne & Shepherd. Kashmir was represented in globetrotters' accounts as an eagerly anticipated paradise. The reality, however, often proved disappointing.

British spaces. Charles Lucas observed, on his visit to Hyderabad, a princely state in southern India, that 'everyone carries about pistols, daggers, guns, etc., with them. Hyderabad does not belong to the British, so that they do as they like'.[27] Hyderabad was not separate, as Lucas claimed, but a princely state, as it was in a subsidiary agreement with Britain and, while governed by the Nizam, was dependent on the Raj. Although Lucas's understanding of the finer points of Indian politics and the organisation of the Raj was lacking, the way that he viewed such sites – along with the activities in which he engaged as a result of these perceptions – was significant in the construction of places of encounter. An emergent theme in globetrotters' letters concerned moving between British and Eastern spaces for an immersive cultural experience.

In India, as Lucas demonstrated, travellers stayed within sites of the Raj, regarding certain places as remote and beyond British reach. Kashmir, a princely state, was viewed as separate: a remote space of otherworldly beauty. In addition, the discovery of Sanskrit manuscripts confirmed it as a site of ancient culture.[28] The combination of picturesque beauty and antiquity proved an irresistible lure for globetrotters. Laird was one of the earliest to publish an account of his visit to Kashmir and the way that he wrote about it is important to consider against the letters of Lucas and Dearmer, as well as Powell-Cotton's diary. Laird emphasised the separateness of the place, noting that to travel there he had to apply to the secretary of the Punjab government to 'facilitate our journey into Cashmere', which was 'out of the world'.[29] Not only did Laird reinforce the idea of Kashmir as distant and outside of the Raj – which held the frisson of difference – but he also included a quote from Thomas Moore's poem *Lalla Rookh* (1817), which describes the Vale of Kashmir and places it firmly on the itinerary of the Romantic picturesque:

> Who has not heard of the Vale of Cashmere,
> With its roses the brightest that earth ever gave;
> Its temples and grottos and fountains as clear
> As the love-lighted eyes that hang over their wave?[30]

Moore himself never saw Kashmir but relied instead on travellers' accounts to craft this image. While globetrotters were expecting the paradise conjured by Moore, confirmed through photographs from the firm of Bourne & Shepherd, the majority travelled to Kashmir in February and March – which was early spring – and rather than encountering an

Edenic site, they found it to be cold and damp with no bowers of roses yet in evidence. The state of Jammu and Kashmir was a relatively new incarnation, created in 1846 with the British installation of the Dogra rulers. Far from being a remote paradise, it was a buffer state, at the forefront of British, Russian and Afghan political frictions. Yet in the popular British imagination, these political realities were overlooked and narratives such as the one Laird produced prepared future travellers to experience Kashmir as an ideal of the behind-the-scenes landscape.

The fact that it was the landscape, and not the inhabitants, that loomed large in globetrotters' narratives indicated that, rather than being a site of encounter with the other outside of British spaces, Kashmir was still a colonial place. The locals were described as dirty and dishonest, inhabiting a paradise that they had done little to deserve. At the same time, the paradise itself did not live up to globetrotters' expectations. When the Lucas brothers visited in 1878, and Powell-Cotton in 1890, the emphasis of their travels was on hunting. However, Lucas still reiterated the separateness of Kashmir, writing to his parents:

> There is a post to Srinagur [sic] but not to anywhere else in Cashmere, so when we are in other parts we shall have to send coolies to Srinagur [sic] for & with our letters. Do not be surprised if you do not hear from me so regularly in future, as we may be for the next 3 months camping miles away from any post town, but I will always send you a few lines when I have a chance.[31]

To be outside of the reach of the post was to be outside of Empire. Lucas's postion outside of the Raj meant that he was figured in his letters as an intrepid traveller beyond borders, but he was also able to lay claim to an elite identity by enacting a type of imperial masculinity. John Mackenzie noted that hunting was an activity that was part of the construction of an elite imperial masculinity. As the nineteenth century progressed, winter hunting tours of Kashmir became increasingly popular. In his novel, *What I Saw in India: The Adventures of a Globe-Trotter* (1892), Louis Tracy, editor of the *Allahbad* newspaper, created the fictional globetrotter Reginald Hooper, 'aged thirty, being of sound mind and body, and carefully ticked by Cook as a globe-trotter, presently bent upon "doing" the country'.[32] Hooper arrived with a number of guns, ready to undertake the hunt in the north of India. However, he also found himself the subject of amusement in the eyes of those stationed in India, who regarded both his hunting skills and exploits with mild derision. In remote Kashmir, young, male globetrotters could adopt and enact an elite imperial masculinity out of the view of those who were actively engaged in the establishment and administration of empire, thus escaping the ridicule and censure to which Tracy's fiction Hooper had been subjected.

Because of its perceived remoteness, Kashmir was also a site where globetrotters could engage in a degree of cultural immersion. However, this too was filtered through the lens of empire. It specifically included adopting an approximation of Kashmiri dress for the duration of an extended hunting trip. When Lucas returned to Calcutta, he commissioned a series of photographs by Bourne & Shepherd to record his experiences, which included several of him in his Kashmiri dress and were staged in the garden of the family with whom he was staying. The Apcars, whom Lucas knew from his school days at Harrow, had a palatial residence in Calcutta. They were of Armenian descent and served as business agents and insurance brokers, as well as running the Apcar Shipping Line between Japan, China and India, and were engaged in colonial society. Alexander Apcar, who attended Harrow with Lucas, was president of the Calcutta Turf Club. The Apcars's reaction to Lucas's photography session, which he staged with his tent and hunting trophies, was recorded in his letter home:

> Got tent pitched & skins head etc. arranged by about 9 o'ck & dressed myself up in the clothes I used to wear in Kashmir & had the whole blessed thing photo'd much to the amusement of all Apcar's servants who could not make me out a bit.[33]

One of the photographs, which he sent home, shows him sitting with his leg slung over the arm of a camp chair, in Kashmiri dress, surrounded by his hunting trophies. His outfit consisted of a woollen turban, paired with a European shirt, open at the collar, and loose European trousers. To these he added a sash around his waist, with a dagger tucked into it, thick woollen cloth wound around his lower legs, bound to them by leather strips, and woven sandals on his feet, which were wrapped in cloth. While not an authentic representation of Kashmiri dress, it indicated that Lucas saw Kashmir as a site of immersion: a liminal space where, if he did not exactly engage with the other, he approximated it through his clothing while maintaining a colonial identity through hunting. These behind-the-scenes activities were recorded for both his family and himself.

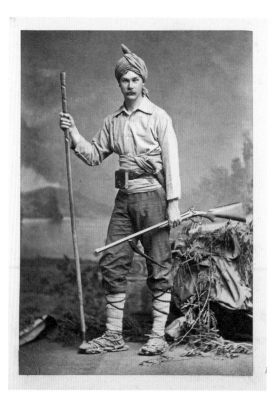

Like Hyderabad, Charles Lucas presented Kashmir as a behind-the-scenes space where he could wear Kashmiri dress and indulge in the pastimes of the imperial elite. He commissioned these portraits to commemorate his Kashmiri experience.

Percy Powell-Cotton spent several months hunting in Kashmir in 1890, and engaged with the space in a very similar way to Lucas. Powell-Cotton was a keen amateur photographer, who captured a camp life spent under canvas, in an approximation of Kashmiri dress, surrounded by hunting trophies; these photographs were identical in style and composition to those commissioned by Lucas. Further, Powell-Cotton recorded in his diary bringing local women to his tent at night: 'Cashmir woman about up to my armpit, good fit, turned her out at 3'.[34] It was one of the only times during his trip to India that he mentioned sexual interactions with locals. Kashmir was far from the gaze of the society of the Raj, where young men could play out ideas of both a colonial identity and indulge in what to them figured as an immersive, transgressive experience, adopting the dress of the other and engaging in sexual interactions with them.

However, the liminality of Kashmir was subject to gender restrictions. Nancy Dearmer and her husband Percy travelled there in 1917 and rented a houseboat on Lake Dal. Instead of a remote paradise, Dearmer's letters record a litany of cold, wet disappointments, culminating in their house-boat or dunga experience:

Percy and I are too miserable and cold in this Dunga. Yesterday was like a bad March day at home and this morning it is just as cold & streaming with rain and we really can't bear it. We have had two rotten nights too, cold & noisy, the pie dogs are a fearful curse & howl by the hour together.[35]

In addition to disappointment with the place itself, Kashmir also proved not to be the remote location Dearmer had anticipated. Another couple that she met in Madras, who were also touring India, took the house-boat next to them. Instead of liminality and potential connection with the other in a remote idyllic setting, Dearmer's experience was that of a well-trodden site where engagement was limited to a circle of individuals with whom she was already acquainted.

Dearmer, however, did access a behind-the-scenes space, and located it not in the far reaches of Kashmir, but rather in central Bombay. She exploited her husband's long-standing professional and social networks to do so. During Percy Dearmer's first marriage, when he was vicar at St Mary's Primrose Hill, in the summer, 'he took a locum tenency [sic], and the family spent August one year at Foyle near Alton, another at Necton in Norfolk, and another at Bradford Peverel'.[36] In mid-October

Houseboats at Srinigar, 1890s: 'View, probably on the Dal Lake, with the hill of Takht-i-Sulaiman in the background. The large houseboat in the foreground is identified as belonging to Henri Dauvergne, the smaller boat behind (with cook's boat and dunga) being the Kay Robinson's.' Nancy Dearmer found the dunga experience to be highly disappointing.

1916, shortly after Nancy's marriage to Percy, which according to an announcement in *The Birmingham Daily Gazette*, 'took by surprise a good many members of this popular clergyman's large circle of friends', the couple sailed for India.[37] Part of the surprise – and also a likely reason for a lengthy trip across the East – was that Percy Deamer married Nancy Knowles just a year after his first wife Mable died of typhus in a field hospital in Croatia. Knowles was fourteen years younger than Percy and the childhood playmate of his own children. In order to facilitate the trip, he had agreed to undertake a series of lectures for the YMCA, and under this arrangement their accommodation, travel and meals were paid for as long as Percy had a lecture. Further, they were able to set the itinerary as they pleased. Considered in conjunction with Percy's past practice of exploiting work connections as a means to holiday, it appears that rather than a mission, this was instead a wedding trip funded by the YMCA. The social network that facilitated the Dearmers's travels grew out of the same Industrial Revolution that created the technological networks of travel. Developing concurrently with Thomas Cook's travel networks, and

under similar religious auspices, the YMCA was founded in 1844 in Britain
by George Williams, a Congregationalist, to improve the spiritual lives of
young
men drawn to London for work. The organisation expanded across the
European and North American continents and, in 1890, the first offices
were established in Madras.

In addition to the economic benefits of Percy lecturing for the YMCA,
the Dearmers had a social network in place, in the organisation of Anglican clergy based in India. Yet for all the perceived privileges that the
network conferred, it also had its drawbacks, and Dearmer was frustrated
by the level of cultural access that it provided. In Madras her hosts were
'exasperating people to sight see with, they wasted so much time over
uninteresting things and hurried over the interesting things'.[38] To remedy
this, Percy renewed his acquaintance with a friend from his student days
at Oxford, to whom he had not spoken in twenty-nine years, but who was
well placed to give the Dearmers an entrée into the society and spaces
of the Raj. G. S. Curtis was head of the Land Office, a member of the
exclusive Bombay Yacht Club and on close terms with the Governor of
Bombay, Lord Willingdon (1866–1941). After a dinner at the Curtis home,
attended by the Dearmers and Willingdons, an invitation to a 'purdah
party' at Government House was extended to Nancy Dearmer, at which
'there were no men over four years old present, except the Band'.[39] The
experience fulfilled her desire to interact with locals and was removed
from the public spaces of Bombay, instead secluded in the grounds of the
socially prestigious space of Government House:

> You have never seen anything like it ... diamonds as big as eggs and
> enormous pearls and emeralds the size of dinner plates. ... Saris of
> thick gold brocade, silver brocade, every colour under the sun, some
> with jewelled borders; jewelled caps, necklace, earrings, nose rings,
> ancle [sic] bangles, girdles. Glittering and sparkling. The ladies drove
> up in coaches (purdah curtains severely closed!) or, the bolder ones in
> cars. ... the ladies were Ranees, wives of rich merchants, and there were
> Persians, Hindoos, Mohammedans, – all sorts. ... it was great tamasha
> and I was lucky to be there. There are women in Bombay who would
> have given their eyes for an invitation.[40]

Dearmer's privileged encounter among the elites of both Indian and
British colonial society combined a level of intimacy and access to a space

where a mutual gaze could be employed. Attendance at the event was restricted by both class and gender and, as such, was an experience open only to elite women. Like Lucas and Powell-Cotton who enacted a version of elite identity in Kashmir, Dearmer was able to do the same through her connection to the Willingdons.

Although it was large reception, it still held with the idea of a behind-the-scenes space, particularly as it was a purdah party and implied a degree of exclusion. Dearmer also asked her mother not to share it, as she wanted to keep private what happened behind the scenes to anyone outside her own social group. What the behind-the-scenes experiences of Lucas, Powell-Cotton and Dearmer confirm is that, in India, they were firmly routed in colonialism. Globetrotters' performances in such spaces reinforced this idea, whether it was the colonial masculinities enacted by Lucas and Powell-Cotton, or Dearmer's attendance at a purdah party, where the other was summoned to attend Government House, a seat of the Raj.

Sites of accommodation, which were, in effect, behind-the-scenes personal spaces, also played a role in reinforcing identities of place and projecting social status. Clubs were a vital institution for male travellers

'General view of the Bengal Club from Chowringhee Road'. For wealthy male globetrotters, clubs in India and throughout the East provided a way of mixing with exclusive society and a means of creating a network of travelling companions. Photograph by Samuel Bourne, c.1867.

The Byculla Club was one of the most exclusive clubs in Bombay; Lucas recorded his own stay there in the autumn of 1877. By the 1890s, Frederick Diodati Thompson noted that, should he return to Bombay, he would have chosen the club even though it was on the wane, to be superseded by the Bombay Yacht Club. Photograph by Bourne & Shepherd, from Charles Lucas's album.

across the East. They were a means of strengthening their network and of cultivating potential travelling companions. The club was also central in creating cultural cohesion among the imperial elite in India, as well as in asserting and bolstering constructs of colonial power. This was certainly the case with the Lucas brothers, who used clubs not only in India but across the East to connect with fellow travellers and confirm their own social status. For example, Charles Lucas and his brother Morton attended Harrow School, whose graduates included politicians, royalty, diplomats and colonial administrators. In Calcutta, the brothers stayed at the elite Bengal Club, where they attended an 'Old Harrovians Dinner' specially organised by the Viceroy of India, Robert Bulwer-Lytton, 1st Earl of Lytton (1831–1891), himself an Old Harrovian. This event was recorded in their photograph albums of the dinner attendees and included a specially printed programme. The Lucas brothers' connections were reflected in their further choices of accommodation: the Byculla Club in Bombay and the Neilghirries Hotel in the elite hill station of Ootacamund. Even in places such as Hyderabad, which Lucas believed to be beyond British rule, he noted to his mother that he was given a letter of introduction from a social contact in India to 'a man there who put us up there, & did everything for us'.[41]

While the club was used to gain business and to make political and social connections, it was also a means of exclusion, not only for women, but for Indians and Anglo-Indians not of high social caste. It was a site of elite protest, too: in the wake of the Ilbert Bill, the Byculla Club in Bombay broke with long-standing tradition and refused to entertain the Viceroy to dinner. However, Nancy Dearmer captured some of the changes to colonial society in India and illustrated that the institution of the club was vulnerable. The Bombay Yacht Club still featured prominently as an indicator of social status and Dearmer was assiduous in recording the number of times she was either invited to lunch or to attend various functions there. But this was very much a part of the cosmopolitan elite. When Dearmer visited a rural club, it did not conform to the assumption that the more rural the club, the more exclusively it became the preserve of the white, male colonial administrator:

> I wonder if you know what the club of a small station is like? ... there is a reading room with the latest papers and magazines, a notice board, with Percy's lectures posted amongst other bills! ... every evening between 5 and 7 cars and buggies and motor bicycles drive up and the club hums for a few hours. In the hot weather it is a god send. People are tired to death of the bungalow where the women have been imprisoned most of the day, and are thankful to get away and to meet their friends ... and so it goes day by day and month by month.[42]

Dearmer conveyed the sociability and domestic qualities of the small club and its importance for women in the community. She also recorded, from an earlier visit to Madurai, the subversion of the club as a homosocial space. This club was for the use of Indian and Anglo-Indian women: 'a charming little place ... P. was not allowed to come in as these are purdah ladies ... there was a billiard room, a library and one or two other little rooms and of course a wide verandah'.[43] For Dearmer, the club was not entirely a place of retreat from the other or a signifier of exclusivity. It also mirrored the changing social and political landscape of India in the early twentieth century.

In China and Japan, which were outside of the formal colonial Empire, the club continued to provide a version of British space and, for male globetrotters, a means to extend social networks. When both Lucas and Powell-Cotton moved from India to China – Powell-Cotton was in the army, but not on active service, able to exploit his connections with fellow officers stationed in India – they lost certain links with colonial society. Clubs in Hong Kong, Shanghai and Yokohama allowed new social networks to be maintained. The club also provided a British space from which to explore and potentially become immersed in the culture of the other. An example of the way that these connections worked can be seen in Lucas's experience in Shanghai. He stayed at the club, but also knew a resident in the city, the cousin of a fellow globetrotter that Lucas met in India. The cousin worked for a Shanghai-based shipping agent, well placed to offer Lucas the opportunity for a behind-the-scenes encounter, and invited him to a late-afternoon party at the home of a local Chinese merchant:

> We were the only Europeans present. I ate some of the 'chow' & smoked their [opium] pipes & drank some very strong Chinese spirit called 'sou chou' it is made out of rice. All the Chinamen crowded around & were much amused ... but I told them that as I had come to a Chinaman's house I wanted to do as Chinamen do. ... we stayed about an hour & I enjoyed it very much. Got back to Club in time for dinner.[44]

Lucas's attendance at a Chinese party was accessed through a European connection, but his insistence that they were the only Europeans present indicated that he regarded it as an authentic encounter in a behind-the-scenes space. It was short-lived, however, and after his consumption of Chinese food and intoxicants, Lucas returned to the British space of the club. In China, the club was a base for cultural exploration, a point from which to experience social immersion and to engage in transgressive behaviours, which for young, male globetrotters were an integral part of behind-the-scenes spaces.

Outside of the club, local lodgings provided a very different experience of the behind-the-scenes spaces in both China and Japan. For example, globetrotters found themselves the subject of the gaze, designated the other by local populations. Although this would have been the case in India as well, it was in China and Japan that travellers demonstrated an awareness of this situation. Just as Laird published his interaction with Japanese 'swells' in his hotel, Gilbert recorded a similar experience in a Chinese hotel and wrote to his mother: 'the natives were very civil & kind, but very inquisitive, examining us, our clothes &c, & asking for tobacco, coming into our room sometimes to look at us rather unceremoniously, but not with any ill intention'.[45] Because these encounters took place

under the agency of local people, there was, for globetrotters, a spontane-
ous quality to them. This differed from their journeys to Kashmir, which
were planned and subject to expectation.

Local accommodation, such as Chinese inns or Japanese teahouses,
offered a more fully immersive experience, but also promised unrelieved
cultural engagement without the option of British spaces as a retreat.
Laird was one of the earliest to set this out, in his narrative of Japan,
where he described at length the Japanese teahouse in which he stayed:

> There are no windows – at least not in our acceptation of the word;
> in the daytime they are commonly open, and you can see in, but at
> night they draw frames covered with paper across, in the same way as
> sliding doors; the paper is pretty tough, and keeps out the air, but the
> house is not very substantially built, and the partitions between the
> rooms are decidedly thin … There are no chairs or beds, and where you
> dine you sleep; they bring you a thin mattress and a thickly-wadded
> dressing gown, very warm and comfortable, great wide sleeves, and
> a very thick collar.[46]

Part of the immersive quality of the teahouse experience was the gradual
removal of those practices or customs that anchored the Western traveller to their own culture. On entering a teahouse, they removed their
shoes. They slept in a room 'insubstantially' divided from the Japanese
themselves, a permeable interior with little in terms of furnishing to
equate with a Western interior. In order to sleep, they adopted Japanese
clothing. In teahouses, the balance of power was held not by the Western
globetrotter, but by their Japanese hosts. Laird detailed his night in the
teahouse as an immersive experience, but absent from his narrative
was a personal connection with the other. In his account, he observed
the other and they observed him, but beyond this gaze there was no
personal engagement.

Laird's room in the teahouse where he slept was certainly a behind-
the-scenes space as well as a a culturally immersive one. But in his
published account, it lacked the social exchange that globetrotters would
style in their letters as an authentic cultural encounter. In a letter from
a Kyoto teahouse in 1879, Lucas recorded that, after a day sightseeing,
he and his companions returned to find that their rooms had been given
to a Japanese party, and that their belongings had been removed to
accommodate these new guests:

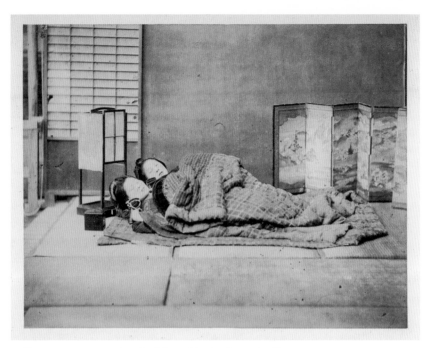

'Japanese women sleeping', from Charles Lucas's album.

At first we were much annoyed but upon enquiring found the rooms had been engaged for this entertainment long before we bespoke them ... we joined in their party although we could not speak a word to them, & had some rare fun for about 4 hours, we danced with them, drank their saki (a spirit made from rice) ... what we thought at first a nuisance turned out first rate sport.[47]

The authenticity of the engagement lay in its spontaneity. It was an interaction that was not sought from a British space, but rather occurred in a Japanese one, and which included both the mutual gaze and cultural exchange. A simple meeting was recorded in Powell-Cotton's diary a decade later, when he noted of the teahouse where he stayed in Kyoto: 'this is just a superior Jap inn, all paper divisions to rooms ... a pretty little girl of 8 or 9 taught me "go bang"'.[48] Gobang or Go was a popular board game using black and white counters in which the aim was to fully encircle an opponent's pieces. It has been played across Japan, China and Korea for millennia and was introduced into Britain in the nineteenth century as part of the fad for all things Japanese. In Powell-Cotton's diary, the inn was a Japanese space where he mutually encountered the other.

Nancy Dearmer's interactions were mediated by her gender and a significant change in her circumstances. She arrived in Bombay as a new bride in October 1916 and left Calcutta bound for China in 1918 as a new mother. Her daughter Gillian was born in January 1918 and christened in St Stephen's Church, Delhi. This was part of the St Stephen's College compound where Percy managed to secure a temporary teaching post and accommodation to coincide with Gillian's birth. The Dearmers then took the decision to return to Britain via the United States. The YMCA again subsidised their travel, in exchange for Percy's further lectures in China and Japan. However, the family's progress was impeded. Their ship took on water outside Singapore; all passengers were evacuated in the early morning and forced to find accommodation in the port. Booking a passage to China on a second steamer proved equally challenging, since ships were, as Dearmer related to her mother, regularly 'commandeered' for war service, leaving passengers stranded, hotels overcrowded and accommodation difficult to find.[49] They finally arrived in Hong Kong in April 1918:

> We went straight to Cooks on landing & discovered that we can get berths on the Shinyo Maru sailing at noon tomorrow. This is luck for the next possible sailing would have been May 15th & that is such a long while to wait. Our YMCA plans have had to be cancelled & this is a pity as the lectures are advertised, but it can't be helped. In these days one has to get along as best as one can.[50]

This was a marked difference to Dearmer's almost leisurely approach to her exploration of India a few years previously. While wartime conditions did complicate travel plans, the Dearmers sailed for India in 1916, having already coped with lost possessions and disrupted posts due to wartime losses of shipping. Sailing from India to Burma earlier in her travels, Dearmer had also dealt with temporary suspensions in shipping schedules due to concerns over possible enemy actions. Her haste to move through the rest of her journey centred around the arrival of her daughter. This, in turn, impacted on her desire to seek out and access authentic spaces.

The family sailed from China for Japan the day after they arrived in Hong Kong. Dearmer noted that there was little to see in Hong Kong, since it was merely a port town and no more, which again was a departure from the travel plans that she had communicated to her mother from Simla in the early days of her pregnancy. At that time, she remarked that the steamers between Calcutta and Hong Kong often missed connections, but that she did not mind 'because Hongkong has good hotels & it would be interesting to see the fringe of China'.[51] When their ship anchored off Shanghai and the opportunity arose to explore a Chinese city, Dearmer chose not to do so, commenting in her letter: 'some people are going ashore for the day, but P & I don't think it's worth while & would be too difficult to manage about Gillian'.[52] Although her circumstances altered her active search for behind-the-scenes spaces, Dearmer simply reconfigured these spaces and encounters. In Tokyo, she reworked popular tourist sites as places that were off the beaten track. In the city, she and Percy used their YMCA connection for advice on what to see. During a social visit with the Anglican Bishop of Tokyo, the American John McKim (1852–1936), they were told about the forty-seven *rōnin*, or masterless samurai. Popularised in Britain by both A. B. Mitford (1837–1916) and Basil Hall Chamberlain (1850–1935), this was the true story of forty-seven samurai who lost the aristocrat they served, Lord Asano Naganori (*r*.1675–1701), who was a daimio or feudal lord. During a visit to the shogun's castle in Edo (Tokyo), Asano was repeatedly taunted by a senior court official, Kira Yoshinaka (1641–1703). These taunts escalated and Asano drew his blade and cut Kira across the face. Drawing a blade in the house of the shogun was a capital offence and Asano was ordered to commit ritual suicide, or *seppuku*; he also lost his titles and lands, and his family was ruined. His servants waited to exact revenge on behalf of their master and eventually killed Kira. Because vendetta killings were forbidden, the *rōnin* in turn were obliged to commit ritual suicide. They were buried in the grounds of the Sengakuji Temple in Tokyo and their graves became a highlight on globetrotters' itineraries. *The Official Railway, Steamboat and Traveller's Guide*, used by Powell-Cotton in 1891, noted in its entry for the site: 'there is practically nothing to see, but many people like to visit it as being the site where the final scene of a historical and somewhat famous dramatical event was enacted'.[53] Dearmer, however, conveyed a very different experience to her mother: 'this morning we visited the shrine. It is very little known by visitors the Bishop says & certainly all the other people there this morning were Japanese'.[54] A well-known site that was popular, but not necessarily recommended, was remade in Dearmer's letters into an authentic Japanese space. Although Dearmer recast the experience as culturally authentic, it was still, in her account, a site of observation of the other, rather than one of interaction.

▲ ABOVE: Tomb of the *rōnin*, Sengakuji Temple, from *A Book of Coloured Photographs of Views in Japan*, 1895. The story of the forty-seven *rōnin* (masterless samurai) who avenged the murder of the master was popularised in Britain through A. B. Mitford's *Tales of Old Japan*, 1871. Globetrotters flocked to the site of their graves at the Sengakuji Temple.

◄ LEFT: Left: A Japanese mother with her baby on her back, from Charles Lucas's album. Nancy Dearmer found that having her own child gave her a way of engaging with Japanese mothers.

Gillian may have hindered Dearmer's access to certain authentic interactions, but the baby facilitated social exchanges of another kind and encouraged a mutual gaze in which motherhood formed a common ground. On a visit to the temple complex in Nikko, Dearmer wrote of her meeting with a Japanese mother who, after admiring Gillian, 'planted her baby on my lap. She then put the loop of her carrying scarf round the baby & with my assistance, hoisted the fat creature on her back & off they went'.[55] Gillian may have initially appeared to impose limitations on Dearmer's search for and desire to access authentic spaces and interactions. However, her presence fostered another sort of interaction that neither Lucas nor Powell-Cotton could access.

PHOTOGRAPHY STUDIOS

Across the East, the photographer's studio was a cosmopolitan site of intersecting modernities, as well as a place where globerotters and locals might interact. For example, in Hong Kong, Lai Afong ran one of the most successful studios in the city; his competitor was Pun Lun (1864–c.1900). A number of photographers moved around the East, most notably Felice Beato. Beato was a British citizen born in Venice, who photographed the Crimean battlefields (1855), the aftermath of the Indian Mutiny (1858), and the Opium Wars (1860), and set up studios in Yokohama (1863) and Burma (1886). Nor was this mobility limited to Western photographers. Japanese photographer Suzuki Chushi (1849–1907) established a studio in Shanghai in 1882 and his fellow countryman Ueno Hikoma (1838–1904) had studios in both Shanghai and Hong Kong in the 1890s.

There was agency in a photographer's gaze. For example, Kusakabe Kimbei, who trained under Raimund von Stillfried (1839–1911), opened the first of his own studios in Yokohama in 1885. He would go on to open four more in the city and one in Tokyo. His images were popular among his globetrotting clientele and a cropped version of a group of Japanese girls bathing appears in Annie Russell-Cotes's published account of her travels, *Westward from the Golden Gate* (c.1900). Both Beato and Stillfried used prostitutes to pose for their images, while Kimbei preferred geisha. In Meiji Japan, geisha occupied a position at the intersection of entertainment, fashion and politics. They represented both traditional society and the new Meiji version of the refined 'modern woman'.[56] They were cultural icons who brought with them a degree of the erotic. For the Japanese viewer, the combination of geisha and the modern, Western technology with which they were captured – in turn deployed

301.

◂ PREVIOUS SPREAD: 'Geyshers', from Charles Lucas's album. ▴ ABOVE: Bathing girls, photographed by Kusakabe Kimbei, from Merton Russell-Cotes's *Home and Abroad*, 1921. This version of Japanese bathers – a semi-nude figure on the far right was cropped by the publisher – appeared in Annie Russell-Cotes's book.

by a Japanese photographer – meant that these images, while seemingly recording the nostalgia of Old Japan, were also representative of the Meiji vision of a new Japan. It was unlikely that globetrotters realised all of these connections but their gaze was guided by the images created by local photographers.

The images of himself that Charles Lucas sent home from the East demonstrate how photographs charted the outcomes of Eastern encounters. The first portraits comprise two half-length *cartes de visite* (page 120), one of Charles and one of his brother Morton, taken in 1877. In the images, they both have their arms crossed in front of them, and are similarly attired in woollen suits. Charles wears a more sober, dark-coloured suit and tie, while Morton's clothing is lighter in colour. The photographs were surrounded by a single, hand-drawn bamboo frame, possibly the work of Lucas's sister, Florrie, who was a keen amateur painter. The addition of the frame gave a sense of enshrining the brothers as they were before their travels.

During their trip to Kashmir in 1878, Morton became seriously ill with what he described in a letter as sunstroke. His health became so precarious that he was sent home from Kashmir, while Charles elected to continue the tour on his own. When Charles returned alone to Calcutta, he commissioned a number of photographs from Bourne & Shepherd to document his Kashmiri journey. In addition to his staged photograph in the Apcars' garden (page 100), he also sat for a studio portrait in his Kashmiri dress. This he sent to his mother with the accompanying explanation:

> After breakfast spent nearly the whole morning at Bourne & Sheppards [*sic*] the photographers, first having my photo taken in Kashmir dress then choosing views of all the places we had been to up country. I shall spend a small fortune on photos before I get home but they will be a lasting souvenir of the places we have seen, so it will be money well spent & will in a way assist me to explain what we have seen.[57]

This image presents a clear departure from the young man in the sober suit at the front of the album. That his Kashmiri dress was recorded in several venues indicated the importance that Lucas's experiences in Kashmir held for him and illustrated his desire to communicate them to those at home, through his recreations of space. Further, by pairing it with stock footage of Kashmir, Lucas located himself in the landscape, as well as conveying the effects of his immersive experience on his construction of self.

There are three further portraits of Lucas in his albums: a single *carte de visite*, possibly from China, and two from Japan. The first, which does not name a photographer but has been placed in Lucas's China album, shows him seated on a studio prop of rocks, wearing a light suit, tie and pith helmet and holding a bamboo walking stick. It was an image that had little to differentiate it from those of the colonial elite, and communicated nothing of the effect of his experiences in Chinese spaces. However, it was taken at the time when Morton had a recurrence of poor health and may have served to reassure Lucas's family that his continued travels had not had an adverse effect on his own health.

The first image of Lucas from Japan was of himself, with three of his temporary travelling companions, to commemorate their successful ascent of Mount Fuji in 1879. It was taken in a Yokohama studio: 'Harman, Ringrose, Davies and I had our photos taken in a group as a souvenir of our trip up Fuji together'.[58] The photograph was labelled 'Fuji Group' and portrayed the young men as alpine ramblers, echoing the images of Grand

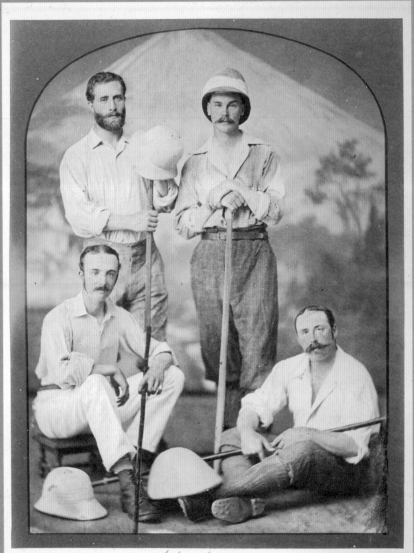

July 21st 1879

◄ PAGE 118: Charles Lucas and his friend Arthur Ringrose dressed in the Japanese fashion to engage in what they believed was cultural immersion. They recorded their experience and its transformative effect in this studio photograph in 1879.
◄ PAGE 119: Arthur Ringrose and Charles Lucas (standing), with fellow travellers Harman and Davies, commemorating their ascent of Mount Fuji at a Yokohama studio in 1879. Their outfits have more in common with alpine ramblers than with local dress. ▲ ABOVE: *Cartes de visite* of Charles and Morton Lucas before they set out on their globetrotting adventures in 1877.

Tour travellers. Although the painted studio background of Fuji and the pith helmets worn by the group indicate an Eastern location, the image nevertheless evokes the social distinction of elite Swiss climbers.

The final image showed Lucas and his travelling companion, Arthur Ringrose (b.1852), dressed in kimonos with two geisha. Taken in Yokohama just days after the Fuji group image, it served a very similar purpose to the studio photograph of Lucas in Kashmiri dress. He noted in a letter to his mother that when he was outside of Yokohama, staying at local teahouses in smaller villages, he would adopt Japanese dress. However, that immersive experience was confined to Japanese spaces. The day before this photograph was taken, Lucas remarked: 'very hot day felt the heat very much, wished I was in the country again & able to go about in Japanese clothes'.[59] Part of travel was the process of becoming the other to those who remained at home, not only through a lengthy journey, but also through the culturally immersive experiences of foreign spaces. This final image of Lucas and Ringrose – in kimonos, drinking tea – documented the outcome of that process. It also illustrated how the adoption of aspects of the other was part of the understanding of a differentiated East. In Kashmir, Lucas adopted an identity that was ultimately an expression of colonial masculinity. The album containing images of Japan, however, reflected a more cosmopolitan immersion. The Japanese image of Lucas and Ringrose was also hand-coloured, an expensive and painstaking process. Lucas's Japanese album not only conveyed his transformation, but also marked his social distinction.

Just as technological developments brought more of the world under the tourist gaze, so too did advances in photography. The equipment progressed from the large wooden cameras and heavy glass plates of the 1870s, when Lucas travelled, to the light and extremely portable Kodak that Percy Powell-Cotton took with him in 1889. This change meant that globetrotters were able to effectively direct their own gaze. Guides in nineteenth-century London represented local knowledge and held the keys to those behind-the-scenes spaces where authenticity could be located. Photographers held a similar position for globetrotters; they not only had access, through local knowledge, to spaces that were off the beaten track, but they also provided a visual documentation of these sites. Powell-Cotton wrote of his encounter with Felice Beato in Mandalay in 1891: 'drove to Europe Hotel, there Beato, a photographer been here some time (a character been all over the world through a lot of campaigns, member of the Club, etc. etc.) gave us information'.[60] The information was regarding a ruined temple site accessed by an overgrown road. Nevertheless, Powell-Cotton set off with his Kodak. He no longer had to rely on a studio session, or on his choice of stock images, to record and re-enact his personal experiences behind the scenes. Powell-Cotton's gaze was still directed by Beato, but at a remove.

By the late nineteenth century, photographers' studios across the East added film developing to the services offered to globetrotters. Nancy Dearmer, who travelled with both a Kodak and a Graflex, regularly had her prints developed throughout her travels. She began this practice from the earliest days of her arrival in India, writing to her mother: 'my films have at least been forwarded from Madras where they go to be developed. Some of them are quite good I think and I enclose a few prints. Don't you love the dear elephant?'[61] Just as she used maps to connect her mother with the spaces through which she moved, Dearmer also sent her own photographs that created a visual connection with the sites.

Using her own camera and having her film developed and printed facilitated a greater degree of social engagement with those that Dearmer encountered. She used her camera to great effect in her early interactions with the family of her newly hired servant, Mumi, referred to initially as the 'Dressing Boy': 'He [the dressing boy] said this morning: "My family wish very much to see the Madam," and as "the Madam" is equally curious to see the family we have arranged to be on view to each other one morning, Madam Kodak in hand!'[62] Dearmer's photographs connected her with home, while at the same time realising the space of the mutual gaze and documenting it. Dearmer not only exercised her own gaze through the camera lens, but she also hand-coloured her own prints, thus creating and enhancing her version of authentic cultural encounter. This was somewhat contested by her fellow travellers, and Dearmer noted an exchange with Mrs Parlett, who shared their accommodation in Rangoon:

> Mrs P... is an interfering person, full of unasked for advice! I was showing her the photographs I have been colouring for you and she said: 'That is quite wrong, you must alter that, no Burmese woman under forty wears pale blue'! Now I copied those figures carefully from life, and only this morning in church I sat near a whole row of maidens, aged about fourteen, half of whom wore pale blue and looked most attractive![63]

While Dearmer may have gained a degree of agency in exercising her own gaze, she was also at a remove from the knowledge and expertise of photographers, who had extensive contacts within the local populations and who knew the location of authentic sites. The result was that Dearmer's own knowledge was superficial and easily challenged.

As Dearmer travelled with her young child, her transformation of self was not tracked in quite the same way that Lucas had done, nearly forty years earlier. Instead of documenting changes to her appearance or adoption of dress, indicating that she inhabited an immersive space, Dearmer photographed her daughter Gillian extensively and noted in a letter to her mother from Nikko: 'I am sending you some photographs of Jillie. They are not too good, they make her face look heavier than it is, but they give an idea of her expressions. I wish every day I could show her to you, she is so lovely'.[64] The camera allowed Dearmer to chart her transformation in a way that was more immediately personal. She used it throughout her travels as a means of social interaction and documentation, but here it excluded all other encounters save those with Gillian.

Following the travels of Lucas, Powell-Cotton and Dearmer from the 1870s to the 1910s allows us to map how globetrotters created a sense of place, by figuring spaces as authentic through connections with the other, as well as through performances of identity. The nature of the interactions that they sought confirmed the identities of the places of the differentiated East: India was the location of colonialism, China of transgression and Japan of cosmopolitanism.

Globetrotters' spatial encounters were opportunities for connection with behind-the-scenes spaces, often acquired through a social connection that enhanced their status as travellers. While immersive spaces encouraged transgression and transformation, their culinary adventures, explored in the following chapter, were an example of active engagement, which moved globetrotters beyond the role of observer and elevated their experiences and knowledge to above those of mere tourists.

3 CONSUMING THE EAST

On a dockside tour in Canton in 1870, Arthur Drummond Carlisle could not resist visiting an opium den, where he described the 'prone' men on beds who were lost to narcotic dreams.[1] He noted that, due to the continued British smuggling of the drug, Chinese consumption had increased nearly 400-fold since 1767. However, Carlisle's sympathies did not lie entirely with the Chinese. He also noted the large pile of tea leaves he spotted immediately after leaving the opium den, which were being scooped into wooden casks for shipment abroad. Carlisle passed the tart comment: 'if we are at all guilty of an attempt to poison the Chinese with opium they try to do us an almost equally bad turn in the matter of tea'.[2] He described what first appeared to be the familiar Chinese 'gunpowder' blend that was, on closer inspection, tea dust mixed with sand and other adulterants bound for Western tables, consumed by unknowing 'barbarians'.[3] In Carlisle's narrative, consumption was used to convey a relationship of mutual distrust between China and Britain. Although these were politicised commodities – tea and opium were at the heart of the Opium Wars – globetrotters mentioned the partaking or rejection of local dishes, such as curry in India, as a means of reflecting wider political concerns and cultural unease. Globetrotters did, however, engage with locals through food culture. In their narratives, food and drink created 'alternative geographies' for India, China and Japan, which were not always predicated on politics or trade, but which brought together cosmopolitanism and the social distinction of Romantic touring.[4]

Food was a powerful means of interaction with local populations in the East. Food culture was integral to the way in which social connections were built and sustained. By consuming or rejecting local delicacies, globetrotters were either engaging culturally with the other (non-Westerners) or they were retaining their dissimilarity and separation. Further, as rules around dining and food were acquired, rather than inborn, the distinctions between what was edible or inedible were cultural and often

tied to social or religious ritual. Abstaining or fasting had the potential
to maintain the balance of power in relationships by highlighting cultural
difference and social exclusion or inclusion. For example, British expatriate communities in Shanghai in the early twentieth century described
local Chinese food as 'disgusting' and refused to eat it, relying instead
on imported, pre-packaged foods from home, or having local cooks copy
British recipes.[5] This separation was reinforced by the physical distance
they kept, living in European sections of the city that were set apart
from the Chinese town. Maintaining a degree of separation between
the other and Western residents in the East was deemed necessary to
avoid what the latter felt was a threat of political contagion, or worse,
cultural assimilation.

Globetrotters were not part of these enclaves, nor were they resident
long enough to fear these outcomes. Their ideas about the edible and
the inedible were different to residents. Dining with civil servants or
British merchants – whose lifestyle abroad was markedly different to that
at home – as well as the Eastern other was a means of fostering cultural
connections and accessing the authentic experience. Food consumed in
the country of its origin and in the company of locals, with the appropriate modes and manners being observed, constituted an experience that
could not be replicated at home. Further, as eating and drinking were

◄ PAGE 126: Arthur Drummond
Carlisle noted of his visit to
a Canton opium shop: 'we
find ouselves in a dingy back
room, round which are ranged
a number of low benches.
On these benches are
reclining six or eight smokers'.
Photograph from Charles
Lucas's album.

◄ LEFT: John Thomson's
photograph of tea being
weighed for export, from his
Chinese album, called to mind
eighteenth-century Chinese
export paintings of tea
production and also reiterated
the importance of China to the
nineteenth-century tea trade.

Chinese food and the accompanying modes and manners of dining were a point of cultural fascination and engagement for globetrotters. Charles Lucas included a studio photograph of a Chinese meal, which he entitled 'Chow chow scene', one of the many images in circulation at Chinese ports. In Lucas's case, the photograph documented his own forays into Chinese food culture mentioned in his letters.

necessary activities, the choice of where to dine, with whom to dine and what to eat offered meaningful social engagement in spaces where political and social taboos could be broken. Dining with the other also meant that travellers placed their hosts on the same social level as themselves, temporarily relinquishing a sense of their own superiority.

Rebecca Earle has written of how, in the conquest of Latin America (1492–1700), part of the Spanish programme of colonisation was based on the assimilation of indigenous people by changing their diet and dress to those of 'civilised' Spaniards.[6] The political element in this connection between food, body and appearance was long-standing and featured in globetrotters' accounts. Egerton Laird wrote of the 'dirty yellow bodies' of the Chinese and that he only ever made the 'mistake' of eating their food once, in San Francisco, because of the 'clean, industrious' appearance they presented there.[7] He portrayed China as inherently dirty, with poor food hygiene that suggested the presence of contagion, noting that, at a hotel in Shanghai, the 'feeding [was] poor' and there were 'smells ... suggestive of cholera'.[8] The foodstuffs of the East were integral to the images constructed at home as part of the much longer political and mercantile interactions with each country. Yet, at certain points in their travels, globetrotters departed from these pre-existing associations to create a new narrative that reinforced their own agendas around social distinction and cosmopolitanism. In some cases, as with tea, this was in direct opposition to the way that it was regarded at home. Globetrotters also wrote letters that revealed how they broke food taboos and indulged their appetite for the experience of mutual encounter.

EXPECTATION AND ADULTERATION

Tea and curry were well known in Britain and already had specific cultural identities attached to them. These identities, or tropes, were used at home as cultural shorthand for a number of histories and political issues. Tea, for example, was a lucrative product and market at the heart of the Opium Wars, as shown in Carlisle's description of his experience in the docks of Canton. In comparison, curry was a culinary symbol of Anglo-Indian interactions and relations that was adopted and adapted in Britain. However, in the aftermath of the Indian Mutiny, curry – as it was eaten in India – came to represent British anxieties.

'ALL THE TEA IN CHINA'

There is a scene in Dickens's popular novel *Bleak House* (1852–3) where his protagonist, Esther Summerson, prepares a pot of tea below a set of early nineteenth-century Chinese export paintings showing the process of tea manufacture from planting to harvesting, drying and shipping. This reminds the reader of the foreign origins of tea and how the product was figured to represent idealised English domesticity. These types of paintings were popular souvenirs for British merchants in Canton in the eighteenth and early nineteenth centuries. The images not only made a connection to the commodities of Anglo-Chinese trade, but they also placed them in a Chinese landscape, albeit one that could only be imagined. That Dickens need only reference the series of export paintings indicated that they were relatively commonplace and invoked a romanticised landscape that located tea in China.

In the course of the nineteenth century, tea production moved from China to India and later expanded to Ceylon. In their narratives, however, globetrotters did not simply relocate the same sites of tea production from China to new locations. Instead, they connected these sites of newly industrialised British tea production, for example Darjeeling, to the Romantic iteration of the Grand Tour of Europe. This took in the Alps and the Rhine in addition to Italy. In doing this, globetrotters created an alternative geography of tea to that of China. They invoked India as a site of the sublime, an act that distinguished them from the pervasive, socially inferior Cook's tourists. The successful transplant of tea from China to Darjeeling created the ideal picturesque landscape, contrasting the orderly yet lush tea plantations with the sublime site of the Himalayas. Historian Romita Ray noted that it was in Darjeeling that conventional ideas of the picturesque were recalibrated. Colonial residents viewed the industrial tea plantations and the railways that transported both the commodity and people as 'picturesque'.[9]

This pairing of picturesque views and the tea terraces was, Ray argued, a means that the British used to simultaneously situate themselves within

▲ ABOVE: Egerton Laird included the iconic view of the Kanchenjunga mountain, with its five distinctive peaks, in *The Rambles of a Globe Trotter*, 1875. It is one of the highest mountains in the world and, for Laird and other globetrotters, it was associated with the alpine views of Switzerland. ▶ OVERLEAF: A European copy of a Chinese export painting showing the drying of tea, from *A Map of China and surrounding lands...*, engraved by Matteo Ripa (1682–1746), *c*.1719. These images of tea processing were in heavy circulation in the West by the late eighteenth and early nineteenth centuries. William Alexander, the artist who accompanied the Macartney mission, prepared images from a tea series for prints.

an Indian landscape and demonstrate a connectedness to the wider Empire, since they, like the tea plants they gazed upon, were transplants. The tea produced on those terraces was, throughout the 1860s and 1870s, extolled in the British press as an important British product. Opinion pieces in publications such as *Frasers* made the point that tea produced domestically in India should be the preferred choice for British consumers, as it was of benefit to the Empire. However, the tea terraces of Darjeeling did not feature in globetrotters' accounts. They focused instead on the Himalayas and the views of Everest and Kanchenjunga, for which the hill station offered a particularly good vantage point. In 1872, Laird dismissively mentioned the tea terraces as an inconvenient encounter on his journey to gain a better view of the Himalayas: 'we came to very extensive tea plantations, but the scrubby tea plant does not improve on acquaintance'.[10] Travelling for leisure, Laird was only away from Britain for a relatively brief period. He did not, unlike longer-term British residents of India, need to confirm his Britishness.

Instead of confirming their connectedness to Empire, globetrotters used Darjeeling in their narratives to demonstrate connections with older iterations of elite touring culture. Their opinions on Eastern landscapes reflected, in part, certain expectations moulded by the itineraries of the early nineteenth-century Romantic Grand Tour, with its extended scope that encompassed Switzerland and the Rhine. Tourists viewed the Alps through the works of the Romantic poets, particularly Percy Bysshe Shelley's *Mont Blanc* (1817), an ode to sublime beauty. Lord Byron's epic, *Childe Harold's Pilgrimage* (1812; 1818), was treated as an indispensable guide on how to observe and experience these sublime sites. In the mid-nineteenth century, increased alpine tourism – under the auspices of Thomas Cook, who offered a package tour to Switzerland in 1865 – meant that elite tourists began to regard sites such as Mont Blanc as well-trodden routes, spoiled by the lower classes. Elite tourists demonstrated their class and status through their knowledge of when and where to express the appropriate Romantic reaction to the sublime experience. Laird quoted extensively from *Mont Blanc* in his account of his time in Darjeeling, musing on the inaccessibility of the Himalayan peaks and their untrodden white snow. By emphasising their untouched quality, Laird signposted their exclusivity: pristine slopes bereft of package tourists.

By the 1880s, the sales of tea produced on British sites, like Darjeeling and Assam, outstripped sales of Chinese teas in Britain. Despite the increase in sales of Indian teas at home, globetrotters continued to locate

Darjeeling as a site of the picturesque. Walter Ryland toured India in 1881, just as Indian teas were ascendant in the domestic market, yet in Assam he had very little to relate about tea cultivation with the exception of the occasional sighting of a tea plant in the wild. His primary aim in travelling to Darjeeling was to see the Himalayas but, as was so often the case for travellers, mists and rains obscured the views and he only glimpsed what he speculated might have been Everest. His plans frustrated, Ryland and his party visited a tea plantation, where he observed the various stages of tea production. He noted ultimately of the excursion, 'we were most unlucky while at Darjeeling in not being favoured with brighter weather, and with more distinct and better views of the magnificent Himalayan mountains'.[11] A decade later, Frederick Diodati Thompson omitted all mention of the tea terraces at Darjeeling when he visited, instead describing his first sighting of the Himalayas as 'the sublimest scene I have ever witnessed'.[12] In the nearly twenty years that separated the earliest globetrotters (such as Laird) from Thompson, Darjeeling was maintained as a site of the sublime.

Tea, therefore, was firmly located in China. Not only did globetrotters erase it from the terraces of Darjeeling to connect with an older, elite touring culture, but they also connected tea to what they thought of as a pre-industrial, Chinese version of tea production. Carew Davies Gilbert collected a series of Chinese photographs illustrating tea production on his travels in 1877. The images clearly drew on the earlier representations shown in Chinese export paintings, although they did also include elements of modernisation with certain mechanised production techniques, indicating that tea production in China was not entirely rooted in the past. However, like in the tea terraces in Darjeeling, mechanisation was not something that globetrotters wanted to see in China. Laird observed the processing of Chinese tea in Foochow, writing that 'the building was very well ventilated, and there being no machinery there was no horrible smell of oil, as in the Manchester factories. From the headdress of the ladies it was a flowery scene, and worthy of China'.[13] Notwithstanding the political associations of Chinese tea production as pre-modern, Laird, and the images that Gilbert collected, located Chinese tea within the realm of the artisan, linking it to the prevalent critique of modernity in the Aesthetic Movement. Tea was part of an alternative, imagined geography, created by globetrotters, that was reflective not only of a desire to see a version of Old China, much like that of Old Japan, but also of a desire to escape modernity.

Photographs of tea processing in China by John Thomson. John Thomson and William Saunders created a photographic version of the tea series, widely collected by globetrotters.

In addition to the processing of tea, Gilbert had two further tea-related images of Chinese landscapes. The first he labelled 'Tea Plantation Yang Le Doon Upper Yantse'.[14] The location of the Upper Yangtze River was significant. In 1877, the year that Gilbert arrived in China, the area of the Upper Yangtze between Ichang and Chungking was newly opened to Europeans and was quickly exploited for the access that it provided to the tea trade. It was not on the tourist trail, however, and Gilbert's letters confirm that, with the exception of Peking, he confined his own route through China to coastal sites.[15] His souvenir photographs of a landscape that he never saw reinforced a vision of China that had its origins in the older imagery in circulation in Britain.

The album, with its images of experiences Gilbert did not have, indicated the way that photographs were employed not only to reconstruct itineraries but also to reinforce expectations. Photography could be used to create a visual document that fused the imagined or expected experience with the actual lived experience. In Gilbert's Chinese albums, these images reconcile his ideal of the imagined Chinese landscape with the documentary qualities of photography, proving that the tea terraces shown in Chinese export paintings really existed. These paintings were produced for a Western market, but by Chinese artists who directed the British view. Gilbert's photographs, on the other hand, were taken by a Western photographer, capturing subjects that many expected to see while also accessing what they had previously been restricted from seeing. Through his photographs, Gilbert created a document that represented not only what Western travellers felt was iconic about China, but also the altered balance of power with Britain.

While tea detracted from the picturesque in Darjeeling, it was an integral element of the Chinese picturesque as constructed by globetrotters. Laird commented on the views near the Taiwan Strait: 'the country is very beautiful, and there are plenty of hills planted on top with the tea plant'.[16] This description of rolling green hills contrasted sharply with his encounter in Darjeeling with 'scrubby' tea plants. When considered alongside Gilbert's images, Laird's comments indicate that tea was part of the alpine picturesque in China. The first photograph of tea terraces in Gilbert's album featured steep-sided mountains adorned by tea plants that stood out in sharp relief. The second of his images, 'Tea Plantation Upper Yantse', focuses more closely on the tea plants and features two small figures in Chinese dress. Their presence was not only an important element in the construction of the picturesque landscape, but it also

▲ ABOVE: Two photographs collected in 1877 by Carew Davies Gilbert, showing tea terraces on the Yangtze river in China. Tea was part of an enduring construction of the Chinese picturesque. ▶ OPPOSITE: This photograph of Darjeeling by Bourne & Shepherd was reproduced in Frederick Thompson's publication, *In the Track of the Sun*, 1893. Thompson commented not on the tea terraces of Darjeeling, but on the view of the 'highest mountain in the world' that this location afforded.

reinforced the perception that, although cultivated, the terraces were sparsely populated and untrodden by Western visitors.

These photographs bear further comparison with one published twenty years later by Thompson, in his description of a visit to Darjeeling. It shows the roofs of the hill station clustered against the Himalayas; Darjeeling is shown as nearly devoid of tea terraces, with the mountains providing the focal point. Although Thompson was travelling in the early 1890s, he used a number of photographs that were in circulation from the early 1870s to illustrate his text. These images, produced by professional photographers in their studios across the East, were part of a set or cannon that, much as the earlier Chinese export paintings had done, encapsulated the East for travellers and their audiences at home. By using a set of images that located the key experiences of the East within a specific geography, such as tea in China, globetrotters fused their new experiences of travel with an older experience, thus conferring social distinction. However, by anchoring these in an older landscape, they also sought a degree of authenticity: to experience tea in China, instead of India, was, for them, to successfully connect with an authentic Old China.

THE ADULTERATION OF CURRY

Just as tea was part of an older relationship between Britain and China, curry was subject to a similarly long-standing relationship between Britain and India, representative of adaptation and assimilation. The Mughals, who politically dominated India from the sixteenth century, transformed simple Hindustani dishes through the addition of luxurious Persian ingredients and cooking techniques. Later, with the first European incursions into India, new ingredients were added, such as chilli peppers from South America, which left a lasting legacy in the form of the Vindaloo. Curry was ultimately modified by the British to become a standardised sauce across regions. But this incarnation was one that only the British and other Europeans consumed, as local populations maintained their own regional tastes. Like the incorporation of Mughal techniques and ingredients, adaptations in the British version of curry was largely limited to Western residents and served to reinforce ideas of difference. These divisions were further strengthened as British residents began to favour imported, pre-packaged food from home.

A version of these Anglo-Indian curries made an appearance in *Mrs. Beeton's Book of Household Management* (1861), a cookery book that was a barometer of popular tastes and tables in Britain. It was a guide to all

Illustration showing curry and Indian cooks, from *Mrs. Beeton's Book of Household Management*, 1892. Versions of curry, representative of Britain's long-standing engagement with India, were on British menus from the eighteenth century. Mrs Beeton's indispensable book was in print throughout the nineteenth and twentieth centuries, and included an illustrated section on Indian cookery that expanded in subsequent editions.

Advertisement for curry powder from *Mrs A. B. Marshall's Larger Cookery Book of Extra Recipes...*, 1899. This advertisement indicated just how popular curry was in Britain. Despite its relative ubiquity, Nancy Dearmer sent her mother curry power she had purchased from the bazaar in Madras, privileging the authenticity of her own experience in India over what was served at domestic tables in Britain.

aspects of running a middle-class household. Although Isabella Beeton died in 1865, a few years after the first edition was published, the book was continually in demand and regularly reprinted and updated throughout the second half of the nineteenth and early twentieth centuries. This makes it a useful tool not only in following changing middle-class culinary tastes, but also in assessing the impact of foreign foods on the British diet. With regard to India, recipes for 'Indian Curry-Powder' and curry for fish, beef, mutton, veal and chicken are listed in the 1861 edition. By 1907, there was a complete section on 'Indian Cookery', reflecting the place that India held in British society and highlighting ideas of its importance as a colony.

In touring the East, curry, like tea, was an expected and almost familiar aspect of the Eastern food-scape and, like tea, there was a concern around adulteration. Adulteration of food within British markets was commonplace in the nineteenth century: bread flour was cut with alum; tea with ash; potted foods like anchovies were coloured with lead; and curry was treated with mercury. The Analytical Sanitary Commission, an independent body, published a number of articles in *The Lancet* in the first half of the 1850s and the issue of food safety was further disseminated to the public through articles, plays and pamphlets that raised levels of awareness and alarm. Poems such as Christina Rossetti's (1830–94) *Goblin Market* (1862), where people buy what they believe is wholesome food only to weaken and die after consuming it, have been read as an example of 'food adulteration literature' that proliferated in Britain in this period.[17] The 1860 Act for Preventing the Adulteration of Articles of Food and Drink relied on merchants to voluntarily reduce the amount of adulterants in food and as a result had little real impact in the marketplace. Food warnings in popular literature extended to children's literature from the 1830s through to the 1880s. This is significant because it was the period when many of the globetrotters mentioned came of age.* They would have been aware of food adulteration, but it would also have seemed a commonplace, albeit scandalous, state of affairs in Britain. Prevalent in British discourse, adulteration symbolised a breach of trust by the provider and, at the same time, an inherent vulnerability on the part of the consumer.

---

* Carlisle was born in 1847, Laird in 1848, Ryland in 1836 and Thompson in 1850. Although Thompson was American, there was a similar situation in that country: the first nationwide legislation dealing with the adulteration of food was the Pure Food and Drug Act of 1906.

This feeling of vulnerability to unscrupulous cooks and suppliers was not an experience that was unique to home. Tourists making their way through Europe had similar complaints. In the East, however, anxieties around adulterations of food also reflected wider political concerns. In this context, consuming curry in India, while allowing travellers to access what was believed to be authentic Indian cuisine, also potentially exposed them to the unwholesome. For example, Ryland spent a large part of the Indian leg of his World Tour in dak bungalows, where a resident cook prepared meals, generally curry, for him and his companions. However, on arrival in Jaipur, he and his travelling companions chose instead to stay at the newly opened Kaisir-i-Hind Hotel where he found a 'much better variety of food'.[18] In his narrative, Ryland confirmed the reputation of the dak bungalow as rough accommodation, especially when compared with the luxury of a Western-style hotel. Ryland's great concern over the food provided at the dak bungalow was that the thick curry sauces could mask adulteration: 'the cook might introduce into the mixture any kind of meat, either that of goats, pigs, fowls or even of camels for all you can

'The Neilgherries. Coonoor. Gray's Hotel (visited 12th November 1877)', 1870s. The hill stations were not only ideally suited to tea cultivation; they were also used by the colonial elite as a retreat from the heat of the plains. Coonoor was situated in the Nilgiri hills of Tamil Nadu near to the exclusive hill station of Ootacamund. Hotels like Gray's catered to residents and also to tourists who wanted to align themselves with the fashionable society of the Raj.

tell'.[19] For Ryland, curry was an inherently untrustworthy food that lent itself to adulteration at the hands of dishonest Indian cooks.

Ryland was travelling through India in 1881, two years before the introduction of the Ilbert Bill, the ratification of which allowed Indian judges the right to pass sentences on Europeans. A strand of the public discourse around the Ilbert Bill focused on the role of servants and how the Bill, when it was passed, would be the undoing of Anglo-Indian households, as their servants would have grown insolent and unmanageable. The khansama, the cook and house steward for dak bungalows and Anglo-Indian households alike, also had the potential to become disrespectful. Locals were equally aware of tourists' anxieties: a 1901 advertisement for the Kaiser-i-Hind, where Ryland stayed, noted that the owner was a khansama who, during the Indian Mutiny of 1857, remained loyal to the British.* The points in the advertisement were meant to reassure globetrotters that here was a servant, a cook, who could be trusted.

The advertisement for the Kaisir-i-Hind also mentioned that not only was the former owner loyal during the Indian Mutiny, but he was also Muslim. He was not bound by the same restrictions as Hindus in regard to food and its preparation. Household manuals for Anglo-Indian families suggested that a Muslim or, preferably, a Christian should fill the role of khansama. Thompson, travelling through India in 1891, engaged a 'Eurasian named Pedro', whose name and background implied links with the Portuguese Catholics and the Christian community in India, to look after his meals.[20] While there was a practical side to selecting a non-Hindu as a cook, the decision also reflected Western perceptions of Hindus as unclean and untrustworthy, and associated in British minds as the perpetrators of the worst episodes of the Indian Mutiny, particularly Cawnpore. Hindu temples, especially those in the holy city of Benares, were characterised in globetrotters' narratives as filthy; Laird described a 'sickening' stench from rotting food left as offerings and 'the worshippers themselves'.[21] Visiting Benares fifteen years later, Thompson went even further, branding the Hindus who worshipped 'Siva and his terrible wife', Kali, as those who 'eat carrion and excrement'.[22] Laird's and Thompson's comments illustrate the long-standing construction of a negative Hindu

---

* The advertisement was a supplement in the *Heritage of India* series (1901–46). The series was written by British writers and aim to impart a greater understanding of India's history and culture from a Western, imperial perspective.

As the 'Holy City of the Hindus', Benares was an important destination for
globetrotters seeking cultural engagement. However, many globetrotters, such
as Egerton Laird, who included this image in *The Rambles of a Globe Trotter*,
1875, documented conditions that they felt were unhygenic.

identity, perpetuated around consumption. Hindus were regarded as
contaminated, spiritually and physically, by their religious practice. The
ongoing debate in Britain on adulteration of foods, paired with the politics of the Indian Mutiny and subsequent Ilbert Bill, influenced the way in
which Western travellers represented Hindus and their food practices.

However, political changes, both domestically in Britain and globally,
were significant in reshaping travellers' perceptions of food culture in
India, or at least those experiences that they communicated in their
private correspondence. Nancy Dearmer was born in 1889, more than a
decade after the legislation of the Sale of Food and Drug Act (1872) that,
unlike the failed Food and Drinks Act of 1860, was a lasting and valuable
measure against food adulteration. Dearmer's childhood, certainly in
terms of the prevalent discourse around food adulteration, would have
been shaped very differently from those of the earlier travellers: Carlisle,
Laird, Ryland and Thompson. She was also travelling through India in
1916, during the First World War, where she observed its impact at first

hand, including encounters with German prisoners of war and members of the Indian army. Hindus, Muslims and Sikhs were deployed not only in theatres of war in the Northern Provinces, but also in the Middle East, as well as further afield, in France. These developments would have had a wider impact and potentially shaped Dearmer's decision to engage a Hindu servant, Mumiswarmy, who was responsible for the preparation of her meals as she travelled the subcontinent.

Not only did she hire a Hindu khansama, but also curry was not rejected in her narrative; it was instead used to render exotic the familiarity of colonial India to her readers at home. In a letter to her mother, she gave a detailed description of the preparation methods for what was seen as an authentic curry:

> In India curry powder is made fresh every morning. You take chillies and ginger, nutmeg, peppercorn and various other spices and these are dried and rolled upon a stone slab with a stone roller, which is to be found in every properly constructed Indian household, Anglo-Indian included.[23]

By linking Indian households, in which she did not stay, with Anglo-Indian homes, with which she did have accommodation, Dearmer sought to achieve an authentic (non-Western) experience by extending her interactions beyond the social layer of the British Raj. This was further reinforced by connecting food with the handmade aspects of curry, thus imbuing it with an artisanal quality that, in Britain, was associated with ideas of authenticity prevalent in public discourse on the Arts & Crafts and Aesthetic Movements. She also highlighted the way in which food represented place, noting to her mother that 'you in England of course can't do this', but promised to purchase some ready-made curry powder in the bazaar and send it home.[24] While Ryland may have rejected curry in 1881, Dearmer not only consumed it in 1916, but also advised and aided her family to approximate the dish at home, thus changing its identity from a symbol of distrust and anxiety, brought about by political and social factors, to a food that represented the cosmopolitan consumption of authentic Indian culture.

BREAKING TABOOS

While food was the subject of anxieties around adulteration, it also lent itself to discourse on contagion, particularly as a means of reflecting

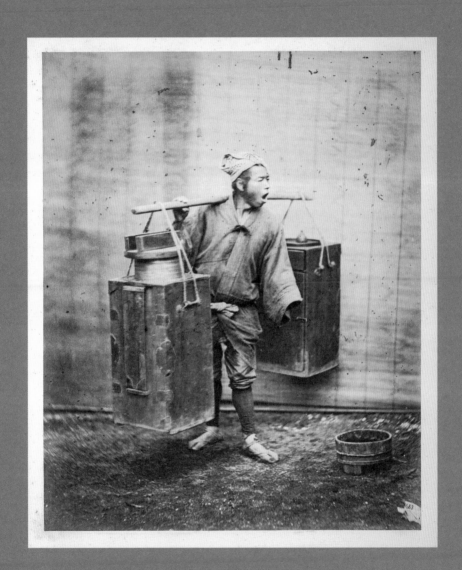

ideals of cleanliness in conjunction with approbation of the cultures
of China and Japan. Chinese cities were epitomised in globetrotters'
accounts as harbourers of dirt and filth, whereas Japan was a haven of
cleanliness. This commentary went beyond mere distinction of cultures
and, like curry in India, was evidence of long-standing relationships
between Britain and China, compared to the relatively shorter interactions with Japan. Consuming the food of the Chinese, who ate ingredients
deemed by globetrotters to be not only inedible – such as dog and cat
– but also supremely unhygienic, meant that globetrotters were doubly
exposing themselves to disease. Added to these cultural tropes was the
very real threat of cholera present across the East in a series of epidemics.
During his stay in Yokohama, Charles Lucas reported cholera outbreaks in
his letters. In Japan, he ascribed the origin to passenger steamers arriving
from China.[25] By consuming what Westerners saw as the inedible food of
the other, particularly in China, globetrotters were potentially exposing
themselves to the contagion of the other. At the same time, local populations, especially in Japan, saw travellers as agents of this same contagion.
For example, Lucas also reported that his fellow globetrotters, en route
from China to meet him in Yokohama, were quarantined in Nagasaki as
Japanese officials feared that they were carrying cholera from China.

In China, as in India, globetrotters' published accounts expressed
concerns about the wholesomeness of their food, paired with political
and social anxieties. Laird was not only concerned about physical
contagion; he also eschewed local food in China in favour of desiccated
soups, biscuits, tinned sardines and Alsop's Ale, supplemented with, he
emphasised, '*pure cold water* from a little stream'.[26] His insistence on
purity stemmed in part from genuine concerns about maintaining good
health while travelling, but also appeared in his text in juxtaposition
with two studio photographs of a Chinese mandarin and an upper-class
woman that he titled 'Chinese Monstrosities'.[27] The mandarin, labelled 'A
"Swell"' is shown with his hand raised, displaying grotesquely long finger-
nails. The woman is reduced to one feature, noted as the 'Feet of a Lady
of "Ton"'. One foot is encased in a small, embroidered shoe; the other is
unbandaged, laying bare the deformities inflicted by foot-binding. These
images simplified and caricatured the Chinese by limiting representation
to single components of their appearance, using them as shorthand for
'barbarity'.[28] Not only, Laird noted, did the Chinese deal brutally with
the 'other' as represented by Western missionaries – who were often the
subject of attacks – but they were also 'barbaric' to their own bodies. In

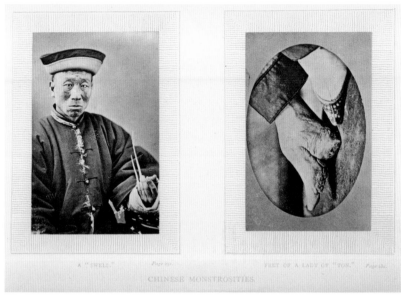

◄ PAGE 147: 'Chow Chow Seller', from Charles Lucas's album. Globetrotters often characterised food sold from street vendors as a potential source of contagion. Although he professed not to have tried it, Arthur Drummond Carlisle enjoyed bamboo omlettes purchased from street sellers in Ningbo.
▲ ABOVE: 'Chinese Monstrosities', from Egerton Laird's *The Rambles of a Globe Trotter*, 1875. Western narratives expressed a fascination with the Chinese practice of foot-binding. It was also one of the exaggerated elements of the appearance of the Chinese upper classes that globetrotters invoked in their writings as a means of conveying a negative image of the country.

Laird's narrative, their moral failings were reflected in their appearance and proclivities, which in turn were nourished by the food that they consumed. To ingest this was to risk being exposed to a moral contagion that shaped Chinese bodies and informed their dealings with the West.

The acceptance or rejection of food was not solely the province of Western travellers. Certain segments of the Chinese population in urban centres such as Shanghai, Canton and Hong Kong embraced Western food culture through the conspicuous consumption of food brought in by tourists and expatriates. In Shanghai, for example, locals who had close relationships with resident Europeans – including compradors, the managers or agents of banking and trading houses, and courtesans – ate these foods. These were specific groups who were employed in various capacities by Western residents, but who also exploited these relationships for gain, both financially and socially. Western food products represented a Western elite and their consumption by the Chinese

▲ ABOVE: Photograph of the Bund Road, from Annie Russell-Cotes's *Westward from the Golden Gate, c.*1900. ▸ OVERLEAF: Photograph of Physic Street, Canton, by John Thomson. This image of a shopping thoroughfare captured many of the elements of a Chinese city that globetrotters reported: the hanging shop signs indicated not only what was sold within but also often included an accompanying motto advocating virtue or hard work. Globetrotters themselves tended to use sedan chairs, making the narrow, crowded streets even harder to traverse.

signified social alignment. They were also used by the Chinese as commodities to trade within their own culture for enhanced social status. For example, courtesans sent packaged food back to their families in rural provinces as expensive signifiers of status, gained through association with and exploitation of Europeans. These groups ate Western food to align themselves with Europeans, who, in their published narratives, consumed the same packaged foods to emphasise their difference from the Chinese.

Not all globetrotters rejected Chinese food. Travelling just one year before Laird, Carlisle recorded a meal taken in Hong Kong in the company of mandarins. Hong Kong itself marked the first point of encounter with China for the majority of tourists. The island was a major British trading concession along with the opening of the treaty ports (Shanghai, Canton, Ningbo, Foochow and Amoy) at the end of the First Opium War. Under British development, Hong Kong became the largest port for international shipping in the second half of the nineteenth century. As such, it was a British space within a Chinese sphere, which for many globetrotters made it an ideal location in which to engage in cultural immersion. The banquet that Carlisle attended began with bird's nest soup, an expensive Chinese delicacy created from the saliva of swallows that binds the twigs of their nests together. The nests themselves were imported to China from Malaysia. They were then cleaned and sold for extremely high prices, and were accordingly presented in globetrotters' accounts as a luxury food and a status dish.* However, Carlisle did not stop at consumption of birds' nests, but detailed the extensive list of dishes he consumed:

> pigeon stew, seaweed soup, pigeon eggs, minced quail, stewed peas, black seaweed, stewed lotus root, sea moss, ducks' feet, shark's fin ... after these eleven courses follow twenty more, whose names had better be given to make the list complete: duck and bamboo, Japan sea snails, meat and seaweed, sturgeon jelly, bêches de mer [sea cucumber], mushrooms, quangsi mushrooms, guarapoo fish, lotus seeds, sweet cakes, fowl and ham, shark's fin with fish balls, frogs, fish maw, pigeon, quail, bamboo omelette, pork fritters and rice, congee and rice, tea.[29]

He confessed to having eaten them all. For a segment of his readership, those involved in trade or politics, his presence at this banquet was a nod to a long-standing history of merchants' dinners. These were generally staged in Canton by hong merchants for Western traders and featured a very similar menu. The meals were a mixture of high-status delicacies, including bird's nest soup, shark's fin and sea cucumber – which Carlisle recorded eating – accompanied by French and Spanish wines. Although they were curtailed just before the onset of the First Opium War, the dinners were later revived and it was likely that they provided the template for the banquet that Carlisle enjoyed in Hong Kong. Chinese merchants continued to use these occasions as a means of building potential business relationships with the West. Although Carlisle himself was not involved in trade, his relations in India were, and it is possible that he was invited due to a family connection. In this context, the banquet

---

* 'I had no idea how expensive the nests were – 54 dollars a "pice," weighing something under a pound'. Baroness Anna Brassey, *A Voyage in the 'Sunbeam'* (London: Longmans, Green, 1879), 391; 'We indulged in some birds' nest soup for dinner, which is a great and expensive luxury'. Walter P. Ryland, *My Diary During a Foreign Tour* (Birmingham, 1886), 199.

was a cultural entrée for a globetrotter. For those among his readership with a pre-knowledge of Eastern trade, Carlisle's presence at the banquet elevated his status beyond that of a mere tourist.

Although Carlisle indulged in Chinese food in Hong Kong, he was at pains, when he travelled to Canton, to point out that it was no longer a version of British space. He styled Canton as authentically Chinese, by noting that the success of the British settlement at Hong Kong had led to a decline in the European population on Shamian Island in Canton, which had been the site of foreign residence since the eighteenth century. Food was central to Carlisle's evocation of Canton as a Chinese space. He began his tour of the city with the markets, focusing on the meat and vegetable shops:

> In the former there are some curious specimens of fish, flesh, and fowl. Besides an abundance of pork, ducks, geese, chickens, and fresh fish, we may see here and there a suspended bundle of harvest rats sun-dried, along with ducks that have gone through a similar process, joints of white meat, which our Chinese attendant makes us understand are of canine origin. ... while there is little doubt that the wealthy classes are great epicures, there is less doubt that the poor people are generally very foul feeders.[30]

In Carlisle's narrative, food represented a stark cultural difference, pairing foods he saw as edible – duck, geese and pork – with, particularly to the Victorian point of view, the inedible meat of rats and dogs, and especially the latter, as Victorians perceived dogs as either pets or strays. The sentimentality surrounding the Victorian pet placed it within the circle of friendship and family; to eat a dog was an act of betrayal. Conversely, stray dogs were disease-ridden and dangerous to ingest. To do so was to align with those who ate the indescribable, like Thompson's references to Indians who ate carrion. Carlisle also made the point that it was only the lower classes who consumed what he saw as inedible, not those who belonged to the same class as the mandarin merchants with whom he dined in Hong Kong. While he might have eaten Chinese food, he had not, he reassured his readers, broken taboos.

The consumption of cat and dog flesh as a symbol of delineation between rich and poor in China was reiterated in globetrotters' accounts. Ryland wrote of 'the low class butchers' shops, where different sorts of joints of cats, dogs and rats were sold.[31] Ten years later, Thompson visited

Restaurants provided a means of cultural engagement as globetrotters and Chinese residents dined in close proximity. In 1881, Walter Ryland recorded the meal he ate in Canton, which included: 'shrimp-patties, and about twenty varieties of sweetmeats, and sweet-cakes, which were all placed neatly on separate dainty little dishes. I did not like the shrimp-patties, but some of the sweet things were quite palatable'. Photograph by John Thomson.

a 'shop that dealt exclusively in the flesh of cats, dogs, and rats, which the lower classes eat with seeming relish'.[32] Yet, in *Walks in the City of Canton* (1875), John Henry Gray (1823–90) insisted that he witnessed middle-class Chinese merchants and craftsman dining in a restaurant where 'no other food than that which consists of the flesh of dogs and cats is eaten'.[33] In addition to Gray's assertion, Carew Davies Gilbert wrote in an unpublished letter to his mother: 'we went to a Native restaurant, & eat [*sic*] cat & dog, the latter was good, not so the former'.[34] In published accounts, tourists such as Carlisle, Ryland and Thompson made the point that they did not break food taboos, yet private letters such as Gilbert's suggest that this was not the case.

The letters of Charles Lucas also highlight that it was in the Chinese city of Canton, instead of the European enclave of Shamian, that social taboos could be broken. Carlisle did this first, by noting the dwindling numbers of Western residents in Shamian. Lucas went even further, to demarcate the separation between Shamian and Canton, noting that the island was surrounded by a wall and had a watchman on duty to keep the Chinese from entering the enclave. To set foot in the city of Canton was, for Westerners, to access the space of the other: in this case, an authentically Chinese site. In a letter to his family, Lucas reported that, while

Charles Lucas's World Tour album, compiled by his mother from the photographs he collected, included what he identified as the interior of a 'flower boat', known o globetrotters as floating brothels. He reassured her in a letter that they were 'so proper any lady might visit them'.

Charles Lucas identified these two portraits as those of popular 'SingSong Girls'. In Canton and Shanghai, these were female entertainers who were trained in singing and dancing; many performed a role in society of sophisticated courtesans. In some ways similar to geisha in Japan, singsong girls were also leaders in culture and style, becoming celebrities. Lucas noted that at a party in Shanghai he 'insisted upon drinking a glass of wine with them which made them the subject of great chaff from all the rest'.

walking through Canton at night, he encountered the flower boats, which he described as 'sort of floating restaurants which a party of Chinese take for a night'.[35] He and his travelling companions joined a boat where a private party was already in progress, noting that the 'Chinamen were very civil to us, they gave us some of their "chow" (food) & pipes to smoke & we listened to the inharmonious strains of the "singsong girls" for some time then went away and back to our houses'.[36] In Lucas's letters, Canton was a place of commensality in almost exclusively Chinese company. It was, therefore, a site of authentic cultural engagement and, being outside of British spaces, a location for transgression.

Like Gilbert, Lucas also engaged in taboo activity. The reputation of the flower boats was that they were, in essence, floating brothels. Thompson referred to them a decade after Lucas's visit as 'the habitation of the frail women of Canton'.[37] When Lucas related his encounters on the flower boat and invited his host in Shamian, a local vicar named Smith, to accompany him on future outings, Smith responded that 'he thought he ought not visit' them.[38] Lucas followed this comment in his letter with a quick assurance to his mother that the flower boats were actually 'so well conducted & proper, any lady might visit them'.[39] Whether or not this was the case, the flower boats were figured by globetrotters as an authentically Chinese space. In his letters, Lucas positioned himself as a social agent who, unlike his host, was not a member of a long-term expatriate community and was therefore able to transgress perceived social codes and rules to access the flower boats. Transgression, whether breaking of food or social taboos, was part of the authentic experience, carrying an alternative set of itineraries and geographical meanings to those put forward in travellers' handbooks.

Breaking food taboos to engage with the other was not limited to globetrotters seeking authenticity. With the influx of Western globetrotters, the number of Western-style restaurants burgeoned. These restaurants were also patronised by local Chinese populations who came to consume mutton and beef, which were part of Chinese food taboos in the latter part of the nineteenth century. Mutton, for example, with its strong odour and rancid taste, was considered unclean. Beef was even more of a taboo, since cattle were seen not only as status symbols for Chinese families, showing that they could afford to keep a cow or ox, but also as helpers in the fields. In essence, they were an extension of the family, seen in much the same way that Western travellers saw their cats or dogs. However, there was also an additional religious dimension, which was tied to the idea that karmic merits were acquired by abstaining from consuming meat, specifically beef. A series of cartoons ran in Chinese-language newspapers in Shanghai, equating the vogue for eating beef with a lapse in morality among young Chinese men. Those Chinese residents who wanted to eat beef and mutton presented it as an acquired taste, indulged by 'fops and dandies' of urban centres in the cosmopolitan spaces of Western-style restaurants.[40] Like the restaurant that Gilbert visited in Canton, these Western-style restaurants were sites where globetrotters and the Chinese might dine alongside each other. In both cases, the seemingly inedible food of the other, instead of the barrier that was presented in published accounts, was actually a bridge to mutual encounter, as locals and tourists attempted to experience an authentic version of each other's culture.

The proliferation of Western-style restaurants, which catered for the increased numbers of Western travellers, was also a feature in Japan. This

ABOVE & PAGE 160: 'Japanese in Western Dress', from Charles Lucas's album. Both Lucas and Carew Davies Gilbert collected these images satirising the Japanese adoption of Western clothing. ▶ PAGE 161: 'Japanese diner in Western restaurant', from Charles Lucas's album. Images like this can be read as a means of ridiculing the Japanese, but the photographs also spoke to a reversal in the balance of power, where Western globetrotters were the ones who were unable to master the modes and manners of Japanese dining.

was tied to the active role that the Meiji government played in construct-
ing, for example, Western-style banqueting halls; the Emperor and his
ministers regularly used them to entertain Western diplomats as part of
the wider programme of embracing Western habits. Unlike in China, this
programme included the use of Western clothing and habits to engage
with the West on what was perceived to be an equal footing. For example, in January 1871, the Meiji Emperor issued a proclamation prescribing
European dress for himself and his court, in an attempt to alter Western perceptions that kimono-wearing Japanese men were feminine and
therefore politically weak. By adopting Western military uniforms and the
dress of Western upper classes, as well as the food of the West, the court
used their own bodies to visually place themselves on an equal standing
with Western powers.

In seeking authenticity, globetrotters did not necessarily appreciate
or understand the meanings inherent in these changes in Japan. Studio
photographs made by Western photographers in Yokohama depicted
Japanese subjects in Western dress and dining in a Western style. The
changes instituted by the Meiji Emperor were viewed through the lens
of satire and lampooned Japanese attempts to master Western culture.
Lucas had a set of these images in his collection of photographs from
Japan, including one trio showing the transformation of a Japanese man
into a European, hand labelled 'Europeanised Japanese'.[41] In the first
image (opposite), the man is shown in traditional dress, presented to the
Western viewer as a gentleman, leaning on a furled parasol much as a
European might lean on a walking stick, itself a visual marker of gentility.
In the second image (page 160) he has been transformed from Japanese
gentleman to Western 'gent' – men who favoured flashier fashion over
taste – attired in ill-fitting Western formal wear that displays little understanding of Western sartorial nuances. The final image (page 161) shows
the same sitter, in the same Western dress, at an opulently appointed
table with a waiter, also a Japanese man in Western dress. Lucas's
comments in his letters home, on the success of the adoption of Western
dress in Japan, reinforce the satire of the images, as he noted that the
railway was 'managed entirely by Japs in European fashions ... [who] look
awful rum little beggars'.[42]

Further, a Westernised Japan undercut the cosmopolitan experience. For globetrotters, a successful visit to Japan was contingent on an
encounter with Old Japan, or what globetrotters perceived as Japanese
society undiluted by Western influences. The aim of Lucas's travels in

the country of Japan was cultural immersion in an idealised world of Old Japan, as he noted to his mother:

> We had such a pleasant time in Kioto without seeing hardly, far less speaking to, another European, quite enchanted with Japanese life ... Nothing I like more than never coming across Europeans at all & living & seeing the customs of the people ... How they must have enjoyed themselves before their country was opened up to the world. I almost wish I had been born a Jap.[43]

Lucas communicated to his family the way in which he engaged in cultural immersion: by staying in accommodation where there were no other Europeans. He also noted how he achieved what he believed to be an approximation of Japanese life, not only by going to places that were outside the urban centres of the treaty ports, but by wearing Japanese kimonos during his stay in the village teahouses.

Yet, while he expressed disapproval of – and possessed photographs mocking – the Japanese appropriation of Western dress, he himself adopted Japanese dress, but failed to express any self-awareness that the Japanese might view his own attempt at cultural immersion with derision. He certainly does not record this as the case, but it is worth bearing in mind Annie Russell-Cotes's own comments on the amusement that her efforts to master chopsticks engendered in the teahouse serving girls. Like the photographs of the Japanese in Western dress, Lucas also preserved an image of himself and one of Arthur Ringrose, dining in the Japanese style and wearing a kimono (page 118). He sheepishly noted, in a letter to his mother, that it was a 'grotesque' image and that he was aware he was 'dressed up'.[44] That he still kept it in his album indicates that, although he was aware of the irony inherent in his adoption of the dress of the other, it still remained a significant moment in his cultural encounter with Japan.

In Lucas's letters, food, in addition to dress, became an important signifier of authentic cultural encounter. The significance of food in Japan was parallel to that of dress. A year after the proclamation on the adoption of Western dress, in 1872 the Meiji Emperor announced that he ate beef and mutton, breaking what had been a taboo in Japanese culture. Eating beef in Japan, as in China, was taboo because of the status of the cow for families and because of the increasing embrace of Buddhism with its strictures against taking any life. That is not to say that the

'Tea house girl', from Charles Lucas's album. In 1874, Egerton Laird wrote of his experience in Japan that 'if it were not for the bright faces of the attendants I am not sure that a teahouse would be bearable'. However, some male globetrotters were often confused by the role of the attendants, prompting Basil Hall Chamberlain's tart comment in *A Handbook for Travellers in Japan* (1891) that the 'moosmes' were not prostitutes and should be treated respectfully.

Japanese diet was completely without meat: although beef was generally not consumed, game, or 'wild meat', was eaten.[45] In the 1870s, beef was consumed by the upper classes in Japan, who in part followed the lead of the Emperor. It took on the aspect of a status dish and, as in coastal urban centres in China, there was a trend of beef consumption among cosmopolitan Japanese dandies.

In Japan, Lucas used food and its accompanying modes and manners to create an alternate geography, which for him represented the authenticity of Old Japan. He did not dine in the Japanese style in Yokohama, where Western-style restaurants were popular, but he did consume Japanese food outside of urban centres. He wrote of a visit to the island of Inoshima, located near to Tokyo and Yokohama, and the tourist track for its shrines. Despite its proximity to Yokohama and its connection to the mainland via a bridge, Inoshima retained a sense of separation. Lucas and his temporary travelling companion, Moseley, took rooms for a week in a local teahouse, where Lucas declared in his letters that he was content to live in the Japanese style. He also included a detailed description of his meal that night:

> We had what Englishmen would consider rather a curious dish, but what Japanese think a great luxury, that is a piece of Octopus. Moseley would not touch it but I managed to get through the portion of a leg. I must confess it looked rather nasty & tasted just like gristle but I am glad I tried it. I always like to taste the native dishes.[46]

For Lucas, food was an integral part of cultural immersion and the experience of authentic Japan. That his travelling companion abstained while Lucas engaged shows a similar presentation of self in his letters from both Japan and China, namely to demonstrate that he was no mere tourist content with superficial encounters. However, it should be noted that the sites of his food transgressions were well outside of his social circle at the club in Yokohama, where he regularly dined with his fellow globetrotters. Additionally, this foray into the authentic experience of food took place with only one other companion, or witness.

From his base at the Yokohama club, Lucas undertook repeated trips, with different companions, to the area around Mount Fuji and to Inoshima. He always booked the same lodgings and, as a result, was able to style himself as an expert on Japan to those newer globetrotters. On a previous trip to Inoshima in early May 1879, when he was accompanied by Moseley, not only did he try octopus, but he also dined on a 'curious native delicacy for dinner – live fish – the fish is brought to the table alive, cut up, regardless of wriggling, & eaten <u>raw</u>, it is not at all bad, I ate a good deal, but Moseley could not be tempted to try it'.[47] This repeated positioning in Lucas's letters of himself as the intrepid traveller, paired with Moseley's reluctance, cast him as a truly cosmopolitan traveller. If not penetrating the country, Lucas was certainly making attempts to intrepidly experience the culture. On a subsequent visit to Inoshima in late July 1879, with a group of friends from Yokohama, he had 'a curious dish for the benefit of those of our party who had never seen it before, viz. a live fish ... It is not at all bad with sauce & a curiosity in its way'.[48] Lucas used his familiarity with the spectacle of native food to establish his own role as an expert traveller, translating the culture for the benefit of his fellow globetrotters. However, his dismissal of the experience as a 'curiosity' also placed it in the realm of the curios, or curiosities, that globetrotters collected from the shops of Japan. Lucas himself devoted large amounts of time to scouring the curio shops of Yokohama, Kobe and

Photograph of a Japanese wayside teahouse, from Charles Lucas's album. Although Japan was styled as a haven of cleanliness by globetrotters, Lucas noted of his stay in a teahouse in Subashiri that he was forced to rise early, having been 'much worried by fleas during the night, had a search & caught fifty-seven in my bed. I counted their corpses afterwards in a glass of water'.

Kyoto, justifying the time and money spent to his mother as wanting their house at 'Warnham to possess a very good collection of curios'.[49] The equation of his experience of the live fish with that of a curio indicated not only that he consumed food to style himself as an expert of Japanese culture, but also that he collected his food experiences, much as he collected his material mementoes of Japan. In his letters, these experiences were, like the curios, something to be sought out; he implied that a degree of connoisseurship about what was good and genuine, versus what was produced for tourists, might be acquired and demonstrated for others through consumption.

Globetrotters used food and dining to construct alternate geographies of social distinction and authenticity. By connecting to older tropes, particularly in the case of tea, globetrotters identified with an earlier, elite travel culture that enhanced their own social distinction. In addition to confirming their own social standing, globetrotters such as Lucas used their experience of food and dining to bridge a sense of separation between the tourist and the other that was reinforced through globetrotters' associations with British residents abroad. In letters detailing his travels in China and Japan, Lucas constructed an itinerary that included food experiences as part of an alternative geography of the authentic cultural encounter. This occurred behind the scenes, outside of European enclaves in Canton and outside of the treaty port of Yokohama in Japan.

The idea of food being a behind-the-scenes experience that represented the authentic was reinforced by the fact that it did not feature overtly in globetrotters' published accounts. These accounts largely equated the food of the other with less desirable apects of their culture; to remain separate was to avoid the filth and contagion in Eastern cities. While dirt and cholera were realities, they also underpinned political situations in globetrotters' writings. The images and food experiences that globetrotters collected represented not only the cultures that they encountered, but also that these things were part of the fashioning and presentation of self. Objects such as the photographs that satirised the Japanese appropriation of Western dress and manners lend themselves, for political reasons, to an alternative reading: they hold a mirror to globetrotters' own use of foreign modes and manners. In addition to depicting the 'Europeanised Japanese', these images were also a reflection of the imbalance of power faced by globetrotters, who were so thoroughly outside their own, familiar, culture. They were indicative of excursions into unfamiliar and potentially difficult social situations. As the images suggest, it was while dining, where a lack of knowledge and manners was at its most apparent, that globetrotters were at their most socially vulnerable. Carlisle described his experience at the Chinese banquet, in the company of mandarins in 1870, noting: 'we have not "implements" beyond china spoons and chop-sticks: the latter, after some awkward experiments, we can wield with tolerable success before the dinner is finished'.[50] This disadvantage marked a reversal of the usual place that Western travellers occupied in the narratives of globetrotting – that of the social superior.

4   COLLECTING THE EAST

In June 1896, following Sir Julian Goldsmid's (1838–1896) unexpected death, auctioneers Christie, Manson and Woods sold his art collections. The MP for the London constituency of St Pancras South and Vice Chancellor of the University of London, Goldsmid was a well-regarded art connoisseur and collector. The lengthy sale, which took place over seven days, reflected the status of his collections. Among the French furniture and Continental porcelains was a discrete collection of 'Oriental Objects of Art', which represented the East (here comprising India, China and Japan) through embroideries, lacquers, bronzes and ivories.[1] Goldsmid travelled to India in March of 1883, ostensibly to investigate the impact of the Ilbert Bill, which he did not support, and acquired some of the Indian material at that time. The addition of Chinese and Japanese items, from two countries that he did not visit, suggests that the art market at home in Britain played a role in materially creating a vision of the East through certain object types that were desirable to collectors.

Goldsmid's 'Oriental' collection was a combination of objects acquired through travel and those purchased at home. In a similar way, globetrotters created the East through objects that were familiar and desirable and those that represented their actual travel experiences. A further comparison of the 'Oriental' pieces in Goldsmid's collection with those acquired by globetrotters – particularly Egerton Laird, Percy Powell-Cotton and Nancy Dearmer – reveals that certain types were consistently collected: Kashmir shawls, Chinese ivory carvings and Japanese *netsuke*. These objects were representative of earlier trade and political connections with the East. For example, after the looting of the Yuanmingyuan in 1860, not only were stolen objects in circulation among Western collectors, but Chinese dealers in Peking also sold items reputed to have come from the Yuanmingyuan as a means of collection enhancement. Objects that were taken directly from the Yuanmingyuan found their way into the royal collections of France and Britain, and pieces with a provenance from the

◄ PAGE 170: Textiles played a dominate role in the displays of the Indian Court, as seen in *Dickinson's Comprehensive Pictures of the Great Exhibition of 1851*, 1854.

◄ LEFT: Advertisement from the *Shanghai Handbook* for *Kuhn & Komor, Art and Curio Dealers*. Curio dealers worked across the East in cosmopolitan port cities. Kuhn & Komor, for example, had shops in Kobe, Shanghai and Singapore. Curio shops were often located in elite hotels.

◄ LEFT: Objects looted from the Yuanmingyuan, as exhibited at the Great Exhibition of 1851. From *The Illustrated London News*, 13 April 1861. Princely objects stolen from the Yuangminyan made their way into royal collections in France and Britain. However, Chinese dealers also sold pieces that were reputed to have come from the Yuanmingyuan as a means of collection enhancement.

► PAGE 175: The Kashmir shawl was an iconic object representing culture and trade. It was adapted for both Eastern and Western markets. For British collectors, it was an object synonymous with India.

Yuanmingyuan were also gifted to museum collections. For example, in 1871, the Victoria and Albert Museum (at that time the South Kensington Museum) purchased a headdress, supposed to have been worn by the Empress, from Captain Charteris (1913–99), who was present at the looting of the Yuanmingyuan. In many cases, it was not possible to differentiate between what was stolen and what was bought in the wake of the looting. However, it was apparent that when those who had spent time in China came home to Britain, their collections – whether looted or purchased – were eventually sold and entered the British art market.*

The relationship between politics, trade and the objects themselves is crucial in considering the meanings that Eastern objects held in this period. Many globetrotters first encountered them in a domestic setting before beginning their World Tour. For example, the vision of India presented in the Great Exhibition of 1851 was based on an accretion of images built over a long period of interaction in both trade and politics. Similarly, Chinese objects were treasured for their craftsmanship while at the same time providing a negative representation of a people who were the subject of British derision due to the outcome of the Opium Wars. Globetrotters often called on these older ideas and layers of meaning to contextualise their own experiences.

However, the significance of these objects in an Eastern context was often misunderstood by globetrotters and exploited by local populations. For example, craftsmen in China played on the misunderstandings that travellers brought with them, producing what were interpreted as courtly objects for the tourist market in the form of small ivory seals with inscriptions identifying them as the former property of the Qianlong Emperor (reigned 1735–96). These were further confused in Western

---

*   These objects appear consistently in the following auction catalogues for Christie, Manson and Woods, which are a sample of catalogues from this period: *Catalogue of a large assemblage of Chinese and Japanese curiosities*, 4–5 July 1867; *Catalogue of ancient Chinese and Japanese enamels*, 1868; *Catalogue of Japan lacquer*, 1868; *Catalogue of a valuable assemblage of oriental, Sévres, Dresden, Berlin, Chelsea, and other porcelains, Gres de Flandres, Wedgwood, Majolica, Chinese and Japanese enamels, Carvings in Ivory, Bronzes*, 1870; *Catalogue of a small consignment of Japanese porcelain and lacquer*, 1874; *Property of Capt. F. Brinkley R.A. of Yokohama*, 1885; *Francis Layborne Popham Esq.*, 1886; *Catalogue of Commissary General Pirkis*, 1890; *Property of Thomas Grey Esq., Nankin and other Chinese and Japanese Porcelain*, 1890.

spheres through the influence that scholars and collectors like Stephen Bushell (1844–1908), who was resident in China as a surgeon, had on the shaping of British perceptions of Chinese objects. Bushell identified what he believed was a court style, thus mistakenly giving a degree of cultural cachet to ivory carvings. Although they created the market for these goods and stimulated it with their demand, tourists often feared that they were purchasing a fake, which in turn undermined the authenticity of their own experiences.

THE KASHMIR SHAWL

In August 1852, the writer and early sociologist Harriet Martineau (1802–1876) described the Kashmir shawl in Charles Dickens's popular publication, *Household Words*, as 'designed for eternity in the unchanging East; copied from patterns which are the heirlooms of caste; and woven by fatalists, to be worn by adorers of the ancient garment'.[2] It is significant that Martineau sought to situate the Kashmir shawl within this context the year after the Great Exhibition, where shawls and Indian textiles comprised a large portion of the display in the Indian Court. The shawls, and other Indian art products, lent themselves to a debate in Britain's public sphere. On one side were arguments from influential designers such as Owen Jones (1809–1874), who felt that there was much that British designers could learn from India. Opposing views, like those voiced by Martineau, implied that India was timeless but had nonetheless declined since its golden age. Views such as Martineau's situated the shawl as a fossilised object, when in reality it was part of a dynamic debate around perceptions of India. Further, this idea of a civilisation in decline had parallels with the way that Chinese objects were portrayed.

Mughal Emperor Akbar (reigned 1556–1605) originally stimulated the Kashmir shawl industry by bringing in weavers from Eastern Turkestan. The earliest extant Kashmir shawls date from the seventeenth century. At this time, they were prized courtly objects that demonstrated the skill of the weavers in their colour combinations, patterns and use of fine pashmina wools. The shawls were a symbol of status in the Mughal courts and were used in the Khil'at ceremony: a means of conferring social standing on an individual and symbolising political alliance. They were presented to local rulers and Western diplomats and traders alike. As such, the shawls would have been recognised by Europeans as objects of value. By the early decades of the eighteenth century, Mughal power was fracturing and Kashmir came under Afghan rule. The Afghans taxed Kashmir shawls

PLATE 18.

London. Chromolithographed & Published by Day & Son, Lithographers to the Queen.

J. B. Waring, Dirext.

GOLD EMBROIDERED CASHMERE SHAWL

heavily but did little to support the industry itself. No longer protected, Kashmiri merchants turned to lucrative foreign markets for their shawls. In 1822, William Moorcroft (1767–1825), an employee of the East India Company, undertook an assessment of the shawl industry. He reported seeing agents, from a number of other Eastern countries, placing orders in Kashmir for shawls that were altered to suit the tastes and preferences of their clientele. The Kashmir shawls imported to Europe were already markedly different in appearance to those worn in India, which in turn differed from those worn throughout the rest of the East.

The shawl appeared on the shoulders of the fashionable Western elite in the late eighteenth century, first in Paris and then in London.* These shawls were long and narrow, with the majority of the design confined to the borders, as worn by Anne-Marie-Louise Thélusson, Comtesse de Sorcy, in a 1790 portrait by Jacques-Louis David. However, as fashion changed in the early decades of the nineteenth century, so did the shawl designs, which began to incorporate large buta cones or paisley patterns on squares with red and green as the predominant colours. By the early 1820s, when Moorcroft made his study of the shawl industry, sections were woven on multiple looms and the pieces were joined together. This production method meant a much faster turnaround time. Instead of a single piece occupying a loom for up to eighteen months, several could be produced in that time. Both French and British agents had considerable input into the styles of shawls made for their markets, further altering their appearances.

The Kashmir shawl had multiple identities in mid-nineteenth-century Britain. It contrasted British modernity with ancient India, as Martineau had done, animating a prominent display in an exhibition dedicated to showcasing British manufacture and growing imperial dominance of the Indian subcontinent. It also figured as a luxury good that socially

---

* Mary Dusenbery cites a portrait by Jacques-Louis David (1748–1825) of the young Anne-Marie-Louise Thélusson (1770–1845), Comtesse de Sorcy (HUW 21, Neue Pinakothek, Munich) painted in 1790. *Flowers, Dragons and Pine Trees* (Garsington: Windsor, 2004), 48; D.N. Saraf attributes the popularity of the shawl to the trend setter Joséphine de Beauharnais (wife of Napoleon Bonaparte and future Empress of France), who first wore them in 1796. *Arts and Crafts, Jammu and Kashmir: Land, People and Culture* (Buldana, Mahrastra: Abhinav Publications, 1998); Eileen Ribeiro places their appearance in Paris in the mid-1780s. *Dress in Eighteenth-Century Europe* (London and New Haven: Yale University Press, 2002), 234.

distinguished its wearer and represented growing ideas of cosmopolitanism through its consumption. For Indian weavers, the shawl was no less a
sophisticated means of catering to different tastes and markets.

From the outbreak of the Franco-Prussian War in 1870, the shawl in
this incarnation began a rapid decline from a luxury object, representing
Britain's mercantile might, to something that was hopelessly outdated
and banished from the pages of fashionable women's magazines. The
factors in the shawl's decline included the eradication of the use of
forced labour, the closure of French markets to Kashmir shawls as a
result of the war, and the rapid improvement in the quality of paisley
shawls, the French and British copies, that flooded European markets.
However, shawl production in India continued to command high prices
for the luxury object. By 1911, Murray's *A Handbook for Travellers in India,
Burma and Ceylon* cited Amritsar – near to Lahore, in the northern Punjab
(located in present-day India, near the border with Pakistan) – as the
centre for the famous Kashmir shawl production, although the author
noted that they were now largely embroidered rather than woven. The
handbook reflected the introduction and popularisation of the *amli*
version of the shawl, on which the designs were embroidered instead of
woven, and which did not exist before the nineteenth century. The *amli*
was produced specifically for a Western market.

Far from being the object that Martineau characterised as representative of the 'unchanging East', the shawl had already undergone a number
of alterations, shaped by interactions between Eastern and Western
markets. In globetrotters' narratives, it was a dynamic object, although
this was also down to personal taste. For example, Arthur Drummond
Carlisle, whose own travels on the European Continent were disrupted by
the Franco-Prussian War, still regarded it as a luxury object. He wrote of
his walk along Delhi's premier street of shops, the Chandni Chowk (Silver
Street), reinforcing the idea of the wealth and splendour of goods to be
found there. In his account, the shawl was not to be glimpsed by the idle
window shopper, but sought out by the connoisseur and collector: 'if
you want to buy in Delhi a two hundred guinea Cashmere shawl ... you
must go up to the native trader's private rooms'.[3] For Carlisle, the shawl
was, even in the land of its manufacture, an exclusive object. To acquire
one was to embark on an authentic experience, involving personal nego-
tiation with the other in the person of the 'native trader', located in his
private rooms, which were behind the scenes in the midst of a diverse
city such as Delhi.

◂ **PREVIOUS PAGES:** Egerton Laird wrote that, even in India, Kashmir shawls commanded high prices. After observing the elaborate weaving process, he wrote: 'one does not wonder now at the immense prices paid for Cashmere articles, as it is all manual labour'. Plate from William Simpson's *India, ancient and modern*, 1867. ▴ **ABOVE:** The Chandni Chowk, or Silver Street, in Delhi was a place where globetrotters could bargain with traders. It was a site of interaction as much as it was place to acquire material representations of their travels. Photograph from Charles Lucas's album.

Cloth merchants in Delhi, from Charles Lucas's album. In 1871, Carlisle noted that a Kashmir shawl could cost 200 guineas, the equivalent of an emerald.

Laird, who travelled just one year after Carlisle, featured the shawl far more fulsomely in his account, elevating it beyond the mere promise of the authentic that it held and embedding it fully in Indian culture. Like Carlisle, early mentions of the shawl in Laird's narrative place it strictly in the role of exclusive commodity. Laird wrote of the great prices it commanded: 'one man calmly asked if I wanted to give 5,000 rupees for a shawl – only £500!'[4] He observed the shawl being worn by men and, by altering what in Britain was a familiar gendered object worn by women, he refashioned it as an object representative of cultural difference. He described its manufacture on a visit to Lahore:

> The main part of the shawl we saw being made was red. Each of the hands had several shuttles, with various colours of wool wound on them, and in turn they threw them through the threads of the warp; and thus are made the wonderful patterns that one sees in red, white, and green; and how they do not mistake the proper shuttle, I don't know.[5]

The Kashmir shawl was an object of art, not machine, unlike the paisley shawl produced in Britain, which epitomised the machine age. Laird, incorporating the shawl into the landscape itself, noted: 'after leaving Serinuggur [Srinigar] the river takes two or three very sharp curves, the origin they say of the pattern on the Cashmere shawls'.[6] The shawl as presented by Laird moved through a series of different contexts: from a luxury object commanding a great price, via its place on the shoulders of the swells of India, to its origins both in highly skilled manufacture and the landscape of Kashmir. In Laird's narrative, it became a single, iconic object that conveyed cultural difference and conjured an authentic experience off the beaten track in Kashmir, which was itself behind the scenes.

Laird also self-consciously and sardonically highlighted ideals of cosmopolitanism, most tellingly in the title of his travel account: *The Rambles of a Globe Trotter*. While he was aware of the inherent frivolity that the name globetrotter conjured, his observation of objects such as the Kashmir shawl revealed a greater depth of perception and experience that belied the superficial image. The idea of a globetrotting traveller was someone who could move easily between countries and cultures, and who communicated ideals of cosmopolitanism as it figured in Victorian thought and discourse. For example, the character of Brooke, a would-be Member of Parliament in George Eliot's (1819–80) novel *Middlemarch*

(1871–2), was portrayed as cosmopolitan, yet Bruce Robbins wrote that Brooke's travels from 'China to Peru' gave him a 'rambling habit of mind'.[7] Cosmopolitanism and its avid consumption of cultural difference, though the subject of satire, was a means for globetrotters to lay claim to a wider global citizenship.

Once the shawl could be copied in large numbers on mechanised looms in Britain and France, it lost its value both as an exclusive import and as an artisanal object. Changes to fashionable dress in Britain further depressed the shawl market. By the early 1880s, women's dress altered from the bell-shaped skirt – over which a draped, triangular shawl provided the perfect accessory – to a tightly fitted bodice, with a relatively streamlined skirt that was gathered into an elaborate bustle at the back. The bustle, with its tucks and drapes, braiding and beading, was part of the display of female dress and a Kashmir shawl not only obscured it but also hung awkwardly, spoiling the desired silhouette. The Kashmir shawl, once the ultimate fashion accessory, became 'fashion's natural victim'.[8] However, the demands of fashion were more complex; instead of being completely abandoned, the shawl was continually reinvented in the latter part of the nineteenth century. It was tailored into short carriage jackets, or 'dolmans', which accentuated the bustle.

The adaptability of the shawl meant that it was the ideal material trope, since it was continually reinvented not only as an object of fashion, but also as a represention of globetrotters' Eastern experiences. This use was apparent in the early twentieth century, when the shawl was again remodelled in Western fashion, this time as a jacket, with a fur collar and suitably narrow, or 'hobbled', hem. An extant version in the collection of the Platt Hall Gallery of Costume in Manchester, made from an *amli*, bears the label 'Debenham and Freebody', a firm that, with Liberty, was at the forefront of selling aesthetic Indian textiles.[9] In 1917, Nancy Dearmer, whose own travel wardrobe was purchased from Debenham and Freebody, bought a number of embroidered shawls from a shawl dealer in Simla, a fashionable hill station for the Raj.* Dearmer had the shawls made into a coat and a burnoose, or large hooded cloak. Her commission, refashioning the shawl into a protective garment worn over her clothes, and hence outside the home, was a means of broadcasting to others her journey to India. The journey itself, she noted in a letter to her mother,

---

* Simla is located geographically in the Indian state of Himachal Pradesh, which shares a northern border with Kashmir and a western border with Punjab.

gave her a greater cosmopolitanism: 'I am awfully glad to be seeing the East, it helps one to understand so much & to get the world in better perspective'.[10] For Dearmer, the shawl was a physical representation of her experience of the wider world as well as a means of fashioning and communicating her personal travel encounters.

Dearmer purchased the shawl during a highly anticipated visit to Simla, yet had it made into something else. This was partly influenced by the fashions of her time, but she also created an object that helped to marginalise the less desirable aspects of her travels. In addition to writing to her mother that travel gave her a greater perspective, she wrote in the same letter that: 'once I leave it [the East] I don't think it will ever call me back'.[11] Her trip to Simla was not one that she enjoyed overall: it was cold and rainy, and the walls of her hotel room streamed with damp. Underlying Dearmer's letters was a sense of dissatisfaction with experiences that never quite matched expectations:

I get homesick sometimes when I think of dear London and all it contains of family and friends and work and play, but I am sure it is a good thing for a person who is so naturally stay-at-home as I am to be made to wander every now and again. I don't mean that I don't love this experience, I do and it is all new and interesting, only I should never stir myself up to adventure...[12]

Dearmer aspired to a cosmopolitanism that she felt was part of her World Tour, although her letters reveal that the ideal was not always attainable. Her Kashmir shawls provided a material means of refashioning an unsatisfactory experience.

CHINESE IVORIES

In 1870, Carlisle observed that the shops in Canton were 'full of the wares of lacquer and ivory for which Canton has long been justly celebrated. ... we are sure to find a most inviting and perfect collection of card-cases, fans, paper-cutters, glove-stretchers, caskets, puzzles and ornaments of many kinds, both tasteful and grotesque'.[13] The items that Carlisle designated as representative of Chinese ivory carving were those produced specifically for a Western market. Unlike the Kashmir shawl, which was an important object in Indian culture – for example, its use in the Khil'at ceremony – Chinese ivory carvings occupied a different place within Chinese society. As Craig Clunas noted: 'Ivory was never a "canonical"

'Peking, Pechili province, China: a dealer in curiosities' by John Thomson, 1869. Porcelains, lacquer and antique bronzes were objects of desire among globetrotters. Carew Davies Gilbert requested additional funds from his mother for the purchase of curios in Hong Kong noting, 'I also saw a very handsome set of 3 old bronzes (£50) I am now only sorry I did not ask for £1000 instead'.

material in Ming and Qing China. It played little part in either ritual or poetic metaphor. No treatises were devoted to its history or to its literary resonances'.[14] Yet ivory, which was a luxury object but not a cultural signifier in China, was designated by collectors at home, and globetrotters abroad, as innately Chinese.

Sir John Barrow's *Travels in China* was one of the early British sources to identify Chinese carved ivories as desirable commodities. In Barrow's eyes, ivory carving was a significant art: 'of all the mechanical arts that in which they [the Chinese] seem to have attained the highest degree of perfection is the cutting of ivory'.[15] Of particular interest to Barrow, and subsequently featuring in the majority of globetrotters' accounts nearly a century later, were carved ivory pieces called 'devil's work balls'. These he described in great detail: they were carved 'out of a solid ball of ivory, with a hole not larger than half an inch in diameter, they will cut from nine to fifteen distinct hollow globes, one within another, all loose and capable of being turned round in every direction and each of them carved full of the same kind of open work that appears on the fans'.[16] His account of these carved ivory pieces conveyed their novelty, but also linked them to the familiar and, at one time, extremely expensive brisé fans, with their carved sticks and guards, that were used in Europe from the late seventeenth century. Published sources like Barrow's, with its glowing descriptions, ensured that these ivory pieces became objects of desire in Britain.

During the course of the eighteenth century, Chinese porcelains, silks and lacquers evoked an idealised image of the East that found expression in chinoiserie. This European interpretation of an imagined, exotic East was presented through stylised landscapes featuring pagodas, elephants and exotic birds, as well as figures dressed in flowing robes and peaked hats, who bore more resemblance to European sophisticates of the eighteenth century than any living Chinese figure. Beyond aesthetic fantasy, the mythical East that chinoiserie created was an 'idealized world [that] complimented [sic] Western visions of a peaceful, Platonic, oriental state and, like those visions, depended on a complete ignorance of Chinese government, culture and society'.[17] This image of China persisted into the early nineteenth century, but it was part of an increasing duality in the way that China was viewed in British society. Chinese objects were used to convey the genius of the people that created them, while at the same time representing the Chinese as backward, and part of a superstitious and crumbling society. It was the Opium Wars and the 'shift in economic power in favour of the British that fostered the decline in the esteem felt for China and the Chinese'.[18]

After the Opium Wars, China was, for the British public, no longer the country portrayed through 'the artistry of Chippendale, the wit of Goldsmith, and the deistic worship of Confucius'.[19] Instead, in public and political discourse, the country was depicted as degraded from its glorious past, which in turn justified British imperial aspirations towards China. This can be seen in the work of politician and theorist John Stuart Mill, who wrote that China, unlike Britain, was the 'antithesis of a strong, healthy, national constitution'.[20] China was evoked more luridly through the images of opium addicts portrayed in the popular press and literature, including Charles Dickens's unfinished novel *The Mystery of Edwin Drood* (1870), which opens in an opium den where a drugged Chinese man 'convulsively wrestled with one of his many Gods, or Devils', snarling horribly.

◄ PREVIOUS PAGES: The flamboyant chinoiserie of Brighton Pavilion was designed for the Prince Regent, the future George IV (*r.*1820–30), by architect John Nash (1752–1835). The theatrical designs, as in the Banqueting Room shown here, drew inspiration from India and China. From *The Royal Pavilion at Brighton...*, 1827. ▲ ABOVE: John Jasper at an opium den in Charles Dickens's *The Mystery of Edwin Drood*, 1870. Dickens situated negative aspects of the East within a domestic British setting: Chinese opium addicts and the character of Neville Landless, who was viewed with suspicion because he came from Ceylon. Illustration by Luke Fides, 1870.

Further, like India, China was represented as part of the unchanged and ancient East, an attractive counterpoint to Western modernity. This view also allowed for greater British agency in China, in regard to both trade and imperial expansion. While the utopia of a China conjured by chinoiserie was known to be untrue, it was still used to evoke the country. Carlisle mused on this lasting and seductive image of China drawn out through its decorative arts when he left Shanghai for Japan in 1870:

The name of China brings up before our mind's eye pictures ... of a well-kept garden where the small-footed celestial maidens sit sipping the most delicate of teas ... houses and temples whose furniture and ornaments are all of the richest lacquer or the finest old porcelain; of a country, in short, which is the favourite haunt of peace and content- ment, of wealth and art.[21]

He pitted two unchanging versions of China against each other in his final analysis. One was the well-known China represented through painted porcelain images, with which his readership would be familiar. He compared this image in the following pages with another, negative version of a stagnating China: one of idle government and Confucian ideals so long followed out of habit that their original meaning had become distorted. Carlisle completed his section on China by noting that this stasis could not be maintained. The objects that epitomised China, like the devil's work balls, were ascribed meaning by those in the West and were, as sinophile and traveller Alicia Bewicke (1845–1926) wrote in her novel *A Marriage in China* (1896), decorative, 'but not strictly useful'.[22]

China was also on show in nineteenth-century Britain and exhibitions of Chinese objects contributed to that way that the country was popularly figured. In addition to Nathan Dunn's (1782–1844) *Ten Thousand Chinese Things*, which featured in a number of London venues, China was also part of the Great Exhibition in Hyde Park in 1851.[23] China, whose policy had been to maintain a largely insular position in global politics, particularly in regard to the West, had 'unusually sent a display' to the international exhibitions.[24] Commodities were displayed – tea, silks, porcelain and lacquer – as well as the more dubious aspects of British trade with China, through the presence of an opium pipe. Also included were carved ivory objects like devil's work balls and an 'ivory chopstick and knife case belonging to a mandarin'.[25] Unlike the other countries that were invited to display at the Crystal Palace, there was no commissioner for China. The catalogue reveals that those who were invited to display in the Chinese exhibition space were overwhelmingly British with a few Europeans. Therefore, the British, rather than the Chinese, created the material image of China at the Great Exhibition. Further, the objects that were displayed were also those that appeared later in the century in globetrotters' collections, indicating both the longevity of this image and the influence of industrial exhibitions in shaping material identities.

Chinese ivories appear in globetrotters' collections, especially that of Powell-Cotton, but accounts are relatively silent on their acquisition and meaning. Powell-Cotton's Chinese collection itself replicates those objects that were displayed forty years earlier at the Crystal Palace and which continued to feature in subsequent international exhibitions. In his diary, Powell-Cotton recorded the acquisition of items during his travels in Canton:

ENTRANCE TO THE CHINESE COLLECTION.
HYDE PARK CORNER.

Nathan Dunn was an American merchant who, during the course of his career in Canton, acquired a large number of high-quality Chinese objects. He opened a Chinese Museum in Philadelphia and toured the collection in Britain with an accompanying catalogue, *Ten Thousand Chinese Things* (1842). It was displayed in a specially constructed pagoda in Hyde Park; later, the structure was transferred to Victoria Park in East London.

ARTICLES IN THE CHINESE EXHIBITION AT THE CRYSTAL PALACE.

A selection of Chinese objects reputed to have come from the Yuanmingyuan were displayed at international exhibitions as a means of representing Britain's economic and military reach. From *The Illustrated London News*, 6 May 1865.

Went to king-fishers wing enamel work, feather laid on sil. Pretty, streets under 6′ wide all paved stone, each shop had sign board many hanging down to ground & about 8″ wide, houses built of grey lined white brick, very crowded. Temple 500 genie lot figures carved & plaster gilt over bit, the old embr. shops, women's petticoats of silk much embr. prices from $2 to $8 & gold ones $10 to more all these 2nd hand, lot of bargaining...[26]

There was little differentiation in Powell-Cotton's narrative between shopping, sightseeing and cultural engagement: all were given equal status and all had the tenor of a commercial exchange. This was further heightened by an additional encounter after his day's shopping. He spent the night in Canton, not in his hotel (where he left his belongings), but after finding 'Susan, an old pimp, din[ner] & then on boat with Chinese woman, boat fairly comfortable'.[27] The mercantile tone of his personal interactions in Canton conveyed the sense that, in China, everything became a commodity.

JAPANESE NOVELTIES

Unlike India and China, Japan had a relatively recent trading relation-ship with Britain. Nineteenth-century travellers viewed the country as a novelty; this perceived newness meant that they often tended to dedicate more space in their accounts to their experiences in Japan than they allo-cated to India and China.* Although Japan did not participate in the Great Exhibition of 1851, there were Japanese objects included in the Chinese displays. Further, the presence of Chinese objects in the Indian Court demonstrated global trading connections and British engagement in the trade between China and Japan. The exhibition of 1862 featured the first wholly Japanese display and, like the Chinese displays of 1851, it belonged to a Westerner, the British diplomat Sir Rutherford Alcock. The display did not entirely meet with the approval of the Japanese embassy that attended the exhibition. However, the exhibition was undeniably influential in that, as writer and critic William Rossetti (1829–1919)

---

* Carlisle devoted fifty-eight pages to India, thirty-eight to China and seventy to his experiences in Japan. Carlisle, *Round the World in 1870*, 24–82, 104–42, 160–230. Just over twenty years later, in 1891, Thompson allocated thirty-two pages to India, nineteen to China and forty pages to Japan. Thompson, *In the Track of the Sun*, 103–35, 65–84, 12–52.

Japanese items from the 1862 International Exhibition (Rutherford Alcock collection). Sir Rutherford Alcock was a British Consul in China after the First Opium War, serving in Fuchow, Shanghai and, briefly, Canton. From 1858–64, he was Consul-General in Japan. In addition to collecting Japanese art and decorative art, he also wrote several books about Japan, notably *The Capital of the Tycoon*, 1863. Illustration from John Burley Waring's (1823–75) *Masterpieces of industrial art and sculpture at the International Exhibition, 1862...*, 1863.

noted: 'the Japanese mania began in our quarters toward the middle of 1863'.[28] Attending the post-exhibition auction for the Japanese displays were buyers for W. Hewitt & Company and Murray Marks & Company, as well as Arthur Lasenby Liberty (1843–1917), who was then a representative for Farmers & Rogers Great Shawl and Cloak Emporium. All these shops specialised in the sale of 'Oriental Wares' and promoted the interior designs of the Aesthetic Movement.[29]

Being relatively new in terms of trade, the novelty of Japan, paired with the popularity of the Aesthetic Movement, propelled Japanese objects from fashion to fad. Inherent in this movement was a degree of cosmopolitanism, in that interiors were created to reflect difference and personal taste rather than conforming to societal rules. The art of Japan in particular was new for British society, becoming the perfect vehicle for the expression of individuality. However, the mania for all things Japanese and their ubiquity in the Aesthetic interior, as well as in shops across Britain, meant that the difference and individuality that they were supposed to convey was instead another means of following fashion. So prevalent were Japanese goods in Britain that Laird wrote in Yokohama that 'I have not bought any curiosities here, as it is so difficult to know what are genuine; and another reason is, I am told London is so over-stocked with Japanese goods that they are cheaper there than here'.[30] While this may have been hyperbole, to which Laird was occasionally prone, it does reveal the popularity and pervasiveness of Japanese objects in both the domestic and mercantile spheres in 1870s Britain.

Japan began actively engaging in industrial exhibitions in the dying years of the Tokugawa Shogunate, the Bakumatsu. Both the Bakumatsu and early Meiji were periods of rapid change in Japan and saw an influx of Westerners: merchants, missionaries, diplomats and tourists. The first display organised by the Japanese was at the International Exposition, held in Paris in 1867, just over a year before the Meiji Emperor was restored to power. This outward-looking programme of cultural activities was a means employed by the Meiji government to express a Japanese alignment and parity with the Western powers that were dominant in the East in this period. By bolstering their status vis-à-vis the West, the

Japanese figures at the International Exposition in Paris, 1867, from *Le Monde Illustré*. The Paris exhibition was the first international exhibition in which Japan officially participated. While the Alcock collections influenced designers and artists, the impact of Japan at the 1867 exhibition was even more widespread. The exhibition was marked by political jostling between representatives of the Shogunate, whose power was on the wane, and the Satsuma clan, who styled themselves as the 'Embassy of the Ryukyu King'. This meant that they were represented as an independent state.

Japanese government used this strategic alignment to renegotiate the unequal treaties that opened Japan to Western trade in the 1850s. This series of treaties allowed extraterritoriality and access for Western trade. By 1858, Yokohama, Shimoda and Hakodate were open to Western travellers. In the ensuing years, this was expanded to another six treaty ports: Nagasaki, Kanagawa, Osaka, Kobe, Niigata and Tokyo. Eventually, major cities, especially Kyoto, were also accessible. Travel to the interior was allowed with a passport, for which travellers had to apply to the British Consul-General, although these were easily procured. An additional means of engaging on an international stage for Japan was taking part in international exhibitions, which were themselves indicators of modernity.

There were two object types that the Japanese consistently displayed: carved ivory *netsuke* (toggles) and okimono (statuettes). For Western travellers, these objects fed into the ideals of the Aesthetic Movement at home, with its emphasis on the handmade. Carlisle focused on *netsuke* during his trip to the Yokohama curio shops in 1870:

> Little figures, carved in ivory, inimitable in their grotesqueness of expression, called by the natives 'nitskis,' and used as buttons to prevent their tobacco-pouches from slipping out of their girdles ... but let none venture in among this seductive array without having both a long credit and some skill in discriminating between the different qualities of the articles; for, on the one hand, contrary to ideas prevalent in England, good lacquer or ivory-work is not to be bought for a mere trifle in the land of its production, the native gentry having as high an appreciation, and being ready to pay almost as long prices for it, as ourselves; and, on the other hand, since the demand for these articles has increased so much by the irruption [*sic*] of foreigners into the market, articles of a much inferior workmanship are manufactured, and palmed off on the unwary or ignorant as equal to the oldest and best.[31]

He identified *netsuke* by name, as one of the defining objects of Japan, establishing their use as troped objects employed by nearly all globetrotters. He also made clear that these pieces had a practical function: as toggles to keep the purse and pouch in place. Carlisle was in Japan just before the Meiji Emperor issued a proclamation, in 1871, prescribing European dress for himself and his court. As a result, large port cities such as Yokohama were flooded with Japanese urbanites in Western clothing, which in turn did away with the need for *netsuke*.

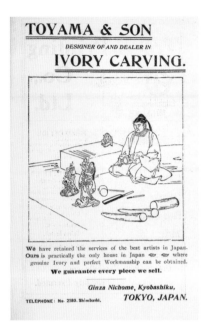

▲ ABOVE, LEFT: Advertisement for 'Designer of and Dealer in Ivory Carving', Yokohama. From the Welcome Society of Japan's *Guide Book for Tourists*, 1910. Carved ivories were a desirable and much sought-after souvenir of Japan. Okimono, carved statuettes, were developed by Japanese craftsman to satisfy the Western hunger for similar objects to *netsuke*, which with the adoption of Western dress in Japan were no longer worn widely. ▲ ABOVE, RIGHT: Plate from *Netsuke* by Frank Morris Jonas, 1928. Although largely out of use by the time this image was published, *netsuke* remained an enduring material representation of Japan.

However, *netsuke* were an embodiment of the Old Japan, made popular at home by A. B. Mitford and Basil Hall Chamberlain, whose writings equated a feudal Japan with a samurai class akin to the tales of medieval knights prevalent in England in this period. The popularity of *netsuke* was in part an expression of nostalgia and a response to the dislocation, both physical and emotional, felt by many in Britain in the face of rapid industrialisation. Finally, Carlisle clearly linked the consumption of *netsuke* to the influx of foreign visitors to Japan, all keen to experience difference. This belied Laird's observation two years later that Japan was a 'new country' and, as such, her people had a love of 'novelty'.[32] Yet it was both the perceived newness of Japan, as a country only recently opened to the West, as well as its untouched quality, that appealed to travellers. *Netsuke* were novel in that they were part of the quaintly elegant Japanese dress; even if globetrotters' encounters with those actually wearing traditional dress was diminishing in urban centres, *netsuke* still represented an ideal of Old Japan that was at once unusual and nostalgic.

By 1918, when Nancy Dearmer was travelling, Japan was on a very well-worn global track. She acquired a *netsuke* there and her treatment of the object, in light of her refashioning her Kashmir shawl, indicated how she ensured a continued experience of novelty and guaranteed that her trip reflected her desired encounters. Her travels were affected by both personal circumstances and global politics. In India, she gave birth to a daughter, Gillian. In Yokohama, the family attempted to settle in a hotel but she noted that, in the aftermath of the Russian Revolution, the city was filled with Russians who were rude, noisy and crowded the best hotels. The family moved to Tokyo in an attempt to find suitable accommodation. From there, her husband Percy made a series of excursions, including a trip of several days to the shrine of Kamakura. On his return he gave her:

> A present, a button made of stag's horn with a medallion inset of gold-bronze & gold. So charming. It is called a netsuke pronounced netski and is used to fasten a pipe to a man's girdle. ... Americans always buy them in ivory, but the ivory ones are simply made for tourists (X. Not always I find, because the one Mr. C. gave me is ivory and a genuine old one.)[33]

Dearmer used the *netsuke* to separate herself from the common tourist by demonstrating her knowledge gained from encounters with local experts ('Mr. C.') to inform her mother of how such objects were used and how to differentiate between the authentic and the tourist pieces.

It is, however, unlikely that she herself saw *netsuke* being worn and used as part of Japanese dress, since she stayed primarily in urban centres where she would have encountered people in Western dress. In addition, as she herself admits, her expertise was faulty, born of brief observation, not of a deep knowledge. This status of superficial traveller led to a point that was consistently repeated in globetrotters' accounts: the worry that they had been duped by local traders, rather than actually purchasing the real thing. To have the genuine article conferred not only a degree of authenticity on their own experience, but also an expertise. Through their travels, globetrotters acquired the ability to delineate between the authentic and the fake. This knowing consumption of difference in turn made them true cosmopolitans, who could appreciate such differences.

Further, their appreciation was practically translated into useful knowledge deployed in the curio shops, which distinguished globetrotters from
common tourists. When Dearmer received her *netsuke*, her husband Percy
suggested 'that I might have the medallion cut out & a brooch made, but
I rather think I shall use the button as it is, on my Kashmir shawl coat
when I have the new collar made'.[34] She fashioned her souvenirs to reflect
her personal aspirations for her journey, but also to convey, by wearing
them, that she purchased these objects abroad rather than at home, thus
gaining social distinction.

COLLECTORS, CULTURE AND ACQUISITION

While on an expensive and lengthy World Tour conferred a degree of
social distinction, by the late nineteenth century the popular associations
with this type of tourism threatened to undermine it. In *Things Japanese*,
Chamberlain playfully created a genus and species. Globetrotting 'types'
were designated, based on their outward appearance and annoying behavioural characteristics:

> "Globe-trotter elegans" who were both wealthy and socially well-con-
> nected; "Globe-trotter independens" who arrived in their own yacht;
> "Globe-trotter princeps" the royal on a world tour; "Globe-trotter
> locustus" the Cook's tourist. The most often sighted of the species
> was "*Globe-trotter communis*": sun-helmet, blue glasses, scant luggage,
> celluloid collars. ... he loves to occupy your time not indeed by gaining
> information from you about Japan ... but by giving you information
> about India, China and America, places with which you are possibly
> as familiar as he.[35]

In this last classification, Chamberlain gave them the attributes of
the sun helmet or solar topee worn by colonial officials in both India
and Africa, paired with the blue sunglasses widely used by British tourists
to both the European and North American continents. The latter were
originally employed by landscape painters in the eighteenth century to
imbue the view that they were capturing with a more picturesque tint.
The glasses were adopted by the fashionable tourists of the late eighteenth century for the same purpose. By the mid-nineteenth century, blue
glasses were used to imply a way of seeing that was superficial. They
were synonymous with European tourists, especially the British, who
had developed the first package tours. These tourists were caricatured

▲ ABOVE: Charles Lucas devoted long mornings to scouring curio shops for prized examples of Japanese art to bring home. This staged image of the curio shop appears in both Lucas's album and that of Carew Davies Gilbert. Rudyard Kipling (1865–1936) accused globetrotters of conflating the curio shop with actual cultural experience. ▶ OPPOSITE: 'Warriors', from Charles Lucas's album. The samurai were part of the ruling class during the Tokugawa Shogunate, in effect the military arm of government. Under the newly restored Meiji Emperor, samurai were displaced by a conscripted army. The two swords, worn as a display of the privilege of their rank, were outlawed. This studio image of sitters dressed as samurai was a popular one among globetrotters, as it confirmed the idealised Old Japan.

as having a desire to experience the picturesque, underpinned by an ignorance of the cultures and landscapes in which they found themselves. In just a few pages, Chamberlain conveyed the popular perceptions of globetrotters. Specifically, he suggested that their social distinction was gained more from the distances they travelled than any genuine knowledge gleaned from their journeys.

The objects that globetrotters collected had the potential to veer into the realm of the superficial, representing what was on display in the shops rather than any specific cultural interactions. In Japan, the curio shop was a space created for Western tourists. Unsurprisingly, studio photographs of these interiors also featured in tourists' collections. These images of the curio shops massed in one space the objects that, for globetrotters, represented Japan. These shops, like the photographers' studios, were places in which to interact with the Japanese themselves but also,

780

globetrotters believed, in which examples of authentic Japanese culture could be procured. In turn, these objects served as tokens that represented a knowledge or interest in both a new and old Japan. One example was a suit of samurai armour acquired by Carew Davies Gilbert in Kobe (Western travellers were allowed access to the port, which was located on the Inland Sea, in 1868). Samurai armour was itself a regular feature in the photographs of curio shops. Gilbert wrote in May 1877: 'I send home from here 2 boxes, containing a suit of armour that used to belong to Nagasawa, a samurai; he is now General of the Rebels who are fighting against the Government in the Southern Island of Kiusu'.[36] Kiusu (Kyushu) was an island that formed part of the Shimonoseki Straits; Gilbert travelled through them and into the Inland Sea, en route from China to Japan. He referred to the Satsuma Rebellion (1877), the last stand of the samurai against the imperial government, which had been in power for a decade. The leader of the rebellion was not Nagasawa, but Saigo Takamori (1828–77). The name Nagasawa may have been misunderstood as either the government leader who was the ruler of the area, Prince Arisugawa (1835–95), or Kawamura Sumiyoshi (1836–1904), a government admiral who was involved in the siege. The siege itself ended with the defeat and death of Takamori and marked a victory for Japan's new modern army. The samurai were a romanticised link with Japanese history and culture. For Gilbert, the provenance given to an otherwise ubiquitous tourist object was both a physical link between places he had actually visited or travelled through and a means of realising Old Japan, while at the same time engaging with the political changes of a new Japan, albeit one he imperfectly understood, given the confusion over the name.

In addition to artefacts such as the samurai armour, tiny *netsuke* continually held sway in the tourist markets. Although the *netsuke* were objects which represented Old Japan, their smallness was a necessity, reflecting the practicalities of travel that dictated globetrotters' selection of objects, since both shipping and customs fees could be extremely expensive. Chamberlain's wry comments indicated that globetrotters acquired a reputation for passing on these added expenses to others. In his definition of '*Globe-trotter communis*' he wrote: 'you will also see after freight and insurance, and dispatch the boxes to an address in Europe which he leaves with you'.[37] Gilbert wrote to his mother from Hong Kong in April 1877 that: 'on receiving the boxes containing the articles ... You must pay all charges for packing forwarding &c. &c.'[38] Nancy Dearmer found that the cost of sending a pair of inlaid bronze vases home to her family from Japan in 1918 was prohibitive, and instead bought a small gold cigarette case as a gift for her brother, since it could be carried easily in her luggage. Costs did not stop at the point of purchase or shipping, but as Dearmer and her husband found, to their relief, that they did not face additional fees at customs on travelling from Yokohama to San Francisco: 'We find our box of Japanese things is well within the amount we are allowed duty free. This is very jolly and we shall be able to have our pretty things'.[39]

Conversely, Merton Russell-Cotes wrote of the large Japanese shrine that he shipped home to Bournemouth, with the aid of the British Consul, at exorbitant cost, thus reinforcing his image as a wealthy globetrotter. In his autobiography, *Home and Abroad*, Russell-Cotes ensured that he would be remembered as a collector on the grand scale. Of the objects collected in Japan, he wrote: 'Over a hundred cases were filled with the curios purchased by my wife and myself'.[40] These curios were purchased in the space of just seven weeks: it was not only an unusually large

Silver and gold Elephant

By Komai, with precious stones and crystal ball.   The Marquis Inouye (Japanese Ambassador) told me it was the finest specimen of Japanese art he had ever seen.

▲ ABOVE, LEFT: According to Merton Russell-Cotes, this shrine belonged to a daimio, a powerful feudal lord during the Tokugawa Shogunate. It was discovered by his guide in a curio shop in Kyoto. Russell-Cotes alleged that he required diplomatic intervention to ship such a culturally and artistically significant piece to Bournemouth. From Russell-Cotes's *Home and Abroad*, 1921. ▲ ABOVE, RIGHT: Russell-Cotes claimed that this incense burner in the shape of an elephant was another high-end curio brought home from Japan, when in fact he acquired it from a British dealer. From *Home and Abroad*, 1921.

number of cases to send home, but it was also expensive. Russell-Cotes was obsessed with self-aggrandisement. Of his vast Japanese collections, the only objects whose acquisition he mentioned in any great detail in his memoir were used to project the image of a wealthy connoisseur. He continually styled himself as an art collector and expert on Japan (acquiring membership in both the Royal Geographical Society, in October 1886, and the Japan Society, in January 1892, albeit in both cases he was an inactive member) but it was at the expense of his wife, Annie, who was the true collector and who was often relegated to the background. The Russell-Coteses' collections also yield a more complex image of their aquisition process and of the way in which the objects created a more nuanced view of their travels, beyond the search for social distinction and wealth projection.

In *Home and Abroad*, Russell-Cotes focused on the acquisition of two objects in Japan. The first was an eighteenth-century shrine, which allegedly belonged to a daimio (feudal lords who were vassals to the shogun). The second was an incense burner in the shape of a silver elephant, mounted with semi-precious stones and attributed to the silversmith Komai Otojiro (1842–1917), whose work was in high demand among those who considered themselves Japanese art cognoscenti. Of the two pieces, it was the shrine that received the greatest attention in Russell-Cotes's narrative. He wrote that his guide located it for him in a curio shop in Kyoto, but he could not offer any further information on its provenance. However, he did note its significance – both as a cultural artefact and as a valuable high art piece – in his account, writing that it was of such artistic and cultural value that it required the aid of Julian Pauncefote (1828–1902), the British Consul, to export the piece. When the shrine is considered alongside the provenance of the silver elephant, it is apparent that these objects functioned as a means of conveying the financial status and self-construction of Russell-Cotes as a collector of distinction. The elephant was actually made by Nakagawa Yoshizane – himself a prominent silversmith – and purchased from a British dealer, George Edwards, who previously displayed it at the Glasgow International Exhibition of 1901. In presenting these status objects on their own, bereft of provenance and severed from experience, Russell-Cotes spoke to the worst aspects of globetrotters, including their superficiality and equation of the curio shop with cultural experience.

While these status objects were the focus of Russell-Cotes's collecting in his own narrative, there are a number of smaller, everyday items that

Merton and Annie either personally used or observed being used that speak of a desire to preserve their cultural experiences of travel. Annie Russell-Cotes saved a pair of wooden chopsticks in their paper wrapper from tiffin in Kyoto. The restaurant where the Russell-Coteses dined was Ikeda's, made famous through its connection to the Ikedaya Affair in 1864.* The chopsticks represented not only the cultural immersion that the Russell-Coteses experienced, dining in the Japanese style, but also, like Gilbert's suit of samurai armour, they were a material means of connecting with Japanese politics and history. These historical associations were further heightened through the popularity of the eighteenth-century story of the forty-seven *rōnin* (pages 111–112). Their graves at the Sengakuji Temple in Tokyo were a favoured tourist site, which the Russell-Coteses visited during their travels.

In addition to Annie's prolific collecting, Merton also acquired smaller cultural souvenirs from sites that he considered significant in terms of history, culture and art. In Nikko, he took the wooden dipper from the water house, opposite the tomb of the shogun. Additionally, Merton and Annie purchased a model of the mausoleum at Nikko and, paired with this smaller, more personal souvenir, they connected with both place and space. The importance of these small, low value objects for Annie and Merton Russell-Cotes was apparent. They were preserved in their museum collection, with handwritten labels attached to them so that they would not be separated from the experience that gave the object its significance. These pieces provided proof of cultural engagement, underpinning the status objects and giving a greater depth to their collections.

Powell-Cotton's collection and his collecting activities followed a similar pattern to that of the Russell-Coteses and focused on capturing particular places through acquisition. Like the couple's focus on

---

* Politically the Bakumatsu period was characterised by a number of changing alliances and warring political factions as pro-imperial and anti-Western groups fought against political and social changes. The Ikeda Inn was a meeting place for a group of *rōnin* – masterless samurai – who allegedly devised a plot to set fires in Kyoto and in the ensuing confusion assassinate key officials of the shogunate. The plot was discovered, Ikeda's was raided, a number of *rōnin* were killed and the rest were arrested. Among those arrested were the owner of the inn, Ikeda, and his family. In the aftermath, the inn was closed and reopened under a new owner.

Japan, Powell-Cotton's diaries reveal that he spent several months in Kashmir, compared to the duration of the rest of his journey through China and Japan that took up to four weeks in each country.* He set up camp in Kashmir in a relatively remote area off the beaten track, where he spent his time hunting. India represented an experience of elite colonial society for globetrotters. Powell-Cotton himself held a commission in the army, although he was not actively serving during his trip; a number of young men stationed in India were part of his wider social network from home. Women who married into the Raj were encouraged by spouses and family to participate in hunting, as part of the female adoption of imperial power and authority in the Raj. However, Nora Beatrice Gardner (1866–1944), who travelled to northern India in 1894, was not part of the world of the Raj; for her, active participation in the hunt was slightly more complicated. She described her own participation in a leopard hunt, using the insistent invitation of the Maharajah of Chamba, Sham Singh (r.1873–1904), a strong supporter and ally of the Raj, to justify her seeming reluctance in taking up the gun: 'the Maharaja [sic] handed me a rifle and begged that I would take the first shot. It was a nervous moment for an inexperienced markswoman before so many spectators, but he would not hear of a refusal'.[41] Her account balanced her engagement in masculine spheres with her activities in traditionally feminine areas, specifically painting watercolours, earning the approbation of one male reviewer, who stated that she was a 'modern woman, but not a new woman'.[42] The term 'new woman' emerged in the 1870s and was applied in the press to describe a woman who was affluent and independent, but generally used to criticise what was viewed as unfeminine behaviour. However, gender restrictions on this type of colonial activity appear, in the context of an Eastern tour, to have really only applied to India.

Although she personally did not hunt, Annie Russell-Cotes collected bird skins as well as taxidermy examples from Australia and New Zealand. Powell-Cotton's hunting activities were confined to Kashmir and his future collecting of zoological specimens and ethnographic studies would be based largely in Africa. The natural history specimens acquired by both Annie Russell-Cotes and Percy Powell-Cotton came from places that were directly under British governance. Outside of India,

---

*   Powell-Cotton, World Trip Diary, Arrives in Canton 16 March 1891, 183. Arrives in the Inland Sea, Japan, 16 April 1891, 195. Departs Yokohama for Honolulu on 5 May, 1891, 208.

Powell-Cotton's connections, travel arrangements and collecting activities did not conform as clearly to an imperial identity. This suggests that, beyond a formal colonial context, Powell-Cotton engaged in a degree of cosmopolitan consumption, represented by a number of small souvenirs; for instance, in China he purchased twenty small gilt 'peach-stone buttons', chopsticks and a brass pipe.[43] In Japan, he acquired an okimono of mice nibbling at a grain sack. There was no perceptible difference between the objects bought by Annie Russell-Cotes and those that Powell-Cotton collected in China and Japan, indicating that, outside of the colonial context of India, there was actually a greater scope for cosmopolitan consumption.

The objects that Powell-Cotton collected, from India in particular, were displayed at his home, Quex Park, in conjunction with older pieces that his family acquired as part of their activities in the East India Company. His collections were a material creation of self, blending family history with individual experience. They conveyed his social standing in Britain and, as a Briton, served to locate Powell-Cotton on a global stage. Annie and Merton Russell-Cotes saw their travels not as part of a longer distinguished family history, but as the beginnings of their creation of identity, as they consolidated their rank in the upper-middle classes.

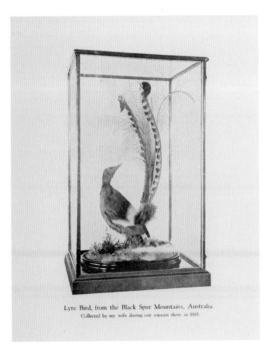

Annie Russell-Cotes collected a number of natural history specimens in Australia, participating in the wider pattern of colonial collecting. From Merton Russell-Cotes's *Home and Abroad*, 1921.

Lyre Bird, from the Black Spur Mountains, Australia.
Collected by my wife during our sojourn there in 1885.

CONCLUSION: COMING HOME

Mr. and Mrs. Cotes at Home.

In the last lines of his book chronicling his World Tour, Arthur Drummond Carlisle wrote of arriving in a fog-bound Liverpool: 'who shall think of the cheerless weather when surrounded by the pleasures of a cheerful English home?'[1] Carlisle anticipated the warm domesticity that greeted the globetrotter's return; he did not record how the globetrotter located themselves and the representation of their travels in this domestic sphere. Globetrotters' letters, once a means of communicating with home, became souvenirs of their trip. Similarly, collections were displayed, on return, in the home, thus embedding their travels into the domestic landscape and documenting significant, albeit ephemeral, experiences of personal transformation. They also conjured the differentiated East of India, China and Japan for family members and visitors alike. While these were small, personal museums to self, Annie and Merton Russell-Cotes and Percy Powell-Cotton created museums that featured their World Tour collections.

A souvenir was a material representation used to evoke the memory of a lived experience; it was not the value of the object itself, but the memory that it enshrined that was important. Both Annie and Merton Russell-Cotes's and Percy Powell-Cotton's collections were preserved in their own museums and galleries, which was very much a product of the zeitgeist of the later part of the nineteenth century, when public museums opened across Britain as a result of the Museums Act of 1845. Between the late 1860s and the outbreak of the First World War, nearly all of the municipal art museums of Britain were founded. The museums that the Russell-Coteses and Powell-Cotton created were a means of building a legacy from their travels, ensuring that their souvenirs were kept within the context of acquisition, thus preserving their significance and distinguishing them from objects available on the art market. Yet the movement of an object or collection from personal souvenir to museum artefact brought with it a new type of authority in the way that it represented a culture or experience. While the context of its acquisition was still very much personal, it became an official cultural signifier, to be studied and analysed by ensuing generations of scholars.

While nineteenth-century museums served a philanthropic purpose, they were also a means of conveying a rise in social position. Another well-known collector and world traveller of the late nineteenth century, Frederick Horniman (1835–1906), also created a public museum from his personal collections. Horniman was, in the 1890s, one of the wealthiest men in London. His museum was open to the public from 1891. Horniman purchased the collections on display at that time through dealers in Britain, at auction, and through specialist buyers who toured the East. Horniman later supplemented these collections with his own, personal objects, which he acquired through travel to India and Ceylon (1894–5) and then on the World Tour (1895–6), thus adding the authenticity of lived experience to his museum displays. However, the lines between

◄ PAGE 208: 'Mr. and Mrs. Cotes at Home'. Photograph from Annie Russell-Cotes's *Westward from the Golden Gate, c.*1900. Merton and Annie Russell-Cotes surrounded by their collections of Western paintings and Eastern objects brought together in an Aesthetic interior. ▲ ABOVE: Photograph of the Russell-Coteses' collection, from Merton Russell-Cotes's *Home and Abroad*, 1921. The Japanese Drawing Room at the Royal Bath Hotel demonstrated the Russell-Coteses conversancy with Japanese culture and served as a draw for potential guests. According to Merton, famous guest Oscar Wilde (1854–1900) once quipped that the Russell-Coteses provided a setting 'for the use and benefit of the public at hotel prices'.

Percy Powell-Cotton's 'Oriental Drawing Room'. Powell-Cotton's own World Tour collections were displayed in his home, which later became the Powell-Cotton Museum.

public and private spheres were blurred, and Horniman continually moved objects between his museum displays and his own residences. This breakdown between public and private was also apparent in the way that the Russell-Coteses used their collections. In the decade following the Russell-Coteses' return from their World Tour, their Japanese collection was exhibited in the Japanese Drawing Room of the Royal Bath Hotel. A photograph of the room from the 1890s shows a densely packed display, with swords and textile panels mounted on the wall, tables filled with lacquerware and okimono, and numerous lanterns hanging from the ceiling. It was during this period, in 1898, that the Russell-Coteses began to build their new home, East Cliff Hall, located directly next door to the Royal Bath Hotel. Given to Annie as a birthday present, East Cliff Hall was a private, palatial residence. The space afforded the couple the opportunity to display their collections in an eclectic style: marble sculptures and Victorian paintings intermixed with Maori axes, Japanese armour and an 'old English weighing machine'.[2] In 1907, the Russell-Coteses formally bestowed the building and its contents on the residents and town of Bournemouth, with the agreement that, although the building would now be a publicly accessible art gallery, it would also continue as their residence for the remainder of their lives. While presented as a joint endeavour, it would appear that Annie Russell-Cotes played a larger role in the creation of the museum; in 1917, she alone made an additional endowment to the town to ensure the future running costs of the gallery, which did not charge an admission fee.

Powell-Cotton also created an Oriental Drawing Room that served as a suitable display space for his World Tour curios. According to Keith Nicklin, a curator of the Powell-Cotton museum, the institution began formally in 1896, 'as a single gallery ... the collection of hunting trophies and curios having by this date already outgrown their temporary accommodation in the Billiard Room of the House.'[3]

The museum would officially open to the public on a regular basis in 1921 and the first curator, George Pinfold, was appointed in the same year. There was a blurring between public and private space, as well as between the individual themselves and the museum that they created. This is more apparent in the case of Powell-Cotton than any of the other collectors examined here. Frederick Horniman died in 1906, Annie and Merton Russell-Cotes in 1920 and 1921 respectively, but Percy Powell-Cotton lived until 1940, thus ensuring that his museum and its collections reflected his later interests, leaving a far different legacy than that of memorial to the World Tour. Powell-Cotton's collections were developed to reflect his interests as a naturalist and ethnographer. His daughters, Diana (1908–86) and Antoinette (1915–97), shared their father's pursuits and often joined him on his travels, eventually conducting their own ethnographic fieldwork in Africa. The Powell-Cotton Museum was very much a family endeavour, with its collections constantly evolving to reflect their changing interests. As a result of these circumstances, the significance of the World Tour collections was diminished. For example, in an exhibition, *Powell-Cotton: Man & Museum*, staged at the University of Kent in 1981, the World Tour collections were allocated a small case at the beginning of the show. The material displayed was described summarily as 'finger rings, combs, opium pipe, etc.', alongside the Singapore collection of Eastern objects that Powell-Cotton acquired on his return from his World Tour. Despite the care taken by the original owners who acquired these objects as material representations of their global experiences, they were still subject to changes in fashion and interpretation.

For globetrotters, these collections were meant to be immutable representations of their Eastern encounters. In addition to preserving their experiences, the collections explained the East to those who did not travel; in the case of Charles Lucas, for sisters and parents, who remained at home. Their souvenirs also prepared the next generation of travellers for what to seek out when they travelled. What Nancy Dearmer encountered on her travels, while highly personal, was also based on the accretion of experiences from the globetrotters who had gone before her. The East of India, China and Japan that globetrotters conjured was created from a perspective that, while foregrounded in the politics of colonialism and Empire, represented the new and thoroughly cosmopolitan experience of the World Tour.

ENDNOTES

INTRODUCTION

1 Maria Hay Murray Mitchell, *In India: Sketches of Indian Life and Travel from Letters and Journals* (London: T. Nelson & Sons, 1876), 57.

2 Jules Verne, *Around the World in 80 Days*, translated by Paul Frederick Walter (Albany: Excelsior Editions, 2013).

3 Egerton K. Laird, *The Rambles of a Globe Trotter in Australia, Japan, China, Java, India and Cashmere*, 2 volumes (Birkenhead: printed for private circulation, 1875), vol. 1, 221.

4 Carew Davies Gilbert, Hong Kong, March–April 1877 (GIL 4/377), East Sussex Record Office, Hong Kong , 26 March 1877, 4.

5 'To see it by moonlight, when mellowly shines/The light o'er its palaces, gardens, and shrines.' From *Lalla Rookh*, quoted in Robert Nicholas Fowler, *A Visit to Japan, China and India* (London: Sampson, Low, Marston, Searle & Rivington, 1877), 49.

6 Laird, *The Rambles of a Globe Trotter*, vol. 1, 198.

7 Ibid., vol. 2, 138.

8 Ackbar Abbas, 'Cosmopolitan De-Scriptions: Shanghai and Hong Kong', in Carol A. Breckenridge, Sheldon Pollock, Homi K. Bhabha, and Dipesh Chkrabarty, eds., *Cosmopolitanism* (Durham and London: Duke University Press, 2002), 212–14.

9 Laird, *The Rambles of a Globe Trotter*, vol. 1, 186–7.

10 John Stuart Mill, *On Liberty*, 129, quoted in Erik Ringmar, 'The Great Wall of China does not Exist', in Agnes Horvath and Marius Benta, eds., *Walling, Boundaries and Liminality: A Political Anthropology of Transformations* (London: Routledge, 2018), 4.

11 Kristen Surak, *Making Tea, Making Japan: Cultural Nationalism in Practice* (Stanford: Stanford University Press, 2013), 67–8.

1 GUIDEBOOKS AND NETWORKS

1 Percy Powell-Cotton, World Trip Journal, Quex Park, Kent, Doc.6.1, 23 January 1890, 62.

2   'Murray's Handbook for Russia', *The Spectator*, 14 October 1865, 20.

3   *A Handbook for India* first appeared in 1859, and the firm's *A Handbook for Travellers in Japan* was published in 1884; *Cook's Indian Tours* was first published in the early 1880s, and Thomas Cook's guide to China was published in 1910; Kelly & Walsh, a Shanghai publisher, printed guides to Nikko in Japan, and Ernest Satow's first *Guide to Japan* in 1881. The Hong Kong newspaper, the *China Mail*, published one of the earliest tourist guides to China in 1876; from 1872, the *Japan Gazette* in Yokohama published guides to Japan.

4   Nancy Dearmer, Mss Eur C326: 1916–18, British Library, bound volume, Bombay, Hotel Majestic, 2 November 1916, 4.

5   Stephen Kotkin, 'Preface', in Bruce A. Elleman and Stephen Kotkin, eds., *Manchurian Railways and the Opening of China: An International History* (London: M. E. Sharp, 2010), xv.

6   Nora Beatrice Gardner, *Rifle and Spear with the Rajpoots: Being the Narrative of a Winter's Travel and Sport in Northern India* (London: Chatto & Windus, 1895), 267.

7   Edward Backhouse Eastwick, *A Handbook for India: Being an account of the three Presidencies, and of the Overland Route; intended as a guide for Travellers, Officers, and Civilians; with vocabularies and dialogues of the spoken languages of India with travelling map and plans of towns* (London: John Murray, 1859), i.

8   'Murray's Hand-Book of India', *The Spectator*, 12 March 1859, 16.

9   Ibid.

10 Lord Ronald Gower, *Notes of a tour from Brindisi to Yokohama, 1883–1884* (London: Kegan Paul, Trench & Co., 1885), 27.

11 Ibid., i.

12 Lynne Withey, *Grand Tours and Cook's Tours: A History of Leisure Travel, 1750 to 1915* (London: Arum Press, 1998), 257.

13 Thomas Cook & Son, *Cook's Indian Tours: Programme of Cook's New System of International Travelling Tickets, embracing every point of interest for Tourists and General travellers in India, including Skeleton Tours and carefully-prepared Itineraries, Illustrating the Chief Routes by Railways, Steamers, Dâk-Ghârries, Ponies, Pâlkees, Jhâmpâns, and other Conveyances, with short Descriptions of some of the Principal Places, and a Glossary of Words and a Conversational Vocabulary, also a specially engraved Map of India* (London: Thomas Cook & Son, 1881), 59.

14 Ibid.

15 Arthur Drummond Carlisle, *Round in the World in 1870: an Account of a Brief Tour made through India, China, Japan, California, and South America* (London: H. S. King & Co., 1872), 55.

16 Thomas Cook & Son, *Cook's Indian Tours*, 65.

17 G. H. Yonge, 'A Tour of Service in Northern India', *Journal of the Royal Army Medical Corps* (1929), 52.

18 W. E. Baxter, *A Winter in India* (London: Cassell & Company, 1882), 62.

19 Frederick Diodati Thompson, *In the Track of the Sun: Readings from the Diary of a Globe Trotter* (London: William Heinemann, 1893), 134.

20 Laird, *The Rambles of a Globe Trotter*, vol. 1, 178, 236–7, 248, 265, 270, 314; vol. 2, 6–7, 24–6, 52, 72.

21 Thompson, *In the Track of the Sun*, 137–40.

22 Laird, *The Rambles of a Globe Trotter*, vol. 2, 158.

23 'Mr. Trevelyan's Cawnpore', *The Spectator*, 29 April 1865, 16.

24 'Mr. Trevelyan's Cawnpore', *Shields Daily Gazette*, 6 May 1865.

25 Erik Ringmar, *Liberal Barbarism: The European Destruction of the Palace of the Emperor of China* (New York: Palgrave Macmillan, 2013), 3.

26 Peter J. Kitson, 'That mighty Wall, not fabulous/China's stupendous mound!' Romantic Period Accounts of China's 'Great Wall', in Julia Kuehn and Paul Smethurst, eds., *New Directions in Travel Writing Studies* (Basingstoke: Palgrave Macmillan, 2015), 249.

27 John Barrow, *Travels in China, containing descriptions, observations, and comparisons, made and collected in the course of a short residence at the imperial palace of Yuen-Min-Yuen, and on a subsequent journey from Pekin to Canton* (London: T. Cadell and W. Davies, 1804), 24.

28 Ibid., 122.

29 Ibid., 124.

30 William Jardine Proudfoot, *Biographical Memoir of James Dinwiddie, Astronomer in the British Embassy to China* (Liverpool: Edward, 1868).

31 Nicholas Dennys, *Guide for Tourists to Peking and its Environs. With a Plan of the City of Peking and a Sketch Map of its Neighbourhood* (Hong Kong: printed at the *China Mail* Office, 1876), iii.

32 Ibid., 36.

33 Ibid., 36–7.

34 Laird, *The Rambles of a Globe Trotter*, vol. 1, 274.

35 Ibid., vol. 1, 273.

36 Ibid., vol. 1, 256.

37 Ibid., vol. 1, 279.

38 Ibid., vol. 1, 277–8.

39 Powell-Cotton, World Trip Journal, Ming Tombs, 4 April 1891, 193.

40 Eliza Ruhamah Scidmore, *Westward to the Far East: A Guide to the Principal Cities of China and Japan* (Montreal: The Canadian Pacific Railway Company, 1892), 42.

41 Dean MacCannell, *The Tourist: A New Theory of the Leisure Class* (London: Macmillan, 1976), 101.

42 Thomas Cook & Son, *Cook's Handbook for Tourists to Peking, Tientsin, Shan-Hai-Kwan, Mukden, Dalny, Port Arthur, and Seoul* (London: Thomas Cook & Son, 1910), 22.

43 Thomas Cook & Son, *Peking and the Overland Route: With Maps, Plans, and Illustrations* (London: Ludgate Circus, 1917), i.

44 Ibid., 2.

45 Ibid., 80.

46 Ibid.

47 Ernest Mason Satow, *A Guide Book to Nikkô* (Yokohama: *Japan Mail* Office, 1875), 4.

48 Ibid., 2.

49 John Milton, *Paradise Lost: A Poem in Twelve Books* (Birmingham: Knott and Lloyd, 1804), book IV, 109, quoted in Laird, *The Rambles of a Globe Trotter*, vol. 1, 203.

50 Laird, *The Rambles of a Globe Trotter*, vol. 1, 203.

51 Basil Hall Chamberlain, *Things Japanese: being notes on various subjects connected with Japan for the use of travellers and others* (London: John Murray, 1890), 140.

52 Ernest Mason Satow and Albert George Sydney Hawes, *A Handbook for Travellers in Central and Northern Japan: Being a Guide to Tokio, Kioto, Ozaka and other Cities; the most interesting parts of the Main Island between Kobe and Awomori with ascents of the Principal Mountains, and Descriptions of Temples, Historical Notes and Legends* (Yokohama: Kelly & Walsh, 1881), i.

2 AUTHENTIC SPACES

1 Gilbert, GIL 4/377, ESRO, Hong Kong , 26 March 1877, 4.

2 Dearmer, Mss Eur C326: 1916–1918, BL, bound volume, On the way to Madras, 7 November 1916, 9.

3 Ibid., Rangoon, 4 April 1917, 178.

4 John Thomson, *Illustrations of China and its People*, 4 volumes (London: Sampson Low, Marston, Low and Searle, 1873–4) vol. 1, 1.

5 Gilbert, Letters February–March 1877, GIL 4/376, East Sussex Record Office, Samcrang Java, 27 February 1877, 12.

6 Gilbert, Japan (Kobe, Nagasaki, Yokohama), May–June 1877 (GIL 4/379), East Sussex Record Office, Kobe, 27 May 1877, 4.

7 Dearmer, Mss Eur C326: 1916–1918, British Library, bound volume, Madras, 10 November, 1916, 10.

8 Gilbert, Letters February–March 1877, GIL 4/376, East Sussex Record Office, Samcrang Java, 27 February 1877, 12.

9 Powell-Cotton, World Trip Diary, QP, Mandalay, 6 February 1891, 173.

10 Ibid.

11 James Buzard, *The Beaten Track: European Tourism, Literature, and the Ways to 'Culture', 1800–1918* (Oxford: Oxford University Press, 1993), 20–21.

12 Dearmer, Mss Eur C326, BL, Palmacotta, 9 December 1916, 40.

13 Carlisle, *Round the World in 1870*, 49.

14 Britta Martens, 'Vatican Ceremonies and Tourist Culture in Nine-teenth-Century British Travelogues', in M. Hollington, C. Waters and J. Jordan, eds., *Imagining Italy: Victorian Writers and Travellers* (Newcastle: Cambridge Scholars Press, 2010), 14.

15 Ibid.

16 Charles Dickens, *Pictures from Italy* (London: Bradbury & Evans, 1846), 200.

17 Carlisle, *Round the World in 1870*, 49.

18 Dickens, *Pictures from Italy*, 172.

19 Carlisle, *Round the World in 1870*, 49.

20 Ibid., 121.

21 Ibid., 212.

22 Laird, *The Rambles of a Globe Trotter*, vol. 1, 188.

23 Thompson, *In the Track of the Sun*, 24.

24 Carlisle, *Round the World in 1870*, 44.

25 Gower, *Notes of a Tour from Brindisi to Yokohama*, 26.

26 Thompson, *In the Track of the Sun*, 18, 148.

27 Charles Lucas, Photo 1224/7, vol. 1, BL, Madras, 9 November, 1877, 53.

28 Chitralekha Zutshi, '"Designed for Eternity": Kashmiri Shawls, Empire, and Cultures of Production and Consumption in Mid-Victorian Britain', *Journal of British Studies*, vol. 48 (2009), 420.

29 Laird, *The Rambles of a Globe Trotter*, vol. 2, 258.

30 Ibid., 247.

31 Lucas, Photo 1224/7, vol. 1, BL, Jehlum 'Dak Bungalow', 27 March 1878, 304.

32 Louis Tracy, *What I Saw in India: The Adventures of a Globe-Trotter* (Allahbad, 1892), 2.

33 Lucas, Photo 1224/7, vol 2, BL, Calcutta, 27 December 1878, 204.

34 Percy Powell-Cotton, World Trip Journal, QP, 22 March 1890, 82.

35 Dearmer, Mss Eur C326, BL, Dunga 484, Srinigar, 20 May 1917, 236.

36 Nancy Dearmer, *The Life of Percy Dearmer, by his wife Nan Dearmer* (London: Jonathan Cape, 1940), 146–7.

37 'Dr. Dearmer's Marriage', *The Birmingham Daily Gazette*, Monday, 21 August 1916, 4.

38 Dearmer, Mss Eur C326, BL, Palmacotta, 9 December 1916, 41.

39 Ibid., Bombay, 23 January 1917, 88.

40 Ibid., 88–9.

41 Lucas, Photo 1224/7, vol. 1, Madras, 9 November 1877, 52.

42 Ibid., Ahmednagar, 15 January, 1917, 78–9.

43 Ibid., Madurai, 10 November 1916, 14.

44 Lucas, Photo 1224/7, vol. 3, Shanghai, 19 March 1879, 31–2.

45 Gilbert, GIL 4/379, ESRO, Kobe, May 1877, 4.

46 Laird, *The Rambles of a Globe Trotter*, vol. 1, 184.

47 Lucas, Photo 1224/7, vol. 3, Kyoto, 2 April 1879, 47–8.

48 Powell-Cotton, World Trip Diary, QP, Kioto, 24 April 1891, 202.

49 Dearmer, Eur Mss C326, BL, On board S. S. *Senator*, 21 April 1918, 512.

50 Ibid., 514.

51 Ibid., Simla, 6 August 1917, 298.

52 Ibid., On board Shinyo Maru, 29 April 1918, 519.

53 *The Official Railway, Steamboat and Traveller's Guide with General Information for Tourists in Japan* (Yokohama: Offices of the *Japan Gazette*, 1891), 13.

54 Dearmer, Mss Eur C326, BL, Imperial Hotel Tokyo, 21 May 1918, 547.

55 Ibid., Nikko Hotel, 30 May 1918, 566.

56 Mio Wakita, *Staging Desires: Japanese Femininity in Kusakabe Kimbei's Nineteenth-Century Souvenir Photography* (Berlin: Deitrich Reimer, 2013), 135.

57 Lucas, Photo 1224/7, vol. 2, Calcutta, 30 December 1878, 206.

58 Lucas, Photo 1224/7, vol 3, Yokohama, 1 August 1879, 153.

59 Ibid.

60 Powell-Cotton, World Trip Diary, QP, Mandalay, 15 February 1891, 85.

61 Dearmer, Mss Eur C326, BL, Bangalore, 18 December 1917, 48.

62 Ibid., Madras, 10 November 1916, 28.

63 Ibid., Rangoon, 1 April 1917, 171.

64 Ibid., Nikko Hotel, 30 May 1918, 564.

3 CONSUMING THE EAST

1 Carlisle, *Round the World in 1870*, 128.

2 Ibid.

3 Ibid.

4 Magdalena Nowicka, 'Cosmopolitans, Spatial Mobility and the Alternative Geographies', *International Review of Social Research*, vol. 2 (2012), 14.

5 Robert Bickers, 'Shanghailanders and Others: British Communities in China, 1843–1957', in Robert Bickers, ed., *Settlers and Expatriates: Britons over the Seas* (Oxford: Oxford University Press, 2010), 279.

6 Rebecca Earle, *The Body of the Conquistador: Food, Race and the Colonial Experience in Spanish America, 1492–1700* (Cambridge: Cambridge University Press, 2012), 17.

7 Laird, *The Rambles of a Globe Trotter*, vol. 1, 174.

8 Ibid., vol. 1, 246.

9 Romita Ray, *Under the Banyan Tree: Relocating the Picturesque in British India* (London: Yale University Press, 2013), 55.

10 Laird, *The Rambles of a Globe Trotter*, vol. 2, 190.

11 Walter P. Ryland, *My Diary during a Foreign Tour in Egypt, India, Ceylon, Australia, New Zealand, Tasmania, Fiji, China, Japan and North America in 1881–2* (Birmingham: printed for private circulation, 1886), 83.

12 Thompson, *In the Track of the Sun*, 122.

13 Laird, *The Rambles of a Globe Trotter*, vol. 1, 292.

14 Gilbert, Photograph albums, ESRO, North China Album, GIL 4/387, image 29.

15 Gilbert, Letters to his mother, ESRO, Hong Kong, March–April 1877, GIL 4/377, and Peking, April–May 1877, GIL 4/378.

16 Laird, *The Rambles of a Globe Trotter*, vol. 1, 293.

17 Rebecca F. Stern, "'Adulterations Detected': Food and Fraud in Christina Rossetti's "Goblin Market"', *Nineteenth-Century Literature*, vol. 57 (2003), 477–511.

18 Ryland, *My Diary during a Foreign Tour*, 32.

19 Ibid., 33.

20 Thompson, *In the Track of the Sun*, 118.

21 Laird, *The Rambles of a Globe Trotter*, vol. 2, 170.

22 Thompson, *In the Track of the Sun*, 124.

23 Dearmer, Mss Eur C326: 1916–1918, BL, Madras, 10 November 1916, 11.

24 Ibid.

25 Lucas, Letters, 1224/7, vol. 3, BL, Yokohama, 31 July 1879, 152.

26 Laird, *The Rambles of a Globe Trotter*, vol. 1, 268.

27 Ibid., vol. 1, 250–1.

28 Ibid., vol. 1, 310.

29 Carlisle, *Round the World in 1870*, 110.

30 Ibid., 119.

31 Ryland, *My Diary during a Foreign Tour*, 196.

32 Thompson, *In the Track of the Sun*, 69.

33 John Henry Gray, *Walks in the City of Canton* (Victoria: De Souza & Company, 1875), 165.

34 Gilbert, Letters, ESRO, GIL 4/377, Hong Kong, 3 April 1877, 4.

35 Lucas, Letters, Photo 1224/7, vol. 3, BL, Canton, 27 February 1878, 16.

36 Ibid.

37 Thompson, *In the Track of the Sun*, 71

38 Lucas, Photo 1224/7, vol. 3, BL, Canton, 27 February 1878, 16.

39 Ibid.

40 Mark Swislocki, *Culinary Nostalgia: regional food culture and the urban experience in Shanghai* (California: Stanford University Press, 2008), 116.

41 Lucas, Photo 1224/6, Japan, vol. 2, BL, Japan, 1870s, photographs 18–20.

42 Lucas, Photo 1224/7, Japan, vol. 3, BL, Kobe, 31 March 1879, 43.

43 Ibid., Kobe, 5 April, 1879, 51.

44 Ibid., Yokohama, 7 August 1879, 156.

45 K. J. Cwiertka, *Modern Japanese Cuisine: Food, Power and National Identity* (London: Reaktion Books, 2006), 26–8.

46 Lucas, Photo 1224/7, Japan, vol. 3, BL, Inoshima, 2 May, 1879, 76.

47 Ibid., Inoshima, 4 May, 1879, 77.

48 Ibid., Inoshima, 30 July 1879, 152.

49 Ibid., Yokohama, 10 April 1879, 59.

50 Carlisle, *Round the World in 1870*, 110.

4 COLLECTING THE EAST

1 Christie, Manson and Woods, *Catalogue of the Important Collection of Old French Furniture, Porcelain, Objects of Art and Vertu and Silver Plate of the Right Hon. Sir Julian Goldsmid, Bart, M.P., Deceased* (London: Christie, Manson and Woods, 1896), Lots 595–609.

2 Harriet Martineau, in Charles Dickens, ed., *Household Words*, 28 August 1852, 553.

3 Carlisle, *Round the World in 1870*, 75.

4 Laird, *The Rambles of a Globe Trotter*, vol. 2, 143.

5 Ibid., vol. 2, 250–1.

6 Ibid., vol. 2, 311–2.

7 Bruce Robbins, 'Victorian Cosmopolitanism, Interrupted', *Victorian Literature and Culture*, vol. 38 (2010), 421.

8 Sherry Rehman and Naheed Jafri, *The Kashmiri Shawl* (Woodbridge, Suffolk: Antique Collector's Club, 2006), 360.

9 Gallery of Costume, Platt Hall, Manchester, 1947.2373.

10 Dearmer, Mss Eur C326: 1916-1918, BL, Srinigar, 26 April 1917, 206.

11 Ibid.

12 Dearmer, Mss Eur C326: 1916–1918, BL, Simla, 10 July 1917, 267.

13 Carlisle, *Round the World in 1870*, 120.

14 Craig Clunas, 'Ming and Qing Ivories: Useful and Ornamental Pieces', in William Watson, ed., *Chinese Ivories: from the Shang to the Qing* (London: British Museum for the Oriental Ceramic Society, 1984), 118.

15 John Barrow, *Travels in China, containing descriptions, observations, and comparisons, made and collected in the course of a short residence at the imperial palace of Yuen-Min-Yuen, and on a subsequent journey from Pekin to Canton* (London: T. Cadell and W. Davies, 1804), 308.

16 Ibid.

17 Shanyn Fiske, 'Orientalism Reconsidered: China and the Chinese in Nineteenth-Century Literature and Victorian Studies', *Literature Compass*, vol. 8 (April 2011), 215–6.

18 Catherine Pagani, 'Chinese Material Culture and British Perceptions of China in the Mid-Nineteenth Century', in Tim Barringer and Tom Flynn, eds., *Colonialism and the Object: Empire, Material Culture and the Museum* (London: Routledge, 1998), 28.

19 Fiske, 'Orientalism Reconsidered', 217.

20 John Stuart Mill, *Principles of Political Economy with some of the Applications to Social Philosophy* (London: Longmans, Green and Co., 1848), 81.

21 Carlisle, *Round the World in 1870*, 157.

22 Alice Bewicke, *A Marriage in China* (London: F. V. White & Co., 1896), 3.

23 Nathan Dunn, '*Ten Thousand Chinese Things.*' *A descriptive catalogue of the Chinese collection owned by Nathan Dunn, now exhibiting at St. George's Place, Hyde Park Corner, London* (London: printed for the proprietor, 1842).

24 Karl Gerth, *China Made: Consumer Culture and the Creation of the Nation* (Cambridge, Mass.: Harvard University Asia Center and Harvard University Press, 2003), 205.

25 *Official Descriptive and Illustrated Catalogue of the Great Exhibition of the Works of Industry of All Nations* (London: W. Clowes & Sons, 1851), 1418–25.

26 Powell-Cotton, World Trip Journal, QP, Canton, 20 March 1891, 186.

27 Ibid.

28 Quoted in Moyra Claire Pollard, *Master Potter of Meiji Japan: Makuzu Kôzan (1842–1916) and his Workshop* (Oxford: Oxford University Press, 2002), 23.

29 Ibid.

30 Laird, *The Rambles of a Globe Trotter*, vol. 1, 193.

31 Carlisle, *Round the World in 1870*, 192.

32 Laird, *The Rambles of a Globe Trotter*, vol. 1, 178.

33 Dearmer, Kyoto, 18 May 1918, 532.

34 Ibid.

35 Chamberlain, *Things Japanese*, 213–15.

36 Gilbert, Letters, ESRO, GIL 4/379, Japan (Kobe, Nagasaki, Yokohama), May–June 1877, Kobe, 27 May 1877, 3.

37 Chamberlain, *Things Japanese*, 213.

38 Gilbert, Letters, ESRO, GIL 4/377, March–April 1877, Hong Kong, 4 April 1877, 4.

39 Dearmer, Yokohama, 24 June, 1918, 580.

40 Merton Russell-Cotes, *Home and Abroad* (Bournemouth: printed for private circulation, 1921), 469.

41 Nora Beatrice Gardner, *Rifle and Spear with the Rajpoots: Being the Narrative of a Winter's Travel and Sport in Northern India* (London: Chatto & Windus, 1895), 128.

42 *The Graphic*, August 1895.

43 Powell-Cotton, World Trip Diary, 18 May 1891, 196

CONCLUSION: COMING HOME

1 Carlisle, *Round the World in 1870*, 408.

2 Simon Olding, 'A Victorian Salon: An Introduction', in Simon Olding, Giles Waterfield and Mark Bills, eds., *A Victorian Salon: Paintings from the Russell-Cotes Art Gallery and Museum* (London and Bournemouth: Lund Humphries in association with Russell-Cotes Art Gallery and Museum, 1999), 10.

3 Keith Nicklin, *Powell-Cotton: Man & Museum* (Canterbury: University of Kent at Canterbury, 1981), 1.

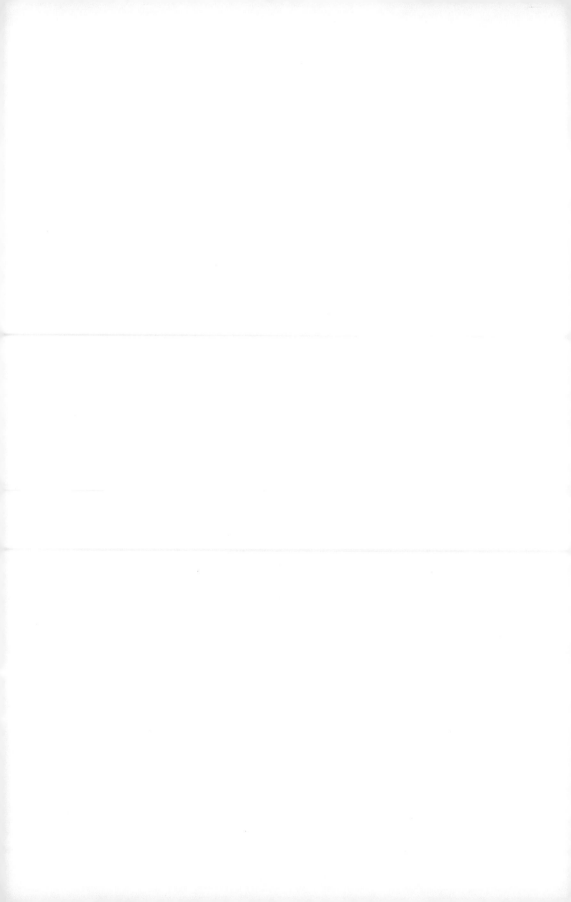

SELECT BIBLIOGRAPHY

Agathocleous, Tanya, *Urban Realism and the Cosmopolitan Imagination in the Nineteenth Century* (Cambridge: Cambridge University Press, 2011).

Alcock, Rutherford, *Catalogue of Works of Industry and Art sent from Japan* (London: International Exhibition, 1862).

Arnold, David, *The Tropics and the Traveling Gaze: India, Landscape, and Science, 1800–1856* (Delhi: Permanent Black, 2005).

Auerbach, Jeffrey and Hoffenberg, Peter, eds., *Britain, the Empire, and the World at the Great Exhibition of 1851* (London: Ashgate, 2008).

Barringer, Tim and Flynn, Tom eds., *Colonialism and the Object: Empire, Material Culture and the Museum* (London: Routledge, 1998).

Barrow, John, *Travels in China, containing descriptions, observations, and comparisons, made and collected in the course of a short residence at the imperial palace of Yuen-Min-Yuen, and on a subsequent journey through the country from Pekin to Canton* (London: T. Cadell and W. Davis, 1804).

Baxter, W.E., *A Winter in India* (London: Cassell & Company, 1882).

Behdad, Ali and Gartlan, Luke, eds., *Photography's Orientalism: New Essays on Colonial Representation* (Los Angeles: The Getty Research Institute, 2013).

Bennett, Terry, *History of Photography in China, 1842–1860* (London: Quaritch, 2010).

Bennett, Tony, *Pasts Beyond Memories: Evolution, Museums, Colonialism* (London: Routledge, 2004).

Berghoff, Hartmut, et al., eds., *The Making of Modern Tourism: The Cultural History of the British Experience, 1600–2000* (Basingstoke: Palgrave Macmillan, 2002).

Bewicke, Alicia, *Intimate China: The Chinese as I Have Seen Them* (London: Hutchinson & Co., 1899).

Bickers, Robert, *Britain in China: Community, Culture and Colonialism, 1900–49* (Manchester: Manchester University Press, 1999).

—, ed., *Settlers and Expatriates: Britons Over the Seas* (Oxford: Oxford University Press, 2010).

Bijon, Béatrice and Gâcon, Gérard, eds., *In-Between Two Worlds: Narratives by Female Explorers and Travellers 1850–1940* (New York: Peter Lang, 2009).

Bincsik, Monika, 'European Collectors and Japanese Merchants of Lacquer in "Old Japan": Collecting Japanese lacquer art in the Meiji period', *Journal of the History of Collections*, 20 (2008): 217–236.

Binfield, Clyde, *George Williams and the Y.M.C.A.: A Study in Victorian Social Attitudes* (London: Heinemann, 1973).

Bird, Isabella, *The Yangtze Valley and Beyond: An Account of Journeys in China, Chiefly in the Provinces of Sze Chuan and Among the Man-Tze of the Somo Territory* (London: John Murray, 1899).

—, *Unbeaten Tracks in Japan: An Account of Travels in the Interior Including Visits to the Aborigines of Yezo and the Shrines of Nikkô and Isé* (London: John Murray, 1881).

Black, Jeremy, *Italy and the Grand Tour* (New Haven and London: Yale University Press, 2003).

Bourdieu, Pierre, *Distinction: A Social Critique of the Judgement of Taste*, trans. Richard Nice (London: Routledge, 1984).

Bracken, Susan, Gáldy, Andrea M., and Turpin, Adriana, *Collecting East and West* (Newcastle: Cambridge Scholars Publishing, 2013).

Breckenridge, Carol A., Pollock, Sheldon, Bhabha, Homi K., and Chakrabarty, Dipesh eds., *Cosmopolitanism* (Durham and London: Duke University Press, 2002).

Bubbar, Prahlad, ed., *Indian Paintings and Photographs, 1590–1900* (Exhibition Catalogue, London: Prahlad Bubbar Mayfair, 2012).

Buettner, Elizabeth, *Empire Families: Britons and Late Imperial India* (Oxford: Oxford University Press, 2004).

Buzard, James, *The Beaten Track: European Tourism, Literature, and the Ways to 'Culture', 1800–1918* (Oxford: Oxford University Press, 1993).

Byerly, Alison, *Are We There Yet?: Virtual Travel and Victorian Realism* (Ann Arbor: University of Michigan Press, 2013).

Carlisle, Arthur Drummond, *Round the World in 1870: An Account of a Brief Tour Made Through India, China, Japan, California, and South America* (London: H.S. King & Co., 1872).

Chaiklin, Martha, 'Politicking Art: Ishikawa Komei and the development of Meiji Sculpture', *East Asian History*, 39 (2014): 53–74.

—, *Ivory and the Aesthetics of Modernity in Meiji Japan* (Basingstoke: Palgrave Macmillan, 2014).

Chamberlain, Basil Hall, and Mason, W.B., *A Handbook for Travellers in Japan, Revised and for the Most Part Re-written* (London: John Murray, 1891; Yokohama: Kelly & Walsh Limited, 1891).

—, *A Handbook for Travellers in Japan, Including the Whole Empire from Yezo to Formosa*, fifth edition (London: John Murray and Yokohama: Kelly & Walsh, 1899).

Chamberlain, Basil Hall, *Things Japanese: being notes on various subjects connected with Japan for the use of travellers and others* (London: John Murray, 1890).

Chan, Ying-kit, 'The Great Dog Massacre in Late Qing China: Debates, Perceptions, and Phobia in the Shanghai International Settlement', *Frontiers of History in China*, 10 (2015): 645–667.

Chang, Elizabeth H., ed, *British Travel Writing from China, 1798–1901* (London: Pickering and Chatto, 2010).

—, *Britain's Chinese Eye: Literature, Empire, and Aesthetics in Nineteenth-Century Britain* (Stanford: Stanford University Press, 2010).

Chard, Chloe, *A Critical Reader of the Romantic Grand Tour: Tristes Plaisirs* (Manchester: Manchester University Press, 2014).

—, *Pleasure and Guilt on the Grand Tour: Travel Writing and Imaginative Geography, 1600–1830* (Manchester: Manchester University Press, 1999).

Chaudhary, Zahid R., *Afterimage of Empire: Photography in Nineteenth-Century India* (Minneapolis: University of Minnesota Press, 2012).

Cheung, Sidney and Wu, David Y.H., *The Globalisation of Chinese Food* (Oxford: Routledge, 2014).

Ching, May-bo, 'Chopsticks or Cutlery?: How Canton Hong Merchants entertained Foreign Guests in the Eighteenth and Nineteenth Centuries', in Johnson, Kendall, ed., *Narratives of Free Trade: The Commercial Cultures of Early US-China Relations* (Hong Kong: Hong Kong University Press, 2012).

Christensen, Allan Conrad, *Nineteenth-Century Narratives of Contagion: 'Our Feverish Contact'* (London: Routledge, 2005).

Christie, Manson and Woods, *Catalogue of the Important Collection of Old French Furniture, Porcelain, Objects of Art and Vertu and Silver Plate of the Right Hon Sir Julian Goldsmid, Bart., Deceased* (London: Christie, Manson and Woods, 1896).

Christie, William, '"Prejudice Against Prejudices": China and the Limits of Whig Liberalism', *European Romantic Review*, 24 (2013): 509–529.

Clifford, Nicholas, '*A Truthful Impression of the Country': British and American Travel Writing in China, 1880–1949* (Ann Arbor: University of Michigan Press, 2001).

Clunas, Craig, 'Ming and Qing Ivories: Useful and Ornamental Pieces', in Watson, William, ed., *Chinese Ivories: from the Shang to the Qing* (London: British Museum for the Oriental Ceramic Society, 1984).

—, *Chinese Export Watercolours* (London: Victoria and Albert Museum, 1984).

Colley, Ann C., *Victorians in the Mountains: Sinking the Sublime* (London: Routledge, 2016).

Collingham, Lizzie, *Curry: A Biography* (London: Chatto & Windus, 2005).

—, *Imperial Bodies: The Physical Experience of the Raj, c. 1800–1947* (Cambridge: Polity, 2001).

Cozzi, Annette, *The Discourses of Food in Nineteenth-Century British Fiction* (Basingstoke: Palgrave Macmillan, 2010).

Culler, Jonathan, *Framing the Sign: Criticism and its Institutions* (Norman: University of Oklahoma Press, 1989).

Cwiertka, K.J., *Modern Japanese Cuisine: Food, Power and National Identity* (London: Reaktion Books, 2006).

Daly, Suzanne, *The Empire Inside: Indian Commodities in Victorian Domestic Novels* (Ann Arbor: The University of Michigan Press, 2011).

de Certeau, Michel, *The Practice of Everyday Life* (London: University of California Press, 1984).

de Lange, William, *A History of Japanese Journalism: Japan's Press Club as the last Obstacle to a Mature Press* (Richmond: Japan Library, 1998).

Dearmer, Nancy, British Library, Mss Eur C326: 1916–1918, single bound volume.

—, *The Life of Percy Dearmer, by his Wife Nan Dearmer* (London: Jonathan Cape, 1940).

Delanty, Gerard, 'The Cosmopolitan Imagination: Critical Cosmopolitanism and Social Theory', *The British Journal of Sociology*, 57 (2006): 25–47.

Denenholz Morse, Deborah, and Danahay, Martin, eds., *Victorian Animal Dreams: Representations of Animals in Victorian Literature and Culture* (Aldershot: Ashgate, 2007).

Dickens, Charles, *Pictures from Italy* (London: Bradbury & Evans, 1846).

Douglas, Mary, *Purity and Danger: An Analysis of Concept of Pollution and Taboo* (London: Routledge, 2002, first published 1966).

Dresser, Christopher, *Japan: its Architecture, Art, and Art Manufactures* (London: Longmans & Co., 1882).

Dunn, Nathan, *'Ten Thousand Chinese Things.' A Descriptive Catalogue of the Chinese Collection Owned by Nathan Dunn, Now Exhibiting at St. George's Place, Hyde Park Corner, London* (London: Printed for the Proprietor, 1842).

Earle, Rebecca, *The Body of the Conquistador: Food, Race and the Colonial Experience in Spanish America, 1492–1700* (Cambridge: Cambridge University Press, 2012).

—, ed., *Epistolary Selves: Letters and Letter-Writers, 1600–1945* (Aldershot: Ashgate, 1999).

Edensor, T., *Tourists at the Taj: Performance and Meaning at a Symbolic Site* (London: Routledge, 1998).

Elleman, Bruce A. and Kotkin, Stephen, eds., *Manchurian Railways and the Opening of China: An International History* (London: M.E. Sharp, 2010).

Elmarsafy, Ziad, Bernard, Anna and Atwell, David, eds., *Debating Orientalism* (Basingstoke: Palgrave Macmillan, 2013).

Fanshawe, H.C., ed., *A Handbook for Travellers in India, Burma and Ceylon* (London: John Murray, 1911).

Farr, Martin and Guégan, Xavier, eds., *The British Abroad Since the Eighteenth Century*, 2 volumes, Volume 1: *Travellers and Tourists* (London: Palgrave Macmillan, 2013).

Farrer, James, ed., *The Globalization of Asian Cuisines: Transnational Networks and Culinary Contact Zones* (New York: Palgrave Macmillan, 2015).

Featherstone, David and Painter, Joe, eds., *Spatial Politics: Essays for Doreen Massey* (Malden, MA: John Wiley & Sons, 2013).

Fiévé, Nicholas and Waley, Paul, eds., *Japanese Capitals in Historical Perspective: Place, Power and Memory in Kyoto, Edo and Tokyo* (London: Routledge, 2013).

Fiske, Shanyn, 'Orientalism Reconsidered: China and the Chinese in Nineteenth-Century Literature and Victorian Studies', *Literature Compass*, 8 (2011): 214–26.

Flint, Kate, *The Victorians and the Visual Imagination* (Cambridge: Cambridge University Press, 2000).

Fogel, Joshua A., *Articulating the Sinosphere: Sino-Japanese Relations in Space and Time* (Cambridge; London: Harvard University Press, 2009).

Frawley, Maria H., 'Borders and Boundaries, Perspectives and Place: Victorian Women's Travel Writing' in Pomeroy, Jordana, ed., *Intrepid Women: Victorian Artists Travel* (Aldershot: Ashgate, 2005).

Fromer, Julie E., *A Necessary Luxury: Tea in Victorian England* (Athens: Ohio University Press, 2008).

Gardner, Nora Beatrice, *Rifle and Spear with the Rajpoots: Being the Narrative of a Winter's Travel and Sport in Northern India* (London: Chatto & Windus, 1895).

Garner, Shaun, 'Sir Merton Russell-Cotes and his Japanese Collection: The Importance and Impact of an Unplanned Trip to Japan in 1885', in Shelton, Anthony, ed., *Collections: Individuals and Institutions* (London: The Horniman Museum and Gardens, 2001), 163–188.

Gartlan, Luke, *A Career of Japan: Baron Raimund von Stillfried and Early Yokohama Photography* (Leiden and Boston: Brill, 2016).

—, 'Bronzed and Muscular Bodies: Jinrikishas, Tattooed Bodies and Yokohama Tourist Photography', in Codell, Julie, ed., *Transculturation in British Art, 1770–1930* (Farnham: Ashgate, 2012), 93–110.

—, 'Views and Costumes of Japan: A Photograph Album by Baron Raimund von Stillfried-Ratenicz', *The Latrobe Journal*, 76 (2005): 5–27.

Gerber, David A., *Authors of their Lives: The Personal Correspondence of British Immigrants to North America in the Nineteenth Century* (New York: New York University Press, 2006).

Gere, Charlotte, *Artistic Circles: Design and Decoration in the Aesthetic Movement* (London: V&A Publishing, 2010).

Gerritsen, Anne and Riello, Giorgio, eds., *Writing Material Culture History* (London: Bloomsbury, 2015).

Gerth, Karl, *China Made: Consumer Culture and the Creation of the Nation* (Cambridge, Mass: Harvard University Asia Center and Harvard University Press, 2003).

Gilbert, Carew Davies, East Sussex Record Office, Letters and Albums from 1877–8 World Tour. Letters: GIL 4/372–379; Photograph Albums: GIL 4/385 (Japan), GIL 4/386 (South China), GIL 4/387 (North China).

Goody, Jack, *Cooking, Cuisine and Class: A Study in Comparative Sociology* (Cambridge: Cambridge University Press, 1982).

Gordon, Stewart, ed., *Robes of Honour: Khil'at in Pre-Colonial and Colonial India* (Oxford: Oxford University Press, 2003).

Goswami, Manu, 'Englishness' on the Imperial Circuit: Mutiny Tours in Colonial South Asia', *Journal of Historical Sociology*, 9 (1996): 54–84.

Gower, Ronald, *Notes of a Tour from Brindisi to Yokohama 1883–1884* (London: Kegan Paul, Trench and Company, 1885).

Graburn, Nelson, 'Key Figure of Mobility: The Tourist', *Social Anthropology*, 25 (2017): 83–96.

Gray, John Henry, *Walks in the City of Canton* (Victoria, Hongkong: De Souza & Company, 1875).

Green, Judith, '"Curiosity", "Art" and "Ethnography" in the Chinese Collections of John Henry Gray', in Shelton, Anthony, ed., *Collections: Individuals and Institutions* (London: The Horniman Museum and Gardens, 2001), 111–128.

Greenhalgh, Paul, *Ephemeral Vistas: The Expositions Universelles, Great Exhibitions and World's Fairs, 1851–1939* (Manchester: Manchester University Press, 1988).

Greig, Hannah, Hamlett, Jane and Hannan, Leonie, eds., *Gender and Material Culture in Britain since 1600* (London: Palgrave, 2016).

Griffis, William Elliot, *The Mikado's Empire* (New York: Harper Bros., 1876).

Guth, Christine, *Longfellow's Tattoos: Tourism, Collecting, and Japan* (Seattle: University of Washington Press, 2004).

Hamlett, Jane, *Material Relations: Domestic Interiors and Middle-Class Families in England, 1850–1910* (Manchester: Manchester University Press, 2010).

Heathorn, Stephen J., 'Angel of Empire: the Cawnpore Memorial Well as a British Site of Imperial Remembrance', *Journal of Colonialism and Colonial History*, 8 (2007): 31–49.

Hight, Eleanor, M., *Capturing Japan in Nineteenth-Century New England Photography Collections* (Farnham: Ashgate, 2011).

Hill, Kate, ed., *Britain and the Narration of Travel in the Nineteenth Century: Texts, Images, Objects* (Farnham: Ashgate, 2016).

Hooper, Glen and Youngs, Tim, eds., *Perspectives in Travel Writing* (Aldershot: Ashgate, 2004).

Hore, J.E., *Embassies in the East: The Story of the British and their Embassies in China, Japan and Korea from 1859 to the Present* (London: Routledge, 1999).

Howes, David, ed., *Empire of the Senses: The Sensual Culture Reader* (Oxford: Berg, 2005).

Huber, Valeska, *Channelling Mobilities: Migration and Globalisation in the Suez Canal Region and Beyond, 1869–1914* (Cambridge: Cambridge University Press, 2013).

Hughes, Kathryn, *The Short Life and Long Times of Mrs Beeton* (London: Fourth Estate, 2005).

Hulme, Peter and Youngs, Tim, eds., *The Cambridge Companion to Travel Writing* (Cambridge: Cambridge University Press, 2002).

Hulsbosch, Marianne, Bedford, Elizabeth and Chaiklin, Martha, eds., *Asian Material Culture* (Amsterdam: Amsterdam University Press, 2009).

Hume, David L., *Tourism Art and Souvenirs: The Material Culture of Tourism* (New York: Routledge, 2014).

Irwin, John, *The Kashmir Shawl* (London: Victoria and Albert Museum, 1973).

Jordan, Caroline, *Picturesque Pursuits: Colonial Women Artists and the Amateur Tradition* (Melbourne: Melbourne University Press, 2005).

Joyce, Patrick, *The State of Freedom: A Social History of the British State since 1800* (Cambridge: Cambridge University Press, 2013).

Joyce, Patrick and Bennett, Tony, eds., *Material Powers: Cultural Studies, History and the Material Turn* (Abingdon: Routledge, 2010).

Keene, Donald, *Emperor of Japan: Meiji and his World, 1852–1912* (New York: Columbia University Press 2002).

Kennedy, Dane, *The Magic Mountains: Hill Stations and the British Raj* (Berkeley: University of California Press, 1996).

Kerner, Susanne, Chou, Cynthia, and Warmind, Morten, eds., *Commensality: From Everyday Food to Feast* (London: Bloomsbury Academic, 2015).

Kopytoff, Igor, 'The Cultural Biography of Things: Commoditization as Process' in Arjun Appadurai, ed., *The Social Life of Things: Commodities in Cultural Perspective* (Cambridge: Cambridge University Press, 1986).

Kostova, Ludmilla, 'Meals in Foreign Parts: Food in Writing by Nineteenth-Century British Travellers to the Balkans', *Journeys: The International Journal of Travel and Travel Writing*, 4 (2003): 21–44.

Kramer, Elizabeth, '"Not So Japan-Easy": The British Reception of Japanese Dress in the Late Nineteenth Century, *Textile History*, 44 (2013): 3–24.

Kuehn, Julia and Smethurst, Paul, eds., *New Directions in Travel Writing Studies* (Basingstoke: Palgrave Macmillan, 2015).

Labbe, Jacqueline M., 'To Eat and Be Eaten in Nineteenth-Century Children's Literature', in Keeling, Kara K. and Pollard, Scott T., eds., *Critical Approaches to Food in Children's Literature* (Abingdon: Routledge, 2009).

Lacoste, Anne, *Felice Beato: A Photographer on the Eastern Road* (Los Angeles: J. Paul Getty Museum, 2010).

Laird, Egerton K., *The Rambles of a Globe Trotter in Australia, Japan, China, Java, India, and Cashmere*, 2 volumes (Birkenhead: printed for private circulation, 1875).

Lasc, Anca I., 'A Museum of Souvenirs', *Journal of the History of Collections*, 28 (2016): 57–71.

Latour, Bruno, *Reassembling the Social: An Introduction to Actor-Network-Theory* (Oxford: Oxford University Press, 2005).

Lester, Alan, *Imperial Networks: Creating Identities in Nineteenth-Century South Africa and Britain* (London: Routledge, 2005).

Levell, Nicky, *Oriental Visions: Exhibitions, Travel and Collecting in the Victorian Age* (London: Horniman Museum, 2000).

Lévi-Strauss, Claude, *The Raw and the Cooked: Introduction to a Science of Mythology: I* (Translated by John and Doreen Weightman, London: Jonathan Cape, 1970).

Lister, W.B.C., *Murray's Handbooks for Travellers* (Bethesda: University Publications of America, 1993).

Lovell, Julia, *The Opium Wars: Drugs, Dreams, and the Making of Modern China* (New York: The Overlook Press, 2015).

Lucas, Charles James, British Library, Letters and Photograph Albums from 1877–9 World Tour, Photo 1224/1–6.

Luther, Narendra, *Raja Deen Dayal: Prince of Photographers* (Hyderabad: Creative Point, 2003).

MacCannell, Dean, 'The Tourist and the Local', *Tourist Studies*, 16 (2016): 343–50.

—, ed., *Empty Meeting Grounds: The Tourist Papers* (London: Routledge, 1992).

—, *The Tourist: A New Theory of the Leisure Class* (Oakland: University of California Press, 1976).

MacKenzie, John, M., 'Empires of Travel: British Guide Books and Cultural Imperialism in the 19th and 20th Centuries', in John K. Walton, ed., *Histories of Tourism: Representation, Identity and Conflict* (Bristol: Channel View Publications, 2005), 19–38.

—, *The Empire of Nature: Hunting, Conservation and British Imperialism* (Manchester: Manchester University Press, 1988).

—, ed., *Imperialism and Popular Culture* (Manchester: Manchester University Press, 1986).

Martens, Britta, 'Vatican Ceremonies and Tourist Culture in Nineteenth-Century British Travelogues', in Hollington, M., Waters, C. and Jordan, J., eds., *Imagining Italy: Victorian Writers and Travellers* (Newcastle: Cambridge Scholars Press, 2010).

Massey, Doreen, *World City* (Cambridge: Polity, 2007).

—, *Space, Place and Gender* (Cambridge: Polity, 1994).

Melillo, Edward D., 'Empire in a Cup: Imagining Colonial Geographies through British Tea Consumption', in Beattie, James, Melillo, Edward and O'Gorman, Emily, eds., *Eco-Cultural Networks and the British Empire: New Views on Environmental History* (London: Bloomsbury, 2015), 68–91.

Mill, John Stuart, *Dissertations and Discussions: Political, Philosophical and Historical* (London: Longmans, 1875).

—, *Principles of Political Economy with Some of the Applications to a Social Philosophy* (London: Longmans, Green and Co., 1848).

Miller, Daniel, ed., *Consumption: The History and Regional Development of Consumption* (London: Routledge, 2001).

Miller, William Ian, *The Anatomy of Disgust* (Cambridge, Massachusetts: Harvard University Press, 1997).

Mills, Sara, *Discourses of Difference: An Analysis of Women's Travel Writing and Colonialism* (London: Routledge, 1991).

Molz, Jenny German, 'Cosmopolitanism and Consumption', in Nowicka,

Magdalena, ed., *The Ashgate Research Companion to Cosmopolitanism* (Abingdon: Routledge, 2011) 33–52.

Murray, Cara, *Victorian Narrative Technologies in the Middle East* (London: Routledge, 2008).

Murray Mitchell, Maria Hay, *In India: Sketches of Indian Life and Travel from Letters and Journals* (London: T. Nelson & Sons, 1876).

Naquin, Susan, *Peking: Temples and City Life, 1400–1900* (Berkeley and Los Angeles: University of California Press, 2000).

Neiswander, Judith A., *The Cosmopolitan Interior: Liberalism and the British Home 1870–1914* (New Haven: Yale University Press, 2008).

Nicklin, Keith, 'Quex for Adventure: The Powell-Cotton Family Enterprise from Field to Showcase', in Shelton, Anthony, ed., *Collectors: Expressions of Self and Other* (London: The Horniman Museum and Gardens, 2001), 147–156.

—, *Powell-Cotton Man & Museum: An Exhibition, Kent University Library, April 21–May 16, 1981* (Canterbury: University of Kent Printing Unit, 1981).

Nishiyama, Takashi, *Engineering War and Peace in Modern Japan, 1868–1964* (Baltimore: Johns Hopkins University Press, 2014).

Nowicka, Magdalena, 'Cosmopolitans, Spatial Mobility and the Alternative Geographies', *International Review of Social Research*, 2 (2012): 1–16.

Oakes, Tim, 'Tourism and the Modern Subject: Placing the Encounter Between Tourist and Other', in Cartier, Carolyn and Lew, Alan A., eds., *Seductions of Place: Geographical Perspectives on Globalization and the Touristed Landscapes* (London: Routledge, 2005).

Olding, Simon, Waterfield, Giles, and Bills, Mark, *A Victorian Salon: Paintings from the Russell-Cotes Art Gallery and Museum* (London and Bournemouth: Lund Humphries in association with Russell-Cotes Art Gallery and Museum, 1999).

Omissi, David, *Indian Voices of the Great War: Soldiers' Letters, 1914–18* (London: Penguin 2014).

Ono, Ayako, *Japonisme in Britain: Whistler, Menpes, Henry, Hornel and Nineteenth-Century Japan* (London: Routledge, 2003).

Osborne, Peter, *Travelling Light: Photography, Travel and Visual Culture* (Manchester: Manchester University Press, 2000).

Pagani, Catherine, 'In Search of a Chinese Picturesque: William Alexander, George Chinnery and the visual image of China in nineteenth-century Britain', in Clark, Antony E., ed., *Beating Devils and Burning their Books: Views of China, Japan and the West* (Ann Arbor: Association for Asian Studies, 2010), 83–105.

Pai, Hyung Il, *Heritage Management in Korea and Japan: The Politics of Antiquity and Identity* (Seattle: University of Washington Press, 2014).

Patterson, Steven, *The Cult of Imperial Honor in British India* (New York: Palgrave Macmillan, 2009).

Pennington, Brian K., *Was Hinduism Invented?: Britons, Indians and the Colonial Construction of Religion* (Oxford: Oxford University Press, 2005).

Pinney, Christopher, *Camera Indica: The Social Life of Indian Photographs* (London: Reaktion Books, 1997).

Pollard, Clare, *Master Potter of Meiji Japan: Makuzu Kōzan and his Workshop* (Oxford: Oxford University Press, 2002).

Powell-Cotton, Percy, World Trip Diary, Letters and Collection, Quex Park, Birchington, Kent.

Pratt, Mary Louise, *Imperial Eyes: Travel Writing and Transculturation*, second edition (London: Routledge, 2008).

Procida, Mary A., *Married to the Empire: Gender, Politics and Imperialism in India, 1883–1947* (Manchester: Manchester University Press, 2002).

Purbrick, Louise, ed., *The Great Exhibition of 1851: New Interdisciplinary Essays* (Manchester: Manchester University Press, 2001).

Rai, Mridu, *Hindu Rulers, Muslim Subjects: Islam, Rights, and the History of Kashmir* (London: Christopher Hurst & Company, 2004).

Ramusack, Barbara N., *The New Cambridge History of India: The Indian Princes and their States* (Cambridge: Cambridge University Press, 2004).

Rappaport, Erika Diane, *Shopping for Pleasure: Women in the Making of London's West End* (Princeton: Princeton University Press, 2000).

Ray, Romita, *Under the Banyan Tree: Relocating the Picturesque in British India* (London: Yale University Press, 2013).

Rehman, Sherry and Jafri, Naheed, *The Kashmiri Shawl* (Woodbridge, Suffolk: Antique Collector's Club, 2006).

Relia, Anil, *The Indian Portrait VI: A Photographic Evolution from Documentation to Posterity* (Ahmedabad: Archer Art Gallery, 2015).

Ringmar, Erik, *Liberal Barbarism: The European Destruction of the Palace of the Emperor of China* (New York: Palgrave Macmillan, 2013).

Roberts, Claire, *Photography and China* (London: Reaktion Books, 2013).

Russell-Cotes, Annie, *Westward from the Golden Gate* (London: W.H. & L. Collingridge, circa 1900).

Russell-Cotes, Merton, *Home and Abroad: An Autobiography of an Octogenarian*, 2 volumes (Bournemouth: for private circulation, 1921).

Russell-Cotes Art Gallery and Museum, *Souvenir of the Japanese Collection* (Bournemouth: Russell-Cotes Art Gallery and Museum, 1931).

Ryan, James R., *Picturing Empire: Photography and the Visualizaton of the British Empire* (London: Reaktion Books, 1997).

Ryland, Walter P., *My Diary During a Foreign Tour in Egypt, India, Ceylon, Australia, New Zealand, Tasmania, Fiji, China, Japan and North America in 1881–2* (Birmingham: for private circulation, 1886).

Said, Edward, W., *Culture and Imperialism* (London: Vintage Books, 1994).

—, *Orientalism* (London: Penguin Books, 2003).

Saraf, D.N., *Arts and Crafts, Jammu and Kashmir: Land, People and Culture* (Buldhana, Maharashtra: Abhinav Publications, 1998).

Sato, Tomoko and Watanabe, Toshio, *Japan and Britain: An Aesthetic Dialogue, 1850–1930* (London: Lund Humphries, 1991).

Satow, E.M., *A Guide Book to Nikkô* (Yokohama: Japan Mail Office, 1875).

Satow, Ernest Mason and Hawes, A.G.S., *A Handbook for Travellers in Central &*

Northern Japan: Being a Guide to Tôkiô, Kiôto, Ôzaka, Hakodate, Nagasaki, and Other Cities; The Most Interesting Parts of the Main Island; Ascents of the Principal Mountains; Descriptions of Temples; and Historical Notes and Legends (London: John Murray; Yokohama: Kelly & Co., 1884).

Schivelbusch, Wolfgang, *The Railway Journey: the Industrialization of Time and Space in the 19th Century* (Oakland: University of California Press, 1986).

Selinger, Vyjayanthi R., *Authorizing the Shogunate: Ritual and Material Symbolism in the Literary Construction of Warrior Order* (Boston: Brill, 2013).

Simoons, Frederick J., *Food in China: A Cultural and Historical Inquiry* (Boca Raton: CRC Press, 1991).

Sinha, Mrinalini, 'Britishness, Clubbability, and the Colonial Public Sphere', in Ballantyne, Tony and Burton, Antoinette, eds., *Bodies in Contact: Rethinking Colonial Encounters in World History* (London: Duke University Press, 2005), 489–521.

—, *Colonial Masculinity: The 'Manly Englishman' and the 'Effeminate Bengali' in the Late Nineteenth Century* (Manchester: Manchester University Press, 1995).

Sivasundaram, Sujit, 'Towards a Critical History of Connection: The Port of Colombo, the Geographical "Circuit", and the Visual Politics of the New Imperialism, ca. 1880–1914', *Comparative Studies in Society and History*, 59 (2017): 346–384

Srinivasa, Roopa, Tiwari, Manish and Silas, Sandeep, eds., *Our Indian Railway: Themes in India's Railway History* (New Delhi: Foundation Books, 2006).

Stanley, Nick, *Being Ourselves for You: The Global Display of Cultures* (London: Middlesex University Press, 1998).

Steinbach, Susie, *Understanding the Victorians: Politics, Culture, and Society in Nineteenth-Century Britain* (London: Routledge, 2012).

Stern, Rebecca F., '"Adulterations Detected": Food and Fraud in Christina Rossetti's "Goblin Market"', *Nineteenth Century Literature*, 57 (2003): 477–511.

Sterry, Lorraine, *Victorian Women Travellers in Meiji Japan: Discovering a New Land* (Folkestone: Global Oriental, 2009).

Stewart, Susan, *On Longing: Narratives of the Miniature, the Gigantic, the Souvenir, the Collection* (Durham: Duke University Press, 1992).

Surak, Kristen, *Making Tea, Making Japan: Cultural Nationalism in Practice* (Stanford: Stanford University Press, 2013).

Sweet, Rosemary, *Cities of the Grand Tour: The British in Italy, c. 1690–1820* (Cambridge: Cambridge University Press, 2012).

Swenson, Astrid and Mandler, Peter, eds., *From Plunder to Preservation: Britain and the Heritage of Empire, c. 1800–1940* (Oxford: Oxford University Press, 2013).

Swislocki, Mark, *Culinary Nostalgia: Regional Food Culture and the Urban Experience in Shanghai* (Stanford: Stanford General, 2009).

Thompson, Andrew and Magee, Gary Brian, *Empire and Globalisation: Networks of People, Goods and Capital in the British World, c. 1850–1914* (Cambridge: Cambridge University Press, 2010).

Thompson, Carl, *Travel Writing* (London: Routledge, 2011).

Thompson, Frederick Diodati, *In the Track of the Sun: Readings from the Diary of a Globe Trotter* (London: William Heinemann, 1893).

Townshend, Dale, 'Ruins, Romance, and the Rise of Gothic Tourism: The Case of Netley Abbey, 1750–1830', *Journal for Eighteenth-Century Studies*, 37 (2014): 377–394.

Tracy, Louis, *What I Saw in India: The Adventures of a Globe-Trotter* (Allahabad, 1892).

Urry, John, *The Tourist Gaze*, second edition (London: Sage Publications, 2002).

—, *Consuming Places* (London and New York: Routledge, 1995).

Verne, Jules, *Around the World in 80 Days* (originally published 1873), translated by Paul Frederick Walter (Albany: Excelsior Editions, 2013).

Voskuil, Lynn, 'Robert Fortune, *Camellia sinensis*, and the Nineteenth-Century Global imagination', *Nineteenth-Century Contexts: An Interdisciplinary Journal*, 34 (2012): 5–18.

Wakita, Mio, *Staging Desires: Japanese Femininity in Kusakabe Kimbei's Nineteenth-Century Souvenir Photography* (Berlin: Reimer, c.2013).

Ward, Kerry, *Networks of Empire: Forced Migration and the Dutch East India Company* (Cambridge: Cambridge University Press, 2009).

Warren, Andrew, *The Orient and the Young Romantics* (Cambridge: Cambridge University Press, 2014).

West, Nancy Martha, *Kodak and the Lens of Nostalgia* (Charlottesville: University of Virginia Press, 2000).

Wilson, Ming, and Zhiwei, Liu, eds., *Souvenir from Canton: Chinese Export Paintings from the Victoria and Albert Museum* (Shanghai: Shanghai Classics, 2003).

Withey, Lynne, *Grand Tours and Cook's Tours: A History of Leisure Travel, 1750 to 1915* (London: Aurum Press, 1998).

Wu, Robert, *Picturing Hong Kong Photography, 1855–1910* (New York: Asia Society Galleries in Association with South China Printing Company, 1997).

Wu, Weiping and Gaubatz, Piper, *The Chinese City* (London: Routledge, 2013).

Yokoyama, Toshio, *Japan in the Victorian Mind: a Study of Stereotyped Images of a Nation 1850–80* (Basingstoke: Palgrave Macmillan, 1987).

Zutshi, Chitralekha, '"Designed for Eternity": Kashmiri Shawls, Empire, and Cultures of Production and Consumption in Mid-Victorian Britain', *Journal of British Studies*, 48 (2009): 420–440.

ILLUSTRATION LIST

All images are from the collections of the British Library unless otherwise stated. (Listed by page number.)
a=above, b=below, l=left, r=right

34. John Murray Collection: Calotype views of India. Photographer John Murray, c.1855–1865. Photo 35 (1).

35l. *Cook's Indian Tours... Programme of Cook's new system of International travelling tickets, embracing every point of interest... in India, etc.,* Thomas Cook & Son, 1881. 010055.g.39.

35r. Charles Ewart Darwent, *Shanghai: A handbook for travellers and residents...,* 1912. 10058.p.13.

36. Clement William Robert Hooper Collection: Album of views of Aden, Madras, Bombay, Andaman Islands, Burma. Photographers Nicholas and Company and others unknown, 1880s. Photo 447/1 (36).

39. Vibart Collection: Views in South India. Photographers Johnson and Henderson, 1850s–1870s. Photo 254/3 (41).

40. Curzon Collection: View of places proposed to be visited by their Excellencies Lord and Lady Curzon during Autumn Tour 1902. Photographer Deen Dayal, 1880s–1890s. Photo 430/21 (46).

42. *A Handbook for India: being an account of the three presidencies and of the overland route...,* John Murray, 1859. T.13122.

43. *Cook's Indian Tours... Programme of Cook's new system of International travelling tickets, embracing every point of interest... in India, etc.,* Thomas Cook & Son, 1885. 010055.g.39.

44. Thomas Cook Archives.

45. *Cook's Excursionist and Home and Foreign Tourist Advertiser,* 25 August, 1873. Lou.Lon.146 [1873].

46. Photographic record of the world tour of Charles James and Morton P. Lucas 1860s–1878. Volume 1: India and Ceylon. Photo 1224/1 (33).

47. Photographic record of the world tour of Charles James and Morton P. Lucas 1860s–1878. Volume 2: India and Kashmir. Photo 1224/2 (2) and Photo 1224/2 (14).

48. Egerton K. Laird, *The Rambles of a Globe Trotter in Australia, Japan, Java, India and Cashmere,* 1875. 10026.g.12.

49. J. Paul Getty Museum, Malibu.

51. Joseph Lee, Proprietor of the Railway Hotel, Cawnpore, *The Indian Mutiny, and in particular, a Narrative of the Events at Cawnpore, June and July, 1857,* 1893. 09059.aaa.26.

53. Richard C. Rapier, *Remunerative Railways for New Countries; with some account of the first railway in China,* 1878. 8235.k.6.

54. Wellcome Images.

55. Trumbull White, *Pacific Tours, and Around the World. Journeys via the American and Australian Line...,* 1900. 10024.bb.35.

56–57. A collection of eighty views, maps, portraits and drawings illustrative of the Embassy sent to China under George, Earl of Macartney. Maps 8.Tab.C.8.

58. Wellcome Images.

62. William Simpson, *Meeting the Sun: a journey all round the world, through Egypt, China, Japan and California...,* 1874. 10026.g.14.

65. Photographer James A. Ricalton for Underwood and Underwood, *China through the Stereoscope*, c.1900. Photo 1188/71 and Photo 1188/94.

66. Photographic record of the world tour of Charles James and Morton P. Lucas 1860s–1878. Volume 5: Japan (Part 1). Photo 1224/5 (55).

67. [A Book of Coloured Photographs of views in Japan], 1895. C.66.k.5.

69. Egerton K. Laird, *The Rambles of a Globe Trotter in Australia, Japan, Java, India and Cashmere*, 1875. 10026.g.12.

70. Isabella Bird, *Unbeaten Tracks in Japan. An account of travels in the interior, including visits to the aborigines of Yezo and the shrines of Nikkô and Isé*, 1880. 010058.ee.53.

72l. *The Far East: An Illustrated Fortnightly Newspaper*, 1 July 1871. P.P.3803.bha.

72r. *A Guide-Book for Tourists in Japan*, Welcome Society of Japan, 1910. X.708/12434.

76. Photographic record of the world tour of Charles James and Morton P. Lucas 1860s–1878. Volume 5: Japan (Part 1). Photo 1224/5 (55).

78. Photographic record of the world tour of Charles James and Morton P. Lucas 1860s–1878. Volume 5: Japan (Part 1). Photo 1224/5 (59).

79. Photographic record of the world tour of Charles James and Morton P. Lucas 1860s–1878. Volume 3: China. Photo 1224/3 (44).

80. Photographic record of the world tour of Charles James and Morton P. Lucas 1860s–1878. Volume 5: Japan (Part 1). Photo 1224/5 (39).

81. Photographic record of the world tour of Charles James and Morton P. Lucas 1860s–1878. Volume 1: India and Ceylon. Photo 1224/1 (72).

82. John Thomson, *Illustrations of China and its People. A series of … photographs with letterpress descriptive of the places and people represented*, 1873–4. 1787.d.7.

83. Allardyce Collection: Album of views and portraits in Hyderabad, Golconda, Ellora, Daulatabad and Aurangabad. Photographer Pestonjee Dosabhoy, 1870s. Photo 302/2 (4).

84. Photographic record of the world tour of Charles James and Morton P. Lucas 1860s–1878. Volume 5: Japan (Part 1). Photo 1224/5 (1).

85. Photographic record of the world tour of Charles James and Morton P. Lucas 1860s–1878. Volume 5: Japan (Part 1). Photo 1224/5 (2).

88a. J. Paul Getty Museum, Malibu.

88b. Photographic record of the world tour of Charles James and Morton P. Lucas 1860s–1878. Volume 1: India and Ceylon. Photo 1224/1 (96).

88. Photograph album of 'Our Indian Trip 1887–88'. Photo 403 (62).

89. Wellcome Images.

93. *The Far East: An Illustrated Fortnightly Newspaper*, 17 January 1871. P.P.3803.bha.

94. Photographic record of the world tour of Charles James and Morton P. Lucas 1860s–1878. Volume 5: Japan (Part 1). Photo 1224/5 (21).

95. Photographic record of the world tour of Charles James and Morton P. Lucas 1860s–1878. Volume 1: India and Ceylon. Photo 1224/1 (46).

96. Photographic record of the world tour of Charles James and Morton P. Lucas 1860s–1878. Volume 2: India and Kashmir. Photo 1224/2 (130).

100. Photographic record of the world tour of Charles James and Morton P. Lucas 1860s–1878. Volume 2: India and Kashmir. Photo 1224/2 (196) and Photo 1224/2 (195).

102. Photograph album of Edward Kay Robinson. Photographers unknown. 1880s–1890s. Photo 291 (24).

104. Views of Calcutta and Barackpore. Photographer Samuel Bourne, c.1867–1869. Photo 29 (4).

105. Photographic record of the world tour of Charles James and Morton P. Lucas 1860s–1878. Volume 1: India and Ceylon. Photo 1224/1 (33).

109. Photographic record of the world tour of Charles James and Morton P. Lucas 1860s–1878. Volume 6: Japan (Part 2). Photo 1224/6 (66).

112a. [A Book of Coloured Photographs of views in Japan], 1895. C.66.k.5.

112b. Photographic record of the world tour of Charles James and Morton P. Lucas 1860s–1878. Volume 6: Japan (Part 2). Photo 1224/6 (26).

114–115. Photographic record of the world tour of Charles James and Morton P. Lucas 1860s–1878. Volume 6: Japan (Part 2). Photo 1224/6 (44).

116. Sir Merton Russell-Cotes, *Home and Abroad. An Autobiography of an Octogenarian*, 1921. 10856.i.7.

118. Photographic record of the world tour of Charles James and Morton P. Lucas 1860s–1878. Volume 6: Japan (Part 2). Photo 1224/6 (67).

119. Photographic record of the world tour of Charles James and Morton P. Lucas 1860s–1878. Volume 5: Japan (Part 1). Photo 1224/5 (48).

120. Photographic record of the world tour of Charles James and Morton P. Lucas 1860s–1878. Volume 1: India and Ceylon. Photo 1224/1 (1) and Photo 1224/1 (2).

126. Photographic record of the world tour of Charles James and Morton P. Lucas 1860s–1878. Volume 3: China. Photo 1224/3 (78).

128. John Thomson, *Illustrations of China and its People. A series of ... photographs with letterpress descriptive of the places and people represented*, 1873–4. 1787.d.7.

129. Photographic record of the world tour of Charles James and Morton P. Lucas 1860s–1878. Volume 3: China. Photo 1224/3 (74).

131. Egerton K. Laird, *The Rambles of a Globe Trotter in Australia, Japan, Java, India and Cashmere*, 1875. 10026.g.12.

132–133. 'The Process of Planting, Growing and Curing Tea', from the original drawing in the collection of Col. Harcourt, 1808. Maps K.Top.116.19–2-d.

136. John Thomson, *Illustrations of China and its People. A series of ... photographs with letterpress descriptive of the places and people represented*, 1873–4. 1787.d.7.

138. Carew Davis Gilbert Photographic Archives. Reproduced with the permission of East Sussex Record Office, copyright reserved.

139. Elgin Collection: photographs relating to the Viceroyalty of Lord Elgin, 1860s–1890s. Photo 15/1 (35).

141a. Isabella Mary Beeton, *The Book of Household Management*, 1892. 7942.dd.9.

141b. Agnes B. Marshall, *Mrs A. B. Marshall's Larger Cookery Book of Extra Recipes...*, 1899. 07945.n.25.

143. Photographic record of the world tour of Charles James and Morton P. Lucas 1860s–1878. Volume 1: India and Ceylon. Photo 1224/1 (66).

145. Egerton K. Laird, *The Rambles of a Globe Trotter in Australia, Japan, Java, India and Cashmere*, 1875. 10026.g.12.

147. Photographic record of the world tour of Charles James and Morton P. Lucas 1860s–1878. Volume 6: Japan (Part 2). Photo 1224/6 (4).

149. Egerton K. Laird, *The Rambles of a Globe Trotter in Australia, Japan, Java, India and Cashmere*, 1875. 10026.g.12.

150. Annie Nelson Russell-Cotes, *Westward from the Golden Gate*, c.1900. X.809/22328.

152. John Thomson, *Illustrations of China and its People. A series of ... photographs with letterpress descriptive of the places and people represented*, 1873–4. 1787.d.7.

154. Wellcome Images.

155. Photographic record of the world tour of Charles James and Morton P. Lucas 1860s–1878. Volume 3: China. Photo 1224/3 (47).

156. Photographic record of the world tour of Charles James and Morton P. Lucas 1860s–1878. Volume 3: China. Photo 1224/3 (38) and Photo 1224/3 (39).

158. Photographic record of the world tour of Charles James and Morton P. Lucas 1860s–1878. Volume 6: Japan (Part 2). Photo 1224/6 (20).

159–160. Photographic record of the world tour of Charles James and Morton P. Lucas 1860s–1878. Volume 6: Japan (Part 2). Photo 1224/6 (21) and Photo 1224/6 (19).

163. Photographic record of the world tour of Charles James and Morton P. Lucas 1860s–1878. Volume 6: Japan (Part 2). Photo 1224/6 (25).

165. Photographic record of the world tour of Charles James and Morton P. Lucas 1860s–1878. Volume 5: Japan (Part 1). Photo 1224/5 (25).

170. *Dickinson's Comprehensive Pictures of the Great Exhibition of 1851, from the originals painted for... Prince Albert, by Messrs. Nash, Haghe and Roberts*, 1854. Cup.652.c.33.

172a. Charles Ewart Darwent, *Shanghai: A handbook for travellers and residents...*, 1912. 10058.p.13.

172b. *The Illustrated London News*, 13 April 1861. P.P.7611.

175. John Burley Waring, *Masterpieces of Industrial Art and Sculpture at the International Exhibition*, 1862–1863. 1800.b.12.

176–177. William Simpson, *India, Ancient and Modern: a series of illustration of the country and people of India and adjacent territories*, 1867. X.108.

180. Photographic record of the world tour of Charles James and Morton P. Lucas 1860s–1878. Volume 2: India and Kashmir. Photo 1224/2 (68).

181. Photographic record of the world tour of Charles James and Morton P. Lucas 1860s–1878. Volume 2: India and Kashmir. Photo 1224/2 (166).

184. Wellcome Images.

186–187. John Nash, *The Royal Pavilion at Brighton*, 1827. 557*.h.19.

188. Charles Dickens, *The Mystery of Edwin Drood*, 1870. C.194.b.358.

190a. Nathan Dunn, *Ten Thousand Chinese Things. A descriptive catalogue of the Chinese Collection [owned by N. Dunn] now exhibiting at St George's Place, Hyde Park Corner, London...*, 1842. RB.23.a.23908.

190b. *The Illustrated London News*, 6 May 1865. P.P.7611.

192. John Burley Waring, *Masterpieces of Industrial Art and Sculpture at the International Exhibition*, 1862–1863. 1800.b.12.

193. *Le Monde Illustré*, 28 September 1867. Lou.F23 [1867].

195l. *A Guide-Book for Tourists in Japan*, Welcome Society of Japan, 1910. X.708/12434.

195r. Frank Morris Jonas, *Netsuké*, 1928. 07805.i.65.

198. Photographic record of the world tour of Charles James and Morton P. Lucas 1860s–1878. Volume 6: Japan (Part 2). Photo 1224/6 (3).

199. Photographic record of the world tour of Charles James and Morton P. Lucas 1860s–1878. Volume 6: Japan (Part 2). Photo 1224/6 (15).

201. Sir Merton Russell-Cotes, *Home and Abroad: An Autobiography of an Octogenarian*, 1921. 10856.i.7.

205. Sir Merton Russell-Cotes, *Home and Abroad: An Autobiography of an Octogenarian*, 1921. 10856.i.7.

208. Annie Nelson Russell-Cotes, *Westward from the Golden Gate*, c.1900. X809/22328.

210. Sir Merton Russell-Cotes, *Home and Abroad: An Autobiography of an Octogenarian*, 1921. 10856.i.7.

211. Courtesy of The Trustees of the Powell-Cotton Museum.

254–255. Porcelain vases from John Burley Waring, *Masterpieces of Industrial Art and Sculpture at the International Exhibition*, 1862–1863. 1800.b.12.

ACKNOWLEDGEMENTS

This book originated from an interest in travel furniture. Those seemingly quirky eighteenth- and nineteenth-century 'metamorphics' that could be broken down and reconfigured in a number of ways – for example a chest of drawers could turn into two travel trunks. Whole suites of furniture could be broken down and moved with relative ease. This naturally led me to consider the mechanics of how people moved around the globe in the nineteenth century. Finally, it developed into a full-blown interrogation of globetrotting and its cultural impact. I am grateful to those at the British Library who have helped this idea along, specifically Rebecca Nuotio and Robert Davies for considering it in the first place. Abbie Day for her careful editing and suggestions, which always improved the text. Sally Nicholls for finding just the right images.

I've been very fortunate to develop these ideas as a PhD student under the patient and always insightful Margot Finn and Lily Chang at University College London.

Special thanks go to the staff at Quex Park, The Russell-Cotes Art Gallery and Museum, The East Sussex Record Office, The Hastings Museum and Art Gallery, and the Asian and African Studies Reading Room at the British Library, for their suggestions and help.

Finally, I cannot leave out the good-natured forbearance of my family: Steven, Godwin, Sibella and Prudence. Who endure numerous museum trips, bookstore trawls, and endless discussions on the school run.

INDEX

Italic page numbers refer to illustrations.

11   Lessons from Japan's financial crisis

12   The Asian bubble and crisis

13   US stock markets: where from here?

Figures

Tables

Foreword

The primary focus of this highly readable and often provocative book is the American stock market during the 1990s and the first few years of this century. It deals with the factors surrounding the remarkable investment bubble and subsequent crash some years later. Although it is essentially a case study, the book makes a broader contribution by addressing more general aspects of stock market behaviour, investment strategy and government policy.

Dr Western provides graphic and, it must be said, chilling insights into the anti-rational aspects of stock market behaviour. For the general reader, and especially those contemplating retirement, the sections dealing with conflicts of interest and the psychology of investment will be extremely unsettling. In the foreseeable future very few people can expect financial security and peace-of-mind after leaving the paid work force. The concept of a guaranteed nest-egg is a thing of the past. As daunting as it may seem to the average citizen, who has grown accustomed to relying upon expert advice and rising markets, there is no alternative but to play a much more active and informed role in the management of their own financial affairs.

The starting point in becoming more financially literate is being aware of the biases in the system. Here Dr Western is especially useful, with special reference to the 1990s he demonstrates the distorting influence of securities analysts, stockbrokers and financial planners and the structural predisposition towards optimism and blind faith. In Dr Western's words, the combination of fear and self-interest 'created a bias toward buy and hold strategies even when the cold truth required sell advice'. However, for most of us, the biggest challenge will be to achieve a higher level of insight into the darker reaches of personal and social psychology. Once again Dr Western offers excellent guidance. His treatment of herd behaviour, the pervasive fear of missing out and the theory of the 'bigger fool' will cause embarrassment and even shame for many of us: 'everyone knows that stocks are vastly overvalued but still play the game on the basis that there are bigger fools in the world'.

The extent to which the stock market relies on reputation and trust is effectively explored and explained. Dr Western describes 'a whole host of unsavoury collapses in corporate governance standards', which undermined investor confidence in the American Stock Market. The resulting bust appears to have had a salutary effect. Dr Western believes that the resulting requirement for greater transparency and tighter audit standards, combined with the trail of ruined careers and high profile convictions, will go some distance in restoring public faith in America's corporate governance. The danger, however, is that the reforms will overshoot to the point where CEO's will become so nervous and risk averse that their companies will stagnate and lose their creative dynamism. Achieving a judicious balance between motivation and regulation is a challenge confronting policy-makers and regulators everywhere.

A major strength of this book is its treatment of the role and influence of Dr Alan Greenspan as Chairman of America's Federal Reserve. Dr Western highlights Greenspan's remarkable impact and stabilizing influence over a seventeen-year period upon governments, traders and investors, not only within America but around the world. He points to Greenspan's ability to 'jawbone' the market down during periods of 'irrational exuberance', and argues that, despite his critics, because 'recessionary fears were real then Greenspan's emphatic reliance on monetary liquidity is well founded'. Indeed, by slashing interest rates to only 1% after the stock market bubble burst, the Fed deserves much of the credit for saving the American economy from deep recession.

Looking ahead and taking a global perspective, Dr Western finds cause for cautious optimism as a result of sustained government policy impetus, a weaker dollar and signs of Japan's overdue revival. He conducts a careful and searching analysis of initiatives by the Bush administration to stimulate economic recovery. However, it quickly becomes apparent that the New Economy presents problems and challenges which are unique and elusive. Despite increased business investment and higher productivity, America continues to experience a 'jobless recovery'. Bush's tax cuts have been significant but they have not been enough to trigger a new generation of business entrepreneurs or to offset the export of jobs to China and India. Clearly, the American economy is delicately poised and while economists may focus on traditional levers such as tax and interest rates, the sentiment of the wider business environment is heavily influenced by the threat of international terrorism and the Bush Administration's open-ended commitment to defeating it.

This book will have a wide appeal. Like the Political Economists of the Nineteenth Century, Dr Western has the increasingly rare gift of applying economic theory to contemporary events *and* of proposing realistic policy prescriptions. In the same tradition he writes in a free-flowing, distinctive style with none of the dry opaque jargon that characterizes the work of so many of his peers. While never timid in expressing his own opinions, he is nevertheless careful to draw on a wide range of sources, explore the evidence systematically and acknowledge alternative viewpoints. Because it is both scholarly and vivid, this book will attract a variety of readers including academic peers, advanced university students and ever ever-expanding pool of general readers with an interest in stock market behaviour.

Dr John Milton Smith
Professor of Management
Curtin University of Technology

Acknowledgements

The brain child of this book is pure curiosity. From teaching classes in the School of Economics and Finance (at the Curtin Business School) I became fascinated with the booms and busts in asset markets. It is with regularity that stock markets both over-shoot and undershoot levels determined by raw economic fundamentals. It is the financial side of economics and markets that drives much of the wild swings in market prices and not just real factors and technological progress. People, and so investors, often over-react to vibrations that shake their precious nest egg and so their retirement life style.

It is my intention to encompass the whole gamut of issues as to why US stock prices went through a euphoric bubble. While living in the United States, it was Professor Ray Canterbery (Florida State University) who spurred my interest in Wall Street, the Federal Reserve and bubbles. The late Professor James Gapinski kept my flame for economics alive and I remain in his debt – he was a good mate of mine. Professor Milton Marquis presented challenging macro and money classes and to Professor James Cobbe for his encouragement as Head of the Economics Department at FSU. Professor Ed Renshaw (University of NY at Albany) offered support and some good ideas for this manuscript.

Back home on the glorious shores of Down Under it was critical that I obtained leave from teaching assignments to complete this book. I wish to thank Dean Michael Wood and Professor Ian Kerr for such grace. With this leave, I worked in a Curtin University research unit – the Institute for Research into International Competitiveness (IRIC). In this institute many of the refinements of this book were forged. Debate was common and many of my colleagues tested my arguments and overview. I would like to thank Professor Peter Kenyon for the provision of resources and support. A special word of thanks to Paul Koshy (IRIC) who greatly assisted with technical figures and tables throughout this manuscript. He was a pillar of support and offered timely advice. Others from IRIC offered comment and criticism, such as Nick Wills-Johnson, Dr Helen Cabulu, Diane Jameson, Professor Guy Callender and Dr Lifen Wu. Tracey Wilson (the secretary) was also very helpful.

Colleagues from the Curtin Business School were also helpful over a long time period, such as Professor Gary Madden (who passed critical comment on Chapter 5 concerning the IT revolution) and Dr Max Kummerow (who generously reminded me of the views of those on the left of politics). My mate, Dr Gary Macdonald, passed critical comment on some of the chapters and assisted with some data presentation.

Professor John Milton-Smith was especially helpful in over-viewing this book and writing a very succinct foreword. He has elegantly shed light on the big picture.

The editors at Routledge, such as Terry Clague, were very helpful and patient, I might add. Vincent Antony and his colleagues cast a careful eye over the manuscript and proved invaluable in cleaning the manuscript and so making it more coherent. Linda Morgan from the Curtin Business School also assisted with the manuscript through its various stages. And of course my mother (Yvonne) and father (Thomas) have been bastions of support over the years.

Introduction

Why the stock bubble?

Real fundamentals could not explain the explosion in US stock prices in the 1990s. Stock prices rose sixfold in this decade while labour productivity only doubled. This large *escalation gap* can be partially explained by investor behaviour in response to biased economic incentives – although some of this behaviour possessed no real base but was indeed pure speculation. There was rational investor response based on tax incentives, generous stock option packages for CEOs, corporate manipulation of profit results, low interest rates, low inflation rates and higher *expected* productivity growth.

However, financial forces have not been emphasized enough and these include the sizable capital flows into US stock and bond markets, the 'dollar bubble', geopolitical forces *pushing* funds into US markets, high levels of corporate financial leverage, margin lending for investors and the rapid growth in the money supply and credit. Much of the escalation gap has its origins in monetary liquidity.

A respectable author such as Schiller (2000) points to this *escalation gap* as being due to exuberance and behavioural forces that include speculation and greed. As in all bubbles these forces are plausible reasons but the fuel that ignites and allows the speculative fire to rage is that of excessive monetary liquidity and credit growth. Another respectable author such as Siegal (2000) points to changing and biased economic incentives such as the lower taxation of capital, lower risk premiums, lower transaction costs and a lower dividend payout ratio for holding stocks – so much so that stocks are a 'one-way street'. Western (2004) emphasizes the significance of financial and foreign capital flow factors that caused much of the explosion in stock prices – above and beyond that can be explained by rational or behavioural forces.

From one bubble to another?

Sound financial theory and asset allocation models argue that rational investors should switch their funds between various asset categories and alter their allocation percentages according to perceived risk-return trade-offs. As the risk of holding stocks increased dramatically so did global and domestic investors flood into the bond market between 2000 and early 2003. Bond yields hit forty-two-year lows and so bond prices forty-two-year highs. The fear of deflation in the United States and the lack of pricing power of US companies pushed investors into bonds and out of stocks. Just as the stampede into stocks lacked rationality so too did this stampede into bonds – the *third* bubble. The question remains whether the rush into US real estate is overdone and prices are at unsustainable highs. This may be the *fourth* bubble that the Fed has to attend to.

What also needs to be noted is the roar of the US dollar (the *second* bubble) in the 1990s (partly as a result of European and Japanese weakness) that further accentuated the roar in US stocks. Foreign investors enjoyed the double gain of US stocks and the US currency.

It therefore follows that a weaker US dollar will generate caution among foreign investors into 2004–5 as will the prospect of higher interest rates at the long end of the yield curve. Conversely, global investors may prefer potentially stronger currencies and so European and Far Eastern stock markets more favourably.

A unique set of circumstances?

There is no doubt that the United States enjoyed a fortuitous set of circumstances in the 1990s or commonly called 'luck'. Japan's economy and stock market collapsed beyond belief and Europe endured high unemployment rates, re-unification problems and sluggish growth. There was also the continued support of Chinese and Japanese investors for US bonds – funding American consumption and indirectly their own exports. Global investors sought the 'safe haven' of the US dollar and US stock and bond markets. Such investors received more justification for placing funds in the United States – as inflation remained docile, productivity growth was accelerating and the risk premium for holding stocks was closing. Moreover, the Fed appeared content to let the growth phase roll and so leave interest rates at low levels. The Fed was also 'accommodating' when Asian stock markets crashed in 1998 and many foreign investors again sought the safety of US denominated assets. In short, there were significant external push factors into US markets and even some attractive pull factors as well – such as low inflation and rising productivity. Foreign capital fed into the US productivity boom by providing the necessary finance (saving) for US companies to innovate.

The question remains, however, as to how US markets will perform when the world economic recovery gains momentum, rhythm and re-synchronization and so the global investor gains greater portfolio choice through rising foreign markets. A weaker US dollar continues to push such global investors into stronger currencies and gold. For US markets to perform solidly under this scenario then US-based investors must take up the slack left by foreign sellers. This also implies a shift out of money market accounts and the bond market and into stocks. A switch that will be based on expected earnings per share being greater than the ten-year bond yield.

How absurd were valuations?

Even the eternal optimist will concede that price–earnings ratio were excessive in the late 1990s. Valuations for some of the high flying tech stocks were between 50 and

100 and could never be justified. Indeed, no US stock has ever justified a *P/E* ratio of 50 let alone a 100. Some of the nifty fifty stocks that sold for *P/E* ratios in the low forties in the early 1970s did justify themselves eventually – twenty-five years later! Nevertheless, investors can and did overpay for stocks during the bubble era as EPS could never reach the heights anticipated and particularly when the ten-year bond yield justified a switch. The eventual killer was profit disappointment – disguised by corporate fraud for a time.

We know from Siegal (2000) that the long-run returns from stocks is around 7.5 per cent and the average *P/E* ratio around 14.5 – so why did investors push *P/E* ratios into the thirties for the S&P and far higher for the NASDAQ? Did they not believe that stock returns revert to their long-run mean – eventually? Or even close to the more recent average of twenty? Did they express no fear that mean reversion would imply a correction in stock prices of 30 per cent for the S&P and double that for the NASDAQ? In reality, the correction for the NASDAQ from its peak was as much as 80 per cent. The collapse in the Great Depression was around 89 per cent.

There were warning signals flashing for the investor. As stated, *P/E* ratios in the 1990s were at least 100 per cent above their long-run trend line. The *Q* ratio was around 1.6 – far above its long-run trend of 0.7 – again implying that stocks were vastly overvalued. A third warning signal was from the Fed model – as EPS fell below that of the ten-year bond. Why not accept the risk-free rate and avoid the inherent risks in stocks? The answer rests in the investor's view that further capital appreciation will accrue to stocks – along with tax benefits. Despite the fact that stock valuations were 'absurd' there was still a euphoria in the investor community that the boom was ongoing and possessed a life of its own. There was money to be made based on the 'greater fool theory' – sell to the next and more gullible investor than the last – or even yourself.

So how did investors and stockbrokers manipulate the business calculus to justify *P/E* ratios of 35 or more? In reference to the NASDAQ the arguments employed included – 'this is the new economy and we have reached a permanently high growth plateau'. The rise, and continued rise in productivity, will justify currently 'high' valuations in the future. Buy now and wait! This time it is different and not play is to miss out! After all, why watch your neighbour grow rich? Greed and jealousy pushed many up the stairs and down the elevator. Collective euphoria and exuberance lured many investors into 'growth' stocks and away from boring 'value' stocks.

Why did investors ignore warning signals?

Another key pitfall of stock valuation comes into play here. It is known as the accelerator or extrapolation principle. The *level* of EPS will justify the *level* of a stock price – for a given yield on the ten-year bond. The *growth rate* of EPS will determine the *growth rate* of the stock price. More precisely, in a runaway boom market it is the *expected growth rate* in EPS that will determine the rise in the stock price. Hence, if a growth stock declares EPS growth in 1997 of 10 per cent, 1998 of 20 per cent then investors may be lured into extrapolating an EPS growth rate of 40 per cent for 1999. This acceleration in EPS can gain a momentum of its own as optimistic investors price into the current stock price a further acceleration of EPS – albeit unrealized. This is the stuff that the 1990s bubble was made of. It was the market's belief in not just rising EPS growth but steep acceleration that generated the rationale for 'high' *P/E* ratios – that were soon to be justified by roaring productivity and the pillars of the new economy. Unfortunately, the pillars collapsed. It was this extrapolation and acceleration principle that clouded investor judgment – perhaps because it was a clever justification for greed?

Why did the stock bubble burst?

As with most bubbles there is no single prick that causes stock prices to shrink and deflation to follow. Just as several major forces drove the US stock market upward so too were there several forces causing it to deflate. The realization that *P/E* ratios were excessive and that bond yields were attractive caused some investors to switch 'early' in the stock cycle downturn. Profit disappointment combined with poor economic visibility and the corporate governance debacle caused many investors to 'sit it out' in the bond market. NASDAQ stocks suffered even more and grossly deflated because of over- and mis-investment in the late 1990s. Such poor investments did not produce profits and even worse caused major write-offs of capital. The September 11 attack and later on the Iraqi War created even greater uncertainty concerning the length and depth of the recession and so corporate profitability. These geopolitical events only added to an already sick and sluggish US economy – that was technically in recession before September 11. In summary, poor investment in IT and corporate profitability that failed to *accelerate* ignited a major revision in risk perception and a quite sudden sell-off in stocks in order to justify lower EPS levels.

Why did Greenspan ignore 'irrational exuberance'?

Chairman Greenspan's stewardship at the Fed has been of a high quality. He oversaw the 1987 stock market crash, the 1991 recession, the Asian crisis of 1998 and collapse of the stock bubble in 2000 and yet he led the US economy through a high growth and low inflation era for most of his seventeen years at the helm. His detailed knowledge of the US economy is exemplary as is his knowledge of economics. And yet there are lingering criticisms of his stewardship from some quarters. For example, why did he seek to slay the inflationary devil in 1994 when it was nowhere to be seen? Why strike at the imaginary Phantom when it is not a 'clear and present danger'? His defense for this strike is that it was pre-emptive in nature – it was good insurance to cool off the economy in the expectation of inflation raising its head.

A more serious accusation is that he allowed a stock market bubble to inflate in the mid-1990s and inflate again after 1998 pushing stock prices to absurd levels that could not be justified over the medium term. The cost of this explosion and then deflation was mainly borne by investors but spillovers into the real economy were inevitable. Job creation collapsed and the unemployment rate rose substantially. Investment collapsed and so a large slice of domestic demand. The real damage to the economy comes through this channel of depressed investment spending – as US companies wait and write off stale investment that has failed to perform. The excesses of the 1990s may take a long while to work off. Although the real economy received a major dent between 2000 and 2003 the real cost of the collapsed bubble rest with both small and large investors that lost anywhere up to 80 per cent of their capital. Those with highly leveraged positions were the hardest hit. Foreign investors weren't impressed either by lower stock prices as the US dollar fell along with US stock markets. There was plenty of pain to be shared by the whole investment community.

So why did Greenspan ignore the stock bubble? First, because 'millions of investors get it right'. It is their choice and their money and so if they get it wrong it is their loss. Second, Greenspan is wary of pitting his judgment against these millions not to say the many 'professionals' that are qualified to trade a market. Besides, if he has superior and/or fresh knowledge concerning stock valuations then why would he not release that information? Third, the cost of a stock market collapse should be shared by those investors involved in the market and not US taxpayers or the real economy at large. So long as falling stock prices do not suffocate the real economy there is little justification for intervention by the Fed. It is only when the real economy is under real threat from capacity constraints, labour shortages or inflationary fires originating in the stock market should the Fed intervene. Greenspan obviously did not believe that serious intervention was warranted. However, he did jawbone on several occasions – particularly his 'irrational exuberance' statement in 1996.

His critics point out that the aftermath of the bubble era has not yet washed through the economic system. The excesses of the 1990s are still to be worn off. There has been a dissipation of wealth that has damaged balance sheets across the board. Investment is lumpy and subject to ever changing product cycles – and so obscelence. Large capital write-offs take time for companies to absorb. The flip-side of the same coin is that the consumer cannot single-handedly do the heavy lifting for economic recovery. Just as Greenspan respected the influence of 'wealth effects' assisting consumer spending so he must acknowledge that losses on stocks in 2000–2 have dampened consumer confidence.

The jury is still out on the costs of the US stock bubble. Perhaps they are overrated and the massive policy push of 2002–3 will more than compensate for the temporary losses on stocks in that era. There are signs in early 2004 that investment is picking up in response to a prolonged period of low real interest rates and monetary liquidity. It is here that Greenspan may have his finest hour.

Greenspan and the markets

As Greenspan's credibility as a policy maker increased in the early 1990s so did fear spread throughout the professional investor community about what he could say that could significantly shift asset values – and within minutes. Professional investors would listen carefully to any hint that the *direction* of interest rates would change sometime soon. They also knew that interest rate hikes and falls tended to be in clusters or a series. Which one would be the last in the series – signalling a 'permanent' change in the direction of monetary policy – for the medium term at least.

Professional traders were alert to signals of 'turning points' or major policy reversals that would provide a green or red light for investing. The Fed would signal a 'bias' in future monetary policy – or state that it is currently 'neutral'. Investors would often wait for Greenspan's testimonies and not take large positions in the market for fear of a clear shift in the future direction of monetary policy. Or they would wait in the hope that Greenspan would say nothing and so remove the shadow overhanging traders in the finance markets.

A degree of caution is required when interpreting Greenspan-speak as 'bad news' maybe good news for the market and 'good news' may in fact turn out to be bad news. This resembles the Goldilocks economy – 'not too hot and not too cold'. Bond traders want bad news concerning the economy to translate into lower inflationary heat and so lower interest rates. Hence, capital gains on bonds would rise. And stock prices would normally rise with a lag – as the future level of interest rates – remain low. Therefore, the inexperienced investor needs to be careful when assessing the impact of Greenspan's words on the markets. Too much good news concerning growth, capacity utilization, retail sales, consumer spending on durable goods, etc. – may provoke a rise in interest rates and so scare off bond investors. Equity buyers must then decide on whether to ignore rumblings in the bond market and so buy stocks. The perversity of this goldilocks economy is that real bad, recessionary news or past data gloom may imply lower interest rates in the near term and so a surge on Wall Street via a calm bond market. After all, Wall Street is more concerned with the future not the past.

Some examples of hints or signals that would influence traders are references made by Greenspan to current or future inflationary heat, demand persistently outstripping supply, wage pressures, labour market tightness, job creation, the unemployment rate, growth being to rapid, gross imbalances or the onset of deflationary forces. Any hint that inflation is subsiding would spell a prospect for interest rates to fall and so a signal to buy stocks. However, such hints could be seen in a negative light – that of imbalances being unsustainable and excess demand pressuring limited resources. Hence, there is the risk that long-term interest rates would rise. Of course, the famous phrase that investors jumped on was that of 'irrational exuberance' uttered by Greenspan. While some signals are clear others are not, perhaps for the reason that Greenspan speaks in the hypothetical and in the abstract. It is therefore very easy for the investor to misinterpret.

What are some examples of Greenspan's words moving the market? First, we shall examine those periods when, somewhat coincidently, the Dow was at or near all time highs. The chairman had a habit of moving against investor enthusiasm in 1994, 1996 and 1997 – all record highs in US stocks – by raising interest rates or jawboning the market down.

How costly was corporate governance failure?

One should not ignore the importance of economic incentives in stimulating economic agents to perform. Such was the case for many of America's CEOs who enjoyed generous remuneration packages with stock options being the cornerstone. The ultimate objective of aligning the effort of the agent with the will of the principal meant that CEOs were granted multi-million dollar stock option packages if the company's stock price reached certain high levels. The CEO then would accrue an *exponential* gain through options while the stockholder would accrue an *arithmetic* gain through holding main stock. Such powerful incentives were effective in raising stock values as the self-interest of the CEOs came to the fore. However, the means by which stock prices were raised remain highly questionable – such as manipulating the accounts, threatening the auditors, silencing the Board and borrowing heavily for company share buybacks. The cost of such stock price manipulation was high. The credibility of Corporate America sunk like stone. The year of 2002 was particularly bad for corporate scandals and the media coverage of them. Investors were reluctant to hold stocks while recent earnings reports could not be trusted and the dust had not yet settled. Bonds experienced good support while Corporate America sorted out its accounting and auditing standards. As of 2004 the memory of poor governance standards has somewhat faded as investors rode the stock rally after the Iraqi war. Perhaps Corporate America was overdue for a jolt to higher professional managerial and accounting standards?

The Fed's enemy: inflation or deflation?

There is one clear message from macroeconomics and that is inflation is not to be tolerated. It is a great parasitic evil that destroys civilizations. Unfortunately, this message is one-dimensional and over-preached. Our objective should be modest price stability and so neither inflation nor deflation. The irony in America's recent financial history is that goods price inflation been very low while asset price inflation exceptionally high. The Fed's mandate is focused more on goods price inflation – of the text book type. This type of inflation has been benign and so the Fed has been able to maintain interest rates at a low level – and more so post September 11. The Fed's monetary policy has been based on 'interest rate targeting' – in the belief that the cost of money can influence spending and stock prices. However, the by-product of low interest rates is a progressive build-up in monetary liquidity and such liquidity contributed in no small way to the escalation of stock prices in the 1990s. It also follows that seeking to reign in runaway asset price inflation is most difficult when employing interest rate rises alone. It may well be that the Fed could not restrain the stock bubble by the use of interest rates – as the required rate hike – would have been far above what the real economy could withstand without plummeting into recession. A more restraining influence throughout the bubble would have been slower growth in monetary aggregates. Conversely, given that the bubble did collapse and that recessionary fears were real then Greenspan's emphatic reliance on monetary liquidity is well founded. After all, the steep fall in interest rates must be at an end – and the monetary pump is the next weapon in line. Greenspan is also correct in stating that America's immediate fear is that of deflation and so there is a dire need to reflate even if it means mild inflation in the short run. He does not want to see Japan's deflationary disease spread to the United States.

What are the lessons from the 1929 bubble?

Markets normally function well and on most occasions there is a degree of rationality. However, the 1929 crash revealed several weaknesses in the financial and regulatory systems of the United States. We have learnt that the conduct and timing of monetary policy is crucial to the economic well being of a nation. If the Federal Reserve in 1928 had raised interest rates faster, and tightened the availability of credit more quickly, the crash of 1929 may have been more akin to a soft landing. If the response of the Fed after the stock market crash had been more accommodating in terms of liquidity there would have been less of a credit squeeze, less pressure on call rates to rise and so less selling pressure on stocks. Thus, the bubble may have shrunk more slowly and deflated without major implications for the real sector of the economy. Allegations of policy mistakes abound as the Fed went the 'wrong-way' and did not pump the real money supply enough – much to the detriment of asset prices and aggregate demand. From this policy debacle came the realization that the economic system needs a 'lender of last resort'. The Fed learnt this lesson and has sought to reassure markets in timely ways that additional liquidity would be provided to asset markets in distress when there was a real risk of spillovers into the real economy. The crash of 1987 was a prime example, and even the Asian crisis of 1997, whereby monetary policy was deliberately loosened in order to reassure investors.

Alas, the control that the Fed had over the credit creation process was incomplete and so lacked the firepower to subdue the flames of speculation. Greater regulatory control by the Fed over the US financial system has been an indirect result of the 1929 crash. Critical deficiencies in stock exchange regulations were also exposed. Overgenerous lending margins by brokers were seen as a major fuel of the crisis and such margins were raised to 50 per cent in the 1930s. Even so, the desire of investors to speculate and employ high gearing ratios was not confined to the 1920s. High leverage and a lack of appreciation of risk have been perennial biases in stock markets throughout recorded history. Just as investment trusts of the 1920s wielded price-making power so did mutual funds achieve similar power in the 1960s. The dangers of margin lending, privately and on mass, have not been learnt well. Instability in the credit creation process has plagued, and will plague, economic systems for a long time to come.

Japan's mess and deflation: what can the United States learn?

Much of Japan's economic misery in the 1990s, and failure to recover, can be traced back to the asset price bubble of the 1980s and to the macroeconomic mismanagement that followed. There were two dark economic clouds that dwelt over Japan for much of the 1990s – an asset price hangover and a debt hangover. Collapsed asset prices spelt massive deflation and damaged corporate-sector balance sheets that in turn translated into economic stagnation in the real sector. Although the origins of Japan's excess liquidity were somewhat different from those of America, the consequences of excess liquidity were, and are, basically the same: asset prices boomed and eventually burst, causing major reverberations in all sectors of the economy. Of key interest to the United States is how Japan's financial sector reacted to prolonged asset price deflation in terms of managing non-performing loans and extending further credit in a high risk corporate environment. Second, how the Japanese government sought to assist the bewildered financial sector suffering damaged balance sheets and a loss of confidence. Third, how effective Japan's traditional policy strikes were in reviving spending flows against a backdrop of spiralling deflation. The United States can learn 'what not to do' from Japan's financial nightmare. Thus far, the huge suffocation effects of deflation have not been felt in the United States – as Greenspan pumped the money supply early in the post-bubble era. Both asset price and goods price deflation have not taken hold in the United States – not yet.

The massive policy push: powerful enough to create sustainable growth?

The Fed has long embarked on an expansionary monetary policy in order to create a cheap credit environment and so stimulate economy activity. As discussed earlier, the Fed funds rate has reached historic lows and yet private sector investment has revived slowly. Sales of interest-sensitive consumer durables did pick up but that was very much a function of aggressive marketing strategies and motor vehicle manufacturers seeking to clear existing stock immediately after September 11. Households took advantage of low and declining mortgage interest rates to re-finance their homes. Extra liquidity could be easily tapped in a rising market and used to purchase home-related items and/or general consumption goods. There are also other channels through which lower interest rates have been effective – by reducing net interest payments made by US corporations to banks and by reducing the spread between corporate bond and government bond yields. Before Greenspan's aggressive interest rate cuts corporate bond yields were dangerously high – partly because investors demanded a higher premium for risk and were also worried about unfunded superannuation liabilities of several big US corporations. Hence, the cost of raising capital was excessively high in 2000–1. No wonder US corporations were unwilling to undertake major investments. Not only were expected rates of return poor and not 'visible' but the cost of raising funds in the post-bubble era was also prohibitive.

Although the earlier-mentioned effects of lower interest rates were quite significant for consumption, the response of private sector investment was muted. Growth theory highlights the importance of modern, fresh vintage capital and high capital–labour ratio that drives medium term growth. The longer additions to the capital stock are delayed the less potent that stock becomes. Technological progress drives long-run growth but even that is often embodied in capital goods in some way. Analysts often point to past economic recoveries and to the central role played by a revival in capital goods spending – for the multiplier effects and chain reaction sent throughout the economy. Why should this recovery be any different? In fact, a subdued pick-up in private sector investment is the Achilles heal of any potential economic recovery in the United States. The immediate future does not look bright as excess capacity remains high in manufacturing and job destruction is rampant. Why should corporations invest in new capacity when existing capacity is plentiful and quite capable of quenching any sizable rise in final good demand?

Moreover, the supply side excesses of the 1990s included both over-investment and mis-investment – in that too much money was placed in so called investment areas that were never going to yield rates of return in line with expectations – if at all. Large portions of investment – particularly during the technology and telecommunications craze – were nothing short of wasted. Ambitions were over zealous and/or obscelence set in quickly. Projects soon became lemons. How does such mis-investment affect US corporations today? It has shaken their confidence, their balance sheet, their angry shareholders and their ability to borrow from banks. Chief Finance Officers (CFOs) of major companies have become tight fisted as a result of the bubble era. Not only will the excesses of past take time to work off but also finding new, profitable investment opportunities in a depressed economic environment become more difficult. There is the added cumulative constraint of major companies waiting for other major companies to flag intent to outlay more on investment – a game of 'wait and see' before becoming more aggressive on the capital outlay front. Such pessimism and delay was mainly confined to the 2000–2 era but as corporate government bond yields have narrowed and stock prices risen, so too have US corporations become less hesitant concerning future commitments in 2004.

On the fiscal front, the US administration passed an aggressive lower tax and prospending bill through Congress. The main features of this Economic Growth and Tax Reform Reconciliation Act are as follows:

- Lower marginal income tax rates
- Child tax credit
- Married joint return relief
- Accelerated depreciation
- Increased expensing for small business
- Capital gain rate reduction for individuals
- Lower taxes on dividends.

The major objective of this 'Economic Growth' package is to reduce taxes and increase the potential to spend. It is both pro-consumer and pro-business. For example, lower marginal tax brackets fell from 15, 28, 31, 36 and 39.6 per cent to 10, 15, 25 and 33 per cent. Those eligible for the 10 per cent threshold have been given additional leeway with increased limits. Those with families were given higher allowances under the child credit scheme and the money was paid to them swiftly. Married people filing joint returns were granted higher thresholds and other benefits. For investors, the reduction in capital gains tax rates from the existing 20 and 10 per cent to 15 and 5 per cent respectively will encourage the buying and selling of more stocks. Likewise, the abolition of the double taxation of dividends is long overdue and will encourage a 'buy and hold' strategy towards stocks. However, some eligibility rules apply to holding periods. Not only are these initiatives valid now but most extend for much of the remaining decade and so can be considered semi 'permanent'. The business community gained relief through accelerated depreciation allowances mainly aimed at 2003–5 period – reducing inventory levels now in order that new durable goods orders would rise. The size of this stimulus must not be underestimated – it is huge by any modern day standard. However, as stated many times in this book – taking monetary and fiscal action to remedy income and spending *flows* may not be enough to offset serious damage to asset price *levels*. Moreover, *over- and mis-investment* can take many years to wear off before new investment springs to life – as past *over-capacity* still hangs over the reviving economy. Hence, economic revival may take longer than normal after a crash of an asset price bubble than a common excess inventory and demand flow slump.

How fragile is the US recovery?

There are several reasons for caution when attempting to assess the strength and duration of the US recovery. The following list of 'weaknesses' is not exhaustive as to why the US economy could be slow to recover but nevertheless provides a fairly broad summary of where the risks may originate.

- Pricing power of US companies
- Capacity utilization
- Sluggish labour market
- Structural weakness – manufacturing
- Growing current account deficits
- Growing budget deficits
- Long end of yield curve
- Deflationary aftermath
- Earnings acceleration – limited?

Where from here?

There are reasons for optimism as a more broad-based world recovery will stimulate US exports. A lower US dollar will place downward pressure on imports. Hence, the US current account deficit may shrink from here. The size of policy impetus is as great as in the Vietnam War years of the 1960s.

- World recovery – synchronization
- Japan's revival?
- A weaker dollar
- Real estate boom
- Lower world interest rates
- Fiscal expansions
- China's explosion.

A bull or bear market rally?

From the above summary – the opposing forces of recovery and recession – and the bulls and the bears – are evenly balanced. It appears that the bulls will win – albeit with doubt – as Greenspan remains determined – for failure is not an option for him or the country. Nevertheless, the structural imbalances in the US economy are cause for concern and American hunger for debt disconcerting. Saturation points may have been reached and a long consolidation period may defer investment plans and cause stock prices to plateau into 2005–6.

1   The bubble era in US stocks

Introduction

When Gordon Gecko pronounced that 'greed is good' in the movie 'Wall Street' he was probably half-right – but what he forgot to mention was that 'fear is bad'. American investors not only listened to, but also believed, what Gordon Gecko (1988) stated

> Greed, for the lack of a better word, is good. Greed is right. Greed works. Greed clarifies, cuts through and captures the essence of the evolutionary spirit. Greed in all its forms, greed for life, for money, for love, knowledge has marked the surge of mankind and greed, you mark my words, will not only save Teldar Paper but that other malfunctioning corporation called the USA.

There were primal motives at work in driving the explosion of US stock prices throughout the 1990s – whereby greed overwhelmed fear. If there was such a thing as investor fear it was of the wrong kind – the fear of missing out. Such an extended boom has not been matched anywhere in US financial history. Booms in stock prices have occurred before, particularly the golden years of the 1960s and not to mention the euphoric episode of 1928–9, but none quite like the extended run of the late 1990s. However, the stock boom of the 1990s was more than a boom – it resembled a bubble or a euphoria that caused a vast overvaluation of stock prices – that eventually had to burst. Moreover, the bubble was triple headed – as the US bond market and US dollar joined in the euphoria. Unfortunately, there have always been serious, if not devastating, collapses in real activity and job growth in the aftermath of a deflating bubble. Policy-makers and Greenspan in particular, were somewhat dubious of the run-up in US stock prices in the late 1990s as there was an inherent fear that a sudden collapse would cause much disruption to economic activity, human welfare and the retirement plans of ordinary US citizens. Just as the lives of ordinary people were damaged in the 1929 crash, so would a routing of US stock prices cause widespread damage across middle-class America. These fears were partially realized in 2000, as US stocks fell and then collapsed into a three-year bear market. The bursting of the US stock bubble, together with an out-of-favour US dollar, raised fear that a major protracted economic slowdown would follow. There are lessons from

Japan's burst bubble as Japan's real economy languished for many years after the bubble deflated. We can go back further – just as in the Bible story – when Joseph proclaimed to Egypt that there would be seven fat years followed by seven lean years and so there is an apprehension that America's euphoric bubble will have to be 'paid for' with several lean years – consecutive or not.

This chapter is somewhat backward-looking in that it examines the major origins of the stock bubble. Brokerage houses pushed the historical fact that stocks have been a superior investment over most, if not all, other classes of assets over a long period of time. This is known as the equity premium puzzle. Hence, brokers pushed a 'buy and hold strategy' or more precisely a 'buy and buy' strategy. Wall Street was depicted as a one-way street and timing was not really that important – just buy and wait – according to the stock pushers. Or 'buy on dips' was another strong investment strategy. Another financial concept is also covered, namely Tobin's Q ratio. When the value of the stock market soars, relative to corporate net worth there is an incentive for companies to invest in relatively cheap physical capital. This substitution effect eventually calls for lower stock prices and the Q ratio to mean revert. This 'predictive tool' pointed to a very high Q ratio in the bubble era that served as a warning signal for stock valuations to fall quite significantly. In essence, stocks trade within a corridor – albeit a wide corridor – and eventually self-correct. So we have two competing investment strategies: the buy and hold strategy (a one-way street) and the contrarian strategy (a two-way street) in Wall Street philosophy.

We now know that US stock markets came off their highs in 2000. We also know that such markets have been extremely volatile since 11 September 2001. What we do not know is how well the real economy will recover and whether corporate profits will improve significantly enough to lead a sustainable rally on Wall Street in 2005–6. Much depends on the ability of the real economy to self-correct – pulling stock prices along – or whether stock prices and stock returns mean revert to some kind of long-run average – that is well lower than the peaks of 1999.

By examining the super performance of US stocks this chapter lays the foundations for major analytical themes examined throughout this book.

Origins of the bubble

Just as Great Britain enjoyed a hundred and fifty years of world domination through technological and commercial superiority so has America achieved the same kind of hegemony over the last century. It is the vast accumulation of US wealth that has the latent power to destabilize financial markets and so the real economy, complicating the task of conducting an appropriate stabilization policy. Moreover, economic growth does not infer economic stability. Quite to the contrary, the trade-off between economic growth and macroeconomic stability is still alive and well, despite the high economic cruise speed of the United States in the 1990s. The US Federal Reserve has a mandate to fight inflation and maintain economic stability in an economic system that is prone to fluctuation or in layman's terms – booms and busts. Why such booms and busts eventuate is still somewhat of a mystery, but the Federal Reserve has to make a value judgment as to whether it should smooth or minimize the effects of the 'business cycle'. The irony of America's massive wealth creation of the twentieth century has been associated with instability not only of output and employment but also of asset markets – and stock markets in particular. Speculation in asset markets, have their origins in some kind of monetary liquidity. That is, not just with expansions in the money supply, easy credit policies or margin lending but also with accumulated or stored wealth. It was America's fat savings pool and vast amounts of capital searching for a home that caused much of its stock market bubble in the 1990s.

Just as Japan experienced a mammoth asset price bubble in the late 1980s due to its massive reserves of accumulated wealth (much of it from exports), so the United States witnessed an asset price bubble of a similar magnitude. The causes are complex, but the vast amount of funds stored in America by both nationals and foreigners is a major perpetrator of the recent asset price bubble. Below are a summary of forces.

Financial forces
- Rapid money supply growth/credit growth
- Foreign capital inflows
- Geopolitical forces
- Margin lending/financial leverage
- Low long-term interest rates
- Low inflation rates
- Lower risk premiums.

Behavioural forces
- Biased capital gain tax laws
- A preference for debt over equity
- Weak corporate governance
- Stock options
- Day trading
- Ponzi games.

Real forces
- Rapid productivity growth
- Expectations of productivity growth
- Expected earnings per share growth.

We shall examine the above causes of the bubble in some detail in Chapter 4. As outlined in this section there are three major driving forces to explain – liquidity, behavioural and real. There is a strong case for arguing that liquidity and behavioural forces dominated the rapid escalation of the stock prices far beyond that can be justified by real forces. The magnitude of this departure from real fundamentals is what a bubble is made of – superficial froth or euphoria – a substance that cannot support airborne stock prices over the long run.

Why the stock bubble?

Real fundamentals could not explain the explosion in US stock prices in the 1990s. Stock prices rose sixfold in this decade while labour productivity only doubled. This large *escalation gap* can be partially explained by investor behaviour in response to biased economic incentives – although some of this behaviour possessed no base but was indeed pure speculation. What remained as rational investor response was based on tax incentives, generous stock option packages for CEOs, corporate manipulation of profit results, low interest rates, low inflation rates and higher *expected* productivity growth.

However, financial forces have not been emphasized enough and these include the sizable capital flows into US stock and bond markets, the 'dollar bubble', geopolitical forces *pushing* funds into US markets, high levels of corporate financial leverage, margin lending for investors and the rapid growth in the money supply and credit.

A well-known author such as Schiller (2000) points to this *escalation gap* as being due to exuberance and behavioural forces that include speculation and greed. As in all bubbles these forces are plausible reasons but the *fuel* that ignites and allows the speculative fire to rage is that of excessive monetary liquidity and credit growth. Another respectable author such a Siegal (2000) points to changing and biased economic incentives such as the lower taxation of capital, lower risk premiums, a lower dividend payout ratio for holding stocks and lower transaction costs – so much so that stocks are a 'one-way street'. This book emphasizes the significance of financial forces and foreign capital flows that caused much of the explosion in stock prices – above and beyond that can be explained by raw fundamentals. The remainder of the escalation in stock prices may be attributed to psychological and behavioural forces. It was abundant liquidity that fuelled the speculative fire.

Stocks versus bonds

Hindsight is God's gift to the economist and so the world. I have just made Mark Haynes of CNBC Squawk Box so very happy! Over a long period of time, stocks have outperformed fixed interest investments. That is, despite wild fluctuations in stock prices and despite uncertainty associated with dividend payments, the rate of return from US stocks has been far higher than those from US fixed interest securities. Acceptance of higher risk derived higher returns from stocks than bonds. However, this superior performance is based on capital gains as well as dividends.

As can be seen from Figure 1.1, the trend line Dow performance (the dark line) has always rested above the nominal interest rate on the one-year treasury bill (T-Bill) – except for a brief period in 1981. Hence, a 'buy and hold investor' could effectively borrow funds and hold the Dow portfolio knowing that capital gains would be greater than the one-year T-Bill rate. Moreover, dividend payouts would accrue to such a conservative investor making the overall returns even greater. As will be discussed later, the risk-free alternative to investing in stocks – namely the thirty-year bond – is a major determinant of stock price fortunes. The ten-year bond is also a benchmark alternative.

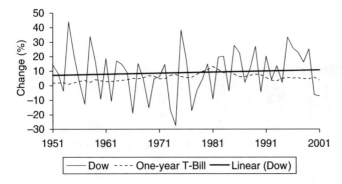

Figure 1.1 Comparing yearly percentage change in Dow and one-year T-Bill rates.
Source: Board of Governors of the Federal Reserve System.

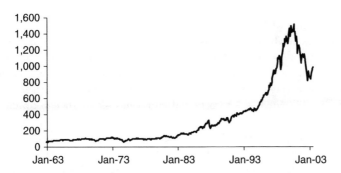

Figure 1.2 Level of S&P 500 (January 1963–July 2003).
Source: NYSE.

The performance of the Standard and Poors (S&P) index is no less impressive, as can be seen from Figure 1.2. In raw terms the S&P rose from around 40 points in 1960 to around 1,500 points in 2000. These were staggering capital gains even after allowing for inflation. For most years the S&P tracked the Dow and capital gains were similar. We can also see that the S&P collapsed to the very low 800s in early 2003 only to stage an impressive rally by year's end.

Was the equity premium significant? It was for most part of the last century. Over longer time periods the superior performance of equity returns over bond yields holds true. From Figure 1.3 it can be seen in the period 1949–99 that stock yields were 8.8 per cent while bonds were only 1.5 per cent – a significant premium. Likewise, in the 1899–1949 period stock yields were 5.1 per cent while bond yields were again far lower at 1.8 per cent. Even in the 1800s a lower but still a significant premium existed. According to Siegal (2002) the rate of return from stocks has been around 7.1 per cent since Second World War while real returns from T-Bills and bonds has

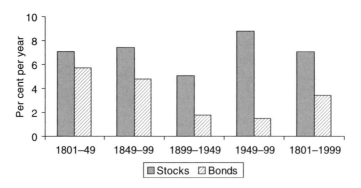

Figure 1.3 Real stock and bond returns.

Source: Siegal (2002) University of Pennsylvania.

been around 1 per cent – yielding a premium of more than 6 per cent. This historical fact is a major reason why stockbrokers pushed investors into stocks in the 1990s
as they claimed it was a *one-way street*. Based on Siegal's research the stocks did outperform bonds over the long run but not so much in the short run – as bond returns
would beat stocks on average two years out of five. So there are times when the risk
fearing investor should switch out of stocks and into bonds – even though timing is
both difficult and critical.

So why did stocks outperform bonds for such a long period of time? This 'paradox'
is known as the equity premium puzzle. Perhaps investors were risk-averse, there was
a large degree of unwarranted pessimism by cautious investors, in part driven by the
residual fear of the Great Depression. Hence, the fact that needs to be explained is
not high returns to stocks but why returns to fixed interest securities were so low.
Why did investors underpay for stocks and overpay for bonds? The type of people
that invested in stocks (risk-tolerant) are vastly different than those that invested
in bonds (risk-averse) and so heterogeneity of investor types might explain why the
premium was so high.

So why then has this equity premium shrunk from around 6 per cent in the
twentieth century to around 3 per cent or even less in the 1990s? For example, even
though the dividend–price ratio for most of the twentieth century was approximately
4.7 per cent, the estimate for the S&P 500 at its 1999 peak was only 1.5 per cent or
less. Siegal (2002) claims that the historical 7.5 per cent rate of return included transaction costs, and so when technological advance lowered such costs, the real return
required was more like 5 per cent. A different explanation of this puzzle is provided
by Hall (2000). He claims that investment in intangible capital has been strong, as
US companies positioned in the new global economy have ample funds to expand
with, control marketing networks, are backed by the powerful copyright lobby
groups and enjoy technological superiority over many international rivals. Forward-
looking investors appreciate the strategic plays of US multinationals and are willing

to pay a premium to buy into this future globally driven dividend stream. This argument of Hall is both powerful and insightful – it is a far-sighted, big picture view.

This equity premium puzzle became less of a 'puzzle' in the late 1990s when the premium disappeared completely. Investors were holding stocks in preference to bonds even when there was no obvious existing premium – as bond yields were higher than dividend yields by anywhere up to 3 per cent. On this basis, the 'premium' appeared to be a discount in the late 1990s. Perhaps investors were over-optimistic concerning capital gains? The crash in stocks was inevitable given that bond yields were higher than stock yields for a considerable number of months. After 2000 the risk premium expanded once again.

Absurd valuations

From Table 1.1 it can be seen that *P/E* ratios (S&P index/EPS $) for the S and P were overstretched at their upward peaks in 1997 (22.2), 1998 (27.7) and 1999 (28.4) in a rising market. In fact, *P/E* ratios were in their low thirties during some months and even higher for the Dow and NASDAQ. But such ratios retreated slowly in a falling market – such as in 2000 (23.5) but rose again in 2001 (29.5) only to collapse in 2002 (19.1). Earnings from stocks (E% – column 7) remained below the risk free rate on the 10 year bond (Y% – column 8) for most of these years – revealing investor optimism concerning capital gains. However, it should be noted is that the acceleration stock prices cannot persistently run ahead of the growth in earnings per share and Table 1.1 illustrates that. Although stock prices rose by an annual average of 25.7 per cent (column 3) during the boom of 1997–9 the rise in EPS was only an annual average of 8.5 per cent (column 5). Stocks could not and did not justify themselves with this meager rise in the EPS growth. Stock prices had to fall and they did. The market collapsed by an average of −15.4 per cent between 2000–2 (column 3) while EPS 'growth' was a negative −1.23 per cent (column 5). We can say that stocks retreated in these three years in response to the unjustified run-up of the three earlier years when stock values rose three times faster the EPS growth. The market pulled back as a result of ordinary non-performance of an EPS annual growth rate of 3.6 per cent over the six years. Stocks rose only 5.1 per cent annually over this time – not

Table 1.1 Comparative returns

	S&P	%	EPS $	%	P/E	E (%)	Y (%)
2002	879	−23.2	46.0	18.5	19.1	5.41	4.61
2001	1,148	−13.0	38.8	−30.8	29.5	3.39	5.02
2000	1,320	−10.1	56.1	8.6	23.5	4.26	6.03
1999	1,469	19.5	51.6	16.7	28.4	3.52	5.65
1998	1,229	26.6	44.2	1.2	27.7	3.61	5.26
1997	970	31.0	43.7	7.6	22.2	4.50	6.35
1996	740	—	40.6	—	18.2	5.49	6.44
Average		5.1		3.6	24.1	4.31	5.62

Source: Board of Governors of the Federal Reserve System and NYSE.

too far above the 3.6 per cent EPS growth rate – reflecting a ratio of 1.42 and not 3 as during the boom. Hence, the S&P self-corrected after it became obvious that rapid growth in EPS was not forthcoming. We should remember that ultimately it is the growth in EPS that will dictate momentum in stock values.

We should also not forget the anchor of stock valuations – namely the risk-free rate on the ten-year bond. If the risk-free rate is 4 per cent then risk-neutral stock investors could pay P/E ratios of up to 25. Or if the risk-free rate is 5 per cent then P/E ratios for stocks of 20 could be justified. Hence we have an array of a P/E possibilities frontier based on whether the risk-free rate is more towards 7 per cent (P/E of 14.4) or more towards 3 per cent (P/E ratio of 33.3). We know that a risk-free rate of 3 per cent is not likely in 2004–5 and so we should not look towards high stock valuations and P/E ratios of 33. Except of course there is a sound expectation that this year's EPS will accelerate and so justify higher P/E ratios at the margin. As of mid 2004 the risk free rate on the 10 year bond is around 4.6 per cent and so P/E ratios of around 22 may be justified – and in fact the P/E is currently trading around this range. From Table 1.1 we can see that the seven-year P/E ratio was 24.1 – whereas valuations in mid 2004 appear below that average. We should also note that the earnings yield (E% – column 7) – from stocks – rests well below the ten-year bond yield (Y% – column 8) for most years between 1996 and 2002 – with the recessionary year of 2002 being the exception. In this year, investors finally sought the safe haven of the bond market – after capital gains in the stock market proved illusory.

The bubble: geopolitical forces at work?

Several international forces were at work in the 1990s that created an extraordinary growth environment for US stock markets. Japan experienced a huge asset price bubble in the mid-1980s that defied the forces of gravity. It burst by 1990, sending reverberations throughout Japan's financial sector and eventually the whole financial intermediation process in Japan ground to a halt. Both the demand for and supply of credit seized up. Slower lending flows and fear concerning job security dampened consumer and investor spending. In short, Japan's real economy suffered at the hand of a weak and fragile financial system under extreme stress. Asset prices suffocated for many years. And so Japan's stock market collapsed from its high of 39,000 points in the late 1980s to a low of around 7,800 points in 2003. Funds flowed from Japan and into more healthy and prospective US stocks *and* bonds for much of the 1990s.

Fortunes in Europe were not much better in the early 1990s as West Germany was finally united with East Germany. Although there was much rejoicing for humanity, not so for bond and stockholders as interest rates soared to attract foreign capital so necessary for the reunification. Europe recovered very slowly from the 1991 recession, unemployment remained stubbornly high and consumer confidence strengthened at a snail's pace. In short, European stock markets were under pressure in the early 1990s as rates of return in the real economy remained depressed. Therefore, there were strong international *push factors* at work in supporting US stock prices.

A worldwide flight to quality, partly as a result of a series of financial crises, pushed even more funds into US assets and into the 'safe haven' of the US dollar. There were crises in Russia, Mexico, Argentina and Asia that reminded all investors of holding a sizable percentage of their investment portfolio in US dollar assets. As Baker (2000) points out, there was a *double bubble* in the United States as an inflated US dollar underpinned inflated US stock prices. Foreigners sought a double-layered capital gain. Therefore, when policy-makers become concerned about the growing size of US current account deficit – to around 5 per cent of GDP (Table 1.1) – they have to appreciate that large capital inflows have generated this ballooning deficit. Why? Mainly because the US investment-savings gap widened and foreigners were willing to finance this shortfall.

It would be comforting to believe that foreigners were lured by high rates of return and that US corporations used these funds productively. Judging by corporate profit announcements since September 11 and the bankruptcies of World Com and Enron the answer would be 'no'. Stiglitz (2002) is particularly critical of America's mis-investment era – 'Money that could have gone into basic research, to improve the country's long-term growth prospects; money that could have been spent to improve the deteriorating infrastructure; money that could have invested in improving both dilapidated innercity schools and rich suburban ones, instead went into useless software, mindless dot.coms and unused fiber optic lines.' Excess capacity often lingers after a recession, squeezing pricing power and profits. The overhangs of the tech bubble will take a long time to wear off.

Did foreign capital flows contribute to the US stock bubble? Greenspan (2000) comments on the size of this capital inflow in the 1990s, 'The latest data published by the Department of Commerce indicate that the annual pace of direct plus portfolio investment by foreigners in the US economy during the first quarter (of 2000) was more than two and a half times its rate in 1995.' This surge in foreign capital inflow coincides with the giant leap in stock prices between 1994 and 1999 – in line with a liquidity driven market. As can be seen from Figure 1.4, the opposite is true post 2000 – private foreign purchases of US equities contracted. However, foreigners still persisted with the purchase of US bonds. The ability of the United States to attract foreign funds has implications for the current account deficit. It hovers around 5 per cent

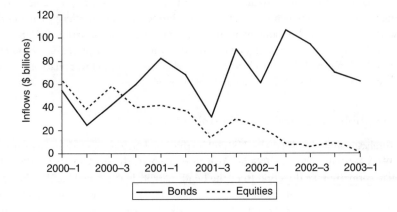

Figure 1.4 Private foreign purchases of US securities.

Source: Federal Reserve.

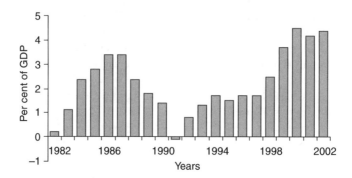

Figure 1.5 US current account.
Source: OECD Economic Outlook (2003).

of GDP (Figure 1.5) and must be financed somehow or close in response to a lower dollar and lower capital inflows.

Even though US financial markets appeared attractive in their own right, the United States nevertheless enjoyed a safe haven status – by default. Rates of return from real capital formation may not be as high as what foreign investors anticipate and such profit disappointment actually caused a massive exit from US stocks in 2000. This exit of funds was based partly on the *expectation* of a collapse in the US dollar, poorer profit results or a sell-off in stocks. In other words, not only did actual profit disappointment set in but also a change in risk perception that further accentuated capital outflows. Therefore, in searching for a trigger that pricked the US stock market boom one has to look no further than the foreign exchange market. A falling US dollar and a three-year bear stock market coincided – each fuelling the other's downward spiral. Global investors wanted to get out of US dollar assets after 2000.

On the other hand, there is also no doubt that other domestic *pull factors* such as low inflation and higher productivity growth assisted in creating a stable macro-economic climate in which to invest. Low real interest rates were a by-product of the low inflation era and a calm bond market underwrote an escalation in US stock prices. While real factors and sound economic fundamentals played an important part in pushing stock prices to historic levels their contribution was relatively minor in comparison to those of financial and behavioural forces.

The bubble: underwritten by a stable bond market?

The relationships between the US dollar, the bond market and the stock market involves very complex interactions. As history dictates, the stock market and the US dollar normally take direction from the bond market. It is the yield and stability of US bonds from which all economic life on earth flows – as investors formulate their vision of future asset prices compared to the risk-free rate. Forward-looking investors also assess the prudence of government policy strategies and form a view of inflation many periods out and so incorporate such views into the thirty-year bond yield. Hence, the bond futures market plays an important part in daily trading strategies. Falling bond yields before the start of stock trading or early in the day send a buy signal to stock traders. This inverted relationship between bond yields and stock prices are revealed in recent US financial history – with a high degree of regularity.

There are exceptions however. For example, during the Asian crisis, when there was a flight to quality, the flood of funds into US bonds was a liquidity effect not a signal to stock traders to buy stocks. Smart professionals were not fooled by this signal. Unfortunately, they were fooled in early 1987 when bond yields rose but the stock market took no heed – it rose despite higher interest rates. Between 2001 and 2003 is another occasion whereby investors were gripped with fear, as they pushed or switched into the bond market driving down yields to forty-year lows. Such investors dumped stocks and switched into bonds – displaying their gross intolerance for risk. Hence, there are times when the traditional bond market signal is false or is the *result* of investor fear of risk. Talk of deflation, as was the case in the United States in early 2003, caused a bond bubble and historically low yields.

As discussed earlier, there are times when the interaction of the trinity runs a little haywire. For example, what is not well appreciated during the bubble era was that both the US bond and stock markets received underpinning support from the US dollar. Up until late 2000, the US dollar slaughtered all currencies in its sight. Foreign investors flooded into US financial markets lured not just by rates of return but also by expected dollar strength. The foreign investment flood of 1997–2000 basically enjoyed very lucrative foreign exchange gains. In short, this financial trinity contains a mutually reinforcing momentum. Perhaps it was not a double but a triple bubble?

This virtuous circle soon turned into a vicious circle between 2000 and 2003 as forward-looking traders sold the US dollar in favour of the Euro and the Yen. Why hold US assets when they are falling in value? Why hold the US dollar when it falls in value? Both US and foreign investors 'switched' into Euro and Yen denominated assets in this era as US bond yields *and* US stock returns collapsed.

Debt, savings and switching

Credit markets were not always as well organized and sophisticated as what they are today. Many people from the older generation that had experienced the Great Depression frowned upon the use of credit and preferred saving for big-ticket purchases via down payments. But such attitudes were formed during low inflation times when the opportunity cost of waiting was low. However, during the 1960s, inflation began to escalate and so the threat of higher prices in the future pushed consumers towards current consumption and a bias towards debt. Tax laws interacted with this debt bias creating a massive impetus for both corporations and households to incur additional debt, as interest payments were tax deductions. Homeowners could gain income tax advantages from being highly geared, as could corporations seeking rapid business expansion during inflationary times. In short, it paid to be in debt. The 1990s era also displayed a willingness of investors and consumers to

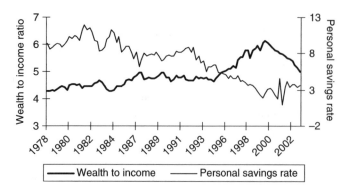

Figure 1.6 Wealth and savings.

Source: Board of Governors of the Federal Reserve.

borrow more in a free and open credit market and to 'under-save' by OECD standards. Some stock market investors tapped their credit cards and refinanced their houses in order to partake in the stock boom.

Switching behaviour was also evident – out of money market accounts and into stocks – in the bubble era. From Figure 1.6, it can be seen that America's personal saving rate has steadily declined from around 10 per cent in the late 1970s to 8.5 per cent in the 1980s to less than 1 per cent by the year 2000. It did rebound somewhat – out of fear by 2003 – displaying an inverse relationship to stock prices. Why such a low and declining saving rate? Households directly (via mutual funds) and indirectly (via pension funds) placed more of their funds into the stock market. Hence, their savings rate is higher than what Figure 1.6 portrays as their funds still remain stored but in a less liquid and more risky form.

More importantly, the wealth to income ratio rose sharply from around 4.5 in the 1980s to over 6.0 by the year 2000. More households have chosen to store their wealth in assets – stocks, bonds and houses – and so this 'switch' partly explains the choice of households to save less in ultra-liquid form. Perceptions of risk had changed – as investing the 'one-way' stock market street would have them. Such a trend is revealed in Figure 1.7, households stored more than 30 per cent of their total wealth in stock markets in the 1990s compared to 15 per cent just before the 1987 crash. Although real estate slightly faded in percentage terms there was a clear switch out of stocks and back into real estate from 1999–2003. This switch was partly by choice and partly by the unexpected collapse in stock values.

Warning signals: why not switch?

There were several warning lights flashing in the 1990s that stocks were indeed overvalued. So why did the majority of investors not switch out of stocks and into bonds, money market mutual funds, gold, real estate or other hard assets? This question has already been partially answered – that stockbrokers pushed the line that investing in

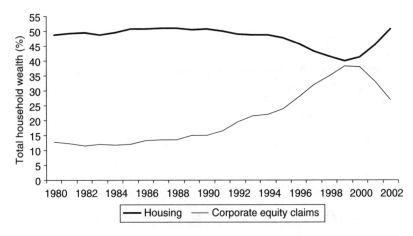

Figure 1.7 Contribution to household wealth: housing and corporate equity claims.
Source: Kopczuk and Saez (2004).

stocks was a 'one-way street' – and pointed to Siegal's research that stocks persistently beat bonds. So why would the individual investor stray from age-old wisdom?

What were those warning signals? The conventional ones included exceptionally high *P/E* ratios, low dividend–price ratios, stock yields lying beneath the ten-year treasury yield (Fed model) and an exorbitantly high *Q* ratio. Not only were stocks overvalued according to these benchmarks but they were *wildly* overvalued. Why were these signals ignored? Perhaps investors believed that these benchmarks were elastic and not fixed? This time was different – so the argument went. Investors were far-sighted and were displaying signs of extreme patience by waiting future, and some would say, distant dividends. In effect, this represented a lowering of the risk premium – caused in part by tame inflation, low long-term interest rates and a surge in productivity growth. One should remember that in 1958 that stock yields fell below bond yields (the great reversal) and the stock market did not collapse but in fact experienced a three-year bull market thereafter.

What of corporate earnings?

As the 1990s progressed so did investors grow more patient in holding stocks at higher-than-normal *P/E* ratios in full expectation that corporate profits would maintain a healthy year-on-year rise. In some years they were vindicated.

What of corporate profits? We know from Table 1.1 that recent EPS (1997–2002) has been around 4.31 per cent and the *growth* in EPS of around 3.6 per cent – whereas for the 1990s it was 4.6 per cent. There would have to be a rapid acceleration of EPS growth to return to the 9 per cent yield of the late 1980s. This is what investors are hoping for – a doubling of EPS yields that will justify a doubling of stock values.

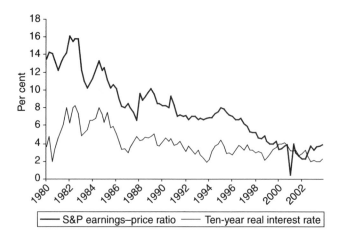

Figure 1.8 Earnings–price ratio and real interest rate.
Source: Board of Governors of the Federal Reserve.

Far-fetched perhaps but even a 25 per cent rise in EPS yields over three years would justify substantially higher stock values.

We know that price–earnings ratio escalated in the 1990s and so earnings–price ratio fell – but how far – and why did investors not take heed? From Figure 1.8, it can be seen that the earnings–price ratio were around 14 per cent in 1980–2, fell to around 9 per cent by the late 1980s and kept falling to 4 per cent by the year 2000. Real interest rates displayed a similar trend but maintained a healthy 8 per cent gap with the earnings–price ratio in early 1980s with still a 5 per cent gap by the early 1990s. However, the gap closed to 2 per cent by the late 1990s and to an amazing zero by 2000! Was there no risk in holding stocks over bonds? Would there be no mean reversion? That is, why wouldn't *P/E* ratios fall back into some long-term average? Investors believed that this era 'was different' and therefore ratios could be justified at their extremities. But minds changed and pessimism set in by 2001–2 with investors herding back into bonds and forsaking stocks because of governance issues, poor reporting standards and the Iraqi war.

Under normal circumstances this trend would constitute a dangerous signal to investors. Why did the risk premium fall so far and why did investors not switch into safe securities and so embrace the risk-free rate? Did they have no fear? Or were they just over confident? Several reasons for this phenomenon will be examined in later chapters but the fact that stock returns were similar to risk-free returns suggests that investors, on average, were confident that capital gains would accrue to stocks – more so than bonds. In other words, the potential for achieving capital gains from holding bonds was less than that from holding stocks – or at least that was the common perception. What is known as the Fed model is relevant here – it states that if the yield on the S&P rests above the ten-year bond rate then stocks are undervalued and if below ten-year bond rate then stocks are overvalued. This is exactly the point of the earlier discussion – the risk-free rate was attractive in the late 1990s and many investors still shunned it. Perhaps they believed Siegal's work – that stocks out-perform bonds over the long run – just sit back and relax!

However, it would only take a mild economic or financial disturbance or an abrupt change in investor sentiment to detonate an explosion out of stocks and into bonds. Such a switch occurred after 2000.

Perhaps the most damning evidence of all comes from an inflated Q ratio. This ratio reflects the incentive transmitted to investors as to whether to invest in financial or physical assets. If the ratio is greater than one then the investor should invest in physical assets as they are relatively cheap compared to buying such assets via listed stock market companies. So a stock market boom can push an investment boom via this relativity and substitution effect. Conversely, if stock prices are low, there is an incentive for the investor to purchase stocks (and implicitly the physical assets they hold) instead of purchasing physical assets directly. Of relevance to America is the surge in stock prices that caused investment to surge as well – and not surprisingly a productivity surge that piggy backed on both. Such buoyancy sounds all very positive but was driven to the extreme – the Q ratio had to return to a more historically normal level – namely a theoretical figure of one or its long run average.

As can be seen from Figure 1.9, the Q ratio (the stock markets total value compared to the fair value of all corporate wealth) escalated since 1990 from around 0.6 to around 1.6 late in the decade. This is cause for alarm as pointed out by Smithers and Wright (2000) – who claim that the Q ratio is 2.5 times its long run average and is likely to rediscover that average in the medium term. These authors state, 'We looked at what has happened when Q has gotten to this sort of level in the US. In every previous instance – 1906, 1929, 1937, 1968 – a bubble has been followed by a crash and a severe recession.' Under this scenario there is a strong prospect for US stock markets to fall by 50 per cent from its height in 1998. Indeed, a fall of this

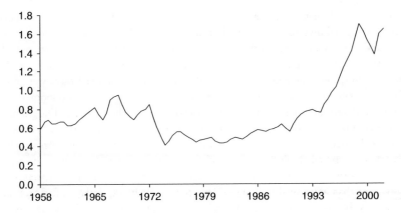

Figure 1.9 Tobin's Q ratio.

Source: Board of Governors of the Federal Reserve Board.

magnitude would be required in order to raise stock yields to a level commensurate with the risk-free rate. This is a pertinent piece of theoretical analysis. Extrapolating the past produces a dire prediction of a major, if not horrific, correction. We do know that stocks retreated very significantly from their highs in 1999 and this so far has been a major correction of around 35 per cent as of mid-2004. Although Smithers and Wright call for a Dow of around 5,500 points (their 50 per cent correction from the recent high) but a more realistic projection is around a 25 per cent correction – or the Dow at 8,625 points. This 'prophesy' was partially fulfilled during the Iraqi War when the Dow fell to around 7,300 points. What is different from the crashes mentioned earlier is that the United States is not in a severe recession as of 2004 and the Fed has strongly stood by with monetary liquidity. Hence, stock prices have rebounded as the Dow rose above 10,300 points by mid-2004.

There is no doubt that a high Q ratio makes it easy for businesses to acquire fresh capital – as the IPO flurry of the 1990s illustrates. But acquiring new capital presumes that it will eventually be channeled into real assets – and these assets will have to yield real rates of return. Just a 'promise to pay' is not enough. Therefore, the kind of 'illusory wealth' stored in US stock markets is a function of substantial 'promises to pay'. If massive amounts of financial capital cannot be translated into tangible, but not necessarily physical capital then the bubble will burst and massive capital losses will inflict investors on a broad scale – just as in 2002–3.

Similarities with 1929

It is often stated that every business cycle is unique and so every boom. Therefore, searching for the same build-up of forces during each boom may be just as elusive as searching for an honest politician. Nevertheless, there may be some commonalities between booms that relate to man's greed, ambition and quest for rapid wealth accumulation. Indeed, there are several parallels between the stock market boom of the 1990s and the crash of 1929. First, the excessive use of financial leverage to purchase stocks and the resultant exposure to greater risk via margin calls is one common feature. Any shock that triggers a sudden fall in stock prices generates a domino effect amidst marginal investors with a modest capital base and an even more modest access to quick liquidity. Second, faith in the 'new economy', the 'new paradigm' and the eternal wellspring of technological progress in driving stock prices are not peculiar to the 1990s, these same beliefs were evident in the 1920s. Indeed there were high-flying stocks in this era that were at the frontier of technological development and some produced long-term sustainable growth while others wilted like summer flowers – never to be heard of again. Third, many of these 'new economy' stocks did not pay dividends nor was there any immediate hope that they would. Nevertheless, speculators ignored the lack of dividend flow in the short run and even the record high price–earnings ratio for the period. Asset backing and capital gain were more important than any trivial cash or dividend flow. Fourth, a speculative fever was evident in both eras whereby marginal, and arguably unsophisticated investors, flooded into the stock market lured by quick-fire capital gains. Economic fundamentals were important up to a point but trading on 'news' and second guessing the fellow investor's move became more important in this game of 'musical chairs'. Fifth, the argument that fund managers view the stock market as a one-way street *over the long run* and so keep pushing funds into the market accordingly can be compared to the 1920s era. A more detailed analysis of the great asset price bubble of 1929 is discussed in Chapter 10.

Where from here?

From theory and long-run historical data we know what should happen to US stock prices over the medium term. That is, they should self-correct or mean revert. When we employ Tobin's Q ratio we know that the numerator can change *quickly* as it is driven mainly by financial forces whereas the denominator changes *slowly* as it is driven mainly by real factors. Hence, for mean reversion to occur it is more likely to occur through the numerator – a lowering of stock prices in a short time frame than a rapid rise in the denominator lead by GDP and productivity growth.

A similar analysis flows from the P/E ratio. What happens to stock returns after an era of high P/E ratios? The answer depends upon whether higher stock prices drove the ratio higher or whether lower earnings drove it higher. As Siegal (2000) points out – annual stock returns were 9.7 per cent for the five years after the P/E ratio peaks and recessions of 1991, 1938, 1921 and 1894 whereas annual stock returns were only 1.1 per cent five years after the P/E ratio peaks and 'recessions' of 1987, 1961, 1946, 1933 and 1929. Hence, it matters *why* the P/E ratio spiked? Depressed earnings may rebound from a recession quickly and so justify a rebound in P/E ratios whereas exuberant buying (based on liquidity) may never justify those same prices again – and so P/E ratios face downward pressure in the bubble aftermath. This analysis is of the same type for the Q ratio – it is numerator that must adjust and can adjust quickly. This is just another piece of evidence against many stocks regaining former glory and former P/E ratios. The Dow and the S&P will have to make do with a modest recovery not a complete retracing to the peaks of 1999.

There are three key macroeconomic variables that will strongly impinge upon the US stock market performance over the next two years – 2005–6. They are the strength of the US dollar, the size of the current account deficit and foreign capital inflows. Foreigners require a degree of certainty when investing in US dollar assets and will be reluctant to fund the large US current account deficits – unless at higher interest rates. These three variables are highly interrelated. US investors do not want higher interest rates at the long end of the yield curve and so are somewhat dependent on strong capital inflows and a stable US dollar to support stock prices.

Conclusion

At the beginning of the decade the Dow stood at 2,634 points; by the end of the decade it had soared to its all-time high of 11,497 points – a stellar performance by any standard. Real returns from holding stocks in the 1990s were more than double the returns from holding thirty-year bonds. This decade was like no other in history, as the rise in stock prices surpassed the long stretch set in the 1960s. However, reality soon paid a visit to paper-rich investors. Paper profits are just that, they are not secure unless they are *realized* – a lesson that many investors learnt in 2000. Just as in 1987, investors stampeded to the exit gate causing stock values to plummet, which in turn generated further panic selling. A dash for liquidity and a safe haven bond market by investors sent shock waves through an already disorderly market. Paper profits turned into concrete losses as investor's simultaneously exited assets and into cash. Therefore, the claim of exceptionally high capital gains in the 1990s is only true to the extent that such gains were realized. Investors with large positions that remained in the market were exposed to sudden shifts in market sentiment and so remained exposed to possible capital losses in the event of a rapid exit to cash or offshore opportunities. Hence, capital gains in the period 1997–2003 were far lower than what nominal index numbers reveal and in some portfolios quite negative. The bubble was well and truly over and Cash once again reigned as King by 2000.

What should also be noted is the *unique* set of circumstances in US history that generated this stock price bubble. There was an abundance of foreign investors pushing and jockeying for position in the richest, deepest and safest market in the world. Not only were foreigners chasing 'blue chip' assets they also wanted to be in the US dollar. This double desire resulted in a double bubble. A plethora of forces were brewing excess liquidity. Besides abundant liquidity, there was a high degree of 'switching' going on – that is, changing attitudes towards credit, leverage and risk – that transferred funds out of low risk savings vehicles and into potentially high risk, high capital gain stocks. Further analysis of the driving forces of the bubble are examined in Chapter 4.

We have witnessed a cooling off in US stock prices in early 2003 – even a collapse – but a rally by year's end – towards 10,400 points on the Dow and 1,085 on the S&P. However, we have also witnessed a tentative revival in both the real economy and stock prices by mid-2004. There are signs of strength in the financial sector and the forward-looking stock market is anticipating a robust revival in the real sector and so economic activity. Have US stock prices returned to a level reflecting basic fundamentals? Is the financial storm over? Can the US dollar reverse its slide? Can US stock prices rally on the back of improved corporate profits and accountability? These questions deserve responses but first we shall examine the historical record of the 1990s in order to familiarize ourselves with the characteristics of the stock bubble and the Fed's response to both escalating stock values and the economy's heat.

2 The great bull run of the 1990s

Introduction

In many ways the effects of the 1987 stock market crash became visible in the real sector years later. The Fed intervened in 1987 with abundant liquidity and stood firm as lender of last resort, saving the real economy from a hard-landing. Stocks took a beating for a while but recovered by 1989. However, there were ill-side effects of the Fed's rescue mission. The economy was awash with funds, and there were spillovers into real estate, creating an asset price boom of some magnitude. Asset price inflation spurred goods price inflation and inflationary expectations were on the rise. The twin overhangs of debt and inflated asset prices cursed the US economy in the early 1990s, posing a macroeconomic management problem for the Fed. Even though the US economy made a sluggish start to the decade, including the 1991 recession, it roared from 1995 onwards.

As surveyed in Chapter 5, given the significant rise in US productivity and efficiency there is a temptation to argue that there is a 'new economy' and a 'new paradigm' for the Fed to respect. However, a fortuitous set of circumstances – indeed unique – for the US economy, abundant liquidity and speculative fever, tempers the view that fundamentals alone were responsible for the US stock market boom of the 1990s. Financial, and not economic factors were the prime drivers of escalating asset prices. Unfortunately, it was a matter of up the staircase and down the elevator for some investors by 2000.

There is no doubt that the United States enjoyed a fortuitous set of circumstances in the 1990s or commonly called 'luck'. Japan's economy and stock collapsed beyond belief and Europe endured high unemployment rates, reunification problems and sluggish growth. There was also the continued support of Chinese and Japanese investors for US bonds – funding American consumption and indirectly their own exports. Global investors sought the 'safe haven' of the US dollar and US stock and bond markets. Such investors received more justification for placing funds in the United States – as inflation remained docile, productivity growth was accelerating and the risk premium for holding stocks was closing. Moreover, the Fed appeared prepared to let the growth phase roll and so leave interest rates at low levels. The Fed was also 'accommodating' when Asian stock markets crashed in 1998 and many foreign investors again sought the safety of US denominated assets. In short, there were significant external push factors into US markets and even some attractive pull factors as well – such as low inflation and rising productivity. Foreign capital fed into the US productivity boom by providing the necessary finance (saving) for US companies to innovate.

This chapter surveys the escalation of stock prices in the 1990s.

Macroeconomic background

When ex-president George Bush sought policy advice concerning the sluggish US economy in 1990–1 he was counseled to 'wait for the self-correcting forces of the market to work'. Indeed, he accepted such advice and waited in the hope that the economy would respond before the November voting date – it did not. Perhaps it was more a matter of Bush losing the election than Clinton winning it. But now it was President Clinton's turn to listen to policy advice – sound or otherwise. For the Clinton administration to be successful, it had to either have Chairman Greenspan 'onside' or at least have Greenspan not work against or thwart the administration's policy strategy. What would be the deal? Obviously Clinton desired growth and prosperity but Greenspan desired growth *with* stability. There needed to be a clear understanding between these two power brokers as to what was and what was not negotiable. Greenspan would not tolerate inflation and he believed that growth could only be achieved if the government got its own 'house in order'. That is, by lowering budget deficits and the national debt, pressure could be taken off long-term interest rates. As can be seen from Figure 2.1, the budget deficit was around 3 per cent of GDP in the early 1990s, diminished in the mid-1990s and turned into a surplus by 1997. The financial markets cheered the Clinton administration's fiscal austerity by lowering bond yields and buying stocks. The path to lower yields at the long end of the yield curve was to reduce the threat of inflation and reduce the crowding out effect of government borrowing.

It was also necessary to assure the finance markets that stop–go policies would not be used to engineer artificial spurts of growth and so raise interest rates in the meantime.

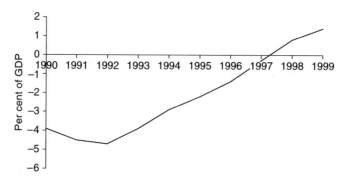

Figure 2.1 Budget deficit.

Source: Board of Governors of the Federal Reserve System.

Credible long-term policies were required to produce long-term *sustainable* growth. If the Clinton administration had in mind reckless expansion there was always the reminder from Greenspan that the Fed would raise short-term interest rates in response to poor economic management. Moreover, bond-holders would censure Clinton's performance by selling long bonds and so raising long-term interest rates. In short, the administration could not afford to provoke either Greenspan or the bond-holding class (Canterbery 2000a).

President Clinton knew there were costs in abiding by Greenspan's blueprint for economic recovery. For example, Clinton had campaigned on spending more on rebuilding America's public infrastructure and education but was constrained in the early 1990s by the quest for deficit reduction. Keynesian demand-side management was frowned upon by America's business community and so any sizable fiscal policy initiatives were likely to meet with stiff opposition. There was also the threat that the owners of capital would 'censure' Clinton policies via the bond market and the US dollar. In order for Clinton to undertake his social reforms he sacrificed a degree of autonomy over economic management, a trade-off that he reluctantly accepted. But there were benefits from agreeing to a low inflation-low interest rate environment whereby private sector investment could flourish. Improving the quantity and quality of the nation's capital stock would raise long-term productive potential via rises in productivity and full employment. More jobs, higher real wages and more prosperity could only increase Clinton's political capital and chances of re-election. In reality, real GDP boomed in this decade to levels not seen since the 1960s. From Figure 2.2, economic growth registered an average of 3.5 per cent. However, the real bonus for the Clinton administration was the collapse in the inflation rate as revealed in Figure 2.3. Despite the recovery in output in 1992 and capacity utilization rates approaching 84 per cent (Figure 2.4), inflation remained subdued amidst eight years of economic boom.

Another outstanding feature of America's economic landscape, besides deficit reduction, was the low level of real interest rates throughout the 1990s. The recession years of 1991–2 witnessed a real interest rate below 1 per cent but still remained less than 3 per cent for the more robust years after 1994 (Figure 2.5). Such a stable,

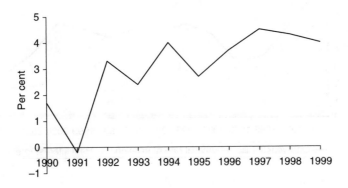

Figure 2.2 GDP growth rate.

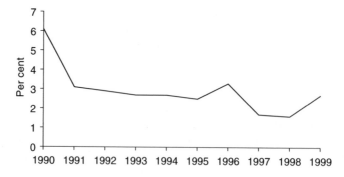

Figure 2.3 Inflation rate (CPI).

Source: Board of Governors of the Federal Reserve System.

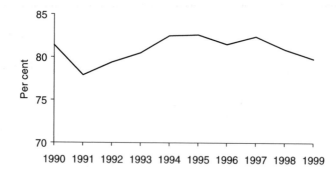

Figure 2.4 Capacity utilization.

Source: Board of Governors of the Federal Reserve System.

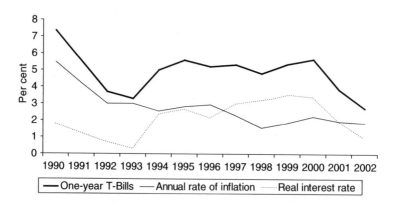

Figure 2.5 Nominal and real interest rates (1990–2000).

Source: Board of Governors of the Federal Reserve System.

low interest rate environment stimulated an investment boom. During this decade, the unemployment rate fell to a thirty-year low of 4.2 per cent. From Figure 2.6 it can be seen that unemployment continued its downward slide from 7.4 per cent in 1992. Ironically, both unemployment and inflation were on recent historical lows *together*. So how did the US economy manage to post rapid growth rates and high employment and yet not experience rampant inflation as a by-product of such 'heat'? As examined in Chapter 5, the US economy pressed up against the Non-Accelerating Inflationary Rate of Unemployment (NAIRU) but did not succumb to excessive inflationary heat. As a result of a robust economy, stock prices, and asset prices in general, soared from 1992 onwards. Rosy expectations beyond the year 2000 also played a part in maintaining high stock prices and sustaining low price–earnings ratio all the way until 1999. We know from hindsight that such ratios were not justified as EPS growth collapsed.

Business profits boomed in the mid-1990s after recovering with a lag from the 1991 recession. Figure 2.7 reveals that business profits (as a per cent of GDP) on average were

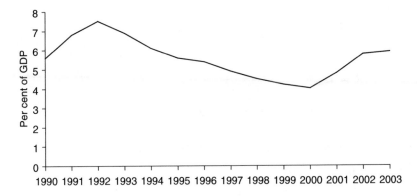

Figure 2.6 Unemployment rate.

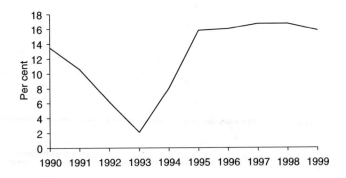

Figure 2.7 Profits.

Source: Board of Governors of the Federal Reserve System.

above 16 per cent after 1995 and well above profit levels of the 1980s. As discussed earlier, real interest rates were low – reflecting low levels of inflation and the Fed's accomodating monetary policy. With the cost of capital lower and consumer credit cheaper, US firms were able to expand sales without crushing profit margins. Subdued wage growth and suppressed unit costs were also major contributors to profitability.

What were the signs that easy credit and a rise in monetary aggregates contributed to a rise in business profits and stock prices? From Figure 2.8 it can be seen that the growth in the M2 monetary aggregate did *accelerate* from 1994, rising from a 0.5 per cent growth rate in 1994 to more than a 7 per cent growth rate in the late 1990s. Rapidly expanding liquidity (and not just rapidly rising productivity growth) fuelled the boom in stock prices. Household debt continued to expand (Figure 2.9). The boom in housing construction can be seen from Figure 2.10. A rebound from a low of less than 800,000 units in 1992 to more than 1.3 million units in most years

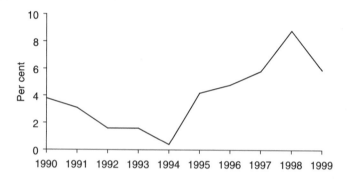

Figure 2.8 Money supply (M2).

Source: Board of Governors of the Federal Reserve System.

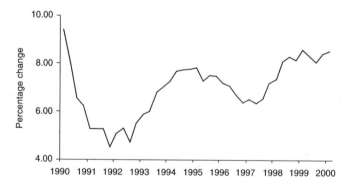

Figure 2.9 Annual change in household debt levels.

Source: Board of Governors of the Federal Reserve System.

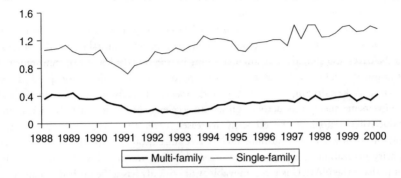

Figure 2.10 Private housing starts (million of units – annual rate).

Source: Board of Governors of the Federal Reserve System.

after 1997 – and maintained such levels into 2003. House values increased along with this construction boom and provided valuable support for stock prices – via re-financing at lower interest rates.

The policy paradigm

Although the Fed charter includes several economic objectives, the interpretation of this charter by Greenspan (2000c) is that long-term sustainable growth is best delivered *via* a low stable inflation rate. He states 'A central bank can best contribute to economic growth and rising living standards by fostering a financial environment that promotes overall economic balance in the economy and price stability. Maintaining an environment of effective price stability is essential, because the experience in the United States and abroad has underscored that low and stable inflation is a prerequisite for healthy, balanced, economic expansion'. By not distorting relative prices and economic incentives, the private sector can invest and innovate and so raise the long-term potential of the economy to deliver higher living standards. In short, low inflation is *the* prerequisite or passport for sustainable growth. Moreover, Greenspan is on public record as stating that history teaches us that monetary policy has been most effective when it has been pre-emptive. That is, strike against emerging inflationary forces before a stubborn critical mass is formed.

Greenspan's logic is also rooted in theoretical monetarism, whereby there are long and variable lags in conducting a monetary policy and so 'waiting' for inflation to mature creates greater risks down the track. Given there are sizable impact lags, and even short-run recognition lags, the restraining effects of tight money and/or higher interest rates effects may be delayed and so the evils of inflation are more prolonged. This is a powerful justification for being vigilant and striking inflation first – as a precautionary measure – so as to not undermine any future expansion. However, there are two basic flaws to this justification. First, the fine-tuning skills required to successfully undertake a pre-emptive strike, or any monetary policy strike for that matter, are enormous – even within calm periods of history. Second, there is strong evidence that old empirical relationships have broken down or become extinct. Monetary aggregates and income velocities, for example, became unstable in the 1990s. The NAIRU also shifted – far lower it seems by the mid-1990s – a shifting target – confusing the policy maker as regards the appropriate economic cruise speed of the economy. A key driving force of this 'shift' was most likely waves of technological improvement causing productivity growth to accelerate by the mid-1990s. Hence, the productive potential of the economy increased faster than what most economists thought possible and was pushing against recognized, but old speed limits – such as capacity utilization constraints, a low unemployment rate and low inventory levels. But perhaps the NAIRU is like a movable wall – it only has to be pushed? Challenges in formulating monetary policy are mounting, as old empirical relationships appeared to have broken down.

Dip and recovery: 1990–1

From Figure 2.11 it can be seen that the 1990s started with a stumble. The collapse of the Dow in July 1990 reflected the short, sharp recession that hit the US economy and the pessimism that prevailed for a time. Despite the mid-year collapse, the Dow only finished down 0.6 per cent for the year. However, a rebound took place quickly and the Dow recovered by 22.4 per cent in 1991. The growth of GDP fell to 1.7 per cent in 1990 and continued to fall in 1991 to record −0.2 per cent. Unemployment rose in both years to 5.6 per cent and 6.8 per cent respectively. In other words, the real economy suffered in the 1990–1 recession but the *forward-looking* Dow actually rose amidst this gloom. Investors predicted a short sharp recession and were basically rewarded for being correct. From Figures 2.12 and 2.13, the S&P posted an average annual gain of 13 per cent whereas the NASDAQ posted a very impressive annual gain of 24 per cent. This was only the beginning of the boom in tech stocks.

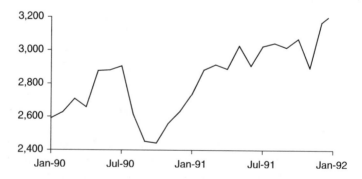

Figure 2.11 Level of Dow (1990–1).

Source: NYSE.

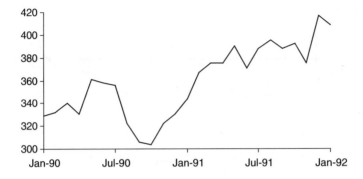

Figure 2.12 Level of S&P (1990–1).

Source: NYSE.

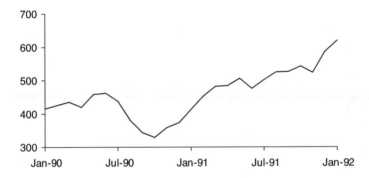

Figure 2.13 Level of NASDAQ (1990–1).

Source: NYSE.

The roaring Dow: 1992–3

With the real economy still sluggish, the outlook for stock prices remained dim with the Dow only posting a 4.4 per cent gain in 1992 but a more solid 13.5 per cent rise in 1993 (Figure 2.14). The S&P performed as well as the Dow (Figure 2.15) but the NASDAQ roared from its low of 460 points in 1992 to 800 points by the beginning of 1994 (Figure 2.16). Unemployment continued to rise in 1992 (6.9 per cent) but fell slightly to 6.1 per cent in 1993. However, GDP growth picked substantially to 3.3 per cent in 1992 and 2.4 per cent in 1993. The economic recovery was underway and stock prices remained quite firm. It is here that we should remind ourselves that EPS growth is tied to long-run GDP growth and that stock prices are ultimately tied to both. Even so we should forget the risk-free rate on the ten-year bond – the bad news came in 1994 as interest rates rose quickly and suffocated stock prices almost immediately – but GDP growth slowed with a lag of a year.

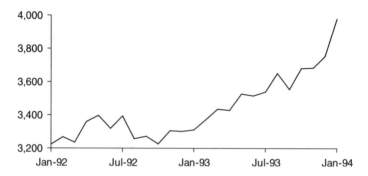

Figure 2.14 Level of Dow (1992–3).

Source: NYSE.

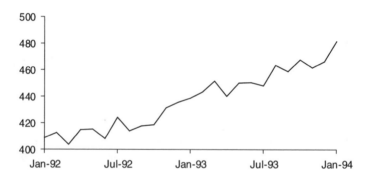

Figure 2.15 Level of S&P (1992–3).

Source: NYSE.

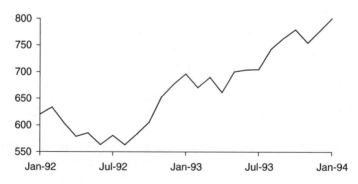

Figure 2.16 Level of NASDAQ (1992–3).

Source: NYSE.

The policy-induced correction: 1994–5

The year 1994 was a poor one for the Dow as the Fed raised interest rates. Optimistic investors were given a beating and the Big Bear visited the bond market. A major rebound occurred in the Dow in 1995 when it posted an impressive gain of 33.4 per cent (Figure 2.17). As for the S&P, it rose by an average annual rate of 16 per cent and the NASDAQ 14 per cent (Figures 2.18 and 2.19). GDP growth was solid in 1994 at 4 per cent but faded somewhat to 2.7 per cent in 1995 – as higher interest rates cooled economic activity with a lag. Unemployment continued to fall, down to 6.1 per cent in 1994 and 5.6 per cent in 1995. In fact, this downward trend would continue for the rest of the decade.

There was a growing anxiety within the Fed that inflation was about to raise its ugly head and the Clinton administration was warned about the Fed's desire to raise interest rates early in 1994. But the signs of inflationary pressure were mixed. It is true that the Employment Cost Index (ECI) rose mildly from 3.5 per cent in 1992 to

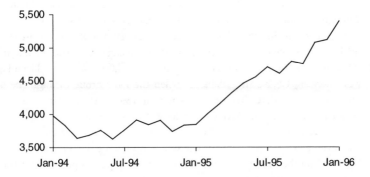

Figure 2.17 Level of Dow (1994–5).
Source: NYSE.

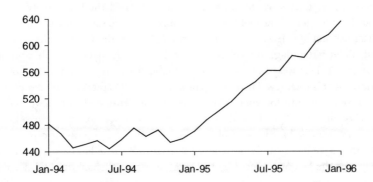

Figure 2.18 Level of S&P (1994–5).
Source: NYSE.

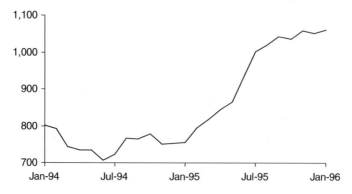

Figure 2.19 Level of NASDAQ (1994–5).
Source: NYSE.

3.6 per cent in 1993. The ECI for services rose from 3.2 to 3.6 per cent in the same period. More importantly unit labour costs did post a substantial rise from 1.2 per cent in 1992 to 2.1 per cent in 1993. However, this index fell to 0.8 per cent in 1994, as did the ECI to 3.1 per cent. Other signs of overheating came from the stock market – the Dow rose from 3,100 points in early 1993 to nearly 4,000 points by the end of the year. I was watching CNBC in Tallahassee when the Dow broke through the 4,000 point barrier and knew that Greenspan was not far away with his dampener against 'excessive optimism'. I did not have to wait long as he acted swiftly.

Between January and April of 1994, the Fed raised the federal funds rate several times to an average of 5.8 per cent for the year – up from a 4.2 per cent average in 1993. The yield on the long bond moved higher to average 7.3 per cent for the year but rose above 7.6 per cent on some occasions. As interest rates began to fall in 1995 so did stock prices rise and by the end of 1995 made a respectable recovery.

Greenspan's rationale for his pre-emptive strike against inflation was premised on two concepts: inflationary expectations would be wrung out of the system and long-term interest rates would fall as investors witnessed the Fed's resolve to raise them at the short end of the yield curve. The former was to some extent achieved but the latter was not – at least in the short-term. However, the yield on the long bond did fall, albeit with a lag, to 6.88 per cent in 1995. Greenspan's gamble paid off in some ways but there was always a lingering doubt that there was a degree of overkill embedded in this strategy. There were costs in terms of capital losses on stocks and bonds as well as output foregone. Was it the recession that we had to have? Was the inflationary dragon kept chained – unable to wreak its normal havoc? Or was Greenspan's strategy based on an old paradigm and old signposts of capacity constraints that were increasingly becoming less relevant? There has been a suspicion to this day that the Fed overreacted in 1994 to 'imaginary threats' that did not represent 'clear and present' dangers. In reaction to such criticisms Greenspan (1997e) commented 'I find it ironic that our actions in 1994–5 were criticized by some because inflation did not turn upward. That outcome, of course, was the intent of the tightening, and I am satisfied that our actions then were both necessary and effective, and helped to foster the continued economic expansion'. Given this criticism it appears that Chairman Greenspan has been a little reticent about imposing his view over that of many millions of investors forming a market view and so has refrained from pricking the asset price boom based on his own personal opinion.

After the dust of 1994 had settled, investors returned in earnest to the stock market in 1995. The inflationary threat had subsided and the there was clear evidence that the US federal budget deficit was receding further – from −3.9 per cent of GDP in 1993 to −2.9 per cent in 1994 and to a twenty-year low of −1.4 per cent in 1995. Such deficit reductions were mainly driven by buoyant economic activity increasing tax revenues and not so much from public spending reductions. The trend was reassuring to investors that anticipated further falls in yields on thirty-year bonds as a partial result of this fiscal performance and perhaps less threatening tax liabilities in the future. In fact, the Clinton administration passed legislation lowering inheritance and capital gains taxes, which further stimulated the rich of America to invest. Hence, the investment climate was ripe for an assault on the Dow.

Up, up and away: 1996–7

The year 1996 produced a real growth rate of more than 3.7 per cent and continued to rise to 4.5 per cent in 1997. Unemployment fell to 5.4 per cent in 1996 and to 4.9 per cent in 1997. Chairman Greenspan attributed much of this heightened economic activity to low interest rates, ample credit availability in a reasonably 'soft economy', a concerted effort to reduce the budget deficit and the easing of Fed policy throughout 1995. In other words, 'sound policies' had provided a stable economic environment in which the private sector could prosper. In fact, the Fed lowered the federal funds rate in December 1995 and in January 1996 to 5.25 per cent. However, in response to heightened economic activity, intermediate and long-term interest rates rose a full point by the middle of 1996. There was a fear that increased economic activity would provoke an inflationary resurgence – in the near future. Hence, the bias in Fed policy was towards restraint by the end of 1996 as both stock prices and interest moved up together.

In reality, inflation remained somewhat subdued in 1996 with a core rate of 2.5 per cent compared to 3 per cent in 1995. There was an acceleration of food and energy prices – oil prices rose by more than 30 per cent in 1996. But there was a deceleration in some consumer and capital goods prices, in fact the CPI (excluding food and energy) was only 1 per cent – a extremely low number compared to previous years. According to Chairman Greenspan low inflation was both a symptom and a cause of a robust economy. Long-term investment in people and capital had been the welcome by-product of low inflation. Such a lack of inflationary heat is surprising in that resource utilization rates were high by historical benchmarks. Indeed, the Fed puzzled over why 'normal relationships' did not hold. Temporary factors were at work to suppress inflationary pressure such as the rising US dollar and weak foreign economies passing on low import prices. However, other forces were also acting as safety valves. The labour market was tight but did not produce wage outcomes associated with such tightness. Perhaps job insecurity caused workers to be less demanding in an environment of rapid technological adoption? With the advent of more sophisticated computer software and the communications revolution, the viability of a wide range of businesses is a month-to-month proposition. The fortunes of labour are tied with this sea of advance. Other reasons cited were domestic deregulation, greater exposure to international competition, greater economies of scale and lower health care costs. However, all of these influences are subject to diminishing returns and so are more like *one-shot* drivers of subdued wage growth.

Despite the fact that wage growth grew a little faster in 1996 than in 1995 there was no spillover into the core CPI. The ECI rose by 3.1 per cent compared to 2.6 per cent in 1995 (Figure 2.20). In other words, despite tightness in the labour market there was no discernable impact on core inflation. How long can this suppressed wage cost growth continue for? Chairman Greenspan expressed concern over this abnormal relationship that departs from previous known relationships between labour market tightness and wage growth and between wage rises and inflation. His response was that respectable rises in productivity had contained unit labour costs even though wage inflation was positive. US companies had apparently lost some pricing power as a rising US dollar kept the lid on import prices, companies desired to maintain market share because of more intensive global competition. In short, the US economy enjoyed wage and price stability much to the surprise of the Fed. Where were the old relationships and more specifically where was the old foe – inflation?

Looking at finance markets, even though there were rises in market interest rates, banks were keen to secure business and so relaxed lending standards. There was also a narrowing of yields between risk-less government securities and corporate bonds. Thus, lending on the prospect of an upswing in the business cycle was vibrant. Home lending was particularly strong and finance companies joined the party. The Fed made the point that the growth rate of mortgage debt increased at a rate of 7.5 per cent – the fastest since 1990. Consumer debt grew at around 8.25 per cent but well below the clip of the previous year. Overall, household sector debt increased at 7.5 per cent but lower

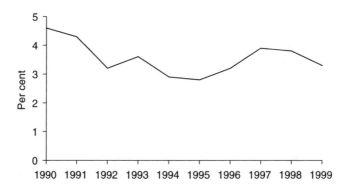

Figure 2.20 Employment cost index.

Source: Board of Governors of the Federal Reserve System.

than the 8.25 per cent recorded in 1995. The level of the household sector debt burden (as a percentage of personal income) approached 17.1 per cent. Banks were obviously wary of credit worthiness and facilitated this shift away from consumer credit towards home equity loans – probably motivated by a quest for collateral. As discussed in Chapter 7, the banks were able to securitize much of their household debt portfolio and so create 'room' on their balance sheets for aggressive business lending. Even though banks were surprised by the deterioration of consumer loan portfolios they were some-what encouraged by the build-up of health in household balance sheets. More than two-thirds of this increase was attributable to surging stock market prices.

Economic strength continued into 1997 and there were signs that consumers had reached limits of capacity and debt burdens were indirectly causing more bankrupt-cies and delinquencies. Credit cards and auto loans were of particular concern but perhaps to be expected on the upswing of the cycle. Credit standards were tightened on consumer loans but relaxed more on home loans. Corporate profits rose a strong 14 per cent during the year but not enough to quench the appetite for external financing for the investment boom. Business loans were easily accessible and yields between investment grade bonds and US treasuries was very narrow – in part due to the capital flight from Asia. Issuing corporate bonds in this favourable climate stimulated investment.

In the first half of 1997 there was a rise in intermediate and long-term interest rates in response to excess demand above the economy's current output potential as witnessed by the strongest surge in imports in many years. Sales of houses also surged, with sales of single-family housing construction topping one million units for the sixth consecutive year. Multi-family units recorded an increase for the fourth consecutive year. As a result of such heat, the Fed funds rate was raised from 5.25 to 5.5 per cent in March. In fact, the FOMC (Federal Open Market Committee) adopted and declared directives that were biased towards tightening. However, the economy began to slow mid-year and inflation was subdued. As the fallout of the Asian crisis became evident in terms of lower export growth and the flood of funds into US secu-rities so did treasury yields fall late in 1997. As a result of this flight to quality, uncertainty surrounding the Asian crisis and the more pessimistic outlook for growth in the United States, the Fed reverted to a 'symmetrical' stance on monetary policy.

In 1995, the gains in stock prices occurred against a backdrop of declining bond rates. In 1996 stock prices continued to strengthen despite the rise in bond rates. The rise in the Dow in 1996 was 26 per cent and 22.5 per cent in 1997 (Figure 2.21). Annual gains for the S&P and the NASDAQ were around 27 per cent (Figures 2.22 and 2.23). This situation was 'classical' in that on the expected upswing of the busi-ness cycle both corporate profits and interest rates rose together. Earnings–price ratio fell to exceptionally low levels. The dividend-price ratio for the S&P fell from 2.19 per cent in 1995 to 1.77 per cent in 1996.

Forward-looking investors saw economic calm ahead and so a lower possibility of disruption to balanced growth. Hence, risk premiums fell and there was an air of expectation that corporate profitability would rise next year and so a pre-emptive strike into stocks was appropriate. In fact, stock analysts were persistent in forecasting an up-beat market.

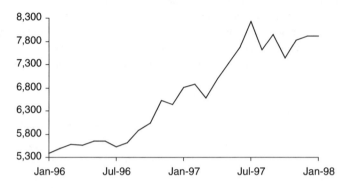

Figure 2.21 Level of Dow (1996–7).

Source: NYSE.

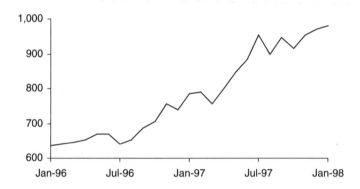

Figure 2.22 Level of S&P (1996–7).

Source: NYSE.

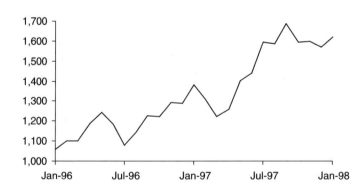

Figure 2.23 Level of NASDAQ (1996–7).

Source: NYSE.

In spite of all this calm Chairman Greenspan issued a 'heightened alert' in his Humphrey Hawkins testimony in early 1997. He remained 'vigilant' for signs of inflationary imbalances that might 'undermine' the economic expansion in place. There may be a need for a pre-emptive action against inflation similar to that of 1994 as the risk of waiting to act may be greater than the risk of waiting for further economic data and clarity of the economic picture. However, Greenspan made it known that the forces of an inflationary build-up are different from cycle to cycle and so a great degree of caution is required before making judgment. Some of his concerns about the potential build-up were old ones. For example, the high rate of capacity utilization, wage earners trading off lower wage increases for job security and the unsustainable acceleration of spending. Rising stock prices bestowed wealth effects on consumers and this combined with 'full employment' and wage growth increased consumer spending. Consumers were optimistic about the future and so released purse strings. Consumer debt levels reached historical highs and credit card delinquencies escalated since 1995. These are reasons why Greenspan questioned the imbalance between spending and capacity as being very dangerous.

On the matter of financial market health Greenspan (1996) offered words of caution as 'participants in financial markets seem to believe that in the current benign environment the FOMC will succeed indefinitely'. Overconfidence is the very reason that financial market participants will not foresee a sharp downturn – and so endure painful capital losses for such misperception. Waves of optimism and financial excesses feed upon themselves causing asset price bubbles and in turn generate complacency. Such economic tranquility is partly driven by historically low-risk premiums for business borrowers. External credit was easily accessible and contributed to the expansion of investment. Greenspan's view of stock valuations in 1996 was 'high' but probably justified on expectations of stronger future earnings. Nevertheless, the low interest rate environment may have created a false sense of security with regard to risk assessment. Stock valuations appeared to be 'fine-tuned' and so very sensitive to changes in expectations. The Fed had some right in expressing concern over widespread low-risk premiums and the markets possible overestimation of returns. However, the Fed did not 'pass judgment' on stock valuations but Greenspan did remind the senate committee in February 1996 of his view by his statement of 'irrational exuberance'.

The plausibility of the US economy reaching a 'new era' or a 'new paradigm' is unlikely in the Fed's view – as history is littered with claims of new eras. In Greenspan's view, the Fed should be ever watchful for even *slow* build-ups in imbalances with the economy, after all that is the central banker's occupational responsibility.

The Fed anticipated that real GDP growth be in 2 to 2.5 per cent range and inflation rest between 2.25 and 2.5 per cent in 1998. However, the Fed continued to *underestimate* the pace of the economic expansion as real GDP actually grew by 4 per cent.

Correction and a major recovery: 1998–2000

Growth continued in the United States at around 4 per cent in 1998 and unemployment fell slightly to 4.25 per cent, its lowest level in twenty-nine years. Despite such a rapid economic cruise speed, the inflation rate remained low, driven in part by soft commodity prices, a decrease in the price of oil and relatively weaker import prices. Businesses continued to invest heavily in innovative and cutting-edge technologies, providing a strong stimulus to labour productivity growth. No doubt global competition and accelerating technological advance were driving waves of innovative investment. Perhaps Schumpeter's creative destruction was a real force of the boom of the 1990s. Even though the Fed expressed concern over labour market tightness, the restraining influence of productivity growth on inflation was acknowledged. Unit labour costs rose by 2.4 per cent but the ECI remained steady at around a 3.5 per cent increase. However, overseas threats, as witnessed by the spillover shocks from the Asian crisis of late 1997 dampened the demand for US exports. There was a great deal of uncertainty over the damage done by the Asian crisis – to their own economies and to US export potential. Greenspan was in a bind as domestic pressures called for a monetary tightening and yet the world in general desired lower interest rates to maintain economic momentum. Higher interest rates and a higher US dollar would hurt Asia even more as they grappled with debt repayment in US dollars.

The Fed anticipated that real GDP would rise between 3 per cent and 3.25 per cent in 1999 and inflation to stay in the 2 to 2.5 per cent range. However, the Fed continued to underestimate the pick-up in growth as a 4 per cent growth rate was achieved.

The growth juggernaut continued into 1999 as the real GDP rose by 4 per cent. Unemployment sat on thirty-year lows of 4 per cent. The crucial wedge in promoting growth without inflation has been accelerating productivity growth causing unit labour costs to actually fall in the second half of this year. Both the general ECI and the ECI for services fell from 3.5 per cent and 3.8 per cent in 1998 to 3.2 per cent and 3.3 per cent in 1999. In response to cost containment and price stability, security analysts continued to revise their forecasts of company earnings upward (a proxy for productivity growth) and so a rationale for further support for stock prices. Wealth effects from buoyant stock prices continued to support consumer spending. The Fed estimates that 3–4 cents in every additional dollar of stock market wealth found its way into additional consumer purchases. Moreover, the boom in capital spending indirectly contributed to an extra 1 per cent growth in domestic purchases since 1995. Given the boom in consumer and investment spending and the growing imbalance between supply and demand, how then did this tightness and pressure on capacity not spillover into inflation? The above productivity wedge explanation remains but also by 'new hires', the net inflow of foreign workers and reliance on foreign imports. These were the safety valves of a booming US economy but not permanent 'solutions' to high speeds of economic growth.

As can be seen from Figure 2.24, the Dow collapsed under the weight of the Asian crisis, falling from 9,000 to a low of around 7,500 points in August 1998. It then recovered in grand style in 1999 to reach a high of 11,497 points. However, the rebound in the NASDAQ was staggering – from a low of 1,500 to a high of around 4,650 points (Figure 2.25). In 2000, the NASDAQ rose above 5,000 points.

A real bubble?

Greenspan issues several words of warning concerning the *dynamics* of the 1990s boom. Accelerating productivity creates greater increases in aggregate demand than

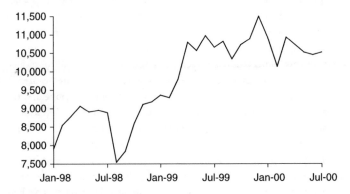

Figure 2.24 Level of Dow (1998–July 2000).

Source: NYSE.

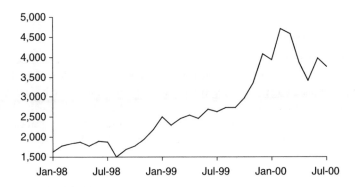

Figure 2.25 Level of NASDAQ (1998–July 2000).

Source: NYSE.

in aggregate supply – in the short term. A prolonged imbalance of demand over supply is not sustainable. Such an increase in competitive excellence generates an increase in the expectations of future productivity improvements, which further stimulates investment and excites further rises in equity prices – much to the benefit of household wealth. Greater spending power is the result in the short term and so tests current capacity. This dynamic-expectation-fuelled boom possesses a life of its own. It represents consumption brought forward based on *future* income growth. The opposite argument is that of Say's Law – supply creates its own demand. Hence, rising productivity increases the current supply of goods and is matched by increasing demand. The caveat of this standard view is that the optimism launched by *accelerating* productivity may cause worker–consumer complacency by increasing debt levels now and pay out of future, but uncertain, income growth. The challenge for the Fed is to dampen expectations of future productivity growth on the basis that this current boom in productivity is maybe transient. On the other hand, if rapid productivity growth is *believed* to be permanent then investors may over-anticipate and over-extrapolate the expansion of EPS and become exuberant. This happened in the late 1990s as investors expected a continued rapid acceleration in productivity growth would transform into rapid accelerating EPS growth. The transformation was far more modest than what investors anticipated.

Appreciating this *'forward-looking productivity paradigm'* is crucial to understanding why aggregate demand outstripped aggregate supply in the United States. It is also crucial to understand why the formulation of an appropriate monetary policy has become more complex. There is the double-headed dragon (twin inflations) to face. Conventional weaponry is not potent enough when seeking to slay this type of dragon. Moreover, the origin of wealth effects may not lie in a productivity surge but in a profitability and a speculative capital gain surge that has caused households to 'bring consumption forward'. What may appear to be a 'virtuous circle' now may be shunted into reverse and renamed a 'vicious circle' at a later date. The Fed should be more concerned with unanticipated asset price deflation that sends shock waves through goods and labour markets. That is, if these wealth effects are more liquidity than productivity driven.

Financial perspectives

To the extent that labour and product markets were tight there should be signs in the finance market of increasing demand for funds. Indeed there was. Such an increase in demand for funds caused corporate bond rates to move up but not enough to offset the *expected* rise in corporate profitability. This gap between the Marginal Productivity of Capital (MPK) and the cost of capital further stimulated stock prices – or known as the Marginal Efficiency of Investment (MEI). While stock prices rise faster than household incomes there is an ongoing potency for increased wealth to spur consumer spending and exacerbate the imbalance between spending and productive capacity. According to the Fed, spending cannot continue to outstrip income growth. Even though interest rates were on the rise in the previous two years, interest-rate-sensitive expenditures did not decline, indicating that real interest rates had not yet reached high enough levels to restore the demand–supply imbalance.

There are additional threats to inflationary pressure in the United States besides tight labour markets and wealth effects. For much of the 1990s, foreign economies remained weak and the US dollar strong but in 2000–3 the opposite transpired and so inflationary pressure may eventuate from this external source. Higher commodity prices in 2003 will add to US domestic costs of production.

As the year 2000 unfolded, the Fed observed the slowdown in consumer spending and sought to explain such a phenomenon in several ways. First, the massive hike in the price of oil was beginning to place some fear in the minds of consumers and entrepreneurs as being more of a lasting than a transient nature. Second, equity prices displayed volatility, as the NASDAQ experienced an early year plunge and then a rebound. Households received less impetus and confidence from this source of wealth. Third, debt burdens were on the rise partly as a result of rising interest rates and partly as a result of surging sales of new homes. Accumulating debt is far easier than the 'acid test' of repayment. Fourth, the stocks of consumer durables have risen since 1997. Perhaps more importantly, such stocks within households have risen sharply – approaching saturation levels. Upside resistance must be reached at some point, as household needs for such goods are temporarily satiated. After all, the US car makers attracted customers with 'no interest' deals and other sweeteners. Hence, the excess demand pressure on productive capacity – in the late 1990s – was showing signs of abating as the economy cooled off naturally.

Conclusion

The 1990s are full of anomalies and paradoxes. When evaluating the conduct and effectiveness of monetary policy over the last decade the Fed would receive a favourable report. That is, the Fed has responded to most shocks of the economic system in a capable and timely manner with the possible exception of its 'pre-emptive strike' against inflation in 1994. The inflation rate of goods and services was far below that of previous decades and the Fed must take some of the credit for this achievement. Paradoxes abound in the 1990s. For example, despite labour market tightness, inflation did not rise as a consequence and the normal pattern of a 'mature recovery' also did not reveal itself. The Fed repeatedly *underestimated* the strength of the real economy and the high economic cruise speed it achieved without igniting inflation – a phenomena at loggerheads with past relationships. There is no doubt that subdued rises in unit costs, driven by a trend rise in productivity growth, has underpinned a major expansion of the real economy. By-products result, as Greenspan points out, there is a lethal by-product in that expected productivity rises feed into consumption *now* via wealth effects.

However, as will be discussed in Chapter 7, economists such as Canterbery, Galbraith, Krugman and Thurow are critical of the Fed's lack of finesse in generating more output growth when inflation is so benign. Unemployment could have been pressured lower without inflationary cost and so the Fed caused America to forego billions of dollars of lost output – and workers lost wages. These economists argue that the Fed has clung to old paradigms that are no longer as useful in policy formulation.

There is another serious criticism, that is, the escalation of asset price inflation. This has been a thorn in the flesh of the Fed as such inflation roared beyond expectation and divorced itself from the normal rate of goods price inflation. The problem is that forces driving the real economy are somewhat *divorced* from those driving the financial economy and this has posed a dilemma for the conduct of monetary policy. We examine further in Chapter 5 the reasons why US stock prices have been driven by rises in productivity and expectations of further rises in productivity – however, this is only a partial explanation of the explosion. This chapter revealed traces of evidence that monetary liquidity, abundant credit and speculation fuelled the asset price bubble of the 1990s.

In the meantime, we digress into a survey of valuation techniques and strategies? Why? Because we wish to explain why stock valuations departed from fundamentals, why 'market efficiency' failed and why 'rational investors' did not appear rational. This is the task of Chapter 3.

3 Valuation methods and investment strategies

Introduction

In Chapter 1 we examined the big picture of the performance of US stocks over the long run. We concentrated on the 1990s bull run in Chapter 2. In this chapter, we examine 'how' and 'why' investors choose to invest in stocks over other types of assets – in essence, a critique of portfolio choice. As we noted in the previous chapter, safely storing wealth over a long time frame poses a whole array of hazards to the investor – inflation, tax regimes, interest rate changes and of course the ebb and sway of the business cycle. The desire for persistent higher rates of return involves higher than normal levels of risk – unavoidable risk. This chapter distinguishes between systematic risk (due to the business cycle) and unsystematic risk (due to insufficient diversification within the basket). It is the former type that wreaks havoc with valuations and rate of return performance. In the boom era perhaps some US investors believed that business cycles were no longer a threat or even had been repealed? Perceptions of systematic risk had definitely tilted towards unbounded optimism. At face value, traditional valuation techniques were thrown out the window. Warnings signals of overvaluation were ignored. This chapter outlines some fairly standard methods of valuing stocks and seeks to explain why there was a wayward departure from economic fundamentals and even the prime fundamental driving stock values – the expected rate of return or expected earnings per share.

Market efficiency would dictate that the market always gets it right. All current knowledge is embodied in stock prices and investors, by and large, fully value stocks correctly. But they did not get it right, as is evidenced by the crash of 2000–3. There are persistent warnings throughout this chapter that no amount of 'scientific method' will ensure success in reaching 'correct' stock valuations. After all, *estimates* of corporate profits are bound to fluctuate and so cause a revaluation of current stock prices. The stock market is also prone to 'news' and unforeseen shocks that knock it about, not to mention frenzied sell-offs triggered by rumour and fear. As discussed in Chapter 1, investor behaviour had changed albeit in response to changing incentives. As Schiller (2000) rightly claims – fundamentals alone cannot explain the wild volatility in US stock prices in the 1990s. As this book emphasizes – it was not just behavioural forces alone that could explain the excessive explosion in stock prices but abundant liquidity and rational investors responding to biased incentives. These 'other' forces – beyond real fundamentals – will be examined in Chapter 4.

Portfolio choice

Before we embark on what criteria to employ when evaluating stocks there is a need to appreciate the whole gambit of portfolio choice. Why not invest in gold, oil, land, housing, bonds, money market funds or even cash or some mix thereof? The answer rests in one's propensity to take on risk and whether the general nature of the portfolio strategy is to be offensive or defensive in nature. It is a generally accepted investment principle that diversification diminishes risk and so the investor should hold a mixture of all or most of the above choices – including stocks. The investor should also consider her age – as less risky assets should be held for each passing year.

There is some evidence to suggest that investor protection and safety stems from the fact that not all of these asset classes move in the same direction – or more precisely are not *perfectly* correlated. For example, gold tends to rise during times of crisis or war. It also benefits from US dollar weakness together with general disillusionment from holding other currencies. There is also a tendency for gold to rise when stocks fall. Given that there is an inverse relationship between stocks and gold there exists an opportunity to be exploited by cautious/defensive investors. Hence, gold can be used as a hedge not just against inflation but also against volatility in stock prices and a weak US dollar.

The price of oil also surges during times of uncertainty and crisis and tends to be relatively low during peaceful times or recession. Economic activity in the OECD is the major demand-side factor driving oil prices – periods of high-income growth and activity supports higher oil prices. Obviously, OPEC seeks to control the supply-side of the equation via quotas and so indirectly maintains a floor on oil prices. Hence, oil prices are to some degree pro-cyclical but still contain a major wildcard element of insurance against uncertainty – and so stock market volatility. Gold and oil prices were highly correlated up until 1980 when higher oil prices spelt higher inflation and more uncertainty. After 1980, the correlation weakened somewhat – possibly because inflation subsided and corporations readjusted their energy input mix.

Most times in US financial history bond prices move in tandem with stock prices. In 'normal' times, bond prices move up and down with stock prices because they are seen as *complementary* assets – as low bond yields (or high bond prices) provide a *green light* for investors to purchase stocks. Lower interest rates stimulate stocks through a variety of channels. This complementary relationship is normally held when *inflation* is persistent. Stocks provide a hedge against inflation over the long run and so there is a pull effect out of the bond market – as corporate profits and GDP growth rise – with interest rates following soon thereafter. Bond prices then come under pressure and so there is more potential for capital gain in the stock market – on the upswing of the business cycle – as expected profit growth overshadows interest rate rises.

However, there have been times when bonds and stocks have not been complementary assets – but rather *substitutes*. Higher bond prices have been a reflection of investors fleeing out of stocks and into the safety of the bond market – driving down bond yields in the process. In this case, the green light flashes the other way – bonds are attractive because stocks lose their gloss in the short run – for fear of capital losses. Thus bonds and stocks are seen as substitutes, as investor fear of capital losses causes this 'switching behaviour' into the safer asset. Such switching often occurs during periods of *deflation* – or the fear of it. The expectation is that *real* interest rates will rise with falling prices. Therefore, investors can exploit this inverse relationship to their advantage – providing they know which way the green light flashes. The key reason why there is some danger in 'switching', however, is that investing in bonds is not always 'safe' as both capital gains and losses can occur – just as in stocks. If the motive for the switch is based on the well-founded expectation that interest rates will fall then there is almost a self-fulfilling prophesy that capital gains will result from the holding of bonds. It is precisely for this reason that investors carefully listen to Fed policy speeches for any hint of a change in the stance or bias of monetary policy. This is why deflationary fears can spur a bond rally as there is ample room for real interest rates to fall and so for capital gains on bonds to be quite stellar.

Investing in real estate has not always been boring – there have been times when capital appreciation from real estate has been very impressive indeed. Although capital appreciation from stocks has often occurred swiftly throughout the twentieth century – the returns from real estate, albeit accumulating more slowly – have not been far behind. In fact, two recent periods of significant capital appreciation stand out – the post 1987 stock market crash 1988–91 and 2000–3. Real estate is both a complement and a substitute for stocks – as are bonds. These two eras just mentioned were periods when real estate was seen as a *substitute* for stocks. Investors fearing a capital loss bailed out of the stock market and into housing, extensions and rental properties in the hope of achieving a capital gain – or at least avoiding a capital loss from holding stocks. However, the 1996–9 era was one of a *complementary* nature – real estate and stocks prices rose together – although not in perfect unison.

Last but not least is cash. The old saying of 'Cash is King' holds credibility in the post-bubble era. Deposits in US banks attract positive interest rates and often provide a safe haven while stocks are crashing due to uncertainty, poor earnings reports or governance standards. Cash, attracting an interest rate, offers a quality that all other classes of assets do not possess – there is no risk of capital loss. Well, almost none. There is always a risk that a US bank may go bankrupt and the deposit insurance may not cover all of the capital loss. In recent US financial history, holding funds in money market accounts has been a safe but inglorious investment. There was a sound rationale for doing so – the fear of a capital loss as stocks sunk in value, the Iraqi war, September 11 and woeful governance standards that caused investors to value what they had – and so preserve their capital. Perhaps the fear of deflation pushed investors into money market accounts?

Professional fund managers employ asset allocation models when deciding how much to invest in stocks, bonds, fixed interest securities and cash. The composition of this mix depends on how much risk they are prepared to undertake. Traditional models place 50–60 per cent in stocks, 20–30 per cent in government securities and the rest in cash. This is not to say that fund managers will not allocate towards gold or oil – that can be done by selecting specific stocks. Even real estate can be held via Real Estate Investment Trusts (REITS) – funds that a wide portfolio of real estate – across states and types. There is the growingly popular investment strategy of buying the S&P index – complete diversification – and so minimize 'avoidable risk'. However, the buying and buying of index funds (including REITS) can be overdone and so self-defeating because every fund manager's manual instructs him to do so. What appears to be a 'pattern' to be exploited can soon be exhausted and capital losses occur on mass.

The *timing* of asset re-allocation is crucial and large institutional funds make much of their returns from switching and not so much from selecting individual stocks or even classes of stocks. That is, it has been crucial to know when to be in stocks and when to exit. On average, the US stock market falls one year in three – there are times to drastically reduce stock holdings. For example, when there is a clear risk and a belief that stocks will fall – as in March 2002 – these professional managers re-weighted their portfolios towards bonds, fixed interest securities and cash. Confident fund managers seized the opportunity to short-sell the stock indices which they did in March–July 2002 and were correct in their prediction.

Diversification and risk

A centerpiece of portfolio theory is that of the Capital Asset Pricing Model (CAPM) which delineates two types of risk. One type of risk, namely unsystematic risk can be diversified away – at least in theory. It is not wise to select one stock or a small few that are highly correlated or buy stocks in a similar industry that may fall on hard times together. Rather than place 'all eggs in one basket' it pays to diversify across a variety of stocks and industries and so minimize this kind of risk. The degree of unsystematic risk declines as the number of stocks in the portfolio rises – to a point. In fact, holding a sample of twenty stocks has been shown to be a reasonable level of diversification. The extreme example is to hold all stocks in the S&P – or just the index. This 'defensive' principle in finance is based on the premise that some stocks in the portfolio are negatively correlated to others – or at least are not *perfectly* correlated. If this were not the case, and all stocks were positively correlated, then this defensive principle of diversification would not be effective. Financial experts refer to the variance (volatility) of stock returns as being good indicators of risk. Highly volatile stock returns reveal the stocks that are the most risky to hold. Financial analysts measure betas to establish which stocks swing further than the market and which stocks swing less. A stock with a beta of 1.5 will rise 15 per cent when the market rises by 10 per cent. Likewise, a stock with a beta of 0.5 will fall by 5 per cent when the market falls by 10 per cent. Hence, if the investor is risk-averse, then a portfolio of stocks with a significant percentage of low beta stocks would be warranted. Conversely, the risk-loving investor believing that a general market rise is imminent may prefer to hold the vast majority of high beta stocks in her portfolio. The investor can diversify away a significant portion of unsystematic risk if she so chooses. Nevertheless, we are confronted with the inescapable 'law' that risk and reward are correlated. Those investors that seek high rewards remain under threat that a high degree of risk accompanies such a quest.

Conversely, there is systematic risk that cannot be diversified away and so is unavoidable. Stock prices and corporate profits tend to reflect the health in the real economy and vice versa. The rise and fall of the business cycle creates risks for the stock investor as most stocks rise and fall together. Forces beyond the control of the

Table 3.1 The risk-return trade-off

Asset class	Compound annual return	Simple average annual return	Std. dev. of return
Small cap stocks	12.5	17.3	33.2
Large cap stocks	10.7	12.7	20.2
Corporate bonds	5.8	6.1	8.6
US treasury bonds	5.3	5.7	9.4
US T-Bills	3.8	3.9	3.2

Source: Ibbotson and Sinquefield (2002).

investor can wreak havoc with an investor's portfolio even if it is neatly diversified. There are times when investors should bail out of stocks completely and push into alternative assets – such as money market accounts, bonds, real estate, gold and oil. As examined in section titled 'Portfolio choice' the returns from these assets are not highly correlated and so there are gains (and safety) from diversification. It is the fact that they are negatively correlated that provides the rationale for diversification across a broad range of assets. This was particularly wise between 2000 and 2002 as gold, oil, bonds and real estate were significant substitutes for stocks.

A recent study by Ibbotson and Sinquefield (2002) highlights the *risk-return trade-off* amongst a few traditional asset classes from 1925–2001. These assets were a sample of small cap stocks, 500 large cap stocks, twenty-year corporate bonds, twenty-year government bonds and three-month US T-Bills. We would expect that government bills and bonds be the safest with the lowest return. Conversely we would expect stocks to yield higher returns but with higher risk (standard deviation). This is what Table 3.1 reveals. Small cap stock had higher returns than large cap stocks, than did corporate bonds, than did twenty-year government bonds, than did three-month T-Bills but risk levels also followed in the same order. Hence, the potency of the theoretical risk-return trade-off is validated by this evidence.

How well do fund managers switch from asset class to asset class in practice? Profit maximization and optimization principles are fine in theory but do the professionals win persistently? Switching involves market timing and so represents a formidable challenge to any investor. Malkiel (1999) provides some very damning evidence against the skill of fund managers to move in and out of cash at the right time. In fact, he claims they have basically done the opposite – they beefed up their cash positions (as a per cent of total portfolio) on stock market lows and held light cash positions on market highs. He states

> Peaks in mutual funds positions coincided with market troughs during 1970, 1974, 1982 and the end of 1987 after the great stock market crash. Another peak in cash positions occurred in late 1990, just before the market rallied in 1991, and in 1994, just before the greatest three year rise in stock prices in market history. Conversely, the allocation to cash of mutual fund managers was almost invariably at a low during peak periods in the market. For example, the cash position in early July 1998, just before the market declined. Clearly, the ability of mutual fund managers to time the market has been egregiously poor.

Hence, we have sound theory that instructs us to switch between asset classes and so be defensive at various times and yet the track record – by the professionals – to implement such theory has been lamentable. Why? Because, in the real world, anticipating turning points in stock markets involves a high degree of luck and not just skill. Placing heavy bets against the flow of the market involves courage – and disgrace if one gets it wrong. Although no one possesses a crystal ball concerning future trends the professional fund managers should respect the laws of probability – and so mean reversion!

News: economic or financial?

There are times when even healthy macroeconomic variables are not enough to lift stock prices. In other words, the reporting of robust GDP growth, high productivity growth, a low inflation rate, a fall in jobless claims, a contracting current account deficit or a fall in the unemployment rate may fail to stimulate stock prices in the short run. One reason for the non-response is that the real economy takes time to accumulate momentum and so investors await a series of good news before they believe in a sustained rally. After all, one sunny day does not constitute a summer. There is also the view that the data is 'old' and stale in that it represents past movements in the real economy. We are only looking in the rear vision mirror. Perhaps more importantly, the 'good news' is overshadowed by a whole host of uncertainties in the corporate sector. In essence, the experience of the US corporate sector in 2002–3 may be seen as a 'profitless', 'jobless' and even a 'jobloss' recovery. Hence, signs of an economic pick-up may not translate into rising corporate profits in the near term. Investors seek tangible evidence of a pick-up in financial and not just economic fundamentals before they re-allocate a greater a percentage of their portfolio towards stocks. Good news on the economy may give heart to investors for a time but it is quarterly profit reporting seasons that justify stocks values or otherwise. Financial variables are closely monitored – such as debt levels, financial leverage, profit margins, cost-cutting efficiency, sales volumes, price discounting and expected profit growth – to name a few. Healthy current profits, and even better, sustained future profits far outweigh any general good macroeconomic news. Corporate profits are the bottom line for determining stock prices and not general GDP growth as such.

Market efficiency

Information is the lifeblood of any market. The stock market is no exception – provide investors with information and they will arrive at a market or equilibrium price. The market efficiency hypothesis claims that the stock market is fully valued by investors based on all current, known information. Given that many millions of people buy and sell stocks, the price outcomes in this competitive market environment should closely reflect equilibrium values – at all times. Rational investors are quick to seek out opportunities – that is to buy stocks that are undervalued and sell stocks that are overvalued – the end result being a fully valued market. It is the 'fact' that investors are rational and 'fully aware' that drives the prediction of the market efficiency hypothesis – that price and value are but the same. Therefore, there can be no mis-pricing or deviations from known fundamentals. Past stock prices contain no predictive power over future stock prices as all that is to be known is already known. The only force that changes stock values is that of 'news' – new information will cause investors to revise their expectations of a company's net worth and profit prospects. And because news is not predictable there can be no way of predicting future stock prices.

A derivation of the market efficiency hypothesis is the notion that the stock market follows a random walk. The market only responds to news that itself is random. Therefore, the market will gyrate around breaking news, absorb it and fully value stocks once again – almost simultaneously. Given that news is random, it then follows that predicting future stock prices is well nigh impossible according to this model and so it is not rational (or profitable) for an investor to select stocks or attempt to pick winners. Many books have been written explaining why the 'buy and hold' strategy is more effective than other strategies and the foundation of this strategy rests on these doctrines of market efficiency and random walk. However, the weakness of this theory is that investors are 'all-knowing' or the market behaves 'as if' they do – via professionals that monitor markets more closely than the amateurs. But more importantly 'all that is to be known' right now is no where enough when dealing with the vagaries of the future and the plethora of shocks that hit individual stocks and the market in general. Investors can all be 'wrong' together based on their complete but finite current knowledge and so price can deviate from true value. Perhaps mass psychology kicks in to cause further deviation during times of gross uncertainty.

So then how do we explain excess volatility of stock prices in the 1990s? The answer is that we cannot if we are relying on the theory of market efficiency alone. If the market is always 'right' in valuing stocks then why did the Dow fall by 509 points in one day in October 1987 or by 512 points in late August 1998? In both precipitous falls there was an absence of clear 'news'. Sentiment and risk perception obviously changed but not in response to one item of news. If markets were that 'efficient' then why do we witness such dramatic collapses from time to time? The very thrust of this book attends to this question of beyond fundamentals or 'real factors' – that there are important behavioural considerations and shifting psychologies that cause the bulky mass of investors to panic. Crowds move in an irrational manner once spooked and fear becomes the dominating driving force.

Investing over the life cycle

Even though the justifications for a 'buy and hold' strategy are strong, there is one problem that confronts all human beings – it is called death. When the good Lord calls we have to go; whether our bags are packed or not. Most of us have a view to retirement, to enjoy to the full our last days on earth in a degree of comfort, free from financial worry and to indulge in a few luxuries like travel (to that glorious land Down Under) from time to time. Therefore, we save (invest) during our working lives and dis-save in retirement. In early years, we may employ aggressive investment portfolios that contain high growth stocks (with high betas) while in later years favour a more defensive portfolio that contains 'old economy' stocks (with low betas).

There should also be greater bias in the portfolio towards bonds and money market positions. The reason is obvious – we can afford to take on more risk when we are young, knowing that volatile stocks will one day rebound and that the stock market rises on average two years out of every three. However, the closer we come to retirement age, the more conservative our investment strategy should become. Even so, for those investors that hold stocks for many years in the belief that they can liquidate at 'high prices' around their retirement year are taking a risk. Recessions tend to last between one and three years and so the value of one's portfolio could be 20–30 per cent down from its recent highs causing retirement plans to be modified or deferred. The moral of the story here is that retirement funds stored in the stock market are not 'on tap' and so should not be viewed as being defacto bank deposits. Values of our stock holdings are no small factor in determining what our retirement year will be.

The fundamentals approach

There is no simple method for valuing stocks. Given that stock prices incorporate 'the future' into current valuations and given that there is a diversity of opinion as to such values then it follows that there are trading ranges for stocks – not point estimates. Nevertheless, a popular valuation method for old economy stocks is that of discounting the expected future dividend stream of a company's earnings. However, most investors accept that companies require capital to expand and so accept that not all earnings are paid out in dividends – and so investors would rather monitor price–earnings ratio. High price–earnings ratio reflect either high stock prices or low earnings per share or both. Earnings growth must pick up eventually in order to justify the faith of eager investors pushing up stock prices to historic highs. A solid discounted earnings flow is a signal to buy stocks and so bid up price–earnings ratio. Conversely, a low discounted earnings flow sends a sell signal to investors. Hence, stock valuations are positively related to estimated, discounted future earnings flows. In this world, the key fundamental – rate of return – drives the stock price. Investors can then compare such an expected rate of return – the EPS – with the known ten-year bond yield. As discussed earlier, investors may pay a premium for holdings stocks over bonds but this gap should be 1 or 2 per cent and not 6 per cent as for much of the last century. Hence, the growth rate in the EPS will be the main driving force of changes in stock prices – over the long run – with interest rates a close second.

So what *P/E* ratios are regarded as being excessive? At the market peak in 2000 the high was 44. Nowhere in the twentieth century did *P/E* ratios attain this height. For example, *P/E* ratios reached 25 in 1901, 32 in 1929 and 24 in 1966 – all previous market highs. Siegal (2002) points to a long-term historical average of around 14.5 but concedes that the economic environment has changed (low inflation, low interest rates, lower taxes etc.) that justifies higher *P/E* ratios in the low twenties. If one looks at the inverse of *P/E* ratios – the rate of return from stocks – the long-term average is 7.4 per cent. Given that stock returns were 13.4 per cent annually from 1982–99 – almost double the long-term average, we would expect both *P/E* ratios and stock returns to revert to their long-term averages – eventually – unless a 'new' trend line for the modern era can be justified.

Another valuation method is that of book value, whereby the value of all tangible assets are totaled up against the value of all stocks outstanding. A price–book ratio (*P/B*) of one is often considered to be cheap. A rather old but valuable study by Fama and French (1992) reveals that buying stocks with relatively book values – a high book equity/market equity ratio (*BE/ME*) – yield higher returns soon after than those stocks with low *BE/ME* ratios. This study also revealed that stocks with high *P/E* ratios were destined to underperform in the near term while low *P/E* ratio stocks outperformed the rest. In essence, this strategy is based on buying undervalued stocks and selling overvalued stocks. Although this study did not differentiate between 'growth' and 'value' stocks there is the inherent recommendation to buy well-recognized stocks that have been beaten up by the market. Another corollary also follows – that big 'over-sized' companies cannot maintain a rapid growth in EPS forever or even the medium term. Big companies with rapid earnings growth for several years eventually fall back to the pack and so the wise investor should stay clear of the market heavyweights at their peak. Besides, fund managers jump on the success bandwagon and overpay for large cap companies – through market weighting and buying indices as well.

So what are fair values to pay for stocks? Much depends on the level of the benchmark risk-free rate. A risk-free rate of 3.5 per cent could justify *P/E* ratios up to 28.6 or a risk-free rate of 5 per cent could suppress *P/E* ratios down to 20 – these are reasonable corridors to expect for 2004–5. Another constraint on valuations is the growth rate of GDP – the long-run growth rate of EPS is roughly constrained by the growth rate of the economy. It is not reasonable to expect EPS to grow at 10 per cent indefinitely if GDP growth is only 3.5 per cent over a long period of a time. If so, corporate profits as a percentage of GDP would explode indefinitely and reduce the labour share of GDP to zero. Hence, long-run EPS growth is constrained by long-run GDP growth – at around 3.5 per cent. However, GDP growth in 1990s was often above 4 per cent and capital did displace some of labour's share and so EPS growth of 4.6 per cent in the 1990s can be understood in this light. As discussed earlier, lower capital gains, corporate and income taxes also bias upward the profit share of national income.

A more specific driver of EPS growth is productivity growth and the suppression of unit costs – any surge from here can push valuations higher. Hence, the low interest rate structure in place now – of 4.25 per cent on the ten-year bond – supports a *P/E* ratio of around 23.5. Any expected acceleration in EPS growth will only push valuations above the 23.5 mark. The US stock markets probably will not receive any further interest rate support from here – as interest rates will most likely rise in 2004. What the market will be looking for is an *acceleration* in EPS growth and not just constant growth – in order to justify valuations in the high twenties. If the United States is indeed on the upswing of the business cycle then the expectation of an acceleration in future profit growth is warranted – into 2004–5. Thereafter, the acceleration in EPS growth will be a formidable task especially in a rising interest rate environment.

The contrarian strategy

Most investors believe, at least to some degree, that the stock market is somewhat predictable and future direction can be anticipated with enough information and technical skill. If this overconfident self-belief did not exist then investors would all be in cash, bonds or just the S&P index. The very fact that they try and pick winners, even within a moderate number of stocks in their basket, illustrates their belief that they can beat the market. Such investors point to the rise and fall of the business cycle and stock prices that roughly move in tandem. If GDP growth collapses then so will EPS and so the wise investor seeks to minimize stock holdings (defensive plays) and maximize bond holdings – particularly as the Fed enters the next easing phase of the interest rate cycle. Hence, bond prices roar and attract capital away from stocks. Although timing the cycle is possible it is not as easy as it looks. The professional investor must be capable of absorbing and interpreting many economic indicators. Some investors boasted of being out of stocks before the 1987 crash but failed to re-enter before it roared once again. The same with the 1998 correction (The Asian Crisis) – some investors timed the exit well but lacked the courage to buy again on the upswing. Alas, there is the recent stock collapse before the Iraqi war where investors shunned stocks only to be left out in the cold as the market rallied from around 7,400 points on the Dow in early 2003 to above 10,200 points by the end of 2003. It is here that a contrarian strategy can be half effective – getting out of a falling market is easy whereas getting back into a rising market is far more difficult – from a psychological point of view. Buying on lows and selling on highs is a great theoretical strategy but very difficult to implement in practice because no two business cycles are the same – or interest rate or stock cycles. If such patterns were stationary, or possessed an anchor, then corridor trading would be easy – alas, the corridors are broken and deviations from trend can be drastic and terrifying especially for those that trade calls and puts.

Nevertheless, the profits from perfect timing are enormous based on the volatility of stocks during any one year.

It is the technical analysts or chartists that claim to have a box of tools that enables them to predict the near term course of stock prices. Their investment strategy is based on the notion that future stock price movements are some functions of past price movements. In other words, there is some cumulative movement, pattern or trend that can be picked up by their analysis and so exploited. Some of their technical jargon includes triple tops and bottoms, heads and shoulders, wedges and the like. Not only is their objective to exploit trends (i.e. the trend is your friend) but also predict major shifts in market direction or turning points. For chartists to be successful, patterns have to persist and be transferable throughout time. That is, past stock price patterns can predict future price patterns and so can be profitably exploited.

As discussed earlier, there is a substantial degree of evidence that a contrarian strategy of buying in gloom (when either *P/E* or *P/B* values are low) has been effective in US financial history. Likewise, buying stocks with low *P/E* ratios and high-dividend yields – again amidst gloom and when they are out of favour on the street – has been more successful than not. This strategy is akin to the 'dogs of the Dow' theory – buy the dogs when they are down and out. They eventually rebound – given time. So why do professional investors, in the main, not employ such a contrarian strategy? The probable reason is that it takes a heap of courage for a professional money manager to buy floundering stocks that other investors do not respect. If such stocks do not recover and other fund managers have not been 'contrarians' then the risk-loving 'odd man out' looks both silly and incompetent. The other reason is that sinking funds into 'sleeping stocks' contains an opportunity cost in the short term. Timing is therefore optimal as a long wait imposes costs.

An interesting article by Barsky and De Long (1990) sheds some light on the rise of price–earnings ratio over time. 'Old timers' often claimed that a multiple of ten was the appropriate benchmark whereas Graham in the 1960s claimed that such ratios should around 15 to 16. Making an assumption that soaring stock prices would always be mean reverting was a courageous assumption – particularly in the 1960s and 1990s. Barsky and Delong (1990) make the observation that the volatility of earnings growth has diminished over the twentieth century and so laid the foundation for higher price–earnings ratio. In their view, major turning points in stock price history have been driven by a change in the investor's estimation of the discounted future dividend stream. That is, investors have readjusted their perception of risk related to the key fundamental driving stocks – the rate of return. Greenspan has expressed some sympathy to this view – that risk perception diminished in the calm waters of price stability in the 1990s.

Much has been said of the old economy versus the new economy stocks and of value versus growth stocks. Such dichotomies can explain why growth stocks with high *expected* earnings have generated exceptionally high *P/E* ratios while value stocks with solid *existing* earnings have generated low *P/E* ratios. What is ironical about this dichotomy is that the new economy stocks have low or non-existent current dividends while the old economy stocks actually do pay dividends. Investors paid absurd *P/E* ratios for the 'high-flyers' because they either believed that future discounted stream of EPS was on a high elevated plateau and sustainable well into the future or that the company's EPS growth would accelerate in the coming years or both. The key here is 'well into the future' – a growth in the EPS well above the market average. We know from hindsight that steep, optimistic projections of EPS were grossly unfounded and the stock prices responded far too sensitively to wild forecasts. True, a tripling of expected EPS growth could triple a stock price and so send it from $33 to $100 but this additional $67 of 'value' is based only on a projection – and often an extrapolation of a brief past trend. No wonder it was a matter of up the staircase and down the elevator for many investors. Historically, no US company has been worthy of a *P/E* ratio of 50 over a long time period let alone a 100!

We know that US stock prices have fluctuated wildly over the years and the opportunity of buying on lows and selling on highs appears both real and rewarding. There have been times when stock price fluctuations have remained within reasonable corridors or bands. Heavy trading and the wise use of options can be effective providing such corridors 'hold' or are not broken. Alas, historical corridors or deviations are broken and it is here that contrarian investors get severely burnt. In essence, the investor can be fooled by 'false opportunities'.

For example, high *P/E* ratios can, at times, beguile the unsuspecting investor. In 1932 *P/E* ratios appeared quite high and so were not transmitting clear buy signals. The irony of this particular year, was that from hindsight, it was a great year to buy stocks. Any investor with a 20–30 year retirement horizon would have enjoyed great returns from this base year even though *P/E* ratios did not appear attractive. The signal was 'false' because earnings fell even faster than stock prices. Blindly follow-ing *P/E* ratios alone can be deceptive – perhaps the absolute price of stocks – relative to their recent peaks would have provided a more reliable buy signal in 1932? Another example is in 1958 when EPS dropped below the ten-year bond yield and yet a three bear market ensued. And more recently there were wild excesses in stock prices in 1987, 1997, 1999 and again in 2003. Investors were excessively fearful in 1987 and 2003 and over exuberant in 1997 and 1999 – the old historic corridors were well and truly broken. With enough patience and enough capital, investors can wait out in the wings and exploit wild fluctuations in stock prices. However, there are penalties from mistiming and not being patient enough – not being in eight straight day rallies can be soul-destroying. Moreover, there is a severe penalty of seeking to time the market – not so much a matter of 'when' to get out but 'when' to get back in. Contrarians often lack courage in rejoining the market flow. Perhaps satisfying behaviour is the key here – to sell on near-highs and be content in leaving 5 per cent for someone else. What is also a lesson from history is that waiting for a 10 per cent correction in stock prices may not be rewarding enough but waiting for a 25 per cent correction has great probability of success. That is, make your trading corridor a wide one!

Serial correlation and mean reversion

If we are to take sides in the debate between the buy and hold strategy (one-way street) and the contrarian strategy (two-way street) we must peruse some of the evidence. The acid test of whether past stock prices can predict future stock prices rests with empirical evidence relating to serial correlation. If today's stock prices are positively related to yesterday's stock prices then a buy and hold strategy or a chartist's strategy of 'follow that trend' maybe warranted. Historical data suggests that there is case to be made for individual stock prices to move in a series – moving up consistently for a few weeks and conversely down for a few weeks. In other words, there are persistent runs or cycles that support the existence of positive serial corre-lation in the very short run. For example, Lo and MacKinlay (1988) found that stock returns over short time periods revealed positive serial correlation up until the 1980s. Other researchers such as Fama and French (1988) claimed that serial correlation was positive in the short run (less than two years) but negatively correlated in the long run (more than two years). Hence, investors could buy low and sell high – using a con-trarian strategy given such negative serial correlation and stock return reversals in the long run. In the short run, however, the strategy of buy and hitch a ride is supported by positive serial correlation and of the visible rallies that last weeks if not months. Both of these strategies coincide with the fact that US stocks rise – on average – two years out of every three and so it pays to be invested in the 'short run'.

Some argue that *P/E* ratios contain predictive power over future stock prices and returns. Schiller (2000) provides some evidence that high *P/E* ratios 'now' predict poorer returns in the future. Returns are often far lower, if not negative – in the next five-year period. The opposite is also true – companies that endure low *P/E* ratios 'now' are more likely to rally and generate higher returns in the future. Poterba and Summers (1988) also find evidence that stocks – winners or high flyers – for say a five-year period often do poorly in the next five-year period. Stocks that are current 'losers' often outperform in the next five-year period.

What this section highlights is the *rationale for contrarianism* – past evidence reveals the highs and lows of *P/E* and *P/B* ratios – that reflect some kind of corridor or limit boundaries that can be exploited by traders. There are grounds for buying puts on the historical highs and buying calls on historical lows. However, historical boundaries or signposts are sometimes broken – as in the late 1990s. A contrarian strategy was not effective – just ask those hedge funds that got it wrong. We can be reasonably confident that stock indices, *P/E* ratios and *P/B* ratios do mean revert – to their long-run average – eventually. But we cannot be sure when – even within a five-year time frame. From hindsight we know that trend chasers and a 'buy and hold' strategy were effective in the boom era – highly leveraged 'hold' positions paid off.

A central issue raised in this book is whether US stock returns will revert to the old long-run trend line (the old mean) of 14.5 or whether they will revert to some new trend line of around 22. The justification of such a new trend line and a 'new era' is based on the *biases* outlined in Chapter 1. Lower taxes have raised after tax EPS and inflation still remains low – keeping the risk-free interest rate down around 4.25 per cent. Massive monetary liquidity injections by the Fed have also raised expectations that EPS growth can expand at a rapid clip. Hence, *P/E* ratios may be justified around the low twenties and therefore will not have to mean revert back to 14.5. First, because the 'new era' of high productivity growth with low inflation can be sustained for a considerable amount of time. Second, the biases are also likely to remain for the medium term – especially the 'low' taxation on capital accumulation. Third, the *floor* for *P/E* ratios relates to the historically low ten-year bond rate whereas the *ceiling* depends on how much EPS can grow year by year. Hence, *P/E* ratios well above 22 may be justified providing EPS growth is positive and preferably accelerating. However, limits to EPS growth are constrained by both productivity and GDP growth. There are no free lunches in the long run.

Investment strategies

As was conveyed to the reader in Chapter 1 the strategy of 'buy and hold' was successful for much of the last century. Riding the bad times and waiting for the booms proved to be a great method to accumulate wealth over a fairly long time period, say 10–25 years. No matter how badly stocks got beaten up since 1945 there was always a strong rebound and to higher levels that resulted in a substantial portfolio gain. To the extent that 'timing the market' is well nigh impossible and that higher productivity growth underpins the long-term upward trend in stock prices it follows to sit in stocks and go for the ride. Just hold the S&P index and wait.

However, most investors are not willing to sit and wait as they witness wild fluctuations in their asset portfolios and so feel pressured to be proactive. As discussed earlier there are historical benchmarks that are useful signposts to switch between stocks and/or switch between asset classes. If there are signposts of predictability, then what kind of investment strategies would the technical analyst recommend? For example, the resistance and support theory that basically rests on the regularity of the Dow exhibiting a cyclical movement within medium term boundaries. There is a kind of trading range that may persist for weeks or even months. Technicians look for resistance near recent highs and support around areas of recent lows. The advice of 'sell high and buy low' appears obvious. Profits can be made from trading within the range. However, if these floors and ceilings are broken the chartist may see a permanent breakout and pursue the visible trend. This requires a substantial courage of course – to forsake the old trading range that is more inline with existing, known fundamentals.

There is an old saying – 'where there is smoke there is fire' and so it is with the stock market in that *volumes* provide a hint of what excess demand exists for a particular stock. Rising prices supported by higher than normal volumes provides confidence that prices will continue to rise in the near term. However, buying a smokey stock is indeed an act of faith – relying on the interest of others and bandwagon effects to draw more investors into the stock. This is really a hot-stock strategy that attracts speculators to take on abnormal risk on the hunch that there is imminent news that will justify a rapid run-up in price. The wise investor (speculator) should then sell on such good news and perhaps move onto the next hot stock craze.

Another strategy from the charts is to buy stocks that are rising and sell those that are falling or non-performing. In other words, don't leave your money in tight range stocks sitting in the doldrums, get out of them and employ your capital in stocks that are in 'favour'. Again, this strategy is dependent on the extension of an existing trend and the notion that optimistic sentiment or investor perception will change only slowly. Stocks that are 'in favour' are often those backed up by a theme or situation, such as oil and gold stocks during the Iraqi crisis.

Some analysts watch closely a 200-day moving average of a stock and buy it when it rises above that average and sell it when it drops below that average. This strategy is based on the notion of revealed buyer support and intensity. A wait and see approach turns into action when the bands are broken. The inherent problem of acting on a 200-day moving average is that the great faith placed in *past prices* and the unwillingness to anticipate future prices changes. That is, why wait until a large price movement has already taken place?

The put-to-call ratio is often used as an indicator of future direction. A heavily biased ratio towards puts indicates that the market is most likely currently oversold and will have to be purchased back in the near term when such puts are due to expire. Watching the markets move oscillate 3 or 4 days before options expire is testimony enough to the highly leveraged options market pushing the primary market around quite wildly at times. Triple witching Friday in the United States is notorious for its breathtaking turnarounds within the same session. The puts may be squeezed due to favourable news or other professional traders seeking to exploit put holders that have left it late to square up the books. Hence, the unwary investor can be caught napping late in the month when markets are volatile in no short measure due to options expiry. The experienced investors wait for the bargains that are temporarily out of line with fundamentals.

The overall health of the stock market is often gauged by the advance–decline line. That is, the number of advancers over decliners in recent sessions. A false impression of stock market performance is when say the Dow rises by 60 points in one session, yielding only 7 advancers but 23 decliners. This is an absence of market breadth and conveys the impression some situation stocks performed exceptionally well while the broader market actually declined. A more bullish indicator is when there are broad market rises – a strong advance–decline line – preferably on heavy volume. Traders prefer the confidence of a broad market rally backed by heavy volumes – a sign of conviction that the market is in a sustained rally and not just temporarily knocked up by superficial news.

The above discussion seeks to canvass a whole range of signposts or trading patterns that can be profitably exploited. We examined signals such as recent floors and ceilings, volumes, advance–decline lines, put-to-call ratios, 200-day moving averages and popular themes. There are some other 'patterns' that are worth mentioning. For example, Friday is normally a 'sell day' as investors are reluctant to hold stocks over the weekend. Some major disaster may occur similar to September 11 and so Monday would bring forth a mad scramble to get out of stocks. This pattern has been evident for much of the period since September 11. This phenomenon is particularly relevant to European stock markets – investors should get out of stocks on late Thursday.

Another pattern that is often discussed on CNBC is the January effect. In recent years there has been a significant January rally in US stock prices. Some analysts point to the end of year tax effects as investors dump poor performing stocks in the last few days of December in order to claim capital losses. After the dumping is over investors reinvest in the market and buy what they consider to be bargains. Perhaps this is herd behaviour at its best and is self-fulfilling as all investors are aware of and seek to exploit the 'January effect'?

What is important to note with any observable 'pattern' is that it will eventually defeat itself. Smart investors will exploit it to the limit and profit from it for a while until there is no more opportunity left. It is here that the powerful can destroy the 'pattern' by preying on the unsuspecting amateur or follower. For example, May is normally a bad month for stocks but not in 2003! Likewise, October is also meant to be a 'sell month' but not in 2003!

Financial fragility

As flagged earlier, the fundamental basis of valuing stocks may not be as scientific or precise as many stockbrokers would lead you to believe. Even if information is plentiful and the company is open and transparent there is no clear or certain way of evaluating *future* income streams as these streams only *estimates*. Furthermore, if information and detail is not plentiful, but rather opaque and shrouded in caveats, then the valuation task becomes much more difficult. The estimated value of an individual stock boils down to a wide range guess.

It was Keynes who coined the term 'animal spirits' in relation to investors being spooked by uncertainty and fear of the unknown. In his view they were prone to large and sudden shifts in sentiment and risk perception. Fear is also cumulative in that what may start out as a few investors panicking and selling off in the face of sharp price falls only snowballed other investors into panicking and accentuating the frenzied sell-off. Such a panic and evaporation of company market capitalization may not have been triggered by any material change in the company's financial fortune but rather by rumour and fear of further capital losses.

Expectations, trading and timing

The sheer volume of trade in stocks, commodities and foreign exchange cannot be justified by investors seeking long-run rates of return but rather traders that turnover large parcels of stock in order to acquire a capital gain.

Trading for short-term profit is about as hard as any profession gets. It involves timing the market, that is, choosing the best part of the fluctuating cycle to purchase in and best part to sell into. True profit maximization requires buying on the low and selling on the high – whether it be daily, monthly or yearly. This art requires a huge amount of knowledge concerning the company or industry or even better – luck. Yes, the rewards are high for getting it right but so too are the losses for getting it wrong! This is why a diversified portfolio is a good insurance policy – even buying the S&P index – to a point.

The importance of expectations is crucial in understanding why stock prices move around so wildly. Anyone watching the markets on TV channels like CNBC or Bloomberg will witness the wild oscillations in stock prices. No one believes that economic and sometimes not even financial fundamentals, can explain such fluctuations within such a short time frame – hours or just a couple of days. The media often report drastic collapses in the market capitalization of a blue chip company prompting ordinary shareholders to ask where has this wealth gone? The answer is that it has left their designated storage vault and evaporated like mist throughout the economy.

What is crucial to note here is that the stock market is forward-looking and 'values' the future as though companies and dividend flows will last forever. They do not. Some fail permanently, others fail to deliver results that meet expectation and so those stocks are normally ravaged for not meeting preset standards of expectation. Investors will often sit in wait of profit announcements by selling off the stock before the announcement date – effectively 'factoring in' any potential bad news. If the news turns out to be bad, then their insurance policy strategy has paid off as they got out well before others on the day. If the news turns out to be neutral or moderately bad then these same investors will most likely buy the stock as a large amount of uncertainty has been eliminated. Such an upward movement in price on such news only bothers the amateur not the professional investor as the absolute worst was factored into the stock. If the news is good then investors will roar back into the stock knowing that their worst fears did not materialize.

What can go haywire with this technique of anticipating future EPS over a long time frame, say ten years, is the fact that the current stock price is very sensitive to the variability of future EPS growth rates. Rumour and over-optimism can cause the existing stock price to double based on a wide range and unsubstantiated guess of discounted future profit flows. This extreme sensitivity generates wild swings in capital gains and losses.

The same principle of 'factoring in' applies to a stock that is likely to produce good news, as investors will drive up the price to the valuation limit in the hope of selling into a large volume of buy orders on the day of the announcement. In essence, this strategy is one of buying on rumour and selling on fact. The upshot of all this is that an unwary investor not listen to the stockbroker's line 'yes, but the fundamentals are right'. Buying and selling on expectations 'news' is not for the faint-hearted as it requires both cunning and intimate knowledge of the stock concerned. The other reason for caution is that full-time professional investors pit themselves against the part-time amateurs and normally win of course with their superior experience and depth of purse.

Why is timing the purchase and sale of stocks so difficult in practice? There are two very important reasons. First, the long-run trend line of productivity growth is upward sloping. It also follows that corporate profit growth is underpinned by such productivity surges. In essence, improved prosperity and ever-accumulating wealth places upward pressure on stock prices as investors seek to store their money and acquire a capital gain or at least a dividend payout. An investor that attempts to 'time the market' faces an uphill battle against a formidable positive bias of rising stock indices over time. This partly explains why the strategy of 'buy on dips' has been advocated by Wall Street for so long. Second, it is also true that US markets rise, on average, two years out of every three. Such rises may not be solely attributable to productivity growth but sheer wealth accumulation achieved through world domination, a favourable tax environment and low inflation. There is also the safe haven status of holding US assets as the world believes in the longevity of the United States as a nation and the reliability of payment. By storing funds in the US bond market the United States enjoys the luxury of consumption and being the world's finest innovator. The claim here is that being in stocks contains the advantage of the profits in bull years far outweighing losses from the bear years.

There are risks in trying to pick the peaks and troughs of the business cycle – that of selling too early and buying too late. Sizable profits can be foregone from mistiming. There are often seven- to ten-day spurts in stock indices that dictate levels for the rest of the year. Hence, the big action can take place without notice and with lightning speed – and so *the* big profit opportunity is long gone. This is why those that proclaim the 'buy and hold' strategy as being optimal as you will be in stocks when the lift-off occurs – not to be there is to miss out.

Conclusion

Perhaps this chapter is a little disappointing for the would-be-millionaire investor. The small investor not only has to beat fellow investors but also more knowledgeable CEOs, company staff, professional traders and stockbrokers not to mention random events such as war or a September 11 attack. There is also the threat of recession and slow reactions from the Fed in terms of interest rate reductions. Even then, if the investor makes a profit there is the Inland Revenue Service to be greeted. To find and exploit a trading/investing strategy that works persistently throughout time is very difficult indeed. Any discrepancies in market value to price will soon be exploited or arbitraged away. Any 'known' trading pattern can also be exploited for a time until all opportunity is extinguished by fellow investors.

There is ample evidence of the potential for a market timer to exploit the wild swings in stock prices and so profit enormously. However, to achieve even a minor slice of these potential gains is very difficult in practice. There maybe times when abject fear pushes wise investors out of the stock market before it crashes but there are also many times when exits were false alarms and the investor foregoes substantial profit. Hence, the 'buy and hold strategy' has proved effective over time as unrealized losses do not hurt as much whereas realized profits after years of patience are sweet. Perhaps the compromise is to sell on twelve-month highs and to buy on dips? But note what was stated earlier – waiting for a 10 per cent deviation or 'correction' may not be enough – as market volatility over the last decade has been greater than this.

We have surveyed several traditional valuation techniques and trading strategies that have revealed how investors 'got it wrong' during the bubble era. Such staggering valuations were not the outcome of employing techniques based on any realistic assessment of future earnings. Moreover, bond yields were attractive and investors did not switch until 2000 and even later. Despite the fact that chartists displayed ceilings that were being broken and new territory being reached investors were content on following the trend. We may conclude that scientific and traditional valuation techniques could not explain much of the bubble explosion. There were obviously biases at work within the macroeconomy, law and Corporate America that overstretched valuations. Human psychology also played a role. More importantly, financial and monetary factors interacted with crowd psychology to ignite the stock explosion. The next chapter continues the search for driving forces 'beyond the fundamentals' for explanations of the 1990s bubble.

4 The bubble era

How rational?

Introduction

This chapter seeks to explain why deviations from 'traditional' valuation methods and investment strategies employed in the 1990s generated an unsustainable rise in US stock prices – above and beyond justified by pure fundamentals. As discussed in Chapter 1, there were broad macroeconomic and geopolitical forces at work. At the corporate level, there were several biases that overstretched valuations. Stock markets are notoriously 'noisy' and prone to wild fluctuations, as they concern themselves with *future* asset prices and income flows. Given such uncertainty about the future, there is much room for oscillation between investor optimism and pessimism. Even though asset prices are driven by economic and financial fundamentals in the long run, they do deviate from such equilibrium values in the short run. History teaches us that what often starts out as being a 'real boom' transforms itself into a 'financial bubble'. Over-trading, speculation, trend chasing, changes in risk perception, crowd psychology and an over-dependence on borrowed money generate volatility in stock prices. Given the bias of many investors for short-run capital gain, rather dividend flow, there is a high degree of sensitivity to 'news' and more importantly the interpretation of that news. Hence, US stock prices moved in line with changes in investor sentiment and percep-tions of risk – a crowd psychology – that not to play was to miss out. Besides, there was money to be made irrespective of whether stock prices reflected fundamentals or not. This chapter examines the rationality debate – why it was rational for the *indi-vidual* to speculate in the short run but not *collectively* rational in the long run. It is also important to examine behavioural biases along with changing incentive structures.

Biases in the one-way street

We know that economic fundamentals cannot explain the majority of the US stock bubble. After all, real earnings per share doubled while real stock prices rose fivefold in the 1990s. We need to look further into behavioural, psychological and incentive forces in order to understand why valuations ballooned beyond historical trend lines. The following forces require examination:

- Mutual/pension funds
- Day trading/margin lending

- Tax biases
- Buy-backs/stock options
- Initial Public Offerings (IPOs)
- Buy/sell advice
- Risk perception
- Rebound ability
- Financial fragility/feedback loops
- Corporate profit massaging.

There is no doubt that the sheer growth, if not explosion, in the number of mutual funds in the United States has encouraged greater participation in the stock market. Advertising and TV finance channels have accentuated the push into stocks. Investors can monitor the performance of their portfolio by the minute as all the way around the nation the stock market averages appear on TVs with monotonous regularity. There is also the thrust, or should I say trust, factor that individuals place with their fund manager. A professional, who 'knows' the market and 'proper' valuations, is managing one's portfolio in a safe and yet aggressive manner. It appears that individuals want it both ways – a high rate of return by employing aggressive tactics – and yet rapid defense if things turn sour. Such individuals want active rather than passive managers that can outperform the market. There was a period in the mid-1990s when active managers favouring *growth* over *value* stocks did outperform the market and so received accolades from their clients. The timely purchase of small cap rather than large cap stocks often proved fruitful as well.

There is also no doubt that the popularity of mutual funds increased dramatically as people placed part of their 401k plans in such funds. As confidence and trust developed with fund managers so were future retirees more willing to place their non-401k funds with them as well. In fact, both mutual and pension fund managers gained from 401k legislation as they were seen as being key retirement vehicles. As defined benefit plans gave way for defined contribution plans so a whole new investment game unfolded. Government regulation pushed risk away from companies and towards employees. Workers were encouraged to allocate their tax-deferred nest eggs between stocks, bonds and money market accounts. They were pushed into being active with their retirement portfolios and not just passive – as in the defined benefit plan. Given the strategy bias towards active management and so risk – the new found choice really favours stocks, that may enjoy a huge run-up in value, versus bonds that most believe are more likely to be passive achievers. Such a choice and emotion is more akin to participating in lotto – take a chance on hitting the big time – even though there is disproportionate risk. So what happened to real estate? It seems odd that a portion of such a large pool of funds could not easily be diverted into real estate funds or indices. However, it should be noted that REITs did grow in popularity by the late 1990s.

As investors became more familiar with how the stock market worked, and how it boomed, so did overconfidence set in. Day trading flourished as investors decided to 'beat the market' via online trading. The objective of such investors was to get in and out of 'positions' in the same day. They wanted volatility in stock prices as profits could be seized by wild swings – even within minutes. Much faith was placed in charts and technical plays as predictable patterns were touted to exist. Alas, many of these investors were really speculators and amateurs at that. Authorities became concerned that the novice trader was not aware of the risks involved and so the NYSE raised the limits for the opening of a margin account from $2,000 to $25,000. This legislative change was aimed at reducing the dependency on borrowed money for such speculative trading.

Unfortunately, borrowing on the 'margin' is like a drug – it knows no bounds. This kind of leverage – even 50 per cent – is a powerful money-making tool on the way up. However, the sword of leverage cuts both ways – investors with a limited capital base can soon get caught in a down draught – and the dreaded margin calls begin. During the boom years, margin debt at online brokers surged. As would be expected with the growth of online trading – the percentage of margin debt to total consumer debt rose significantly throughout the 1990s. The lethal combination of day trading and margin lending caused many speculators to come to grief after market collapse of 2000. Outstanding margin lending peaked in 2000 and shrunk during the market collapse.

Investor behaviour appears quite rational in the light of America's tax incentive structure. For example, the bias of an incentive structure towards capital gains has been long embedded in the tax system. The capital gains tax was cut from 28 to 20 per cent in 1997 and 18 per cent in 2001 for assets held more than five years. Brokers were keen to advise their clients not to sell profitable stocks two and three years before this 1997 legislation was passed. Why not wait and take advantage of the tax cut? Moreover, other sellers were in a similar position and so buyers knew of this deferment strategy. What also needs to be remembered is that capital gains taxes are lower than income taxes anyway – particularly for the middle classes. Thus, there was a preference or a bias for gains to be locked into stock price rises than in dividend payouts. There also existed a bias to hold stocks in a rising market for a longer period than it otherwise would be and so time the payment of taxes. Corporations responded to this tax bias by favouring the retention of profits in order to strengthen future earnings flows and so stock prices. The by-product of this bias was a decline in the dividend–price ratio in the 1990s to around 1.5 per cent and collapse of the dividend–earnings ratio to an all time low of 32 per cent. However, this behaviour of investors to prefer unrealized capital gains – and so defer selling – further contributed to an escalation of stock prices. Any sudden fear could trigger a stampede to the exit gate – and into bonds. This occurred in 2001–2.

The above bias away from dividend payouts and towards capital appreciation was not only driven by tax considerations but by other forces as well. As stock options became a common inducement and reward for corporate executives so did buy-back schemes rise in response. Not only were accumulated profits used by US corporations to buy back their own stock – borrowing to fund buy-backs was also employed by some companies. Such a strategy delighted stockholders but delighted even more company executives that were privileged enough to hold stock options. Rising stock prices impacted disproportionately on stock options and many executives acquired 'windfall gains' of millions of dollars in remuneration. Corporate America had found a temporary money-making machine that possessed enormous power to push overvalued stocks even higher.

In the author's view, corporate sector self-interest had reached its limits, as the most singular goal of Corporate America was to maximize its own stock price – regardless of the cost. In fact, US corporations were net buyers of stock in the late 1990s – their own stock at that. Not only did corporations use accumulated profits to indulge in stock buy-back programs but they also borrowed – often at interest rates above their own profit rates – to meet this singular goal. Such a strategy produced dire long-term consequences. It was not a sustainable ploy to highly gear a balance sheet in order to artificially support a stock price. Buy-backs are somewhat legitimate and clever if prices paid are below fair value but a terrible waste of company funds if buy-back prices are above fair value. There are SEC rules that attempt to protect existing stockholders 'artificial' attempts by management to prop up its own stock price. For example, a corporation could not buy more than 25 per cent of average trading volume in its own stock compared to the previous month. It should be noted that buy-back rules were relaxed post September 11 as the SEC wanted to encourage the buying of stocks during this time of gross uncertainty. The message here is that the explosion in stock buy-backs is too highly correlated with the explosion in stock options to be passed off as a coincidence. In essence, there has been a transfer of stock-holder wealth to corporate executives of some magnitude. The SEC and other author-ities have expressed concern over the 'expensing' of stock options – as the ordinary investor is not fully aware of impact on bottom line profit figures and/or is aggrieved by the magnitude of the hidden expense.

As the popularity of holding stocks rose in the 1990s so did Corporate America seek to exploit this trend by the issuance of IPOs. Underwriters played a big role in pushing new issues together with molding a marketing strategy that would appeal to the public. It was important to price IPOs at a value that would cause it to be well bid if not oversubscribed. After all, the underwriter did not want to be left carrying the bulk of the stock. Public hunger was not only for new stocks but also for new *themes* that may turn out to be money-making machines. There was also a public per-ception that IPOs were underpriced and undervalued because of the underwriter's fear of clearing the issue. Historical evidence tells us that IPOs are great short-run winners and terrible long-run losers. On the first day of listing it is common for IPOs to trade 5–10 per cent above their official offering price. During the bubble, there were staggering early gains of anywhere up to 400 per cent in just a few days. No wonder investors indulged in a mad scramble to acquire these stocks! However, despite very quick gains, the evidence of performance over the long haul is very poor – most IPOs over the last twenty years have significantly underperformed equities by as much as 35 per cent (Cunningham 2002). This looks just like the manifestation of the greater fool theory – investors know they have to get off the roundabout sooner rather than later – and before others do.

Security analysts displayed their bias in an industry that basically wants the mar-ket to go up – most advice was 'buy' advice, if not 'hold' advice during the bubble. Security industry health, remuneration and commission based on 'performance' were all biased towards a rising market. Sell advice was few and far between, perhaps because CEOs did not take kindly to their company being isolated as a floundering company that investors were encouraged to dump. Security companies and their analysts would be deprived of news and information relating to a whole host of issues if they insisted on clinging to a sell recommendation. Fear created a bias towards buy or hold strategies even when the cold truth required sell advice. Another obvious conflict arose when securities firms sought to appease existing clients (some with outstanding loans) by painting a rosy picture of a company's business prospects in order to support their stock price. Research standards were compromised by the 'closeness' of sales and research divisions. The end result of such buy advice was to encourage investors to buy stocks – whether the fundamentals justified such a strategy or not.

Besides the biases mentioned earlier towards buying stocks was the notion that there was a game to be played and fortunes to be won. Small investors in particular play the game because they want to win big with modest funds and realize their dream of ultimate prosperity. Large institutional investors want to win big as well but for different reasons – they want to maximize their prestige as money handlers and money makers. Success begets more pension funds and more discretionary investment money. However, both groups can be spooked easily. There is a large literature on financial fragility and its emphasis on the herd behaviour of investors. Could it be that US investors indulged in a type of pyramid or chain letter game? That is, everyone knows that stocks are vastly overvalued but still play the game on the basis that there are bigger fools in the world. The early *insiders* benefit from first-mover advantage and sell to *outsiders* and they in turn sell to a new wave of outsiders. Profits accrue to the insiders so long as the new base of the pyramid gets larger (and more stupid) than the previous layer. What is the rationale for playing this game when there is a suspicion in the hearts of many investors that underlying fundamental values are 'soft'. Cost–benefit analysis applies here, in that the many years of speculative capital gains from turning over stocks may outweigh the sharp loss incurred in the end period. Or even better, the smart investor realizes capital gains and exits before the rest of the investor herd. This is the prime strategy of the professional speculator – true 'hit and run'. Alas, such strategies have much theoretical sex appeal but are more akin to the lights being out. Daylight can bring forth much horror, as speculators realize that an orderly exit is not possible without accepting large capital losses. Abrupt changes in investor sentiment or shock news cause panic to set in. Hence, the pyramid collapses in a heap when it becomes *known* that stock values are not justified by fundamentals. This lack of value is not a total shock to investors but the *timing* of the news may catch the professional speculator by surprise. Even in this pyramid game there is a degree of rationality – not to play is to miss out. That is exactly what happened in the 1990s – many investors were gripped by the greater fear of missing out than they did of standing by and watching their next door neighbour grow rich. New waves of investors joined the capital gain feast out of sheer envy. Judging by past stock market records, the lower layers of the pyramid have enjoyed success and have not been backward in coming forward when informing their neighbours of recent stock market conquests.

There is also the belief that bubbles feed on themselves and so gain a cumulative momentum. Schiller calls these 'feedback loops' whereby each *layer or wave* of stock price rise creates the impression in the minds of investors that there is an upward trend feeding upon itself. Human beings are creatures of habit and the past – they form expectations adaptively based on the recent past. Hence, recent trends can be willingly extrapolated and amplified to produce further price rises. There is also a well-known gambling technique that comes to the fore – that of playing with house money. A series of wins (profits) can cause investor arrogance and dare – excess risk-taking and doubling up – in the belief that it is 'house money' and not 'earned'. Human beings do tend to spend money willingly or reluctantly depending on its source – a gift, money from a will, lotto winnings or rapid stock market gains can be spent more freely from a psychological point of view.

This leads to a whole array of psychological factors that impinge on how an investor forms a strategy – or acts and reacts to waves of information. Cunningham (2002) points to many human biases and mental accounts that distort the investor's decision-making ability. There is an *availability bias* as employees use most of their 401k plans to buy their employer's stock in preference to other stocks. People use 'target' prices and 'reference points' for stock price levels and hang on doggedly to meet them. Conversely, realizing capital losses becomes an obstacle in the mind – hang on until the market recovers – despite what fundamentals say. This is a *commitment bias* – I have made a decision to buy Enron and I am right! I will see it through until stock price recovers to where I entered the market. Investors also indulge in *pattern seeking* when perhaps all that is visible is a series of unrelated random events. This is the old '*oasis in the desert bias*' whereby investors see what they want to see! There is also the comfort of *social proof* as investors feel convinced that the market is right and that following the herd is indeed wise – there is safety in numbers. Last but not least is the inability of investors to calculate or even recognize probabilities – this is why people buy lotto tickets even when they know that they will not win. They will pay a higher price for the chance of winning big and this is probably why small investors are willing to speculate in the stock market.

The rebound ability of US stocks is well canvassed by Siegal (2002). He points to the following 'stylized facts' for supporting the buy and hold strategy.

- Stock returns fell short of the risk-free real rate of return on the ten-year bond (3.5 per cent) – only 25 per cent of the time.
- Stocks broke the long-run trading corridor of one standard deviation from the mean – only 25 per cent of the time.
- Stocks have risen on average two years out of three in the last 100 years.
- The longest it has ever taken since 1945 to recover an original investment in stocks has been 3.5 years (1973–6).
- The 'buy on dips' strategy has been effective in main since 1946 and especially since 1982.

What the information stated earlier tells us is that investors favour stocks over most classes of assets for their proven rebound ability. The trend for stock values has been upward for over 150 years and buying on dips makes sense – ex post. Siegal (2002) also points to the high valuations of the nifty fifty stocks in 1972 – with *P/E* ratios of 41.9 – and 'proves' that even buying this basket at their peak would have yielded about the same return as the S&P index. Moreover, he mentions that some of this basket such as Pepsico, Coca Cola, Gillette, Anheuser-Busch, Pfizer, Eli Lilly, Merck and so on – performed better than the S&P index – even buying them at their 1972! How much more then from buying on dips in 1973–6 stock plunge? Even mistiming the buying of stocks was effective enough. Many US investors believed that buying stocks in the 1990s was 'correct' – given enough patience. Dollar cost averaging was a technique often touted as a complement to a buy on the dip strategy.

The corporate massaging of company profit statements was also beguiling to investors. There were a whole host of unsavoury collapses in corporate governance standards that came home to roost on Corporate America the 1990s. Not only did corporate greed manifest itself with the issue of IPOs and stock options but also with very poor accounting and disclosure standards. Corporate profits were bloated for many reasons and by many devices. It became a common trend for US companies to report higher pro forma earnings than GAAP (Generally Agreed Accounting Principles) earnings by leaving out certain expenses or claiming they were 'one-off' disturbances. It therefore followed that true EPS were a lot lower than what most companies had portrayed years earlier. Poor governance is the major focus of Chapter 6.

As previously stated, economic fundamentals alone could not explain the huge escalation in US stock prices in the 1990s. The growth in real EPS was only 4.6 per cent for this era – not far from real GDP growth of 4.4 per cent. We know that the EPS growth rate cannot exceed the real GDP growth rate for any length of time. So why did stock prices rise sixfold? These biases outlined above go a long way to explain why stock prices deviated so far from their long-run trend – excess exuberance, biased incentives, lower transaction costs and monetary liquidity.

Where were the arbitragers?

Economists argue that all markets possess self-correcting properties and the stock market is no exception. Just as flexibility in prices and wages restore equilibrium in goods and labour markets, so does arbitrage smooth deviations from fundamentals in stock markets. Significant deviations from economic fundamentals cause arbitragers to step in and sell-off 'overvalued' stocks and buy 'undervalued' stocks. Hence, the market is stabilized by profit-seeking arbitragers or 'rational speculators'. These arbitragers base their analysis on fundamentals. On the other side of the market there are trend chasers or liquidity traders. These traders are perhaps unkindly called 'irrational speculators' that ride and follow the market. Their style of analysis is based on the sentiment of their fellow investor and herd behaviour. They seek to anticipate how the market will react to *breaking news* not so much how it will react to fundamentals. This in effect is a game of second-guessing as to how one's fellow investor will react to news. After all, the major thrust of speculation is to make capital gains from other 'players' and this strategy is akin to Keynes perception as to how best to judge the winner of a beauty contest. That is, watch the reactions of *other judges* as the contestants come out on stage – and subjugate your own views as a judge.

It appears that the 1990s witnessed a plethora of traders that chased if not created the upward trend. This is known as momentum trading. Rising stock prices signal further rises to follow and so brokers warn – don't fight the tape. Even so, when warning signals flashed they were rationalized away by stockbrokers and fund managers. This time it is different! They claimed – we know that *P/E* ratios are high by historical standards but we are buying forward in anticipation of next year's dividends and maybe the year after as well! Buying 'growth' has its perils. Besides, the new economy had arrived and one didn't worry too much about *P/E* ratios anyway – it is the richness of the big picture that counted – so the story went. In this era, there was a great temptation for many 'investors' to become speculators – including the institutions. Perhaps they placed too much faith in the greater fool theory?

So how much of a problem are speculators for stock markets? If you believe Friedman (1953), there can be no destabilizing speculation. To the extent that speculators buy when prices are high and sell when they are low – they make losses and exit the market. This is the rationale discussed in Chapter 3 of selling overvalued stocks and buying undervalued stocks. Johnson (1976) also supports this view by stating that for every destabilizing speculator there is a stabilizing one and vice versa. In this classical world, speculators stabilize the market. However, as discussed more fully in the section 'Old benchmarks and turning points', there is a great temptation for potential arbitragers to wait, and even follow the market, until the outside limits of price fluctuation have been tested. Then they move. There is not enough evidence to suggest that stabilizing speculation was a major feature of US stock market history in the 1990s. Quite to the contrary, speculators were all too willing to ride on the bandwagon and not bet against a roaring market. Not to play was to miss out. Quite clearly then, the US stock bubble of the 1990s was a direct function of excessive speculation? Why? Because there were too many biases in the system – favouring stocks over bonds.

Old benchmarks and turning points

In Chapter 1 the topic of mean reversion was raised. Why did investors not believe in old benchmarks? That is, why did they not fear that *P/E* ratios would revert to their long-run trend of 14.5? Conversely, why did they not believe that total stock returns would mean revert to 7.4 per cent? After all, we know that *P/E* ratios were well above 30 for much of the 1990s? We also know that real stocks returns averaged 13.4 per cent p.a. from the market lows of 1982 to the 1999 highs. These figures were grossly above long-run trend values and yet investors ignored them. The magnitude of overvaluation was quite staggering. Even using the long average *P/E* benchmark of say 14.5 – and a boom in *P/E* ratio of 35 – US stock markets were 'overvalued' by a factor of 2.5.

It is the *Q* ratio that has strong historical qualities of mean reversion and estimates of *Q* during the boom years were as much as 2.5 that of its theoretical norm. Another benchmark employed to gauge the extent of stock market overvaluation is the Fed model. There were times when the yield on the ten-year bond was about twice that of the average EPS of the S&P. This reaffirms the view that US stock markets were grossly overvalued according to historical benchmarks. However, the magnitude of the overvaluation is debatable. It is more likely that incentive biases have pushed justifiable *P/E* ratios into the mid-twenties and so a stock price correction of 20 per cent is more plausible than one of 60 per cent.

Nevertheless, we can only surmise why it took so long for the US markets to self-correct. The near 40 per cent correction in the Dow from its 1999 peak to its 2003 low appears an overreaction – even from a theoretical perspective. Most of the explanations for excessive exuberance – overshooting on the way up – were explained in the earlier part of this chapter. The excessive pessimism – overshooting on the way down – can easily be explained by September 11, the Iraqi War and poor governance standards. Perhaps investors hold the middle ground between greed and fear in 2003?

Was it a speculative bubble?

The rise, rise and then fall of the NASDAQ can easily be labelled as a bubble. *P/E* ratios were never going to be sustained from their 1999 levels. The Dow and S&P indices were, from hindsight, for all intents and purposes a 'bubble' as *P/E* ratios had to return close to some long-run average. The stock market resembled a casino whereby there was ultra-fast money to be made in the pursuit of capital gain. Although there was underlying strength in the real economy (productivity growth) it nowhere near matched the escalation of stock prices. The financial economy had diverged from the real economy as it had done in 1929.

If investors buy stocks with the motive of receiving a dividend flow from a long-term held stock and so value that stock according to expected rates of return – then the stock market has a high probability of working efficiently. Asset prices are driven by a prime fundamental – the rate of return. However, another kind of efficiency is at work here – an efficient capital market allocates capital towards companies undertaking real capital formation and innovation. In this virtuous circle – a more efficient economy reinforces a more efficient stock market. However, stock values have to 'justify themselves' – after all, patient investor/consumers are forgoing current consumption in order to consume more later. Compensation is needed for that sacrifice. Just as importantly, there is the implicit belief that US companies are seeking out productive investment opportunities not recycling funds into high-risk casino-type ventures. Hence, patient investors seeking out *long-term* capital gains in a capital market are not likely to create a bubble in asset prices. Likewise, US companies delivering real returns in line with expectations reduce the possibility of a bubble developing. This is what did not happen. US companies did waste funds through mis-investment and over-investment and did not meet investor expectations of returns. However, US companies did not just fail to generate above normal returns they were the cause of their own failure by being net buyers of their own stock – pushing valuations to unsustainable levels.

However, if investors are obsessed with acquiring *short-term* capital gains with little regard for 'peanut' dividends (apologies to Jimmy Carter), the stock market will resemble a casino. Canterbery (2000b) holds no punches when referring to the casino mentality of US investors in the 1990s. If the investment horizon is long in the minds of US investors, then we would witness far lower turnover rates for both stocks and bonds. In other words, the 'buy and hold' strategy would prevail. However, high turnover rates in forex, bond, stock and derivative markets – above and beyond that justified by news of changing fundamentals – provides more than a subtle hint that a speculative philosophy pervaded US financial markets in the 1990s.

Although any strict definition of a speculative bubble is not easy to come by, there is the common bond of all bubbles – that of purchasing an asset for the express purpose of resale for a capital gain. The NASDAQ bubble was just that as speculators displayed little concern that their stocks did not pay dividends and *knowingly* would not for some years. Much of the justification for paying excessively wild *P/E* ratios rest in the belief that the profits of technology companies would grow exponentially, would accelerate or just reach such a high plateau that they would last indefinitely. Hence, the rosy future discount flow of earnings was factored back into today's current valuation. But the *P/E* ratios were nevertheless absurd. No US company can generate a 10 per cent growth rate in EPS indefinitely – high flyers always fall back to the norm of around 4.5 per cent (the GDP growth rate) – as the euphoria subsides.

Another telltale sign of a bubble is the opportunity value of the asset held. For example, during the Dutch tulip bubble, one tulip bulb bought three homes in Amsterdam in the 1620s (Thurow 1996b). Could anyone believe that these relative values made any sense whatsoever? On the issue of whether a bubble is in play or not, Greenspan (1997f) makes the comment 'But identifying a bubble in the process of inflating may be among the most formidable challenges confronting a central bank, pitting its own assessment of fundamentals against the combined judgment of millions of investors.' Hence, in his mind at least, there was an identification problem. Millions of investors could not be wrong – could they? Perhaps there is not safety in numbers, not even on the road to hell.

If Greenspan was alive and well in Holland in the 1620s, could he at some point, make an assessment that three houses per tulip, two houses per tulip or one house per tulip etc. ... would constitute a bubble? Or would he sit on the fence, making the same arguments that millions of rational investors have got it right and so why not let asset prices subside in the fullness of time? Of prime concern is the Fed's ability and courage (or lack thereof) to call a bubble a bubble. Of secondary concern is what action, if any, could have been taken to deflate that bubble. We shall discuss such issues more fully in Chapters 7 and 8.

The 'New' new economy

If US investors could take back the 1990s and start afresh they would not be hijacked by the propaganda concept that the new economy had arrived and the old economy was in the throws of senility. The prospects of new economy stocks roaring, capturing new ground in market share, generating super-profits and generally setting new highs in *P/E* ratios was the ethos of the day. It was argued by the stock-broking fraternity that a watershed period of new innovation had begun and the real growth stocks were in the new economy and just as importantly would most likely suffocate or dampen the growth prospects of old economy stocks. According to this paradigm, prudent investors should switch or at least heavily bias their portfolios towards new growth stocks that would disproportionately soak up the discretionary spending dollar. Thus the old debate of whether to invest in growth or value stocks was re-ignited. From hindsight, a bias towards growth stocks won the day between 1996 and 1999 and value stocks enjoyed a revival from 2000 onwards. Although it should be noted that high beta stocks performed better than low beta stocks in this bracket, in reality, the new economy never arrived or blossomed in the way stockbrokers had envisioned. Investor expectations were too high to begin with, were beguiled by the investment community along the way and were cursed by their own greed and gullibility when the 'growth party' ended. Perhaps Greenspan's faith in the depth of markets – 'millions of investors get it right' – was misplaced. In reality, millions of investors got it wrong as they believed too much in the power of the 'new economy' to deliver long-run super-normal profits. All companies can't be above average in the growth stakes.

The 1990s: a deviation from fundamentals

There are a combination of reasons why US stock prices did not reflect market fundamentals in the 1990s. Many of these reasons were canvassed in explanation of the bubble experience. The basic underlay of the 1990s escalation in stock prices rest with the new-found tranquility of low inflation and so low long-term real interest rates. Investor perception of risk subsided in response to such bond market tranquility – driven by the inflationary tiger falling into a coma and foreign investors from Japan and China feeling content to hold US bonds.

It is here that gullibility and expectations played an important role in arriving at a commercial view of what future rates of return would evolve. Sensitivity to 'news' is a direct function of the expected discounted future dividend stream flowing from the stock held. Such a dividend flow is not known with certainty but is surely shaken when breaking news alters perceptions of risk. In this world of uncertainty, changing expectations may affect asset prices as much as changes in fundamentals themselves. It would be false to assume that risk can be accurately assessed or even abolished by diversification. There is some degree of unavoidable risk in the real world that cannot be eradicated by portfolio diversification.

There is also a problem in relying on 'technical analysis' and sophisticated econometric models that rely heavily on past relationships and do little more than extrapolate the past (Barsky and De Long 1990). Historical trends are just that; historical and only may shed a dim light on current trends. To the extent that stock analysts are captive to past empirical regularities their ability to predict major turning points in stock prices is severely limited.

On a more human level, there is an optimism bias of investors towards rising stock prices and boom conditions than a belief in sharp losses and gloom. Most, but not all market participants, are biased towards good news, an upward spiraling market and profits. Fear of devastating losses is offset by the security of moving with the market and so millions of other investors. There is a feeling of safety in numbers, as the market 'must be right.'

It is not only trend chasing or moving with the market, the domain of individual investors but institutions as well. Chartists often look for ceilings and floors, if such barriers are broken then trigger responses are activated. Clearly then, such trading activity is *pro-cyclical* and adds to market volatility. Trading strategies of mutual funds, and index funds in particular, seek to profit from following the market trend – irrespective of what fundamentals may dictate. Such a repetitive, high turnover, hit and run strategy can be extremely profitable with the right touch and timing.

Short-run volatility may be based on knee-jerk reaction to news or herd behaviour caused by panic. If large trading institutions employ the same econometric models and forecasting techniques then there is self-fulfilling institutional trading behaviour that generates greater volatility in stock prices. Why should fund managers take a risk by not following the market – it is their reputation and job security on the line? Why be a contrarian investor that departs from the pack and suffer the humiliation of devastating losses when other professional investors have succeeded in unison? Fear and shame account for part of the herd-like behaviour that is observable in stock markets.

When do arbitragers not really act like arbitragers? They may wait until the outside boundaries of volatility are truly tested before they respond. In the meantime volatility continues. Even worse, arbitragers may join risk investors as they *move with* a volatile market and so accentuate 'the trend', as it is more wise and more profitable than attempting to fight a runaway market (Shleifer and Summers 1990). It matters not about the irrationality of a collapsing or soaring market but what does matter is to anticipate the mood and mind of such a market. Cumulative movement and a market frenzy feeding on itself should be treated with caution. It is the large trading institutions that have the power to move stock prices but often abide the rule – 'the trend is your friend'. Market professionals in periods of high volatility assess fellow investor sentiment as a priority rather than focus on fundamentals that may be obscured for a time. Such an approach to investing is akin to a game of second guessing one's fellow investor's next move, her strategy and her portfolio mix. Failure to ride a popular trend is to forgo profits amidst a market runaway.

It should also be noted that market professionals *desire* volatility in financial markets, as any movement in stock or bond prices spell potential profitability. If stock prices remained dead constant until the release of actual dividend results this so-called 'market' would be a very low volume, boring place that would attract nowhere the attention that it currently receives. It is the quest for short-run capital gains that dominates market play. However, arbitragers eventually perform their arbitrage function after the 'dust has settled', that is after wild swings have exhausted themselves, and profits now rest in taking stock prices back towards some equilibrium value – according to accepted market sentiment and medium term fundamentals.

If stock markets were rational, they would only respond to news concerning fundamentals and rates of return in particular. However, we observe significant changes in stock prices on days when there is no news concerning stocks in particular or the market in general. There is also discussion of the impact of weekend effects on stock prices. Hence, the trading paradigm that professional investors move on the basis of what other investors might do is relevant here.

Obviously changes in expectations of future dividends and stock prices, or investor sentiment, affects stocks prices now even if now new information becomes available. Hence, changes in risk perception are crucial for stock prices. It is likely that investors overreact to news in the short term and some investors revise their expectations after their 'mistake'.

At face value, *P/E* ratios of US stocks reached historic highs in the late 1990s. For example, the *P/E* ratio for the S&P reached a massive 44 in January 2000 (Figure 4.1). This surpassed the previous historic high reached in the 1929 bubble. Even the golden years of the 1960s only breached a multiple of 20. As mentioned earlier,

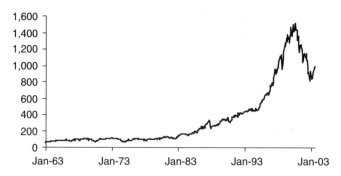

Figure 4.1 Level of S&P 500 (January 1963–July 2003).
Source: NYSE.

research by Schiller (2000) reveals that the price-earnings ratio is good predictor of future (ten year) returns. He claims that years with low price–earnings ratio have been followed by high returns whereas years with high price–earnings ratio have been followed by low or negative returns. We know that *P/E* ratios and returns fell in the 2000–2 era – a partial correction from great heights. Even recent dividends are just over 1 per cent and so rest far below the historical average of 4.7 per cent.

Wealth storage and far-sightedness

Experienced investors know that the current valuations of stocks have little to do with current earnings or the current economic environment, but rather with *future* earnings and the *future* health of the economy. Hence, the recent US stock boom is very much a function of far-sighted investors looking farther than at any time in recent financial history. It appears that risk premiums fell dramatically as far-sighted investors saw distant horizons far more clearly than ever before. In the 1970s, investors were uncertain, anxious and near-sighted as US finance markets were under an inflationary cloud – caused in part by the oil crisis and fear. In other words, investors feared opaque storm clouds on the horizon and required a higher risk pre-mium as compensation for news that might adversely affect earnings and therefore stock prices. High *P/E* ratios for high-tech stocks are but a reflection of investor opti-mism and far-sightedness. However, from hindsight such vision was not correct and stock valuations could not be justified – and so the shrinkage of the risk premium was also unfounded.

Such far-sightedness (or lack of fear) is based on several pertinent trends that have become evident since the 1980s. From an economic perspective – the inflation rate became *less volatile* and trended downward. As Taylor (1998) claims – *both* output and inflation in the United States became less volatile since the early 1980s. As a result, interest rates also trended downward. From a financial perspective, corporate earnings and dividends displayed less volatility. Hence, price-earnings ratios rose accordingly. Therefore, a whole host of reduced volatilities made the business or rate of return calculus that much easier. Such far-sightedness appears rational as it is built on a more mature, stable economy. Hall (2000) cites several reasons as to why the US economy is more stable – such as a larger service sector, greater Federal budget stability, better control of inventories, less external shocks and above all, a more sophisticated and reactive monetary policy. All of this adds up to a finer business calculus and explains why investors were content to ignore risk that they previously feared.

The bubble and its subsequent collapse proved the point that funds stored by investors were not safe and definitely not 'on call'. Some individual investors have already been caught losing their life savings as they were 'misled' into thinking that investing in stocks was just the same as investing in bonds or placing funds in a bank. Wild fluctuations and/or poorly selected individual stocks caused personal disaster in many cases. It should be of great concern to Greenspan that US fund managers, and individual investors alike, have treated the US stock markets like on-tap storage facilities – *or a giant financial warehouse.* Yes, there were tranquil times and the US financial markets had few natural predators as of 1999 and so an 'orderly exit' scenario from the markets was believed by most. From hindsight, this was only a half-truth. We can learn from the Asian crisis as it came like a thief in the night. An orderly exit is not a God-given guarantee, as Greenspan (1999c) often refers to abrupt changes or events that may spook the markets into a frenzied sell-off.

Greenspan's defense of the NASDAQ bubble

With some of the high-tech NASDAQ stocks displaying 'wild' *P/E* ratio of between 50 and 100 there is no wonder that some investors question the wisdom and sustainability of such ratios. Even though estimating future earnings streams for select high-tech stocks is fraught with danger – a 'shotgun strategy' may prove effective. That is, buy a sample bunch and hope that a few reach profitable maturity.

Therefore, there is a degree of investor rationality in holding a portfolio of high-tech stocks on the basis that even if only a few grow in maturity and realize super-profit expectations. However, from hindsight this strategy proved ineffective – ex post – as all NASDAQ stocks collapsed together with very few exceptions. Rationality is in the heart of the beholder *at the time.*

There is a very clever acknowledgment of this portfolio and lottery approach expounded by Greenspan (1997c).

> You would not get this kind of hype working if there weren't something fundamentally sound under it. The issue really gets to increasing evidence that a significant part of the distribution of goods and services in the country is going to move from conventional channels into some form of Internet system, whether it is real goods and services or a variety of other things. The size of the potential market is so huge that you have these pie in the sky types of potentials for a lot of different vehicles. And undoubtedly some of these small companies whose stock prices are going through the roof will succeed. They may well justify even higher prices. The vast majority, however, are almost certain to fail. That is the way the markets tend to work in this regard.

In other words he concedes that portfolio managers are justified in holding a wide range of high stocks in the hope that the profits from the winners offset the losses from the losers. Moreover, he stresses the fundamental transformation of the way business does business – substantially lowering unit costs in its path. Therefore, beneath 'the hype' there are sound fundamentals – at least for some companies.

Greenspan (1997c) goes on to reiterate this lottery principle.

> There is something else going on here though which is a fascinating thing to watch. It is, for want of a better term, the 'lottery principle.' What the lottery fund managers have known for centuries is that you can get somebody to pay for a one-in-a million shot more than the value of that chance. In other words, people pay more for a claim on some big payoff and that is where the profits from lotteries have always come from. And what that means is that when you are dealing with stocks, the possibilities of which are either going to be valued at zero or some huge number, you get a premium in stock prices, which is exactly the sort of price evaluation process that goes on in a lottery. So the more volatile the potential outlook – and indeed in most of these types of issues, that is precisely what is happening – you get a lottery premium in the stock.

It is not only professional portfolio fund managers that want to hit the big time but also individual investors that are lured by the possibility of large capital gains and are prepared to accept higher (known) risk in order to participate this game to glory.

Given that Warren Buffet has been an extremely successful investor it may be wise to listen to him on investors or players of the stock market game that wish to 'hit and run' knowing that losses must someday visit someone. Buffet and Cunningham (1997) states

> The line separating investment and speculation, which is never bright and clear, becomes blurred still further when most market participants have recently enjoyed triumphs. Nothing sedates rationality like large doses of effortless money. After a heady experience of that kind, normally sensible people drift into behavior akin to that of Cinderella at the ball. They know that overstaying the festivities – that is, continuing to speculate in companies that have gigantic valuations relative to cash they are likely to generate in the future – will eventually bring on pumpkins and mice. But they nevertheless hate to miss a single minute of what is one helluva party. Therefore, the giddy participants all plan to leave just seconds before midnight. There's a problem, though: They are dancing in a room in which the clocks have no hands.

Although Greenspan's interpretation of the tech-stock craze appears wise and worthy justification – we know from recent history that the shotgun strategy failed – as most high-tech flyers fell precipitously from grace *together*. This is not to say that after the dust settles and the new economy stocks mature, that dividend streams may reward faithful investors for many years to come. However, the speculative element of this tech craze was high and many big name stocks fell by more than half in value, some of which will never obtain former glory. We must all pay for our sins here on earth and write off that which we have realistically lost.

Domestic origins of the boom

Given the exponential explosion in stock prices in the 1990s it is logical to ask what forces drove this upswing? From Chapter 1, we know that both households and corporations have become increasingly reliant on storing wealth in stock markets. Official savings rates have declined accordingly. This switching behaviour is based on the belief that stock indices always go up – given enough time. Besides the greater faith placed in stocks for the long haul, the use of leverage is another means by which the market pumped itself to greater heights. The popularity of margin lending raises its head as stockbrokers have in the main been generous with margin-lending requirements. Eager brokerage houses reduced margin-lending requirements in order to push hot stocks and attract business. The margin-lending rate stands at 50 per cent, compared to 10 per cent in the 1920s, but even this rate created a strong upward bias in stock values. At face value, it appears that many day traders drew upon credit cards and household mortgages and so used such funds as deposits for leveraged trading.

Other forms of liquidity drove the market higher. Drawing on liquidity from mortgage refinancing and substantial rises in home equity had its risks. It appears that such additional funds, at least up until 2000, were used partly for consumption and partly for re-deployment into stocks. Thurow (1996b) criticized this practice of dipping into home equity – 'From a savings perspective the tax laws permitting home equity loans will probably prove to be one of America's biggest economic mistakes.' In effect, Americans have transferred part of their wealth out of their low-risk home investment into higher-risk stock investments. Perhaps the change in the Tax Reform Act in 1986 that phased out the deductability of the non-mortgage debt pushed householders into greater financial leverage over the family home. Much of this increased borrowing flowed into the stock market and so US house prices are indirectly tied to the fortunes of US stock prices. A major unexpected fall in US stock prices has the potential to devastate house prices, as bank loan repayments still have to be met. If investors collectively believe that a stock market fall is *permanent* then a scramble for liquidity is likely via home selling and downsizing. This linkage is not different to that experienced by Japan in the late 1980s – as discussed in Chapter 11.

Should we claim that margin lending is dangerously fuelling high stock valuations and therefore should be raised? There is a degree of validity with this concern but the broader issue of financial leverage also deserves attention. Financial markets provide a vast array of highly leveraged products such as stock options and futures that have overshadowed the importance of margin lending. In short, US financial markets are deregulated and open – and so if investors demand high degrees of leverage they can obtain it. In short, anyone has the right to hang themselves with their own rope if they so choose. To the extent that negative externalities arise from a stock market crash, the Fed has the power to demand higher credit and margin-lending standards but greater regulation of derivatives trading is another more difficult matter.

As discussed in Chapter 1, another key reason for pumped up liquidity in the US financial system is the foreign money that poured into the US financial system for much of the 1990s. Such a surge of additional liquidity superimposed itself on an already vibrant financial market creating the fuel for a stock market bubble. If this view is symmetrical then a reduction in foreign capital flows and the consequent widening of the current account deficit should have adverse effects on liquidity (the Fed not withstanding) and so deflate stock prices. We have witnessed such a trend in 2000 and 2002 as the stock market endured two straight bear years. However, after the Iraqi war in April 2003 US stock markets rallied – up some 30 per cent from their pre-war lows – and so avoided the shame of a three-year straight fall. These markets continued to rally in early 2004 along with the US dollar and a stabilization of capital inflows.

Conclusion

The US stock market overinflated in the late 1990s to the point of being labelled an asset price bubble. History teaches us that the aftermath of an asset price bubble is particularly deadly as the financial sector is suffocated into stagnation – creating financial sector disintermediation. A hesitant financial sector can transmit ongoing suffocation that in turn chokes the real economy for years after the original financial breakdown. This chapter explored the hypothesis that traditional valuation techniques failed or were ignored by investors. Deeper and perhaps less tangible explanations of bubble were examined – herd behaviour, greed for capital gain, biased tax incentives, poor corporate governance, stock options, IPOs, margin lending and the growth in the power of giant institutions. The investment environment was biased towards trading in stocks and bonds – pushed along by government rules and investor behaviour. Further fuels of the speculative bubble were abundant domestic liquidity and geopolitical forces that pushed foreign funds into US assets.

There is an alternative view – that of a 'real bubble'. This view that the US economy underwent a surge in real productivity growth that enlivened the real economy and so stimulated corporate profit growth remains somewhat indefensible. In this view – held by Greenspan – stock valuations were underpinned by strident gains in productivity growth and the expectation of further growth. The author finds this latter view somewhat porous as the magnitude of the surge in stock prices went far beyond the rate of increase in productivity gains. As will be discussed in Chapter 5, there is case for strong productivity growth and some kind of technological renaissance pushing up stock prices but the notion that economic factors drive stock market fluctuations has never been an accepted financial investment pillar of wisdom.

On the issue of rationality, the speculative bubble in US stocks may have been a 'rational bubble': that is, what was rational for the individual was not rational for the collective investment body. There was a degree of *individual* rationality in this stock market boom – if moving with the investor herd yields lucrative profits – as it did in the 1990s, then investors were justified in hitching a ride, that is, irrespective of movements in economic or financial fundamentals. What happens to overcommitted investors when the game of musical chairs comes to an end? This is the Cinderella story all over again. The answer is huge capital losses but not for those that traded and then exited before the music stopped. Given the extended rise of US stock prices and low yielding alternatives it is not difficult to understand why investors and institutions went for the ride.

What was the Fed doing amidst all this hype in stock markets? Did the Fed turn a blind eye to asset price inflation? In Chapters 7 and 8 we examine the role of the Fed in influencing economic activity, inflation and stock prices together with the challenges that it faces in the twenty-first century. But first we examine US productivity and 'new economy' story in Chapter 5.

5 The new economy
Has it arrived?

Introduction

There have been many inventions throughout history that have transformed 'old' slow-moving economies into 'new' dynamic ones – and so changed forever the way ordinary people live and conduct business. The railroads of the 1800s, the motor vehicle, the airplane, containerization, TV, computers and the internet are examples of the vehicles of transformation. Vast improvements in welfare have resulted, as great strides in efficiency released resources for better uses. We now enjoy more music, theatre, movies, art, sport and CNN as direct result of technological inventions that have freed mankind from arduous, back-breaking, mundane tasks.

Given that waves of technological shocks have hit and reshaped the US economy, and that living standards have risen dramatically, it begs the question of why such progress is not revealed in the productivity statistics? Why does it appear that there is such a gross underestimation of economic well-being? One reason cited is that the *quality* of products has improved exponentially and is not accurately captured in the statistics. Second, with superior machines and capital stock, the burden and boredom of work has slumped dramatically. It is the quality of the capital stock that has eased the pain of work, caused output to explode and generated an explosion in the great variety of goods. However, despite major waves of innovation in the United States – it is premature to claim that the 'new economy' has arrived. After all, the collapse of the stock bubble is testimony to that. Technological progress and innovation has *incrementally* raised economic prosperity in the United States but the repeal of the business cycle has not occurred. There is no doubt that massive structural adjustments are visibly underway in the US economy but it is more than a giant leap of faith to claim that this 'new economy' is repealing the old laws of economics and that economic prosperity is more permanent. In essence, this is an admission that the stock bubble of the 1990s was not well based on the arrival of the new economy. It never arrived. This chapter examines some of the explanations for the roller-coaster ride of productivity growth over the last forty years. It also provides reasons for caution against the proclamation of a new and permanent plateau in productivity growth for the twenty-first century. There is always the danger of pushing stock prices higher on the basis of higher – but not yet permanent – productivity levels.

Productivity growth and the stock market

Throughout this book the power of monetary liquidity, margin lending, foreign capital flows, tax laws, behavioural factors and speculation have been emphasized as the key driving forces of the 1990s stock bubble. Productivity growth was important in providing a real floor for rising stock values but could not explain the escalation in the late 1990s. Unless of course, the Greenspan view of *expected productivity growth* – explained in pp. 49–50 – is plausible. The rise in US labour productivity growth almost doubled (2.1 per cent) between 1999 and 2000 compared with (1.3 per cent) in the 1973–94 era. However, the S&P rose sixfold during the 1990s. From Figure 5.1 it can be seen that labour productivity continued to surge well into 2003 – at an average of above 4 per cent since 2000. It is true that productivity growth in the IT sector was far higher at around 7.35 per cent between 1990 and 1995 and 9.31 per cent between 1995 and 2000 (Jorgenson *et al.* 2003). Not even these productivity growth rates could justify the extent of the NASDAQ bubble of a tenfold increase in the 1990s.

Perhaps the *acceleration* in productivity growth was expected to translate into the *acceleration* of earnings per share growth? This is a corollary of Greenspan's *expected productivity growth* story – investors purchased stocks in the belief that *accelerating* productivity growth would generate a sustainable corporate earnings boom – a new plateau. We know that this did not happen. Although the prospects of rising corporate profits appeared real at the time – the magnitude of the productivity bubble was nowhere enough to justify the magnitude of the stock bubble. From hindsight, investor expectations of profit growth were unrealistic.

There were good reasons why the power of the productivity surge was insufficient to support the surge in stock prices. The flagship of the investment boom was the IT sector. And yet, the relationship between IT and productivity is 'murky' according to the McKinsey quarterly. More information and knowledge flow is useful but not

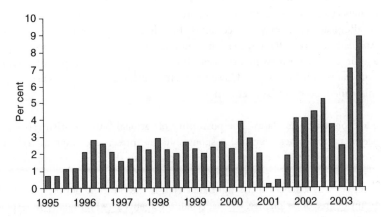

Figure 5.1 Productivity growth (year–year, per cent change by quarter).

Source: US Bureau of Labour Statistics.

necessarily paramount in generating economic growth or corporate profits. As Feldstein (2003) points out the size of the IT sector is still relatively small compared to the overall GDP and therefore does possess enough pulling power – yet. Most economists agree that the basic origin of rapid productivity growth comes from and will continue to come from the IT sector. Although we may look forward to a higher level of productivity growth in the future it does follow that GDP growth will maintain a high speed. However, the jury is still out as to the power of transmission from productivity to corporate profits and from the acceleration of productivity growth to the acceleration of corporate profit growth. Other financial and monetary forces are powerful drivers of corporate profits in the short run.

We need to address two structural breaks in the time series data in the 1990s. Do we have *new and steeper* trend lines in both stock prices and productivity growth that reflect higher long-run averages for the future? We need to appreciate the following points before reading the rest of the chapter.

- The huge escalation in stocks prices from 1991–2000.
- The significant leap in productivity growth in the same era.
- The build-up of incentive biases.
- The link between productivity growth and EPS growth.

A rational bubble?

Despite the appearance of the IT and dot.com boom being a 'bubble' some economists argue in favour of rationality. Indeed, in their view, the label of irrational exuberance is an unfair one. For example, Cooper and Madden (2004) state

> Given the link between stock market behaviour and the ICT sector with the birth and subsequent bust of the dot.com bubble, it is perhaps understandable that irrational exuberance is now being offered as a reason for the telecommunications crisis. However, this idea is potentially misleading since it characterizes as illogical what may be complex but logical reactions to uncertainty. Acquisition access, the payment of license fees that are too high viewed ex post, and unrealistic business models have all been proffered as examples of irrational exuberance (OECD 2003). However, such firm behaviors, even when ex post misguided, need not be irrational.

These authors go on to claim 'The possibility of rational bubbles arising from the interaction of component rational responses in the presence of asymmetric price adjustment suggest different implications for policy. In this circumstance irrational exuberance is an irrational explanation.'

Hence, there is a school of thought that claims the dot.com bubble possessed a significant degree of rationality, that is, economic agents acted rationally in response to the information set that confronted them *at the time*. This position is different from claiming that the boom years were rational – ex post.

Old questions and old answers

Amidst the huge wealth creation era of the 1960s came the debate among business-men, investors, policy-makers and economists that the 'business cycle was now obsolete and a thing of the past'. In other words, the wild swings in income and real activity had all but died, leaving in its wake the tranquility of a stable, high growth economy that had acquired a 'natural' high economic cruise speed. Poverty was a problem of those that did not choose to join the 'investment club' or did not choose to work. Such people were often referred to as the hippies and flower-power people of the 1960s. Other respectable middle-class people, so the story goes, could enjoy the new promised land of prosperity – as poverty had been outlawed by the 'new' growth forces of organization and technology. The problem with this view of permanent prosperity is that America's *financial* wealth was partly a function of speculation and greed – inflated stocks values and so potential capital gains – were not bonafide rates of return unless they were *realized*. They were often not – as in any stock market boom, holders of assets could not exit simultaneously without causing asset prices to collapse and financial wealth to evaporate. The lesson here is that the law of the business cycle has not been repealed and that capital losses and corporate bankruptcies are an ongoing fact of life.

Associated with this 'new plateau of prosperity' debate was the arrival of the 'new economy' reflected in the high flying stocks of Ampex, Brunswick, Polaroid, Sperry-Rand and Xerox – in the 1920s. The old economy stocks still remained profitable but offered both lower growth results and so lower capital appreciation potential. Do these arguments ring a bell for those stock market investors of the twenty-first century? They most certainly should! Such debates can be found on the internet in recent times. Given what we know about the 1960s onwards, the new economy soon became the old economy and new waves of technology did not abolish the wild fluctuations of the business cycle. Investment in IT industries was heralded as the catalyst of the new economy and the engine of a new plateau of prosperity. Such investment failed to deliver and so was a false dawn of new-found prosperity.

The productivity slow down debate

We know that labour productivity growth faded considerably in the 1970s (1.1 per cent) and 1980s (1.3 per cent) – far below the rate set in the boom years of the 1950s (3.0 per cent) and 1960s (2.6 per cent) (Roubini 2000). Perhaps the poorer perform-ance was just a function of the exceptional and the earlier mentioned trend in pro-ductivity growth of the postwar years. In other words, a pace that could not be sustained over a thirty-year period. So what were the likely causes of the productiv-ity slow down? The oil crises in 1974 and again in 1978, standout as being prime movers of inflation as the real energy prices to final consumers rose by 23 per cent between 1973 and 1975 and by 34 per cent between 1987 and 1980 (Jorgenson 1988). To that extent energy and capital are complements, the higher price of oil caused investment to slow – at least in key industries. As relative prices were disturbed, there was a stimulus to switch out of energy-intensive and now obsolete, capital equipment into more energy-friendly investment. Not only did rising oil prices create greater obsolescence in the existing capital stock but also generated much under-capacity. Unit costs were pressured accordingly. There is also a 'time to build' and 'time to adapt' issue whereby new fuel-efficient technologies were introduced gradually over the course of the 1970s. However, if this high price of energy story is to explain the productivity slow down of the 1970s then why did a boom not take place in the mid-1980s when the price of oil fell substantially in real terms? There should be symmetry in explanation – but there is not. Some economists claim that energy costs were not a large portion of GDP in the 1970s and therefore could not explain the productivity slow down.

However, such oil price shocks may have 'shocked' lobby and interest groups into serious defensive action. According to Olson (1988) collective action is important in explaining this productivity slow down as lobby groups clamoured for protection against higher *expected* inflation by raising price and wage claims in anticipation. The roller-coaster ride of inflationary expectations possessed a life of its own and so raised unit costs. Coalitions in older industries could block innovation that threatened their own short-term welfare and so protect themselves by rent-seeking activities. Fights over the profit-wage share of the national cake and wage–wage inflation typified the conflict over the distribution of income.

During such inflationary times there was an adverse affect on savings and investment, as there were greater incentives for households to hold assets and not cash. Large budget deficits contributed to inflation and 'bracket creep' pushed many Americans into higher tax brackets skewing economic incentives away from work and thrift. This inflation-tax interaction adversely affected productivity growth.

Could the productivity slow down be explained by a slowing of technological progress or a slowing in the adoption of new ideas? Keeping up with the technological developments of the war era was always going to be a tough task. Perhaps the observed decline in R&D in the 1960s operated with a lag or the number of patents issued in the 1970s declined thereby adversely affecting technological progress. What is more likely is that the *adoption* of new knowledge was slower in an environment of uncertainty and businesses waited for a clearer economic picture to emerge (Griliches 1988).

Despite the plausibility of the reasons mentioned earlier, it does not appear that these channels were large enough to cause a collapse in productivity growth in the 1970s. Perhaps productivity growth is pro-cyclical? It tends to rise in booms and fall in recessions? Thus, some productivity growth is permanent and durable whereas the remainder is temporary and fleeting. Moreover, productivity fluctuations may be more related to the profit cycle? That is, lower profitability is picked up in the statistics as lower productivity. Or perhaps there have been large improvements in welfare that are not picked by measured productivity statistics, such as vast improvements in quality?

Even though there was a productivity slow down in 1974–94 (1.3 per cent) the US stock markets still performed well over the latter part of this time period – that is, from 1982 onwards. This paradox should be appreciated as the health of the real economy is not always the prime driver of stock values over the medium term. It is the switching of wealth from one asset category to another and/or just sheer wealth that enters the stock market that explains why stock prices rise faster than that dictated by productivity growth. Besides, it is profitability of the US corporate sector, and not GDP growth in general, that drives stock prices in the medium term. Perhaps US companies enjoyed the lower price of oil in the 1980s as well as lower unit costs?

Sources of productivity growth

From a theoretical perspective, the accumulation of capital and labour can only produce a spurt of transitional 'growth' for a time. Even raising the capital–labour ratio only produces temporary short-run growth as diminishing returns eventually set in. Given that the US economy has reached a stage of maturity, there is only minor impetus to labour productivity from the sources mentioned earlier. However, the 1990s may be a mild exception as the vibrant US economy experienced a rise in the labour force participation rate, drew more heavily on migrant labour and added modern, cutting-edge capital to labour at a rapid pace. Hence, the US economy appears to be in a transition phase – moving from one steady state to the next. As once stated, 'necessity is the mother of invention' and so it is with US firms facing squeezes on profit margins. Given that many US businesses lack pricing power, there is a distinct lack of ability to pass on price increases in highly competitive markets. Therefore, firms have sought to lower unit costs, not just by wage suppression but by operating more 'lean' and so raising productivity growth. New-found surges in efficiency have stemmed in part from more investment in capital stock; plant and equipment – thus raising both the quality and quantity of capital per worker.

There is also a case for arguing that the investment surge in the United States has been stimulated by external factors – greater openness, globalization, increased competitiveness, weak foreign currencies and weak foreign economies. It has been the threat of entry and the *threat* of foreign competition that has *forced* many pockets of US industry to raise efficiency and competitiveness. For example, when the international price of taconite fell in the 1980s – the Minnesota steel and iron ore industries responded by doubling labour productivity (Miller and Schmitz 1996). The deregulation of the US telecommunications industry forced a wave of technological improvement that pushed labour productivity higher. As Greenspan (1997g) states, 'Increased deregulation of telecommunications, motor and rail transport, utilities, and finance doubtless has been a factor restraining prices, as perhaps has the reduced power of labour unions.' It was the US policy commitment to openness, in the face of stiff foreign competition that forced US businesses to find ways of lowering costs – notably via modern capital injections. On the demand side, US businesses had good reason to innovate and raise the capital–labour ratio by quantity and quality. However, there was good news on the supply side of the fence – foreign capital flooded into an already liquid US market, making it easy for US companies to tap financial markets – with corporate bonds or borrowing through commercial banks. Foreign competition alongside foreign money revitalized US businesses – at the cost of US manufacturing jobs. The surge in equipment investment can be seen from Figure 5.2, averaging 12 per cent p.a. from 1993 onwards.

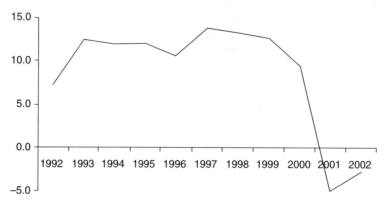

Figure 5.2 US equipment and software investment (1992–2002).
Source: Board of Governors of the Federal Reserve System.

The IT and communications revolution

Even though the US economy has been dominated by services for several decades, the explosion in the use of personal computers, the internet and the rapid proliferation of the virtual firm has revealed the advent of the true 'knowledge-based' economy. Innovation and adoption have been the trademarks of US prosperity as US businesses have seized opportunities to smash unit costs. Several examples are often cited. New technology allowed the steel industry to build mini-mills; small-scale plants capable of producing rolled sheet steel for the automobile industry. The pharmaceutical industry has enjoyed advances in biomedicine to the point that it can design drugs for specific illnesses from the molecules up. This industry employs the internet to gain data on individual medical histories (from volunteers) to continually up-date its knowledge base. In manufacturing, there have been rapid advances in the power of computer microprocessors (semi-conductors) causing the price of information processing to plummet (Greenspan 1997b). A simple, but an excellent example, of vast gains in efficiency in the service sector is the electronic scanner. The pricing of goods is less labour-intensive and movements in sales and inventories can be monitored far more efficiently than ever before. In banking, the ATM has increased bank efficiency and customer convenience. In education, web-based learning is growing in appeal, as universities seek to tap large volume offshore markets and so gain market share.

Major improvements in information technology have revolutionized the telecommunications industry. Giant networks have been developed in a relatively short time frame with the internet being the King of the networks. As a result, the 'new industry' of e-commerce has sprung up. Companies worldwide have jumped on this global network to advertise their existence and wares. There is even a competition between companies for the most glamorous and enticing home page. Such glamour and variety encourages individuals and businesses to surf the net, building commercial knowledge and awareness in its wake. US businesses can now be truly global enterprises without incurring any massive expense.

Not only has the internet been a major network carrying both public and private, and commercial and non-commercial information but other networks have flourished targeting private, commercial users. Cable TV and mobile phones come to mind. As the size of the network grows there is a positive externality or greater value bestowed on existing users. There is a positive feedback cycle that encourages more people to 'join the club' and so the cycle continues. Network providers play upon this feedback cycle and club by advertising its size and expansion and by warning potential customers against joining other networks that will only diminish in size in the future. In essence, the potential customer is warned about switching costs to other networks or if they do 'defect' they run the risk of not being connected, as the dominant company controls the dominant network. Differing network standards and switching costs only complicates the consumer's decision. In the meantime, a dominant company like Bell can secure above normal profits.

Given that the rate of GDP growth is a *flow* concept, any improvement in the *flow of information* is bound to have a positive impact on economic growth and productivity. As the cost of transmitting information has fallen so have businesses seized opportunities for cost reduction via more efficient information technology. Managing inventories is a good example. An efficient distribution system results from the little need to 'physically carry' a wide range of goods as they can be ordered quickly 'online' from suppliers. Moreover, specific customer design orders can be negotiated over the internet – with modifications made easily – and so the manufacturer does not have to bare the risk of customer rejects or changes of heart. As Greenspan (1997g) comments

> Increased flexibility is particularly evident in the computer, telecommunications, and related industries, a segment of our economy that seems far less subject to physical capacity constraints than many older line establishments, and one that is assuming greater importance in our overall economy. But the shortening of lags has been pervasive even in more mature industries, owing in part to the application of advanced technologies to production methods.

This lower inventory to sales ratios is revealed in the national statistics – seen in Figure 5.3. From above 1.52 in 1990 to 1.39 in 1998 reveals just how much smarter business is working with regard to holding costs and managing unwanted inventory levels. New distribution channels have changed the structure and shape of a firm. The virtual firm has eliminated the role of many middlemen and has increased the speed and flexibility with which an electronic firm can meet customer demand. Established distribution networks, along with all associated privileges, is under some threat as virtual firms transcend and circumvent traditional physical networks. For example, more than 400 new internet surfers join every hour and around 64 million people use the internet each month (Bell 2000). The profile of net users is one of being educated, young and/or affluent. More than 40 per cent of households in the United States have access to the net and rising (Bell 2000).

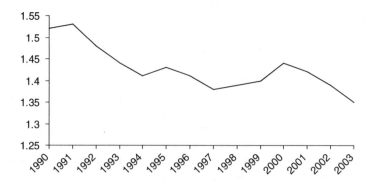

Figure 5.3 Inventory to sales ratio.
Source: Board of Governors of the Federal Reserve System.

There is no doubt that e-commerce has gained in popularity as it possesses several advantages for both the customer and the seller. There is a wide selection of products to choose from those that are visually displayed, search costs are low, convenience high and service delivery is normally prompt. For the business, storage costs are reduced as a multitude of individual suppliers are notified when orders have been placed. This decentralized sales system saves on transport costs to the 'old centre'. Another strength of e-commerce is that it broadens and deepens the market – reaching distant customers out-of-state and worldwide. A reduced sales force is also a benefit as the 'store' is visual not physical – akin to a self-service supermarket. However, some electronic retailers have acquired their own warehouse distribution centres in an effort to provide complementarity to their existing visual networks. This provides at least a hint that electronic firms are not substitutes for traditional firms and conventional physical buying but *reinforce* sales in such mediums. E-tailers are beginning to realize that a hybrid company that incorporates both brick and mortar with cyber-space is not just a compromise but a commercial reality. Customer surveys often highlight a high degree of customer dissatisfaction with a lack of personal service and the inability to make direct contact. Jungle-like web pages often cause customers to get lost several layers down. Returning goods is also high with e-tailers. What has become evident is that the internet is a great *communications* medium but a far weaker *distribution* medium. In other words, it facilitates a vastly greater flow of information and allows decentralized markets to link together well but does not guarantee an explosion in sales.

Where e-commerce appears to offer greater potential is via business-to-business links. New websites enable buyers and sellers to find each other and strike deals far more easily. Searching for suppliers and gaining quotes and particular specifications is also less tedious. Competition is enhanced among suppliers as potential buyers have a greater appreciation of market prices, qualities and delivery times. Firms can hold auctions and so test the market. Hence, procurement costs and the traditional relationships between the firm and its suppliers have been altered. For suppliers to gain market share is one matter but to keep it in a wide, well-informed market is another matter. The threat of entry or 'buyer switching' keeps suppliers on their toes.

IT and communications: drivers of productivity growth?

No one denies that rapidly declining information processing and the proliferation of communications networks has stimulated innovation and lifted productivity growth. But by how much is the question. Opinion on the potency of this 'revolution' is divided. Research conducted by Roach (1987) is critical of low office productivity in the service sector, even those sectors with high-tech capital – output per information worker decreased by 6.6 per cent between 1970 and 1986 while output per production worker rose by 16.9 per cent. Research by Gordon (1998) has remained skeptical of IT driving the pick-up in labour productivity – cyclical factors are more important. Returns to IT capital are modest and much of the push has come from the *production* of computers not their use. Research by Berndt and Morrison (1995) find that IT is not correlated with productivity in most manufacturing industries. The marginal productivity of IT capital is not much different from other types of capital and so impact on the economy in general is somewhat dubious.

The alternate view that IT has contributed to productivity growth is supported by Siegal (1997). He is critical of measurement problems and claims that computer investment is strongly related to multi-factor productivity. Striking results were found by Brynjolfsonn and Hitt (1994) for the service sector, they claimed that gross marginal product averaged over 60 per cent per year while gross marginal product of non-computer capital ranges from 4.14 per cent to 6.86 per cent. They also claimed that IT contributed as much to output in the service sector as compared to the manufacturing sector. Jorgenson and Stiroh (1995) claim that computers have contributed between 0.38 per cent and 0.52 per cent to output growth between 1972 and 1992. Such results are similar to those of Oliner and Sichel (1994) of 0.4 per cent for the US economy. These researchers also claimed that two-thirds of the 1 per cent step up in productivity growth in the mid-1990s was attributable to IT – if the *use* and *production* of computers are included (Oliner and Sichel 2000). Hence, the contribution of IT to output and productivity appears robust.

Some commentators refer to a 'productivity paradox', that is high expectations that the IT revolution would act as a giant engine of productivity growth but failed to deliver. As Krugman (1996) points out, the desk top computer may be fifty times more powerful but that does not mean it is fifty times more useful! More information is better than less, but there are absorption constraints by mere mortals. In fact, it is likely that US businesses are suffering under an 'information overload', a plethora of data unmatched by an increase in analytical skills. If you ask a stock analyst which way will the Dow go today ... she will not know with any certainty, even though she has more statistics, charts and historical evidence at her finger tips. Therefore, one view is that expectations were too high and unrealistic – as computers represent only 2 per cent of the nation's capital stock, compared to the railroads 12 per cent in the 1800s. As discussed earlier, the marginal product of capital for IT may be high, but operates off a small base or percentage of GDP and so cannot 'deliver' large productivity gains – at least not yet. This is a crucial argument – how broad and widespread is the use of IT in lowering unit costs – across all industries.

Another view is that IT increases consumer and worker *convenience* by leaps and bounds. For example, when a bank installs more ATMs it raises productivity by reducing the numbers of bank telling staff. But if those displaced workers are retrained as loan officers, the overall number of workers by the bank will not change. If output is unchanged along with employment, then any significant leap forward in productivity will not reveal itself. Despite the fact that less work effort is required and despite the fact that customers have a convenient 24 hour service and despite the fact that the level of human welfare has risen – the productivity growth rate remains unchanged or in disguise. Hence, economic welfare has increased via more IT but measured productivity has not – in this example.

Yet another view is that productivity gains from new technologies trace a non-linear path. There is a J-curve effect. Initially, a technology surge reduces average productivity while teething problems are sorted out, as complementary technologies develop and as diffusion filters throughout the economy. Diffusion may be slow but picks up as new synergies are realized. Bluestone and Harrison (1997) claim that 'we have been wandering in the information technology desert for close to three decades'.

US government and productivity growth

An influential paper on economic growth by Paul Romer (1991) has shed more light on the importance of government support for research and development via patents and subsidies. The major reason being that researchers (and commercial enterprises that employ them) require monopoly profits for a time, to compensate them for large fixed or sunk costs. Patents provide researchers with the incentive and security to invent and create new knowledge in the first place. If property rights were non-existent and barriers to imitation were few, then the amount of resources devoted to research would diminish. It is because positive spillovers for the community at large exists that the US government does provide legal support for new inventions. The current US administration acknowledges the necessity of maintaining and increasing the flow of innovative ideas to the economy by stating 'government support for basic research is critical in a knowledge-based economy, where growth ultimately depends upon the flow of new ideas'. Why basic research? Because there were inventions in the past that were not explicitly intended for commercial use and/or were employed more fully when other complementary inventions were exploited. In other words, General Purpose Technology (GPT) has an important role to play in society because of the potential spillovers and even commercial value realized at a later date. The original inventors may not have the resources to upgrade the technology or improve its applicability to the commercial world. Nevertheless, the US government has a responsibility to expand the stock of knowledge despite low levels of commercial relevance. In fact, the internet itself is an example of a GPT, as it was originally an exercise in connecting several government databases in different locations but grew over time to include a plethora of sites and users.

However, for the United States to promote research and innovation is easier said than done. Basically for the reason that Romer and others have pointed out – there is a fine policy line between protecting monopoly profits and thus stimulating invention, and promoting competition and thus lowering prices. Various US administrations have displayed concern over mergers and monopoly power and have been ever vigilant with a competition policy and the enforcing of anti-trust legislation. For example, the Telecommunications Act of 1996 removed barriers to entry in telecommunications markets by forcing regional Bell companies to allow other competitors into the local telephone market. The obvious example is that of Microsoft, whereby an 'industry standard' is set and other competitors are tied to the chariot wheel of Microsoft's products and network of users. Competitors and product developers are prevented from building a critical mass sizable enough to challenge the incumbent. There are always dangers of size, as consumers may be exploited and the 'too big to fail' threat hung above the community's head. However, inventions normally require large amounts of upfront investment, with the associated risk of failure, and these sunk costs need to be written off against large sales volumes in the future. Perhaps, the relevant question for the US administration is how long should patents be valid? When should competition be stimulated in some of the new economy industries? For example, what kinds of laws, including tax laws, should be imposed on electronic commerce? The economist's answer is that of self-regulation and eventual competition that will substitute for government legislation.

Has the US government made a contribution to rise in productivity growth? The answer is 'yes' but in an indirect way, by upholding intellectual property rights in a flourishing knowledge-based economy and by acknowledging the need for corporate inventors to acquire monopoly profits for a time. There are other channels through which productivity has been given a boost. As US budget deficits have declined and even turned into surplus so has additional 'room' been created for private sector investment. As discussed in Chapter 3, lower taxes are always welcome by the investing class. Macroeconomic stability, and in particular low, stable inflation rates underpinned the investment boom of the 1990s. In these ways, the US administration has indirectly supported the surge in US productivity.

Productivity growth: how permanent?

As with all upswings of the business cycle, there is a cyclical element embedded in the growth rate of productivity. In other words, productivity growth appears to be pro-cyclical, rising in booms and falling in busts. Therefore, the degree of structural improvement in productivity growth, the part that is more enduring, can be somewhat camouflaged in a strong economic recovery. Greenspan (2000e) refers to data that portrays the acceleration in productivity growth since 1996 but warns of the possibility of 'overstatement'. And yet in July 2000 he claims 'So far there is little evidence to undermine the notion that most of the productivity increase of recent years has been structural and that structural productivity may still be accelerating. New orders for capital equipment continue to be strong – so strong that the rise in unfilled orders has actually steepened in recent months'. The gains in productivity stem from several sources mentioned earlier. The boom in capital spending in recent years has significantly increased the quality of capital per worker, as such investment is heavily knowledge laden. Just as important as the cutting-edge quality of capital investment is the fact that prices of such capital goods have fallen dramatically and so assisted the proliferation of use of such goods economy-wide.

What have been the temporary or one-shot driving forces of productivity growth? The answer rests in monetary and financial factors and the vast inflow of foreign capital in the boom era. Easy access to external finance pushed many CFOs headlong into the investment craze. Just as importantly was the shrinkage in risk perception – fund managers were willing to discount future profit flows more heavily – as inflation and real interest rates fell. Less risk spelt less fear and so more investment. As the reader is well aware – take these transient forces away and transient or superficial productivity growth should also disappear.

Why has productivity been slow in revealing itself in the statistics? One answer comes from Professor David (1990) – who point out that it takes time for *synergies* to develop between different forms of capital and technologies. He cites the example of the dynamo, invented in the mid-1800s, but required the complementary technology of the electric motor before such technology was adopted in any widespread fashion in 1920s. The complementarity of technologies and their powerful interactions take time to fuse and explode. The application of the laser did not really blossom until the extensive use of fiber optics. So, we may be in the midst of a major productivity upswing as recent IT breakthroughs are filtering through the economic system.

Productivity and the stock bubble

It is most unlikely that the surge in US productivity growth was strong or widespread enough to cause the massive surge in stock prices post 1995. After all, productivity growth was still alive and well in 2000–2 and yet stock prices plummeted for more than two-and-a-half years. The incentive biases (financial and behavioural) canvassed in Chapter 1 were more than likely overwhelming forces that caused a structural break in the time series data during this era, that is, investors responded to low inflation, low interest rates, tax breaks and abundant liquidity while CEOs responded with stock options, buy-backs, book-cooking and IPOs. Financial biases heavily favoured buying and holding stocks given the calm financial sea and low levels of risk perception. To the extent that some of these forces are not transient there may be a new and higher trend line in stock prices and *P/E* ratios – that supercedes the old trend line *P/E* ratio of 14.5. If so, this is good news for the stock market in 2004 through 2006.

However, there may also be a new trend line – or new plateau – for productivity growth at 2.5 per cent – and way above the old trend line of 1.4 per cent. Thus, stock prices can receive support from this source as well – provided that it is permanent and not temporary. Given that we may have two new and higher trend lines than the past then we can argue that *P/E* ratios of around 22 can be justified – a mid-point between the euphoric *P/E* ratios of 33 in the boom era and the 'old' long-run trend line of 14.5.

Conclusion

The view that the US economy is riding on a giant wave of productivity growth has a sound theoretical base. Real business cycle theorists remind us of the potency of real factors in driving economic growth – especially that of technologically driven productivity growth. The preferences of worker–consumers also matter as they respond to wage and interest rates and the set of economic incentives before them. US workers have revealed a propensity to work more but not save more during the current boom – not quite fitting the typical response of real business cycle theory. If worker-consumers believed that this productivity boom was *permanent* then they should offer less labour, as their permanent incomes have been raised forever. However, a declining saving rate provides some evidence that ordinary Americans believe that this current technology boom is going to raise their living standards well into the future.

The opposite view is that the current productivity boom is *temporary* or just an aberration. Hence, low savings rates may represent the belief that considerable capital gains can be extracted from a runaway stock market – enough to feather a comfortable retirement nest. In this view, the expectation of a current technological wave coming to an end causes many speculators to ride the wave of capital appreciation while the wave is still rolling – and then cash in. Some did in 2000. There is also the flood of capital inflows that in many ways propagated the tech bubble and financed the investment expansion of the 1990s.

The IT and communications revolution have made a contribution to US productivity growth but there is considerable conjecture as to the size of that contribution. Evidence from this chapter suggests that the impact of IT in driving the technological boom is somewhat overstated. Perhaps there are long lags involved or perhaps the still small share of the IT industry in the total economy accounts for the low impact. More information is probably worth more than less – but at the end of the day you can't eat information – there are probably thresholds of manageability. The even larger question as to whether a large technological wave drove the 1990s boom in the US economy and stocks is also uncertain. Just because a burst of new technology related investment is observed – it does not follow that future returns will justify current investment surges. Such surges may also be liquidity driven, merger driven, IPO driven and even high Q ratio driven as US companies can access funds on easy terms and so 'invest'. The jury is still out on whether the US economy is experiencing a full-fledged technological overhaul. The true test of the durability of the US productivity boom will be whether it is knowledge-based and whether unit costs across the economy decline substantially. If this be the case, then stock values will enjoy strong support for the rest of the decade. This is just another way of stating that permanent productivity growth that impacts on broad economic activity will be far more conducive to rising stock prices than transient productivity growth that is highly localized – in just high-tech areas.

6 Governance issues
Old and new

Introduction

Just as American's placed much faith in their banking system for the safe storage of their money – so too have they trusted the US stock market in a similar fashion. Alas, some of this trust has been misplaced as an array of corporate scandals and bankruptcies have shaken investor confidence in the ethical standards and business practices of Corporate America. Not only have many stocks fallen in value, but more disastrously, some companies 'lost all' and went into receivership. As discussed earlier in this book, investors learnt the hard way that their funds were not safely 'on call' in US stocks. America's CEOs have been placed under the spotlight as too many big name US corporations reported 'false' earnings figures and/or were 'loose' in forecasting future earnings growth. Accounting standards were too low for investor security and accounting trickery defrauded investors of billions of dollars. This chapter examines why both government and self-regulatory frameworks failed to provide creditors, shareholders and the investing public a high degree of protection. The new regulatory framework based on the Sarbanes-Oxley Act seeks to remedy many of the weaknesses in the old system and so will be examined. The major objectives of the new regulatory framework are to restore investor faith in the stock market, to raise the overall standard of corporate governance and to ensure a higher degree of investor security in the future. The means to achieve these objectives are wide ranging but include – improved accounting and auditing standards, a redefinition of directors' responsibilities and higher levels of board independence. This chapter examines the origins of corporate governance failure and the US administration's regulatory response.

Market versus government failure

Not only was there gross corporate failure in the United States but government failure also. A series of deregulation initiatives created strong incentives for corporate executives and the accounting profession to take on risks and be more 'flexible' with respect to business practices. For example, tearing down of the fire walls between investment and commercial banking. For nearly half a century the Glass-Steagall Act separated investment and commercial banking. The rationale was based on a conflict of interest that may have arisen from recommending that investors buy a stock that the investment bank has a close commercial relationship with. There is a temptation here to paint a rosy picture of a stock's future earnings potential while that same company is heavily indebted to the investment bank. In principle at least, there is a bias to disseminate favourable research reports for those companies that are sizable clients – on the commercial lending side of the bank's operation. This does not state that deregulation initiatives failed but that they possessed unwanted by-products – such as a moral hazard and loose attitudes towards risk.

In 1995, Robert Rubin of the Clinton Administration decided that this separation and compartmentalization of the banking industry should end. Banks should be allowed to become more integrated in function and hence larger. Conflicts of interest did arise and integrated banks did succumb to the temptation of allowing research and stock recommendations to be biased by close client banking relationships.

Brokerage houses faced similar conflicts of interest and several of these firms faced SEC (Securities and Exchange Commission) investigation. Again, the crucial issue was the 'biased' research reports for existing commercial loan clients that were too big and too important to 'lose' as clients. Hence, professional judgment concerning buy, sell or hold was clouded by CEO directives, biased research reports and the lust for profit.

This is not to say that deregulation did not deliver benefits in terms of greater competition within the financial sector and a greater variety of products and services for the customer. These are the major motivating forces for deregulation. However, costs can and did arise via moral hazard – corporate managers chased greater market share and were more 'flexible' towards customer needs. Greater openness in the financial sector brought with it associated costs but most professionals would argue that the benefits outweighed the costs of deregulation.

And yet, from hindsight, regulatory responses to obvious accounting shortcomings and non-disclosure of high-risk exposure appeared both slow and porous. How much regulation is enough – that is, how to find an *optimal balance* between all parties concerned? There is a trade-off between the government's desire for security, transparency and fairness and the private sector's desire for innovation, profit and risk. Given the recent array of corporate scandals, the power and resolve of the SEC is being tested in the post-bubble era to implement an optimal mix of regulation that provides protection to shareholders, potential investors and creditors and yet does not significantly stifle incentive or risk-taking – so essential for dynamic long-run economic growth. It therefore appears that earlier government deregulation waves did not achieve optimal balance – they created too much choice, moral laxity and an excessive tolerance for risk. Recent re-regulation efforts represent an effort by US authorities to restore such balance and so warn CEOs that fraud and wrongdoing will be punished. At the heart of these recent reforms lies the importance of honest profit reporting and disclosure.

It is here that an age-old debate comes to the fore – that of the costs and benefits of self-regulation. Corporate America has long seen itself as a guardian of its own destiny, preferring self-regulation and 'in-house' solutions to problems that arise. Professional bodies commonly have a code of ethics and business standards that are to be followed by all members. The NYSE and its members set listing standards and breaches invoke disciplinary action. The benefits for the body collective are uniform professional standards, the preservation of long-term reputation and so respect and recognition from the public – prerequisites for an efficient capital market. It therefore follows that any member violating professional standards and ethics should be punished – as the reputation of the whole association can be tarnished – if not permanently damaged. The same principle applies at the individual level – a professional that indulges in unethical behaviour and is caught – will suffer damage to his reputation. The loss of many years of future income should deter professionals from any illegal or unethical behaviour – as it may cost them their livelihood. This is the lifeblood of self-regulation – the fear of losing reputation. The Bush administration has publicly supported the concept of self-regulation with the caveat that more refinement and self-discipline is warranted. Moreover, the US corporate scandal debacle, according to President Bush, was caused by a 'few bad apples' and was not the fault of the self-regulatory framework itself.

So why then did so many corporate executives risk their reputation and future livelihood by unethical and illegal activities? First, because the probability of getting caught was not that high. Non-disclosure, delay, non-arm's length board members, the concentration of power and appointment of 'friendly' auditors meant that CEOs had much control over the timing and quality of information that was released. They had control and believed, at least for a time, that they would not be exposed. Second, the benefits from misusing power and cheating in terms of insider trading and unloading vast amounts of stock options without anyone knowing for a while – far outweighed the risk of being caught. Given that even one CEO could appropriate anywhere up to $120 million – and then leave the company – would most likely far outweigh the loss of reputation. The sheer size of the sums involved was too tempting for some executives, knowing that the sacrifice of a lifetime's income flow (at the age of say forty) was indeed small pennies to sacrifice. Brazil is a nice place I believe. Third, even if caught and convicted, the sheer size of the sums involved may still warrant a medium term holiday in prison. Besides, with memory loss being what it is these days and a plethora of clever lawyers to choose from, there still remains a high probability of only a minor penalty being incurred or even complete acquittal.

In essence, this is where self-regulation broke down in the United States – the incentives to cheat were so huge and the ex ante likelihood of being caught so low. It is very difficult, if not impossible, for government regulation to harness human nature completely – otherwise the whole management function would crumble and risk-taking would diminish to zero. *The driving forces of corporate corruption are greed and inflated egos.* Government's cannot abolish these inherent human characteristics and so government regulation may fail where self-regulation also failed. Perhaps those to the right of politics favour 'carrots' whereas those to the left of politics favour 'sticks'. It appears that while the principle of self-regulation has not been abandoned there has been a shift in political thinking towards a greater external regulatory framework. The bias is now towards government imposed penalties and not corporate designed incentive packages – in order to align the interests of the agent (CEO) with the principal (stockholder).

An expert on the regulatory response, including the Sarbanes-Oxley Act, is Professor Larry Ribstein (2002) – his assessment on the debate discussed earlier is as follows

> ...despite all the appearances of market failure, the recent corporate frauds do not justify a new era of corporate regulation. Indeed, the fact that the frauds occurred after 70 years of securities regulation shows that more regulation is not the answer. Rather, with all their imperfections, contract and market-based approaches are more likely than regulation to reach efficient results. Increased post-Enron reforms, including Sarbanes-Oxley, rely on increased monitoring by independent directors, auditors, and regulators, who have both weak incentives and low-level access to information. This monitoring has not been, and cannot be, an effective way to deal with fraud by highly motivated insiders. Moreover, the laws are likely to have significant costs, including perverse incentives of managers, increasing distrust and bureaucracy in firms and impeding information flows. The only effective antidotes to fraud are active and vigilant markets and professionals with strong incentives to investigate corporate managers and dig up corporate information.

Incentives and trade-offs

Much of US corporate failure can be explained by greed and the biases explained in Chapter 4. Game theory has something to offer here, as there are many 'players' in the stock market game – not all sharing common interests. Each player seeks to gain a share of the corporate pie (stock values) – sometimes at the expense of other players. Greed and conflict of interest lead players to indulge in unethical and illegal behaviour in an effort to jockey for a better capital gain position. A comparison of a 'game of musical chairs' with the stock market 'casino' is a relevant one here. Sometimes the investment game boils down to winners (executives/managers) colluding against losers (shareholders/creditors).

For any regulatory framework to be successful, and so meet its objectives, it must incorporate and respect self-interest and so *align* the incentives of the principal with those of the agent. There are unavoidable agency costs. In this modern world dominated by large companies – the separation of ownership from control – presents a serious power dichotomy. It is often said that a potent vehicle of aligning manager and shareholder interests is that of granting stock options for the manager – triggered at a 'high' stock price level. This causes the manager to strive for higher and accelerating profits – partly out of self-interest and partly out of managerial responsibility. The short-term aim of shareholders is higher profit levels and so by sharing a greater portion of profits with managers there is greater harmony and zeal towards that common goal. Hence, the manager's remuneration is largely performance based and so shareholders should not complain if stock price and/or profit targets are met – and the CEO draws a huge bonus.

At least that's the way the story runs. Well, what's wrong with the story? First, the lengths to which creative and crooked accounting was undertaken by corporate managers is partly explained by their pot of gold (stock options) resting on a few consecutive years of rising profit growth. Why not cook the books, exercise the options and then leave? Second, the incentive structure is hugely biased in favour of the CEO as his gains are *exponential* while the shareholders gains are *arithmetic*. Both gains should be tied to some arithmetic formulae – the CEO be granted main socks and not options. Third, there is a real cost to paying managers with stock options as they have not been expensed in the past. Profits are eroded and there is less to pay the real residual stakeholders – the shareholders. It is not just the cost to the shareholder that caused a major uproar against the accounting profession but the fact that it is partially hidden. It is only recently that large companies have tried to put an estimate on this cost – possibly around 8 per cent of profits. However, this theory of alignment and self-interest is based on performance not failure. So why then have so many lucrative packages been cashed in when stock prices have fallen? In theory, a poor or 'negative' bonus should accompany a poor company performance.

So why then did America's CEOs perform so badly when their incentive structure was so lucrative? Perhaps the profit benchmarks were set too high and a kind of moral hazard set in? All managers tried to be better than average. Or perhaps it was just plain greed – the exponential incentives were too great – and managers yielded to temptation? Maybe the carrots were too sweet and the sticks too soft? There is the issue of real fundamentals here, the economy can only grow at around 3 per cent per year and so achieving 'above normal' corporate profits year in and year out is not possible. Even great growth companies can only deliver supernormal profits for a while. This belief in the supernormal is at the heart of corporate governance failure – CEOs thought themselves far superior to other CEOs – and in reality were beguiled by their own egos. Peer pressure did the rest – too much competition between CEOs (or should I say too much jealousy) – poured excessive fuel on ambition. At face value at least, theory can explain the corporate fraud debacle as the *financial* incentive structure was too lucrative and not constrained by the long-run real *economic* growth rate of the economy – as non-verifiable corporate profits were overstated in the short run. What is consistent with cost-benefit analysis is that the huge pot of gold was worth running off with – by the sheer laws of probability.

One should remember the stock broker Budd Fox in the movie 'Wall Street' who was trapped and blackmailed by Gordon Gecko the greed merchant. The young man was lured by ambition and fame and not just money. He wanted to emulate Gordon Gecko and be a raving success. He also believed the he would not get caught by government authorities and continued to 'live on the edge'. He crossed the line into illegality and did get caught. There were too many pressures from Wall Street that beguiled him to be above average.

What are the challenging issues?

There are many examples of corporate misbehaviour, if not fraud. In many ways, corporate executives, as well as the accounting and legal professions crossed a fine line between what was clinically legal and what was not. The drive to maximize profits and minimize taxation is not new but the audacity and arrogance with which

Corporate America pursued these goals set new highs. We know of the downfall of Enron and Worldcom and the tarnished reputation of Arthur Anderson the auditor. The bloating of revenues and profits was not the sole domain of these two giants but many other respectable corporations got caught up with book-cooking as well – such as Merck and Xerox. Charges of insider trading were made against Sam Waksal (ImClone Systems) and Martha Stewart.

Other corporations such as Qwest, Global Crossing and Bristol Myers Squibb also face investigation by the SEC for allegedly violating accounting rules. The overall picture of corporate governance in America is a poor one. There is gross dissatisfaction and disillusionment with both professional and ethical standards. Intense media coverage has broadened the exposure of corporate misdeeds into the public arena. Not only have distraught smaller investors vented their anger over devastating losses but the public also displayed its outrage on moral grounds.

So what are the major issues of concern? What are the misdeeds of Corporate America that are so wrong? The olds sin is that of *insider trading*. Executives and employees of a company may take advantage of special knowledge of a company's prospects and so buy or sell that stock in order to profit – before anyone else can act. Even delaying the release of relevant information is both unfair and illegal.

Second, the inflating of revenues and deferring of costs – with the intent of *pumping up profits* – is seen as cooking the books. Such 'profits' are fake, false and misleading. The divergence between Pro-Forma and GAAP-based profit reports widened in the 1990s as CEOs indulged income smoothing and treating distant income flows as they were certain to arrive. This pulling of levers and strings is aimed at deceiving some investors, if not all. The size of this false reporting for the NASDAQ was staggering as Cunningham (2002) points out – 'One way to gauge the costs of believing in the spurious accounting of the late 1990s examines the difference between the gains reported in that period with losses revealed later. For the four quarters ending in mid-2001, 4,200 Nasdaq companies reported combined lossess of $148.2 billion, compared with $145.3 in profit over the prior five years combined.' This is a massive reversal and face-about-turn as you will ever see. Massaging the accounts to present a rosy trading picture was aimed at protecting the managers of corporations from shame, firing, and of course their precious nest egg of stock options from diminishing in value. However, the downside of such massaging is the threat of law suits – albeit well after the event.

Third, the use of Special Purpose Vehicles (SPVs) – other companies that can be used to 'hide' debt and so keep off the balance sheet of the parent company. The principle here is that all accounting 'negatives' are placed in the SPV, well away from scrutiny and the main company 'picture'. There has always been great conjecture as to what should and what should not be disclosed in a company's balance sheet. Most investors would argue for more disclosure rather than less and for less information to be buried footnote form. The existence of large derivative-related liabilities being hidden as 'off-balance sheet' items caused much consternation in the investor community as witnessed by the Enron and Long-Term Capital Management debacles. This era was no doubt one of creative accounting and crony capitalism.

Fourth, the non-arm's-length relationships within the company framework that inhibits any independent criticism of company wrongdoing. For example, CEOs appointing key personnel to the company's board – in the belief that they will be 'loyal' and not make waves. Appointees are often part of the 'old boys club' or old friends from college days that can be 'trusted'. Such appointments restrict true scrutiny and criticism of company affairs – a suffocation of any independent watch-dog role as it were.

Fifth, the conflict of interest that arises for an accounting firm when it undertakes both audit and non-audit work. This is the conflict that exists between auditing and investment banking. Accounting firms make far more money from investment advice than from auditing. The independence and quality of research is also compromised in order to keep the investment banking client content.

At the heart of the mangled corporate governance issue is the insider–outsider dichotomy. It is the insider that has the vast majority of power and knowledge, whereas the outsider is just that – possessing weak rights of reply, ill-informed and individually powerless. The incentives to exploit this lopsided power relationship have been irresistible for some executives in Corporate America.

Wall Street in the 1960s: fresh challenges

Recent failures of corporate and public governance are not new – there were similar stresses and strains in the 1960s when the 'new flood' of investors arrived – seeking large capital gains. Vast amounts of 'new-found' wealth were placed or stored in US stock markets – challenging partnership brokerage firms, market forecasters, government regulators and policy-makers alike. Something like seven times as many Americans held stocks by the end of the 1960s than during the height of the 1929 boom. Such a surge of investors into stock markets was driven by sheer speculation – as ordinary citizens increasingly dabbled in common stocks lured by tax-free capital gains.

The securities industry was seen in a certain light in the old days. Between 1930s and the early 1960s the US stock brokering fraternity portrayed the image of being the establishment and some kind of private club. Discrimination was at work as men were preferred over women, old over young, protestant over catholic and white over black. This industry was, and still is, 'well-connected' with Washington. Much political lobbying is undertaken so as to not diminish the privileged position of the 'club'.

There is one key ongoing trend that has challenged regulatory authorities for years – the rise of big institutional investors. The nature of the investor–speculator changed from the individual to the institution as mutual funds, and to a lesser extent, hedge funds made their appearance in the 1960s. By their sheer size, the mutual funds could affect stock prices in their day-to-day trading let alone in securing long-term strategic positions. In collusion, they could manipulate stock prices and so trap unsuspecting small investors who watched the market for clues of takeover or merger activity. Hence, profitability was a function of well-disguised deception. After the crash of 1962, the power of mutual funds was evident, as they bought in gloom and were also able to withstand margin calls in contrast to their small shareholder–speculator counterparts. No longer were individuals and small traders the lifeblood of stock markets in the United States but institutions with deep pockets. In fact, the portfolio managers of the 1960s were akin to the pool managers of the 1920s. As discussed earlier, the expansion of pension funds and 401k biases – from the 1980s onwards – have pushed a flood of money into the 'one-way street' of stocks.

Just as in the 1960s, new waves of both individual and institutional investors flooded into stocks in the 1990s. This time foreign investors played a major role in ballooning the market. What challenges US regulatory authorities is to protect new investors from themselves – those that are inexperienced and have never drowned in a recession. Moreover, such authorities seek to protect the outsiders from the insiders and new investors from the powerful.

Past pressure for regulation

Just as the Great Depression served as a catalyst for regulatory reform in the mid-1930s, so did the changing corporate face of America in the form of more 'conglomerates', the growth of mutual funds and the portfolio manager in the 1960s stimulate the SEC into more action. Such trends typified the growing problem of principal–agent whereby the small shareholder and creditor depended heavily on the judgment and honour of their broker. Given the amount of money being 'invested' in Wall Street and the privileged position held by stock-brokers, there were bound to be abuses of power and trust. Brokers used inside information to their own advantage, deliberately distorted stock prices and volumes in order to attract investor attention and traded on their accounts on the trading floor. Nevertheless, stock-brokers were not prosecuted under any insider trader provisions of any legislation. The US regulatory authorities became growingly uneasy by the increasing visibility of the insider–outsider dichotomy and its potential damage to the long-run reputation of Wall Street. In response to several scandals and alleged misdemeanours the SEC increased its surveillance of stock exchange members.

Corporate scandals were not the sole domain of the 1990s. Amidst the boom times of the 1950s were visible undercurrents that high-flying individuals and brokers themselves were not acting properly in accordance with existing legislation or a basic code of ethics. The American Stock Exchange (AMEX) was rocked by several scandals and investigations. Research by Brooks (1999) paints the following scenario of intrigue and reform. An investigation into the stock trading and conduct of Jerry and Gerard Re (a member firm) in the 1950s witnessed their expulsion from AMEX in 1961. Further investigations revealed that the current head of AMEX (McCormick) was implicated in these matters and was associated with the two Re's brothers. The new-found vigour of the SEC under Jackson pursued McCormick until he resigned as chairman of AMEX. Such conflict is a classic case of the regulator (SEC) versus the industry (AMEX) whereby the latter is accused of misusing privileged power against its own clients and the public in general. The SEC won this battle as the old executive guard of AMEX were forced to stand down and so enable some fairer trading laws to be put in place. It appears that self-regulation failed in a rapidly growing industry such as US stock markets much to the bitter dismay of both AMEX and the NYSE. Obviously some member brokers were clean, honourable and cherished their own reputation and so naturally felt victimized by their colleagues dishonesty and greed.

As a result of the crash of 1962, the head of the SEC (Cary) initiated a special study into AMEX. Several recommendations followed such as greater screening of character for aspiring stock brokers, the tightening of insider trading rules, higher disclosure standards for new issues, lower brokerage fees, the abolition of floor trading by specialist brokers on their own behalf or if not members be required to pass an examination before they became full-fledged floor traders and the abolition of front-end fees by mutual funds for putting together a large deal. In August of 1964, some of these recommendations became law but more importantly Wall Street had been given a wake-up call that the cowboy days of fraud and manipulation were not acceptable and the SEC would convict those brokers that still wanted to ignore 'the call'.

The corporate world produced individuals that were willing to bend rules to the limit in order to achieve the rapid accumulation of wealth. High leverage was a common feature of the downfall of several high-flying Gurus. For example, Lowell Birrell commanded several corporations and issued himself unauthorized stock to later sell these shares on the open market. Even though chased by the law in the late 1950s, he managed to secure a nice lifestyle in Brazil free from US prosecution. Eddie Gilbert was another high-flying, highly leveraged entrepreneurial corporate leader who exploited the weak regulatory environment of the early 1960s and ended up in the same place – Brazil. The crash of 1962 squeezed him badly on calls. Buying stocks on margin and exploiting high leverage ratios were the major reasons why both men fell from grace and stability.

There are lessons here for the modern day. The insider–outsider dichotomy has not disappeared over the years. Various types of manipulation can be undertaken by the insider to jack up the company's share price in the belief that he can sell to the duped outsider. The 'new waves' of investor clientele has made this task easier – as in the 1960s. Small investors and creditors are still being deliberately deceived by large institutions and corporate executives as in the past. Accounting trickery, especially in relation to merger activity, ballooned stock prices and expectations in the 1960s – as in the present. In summary, the key problems surrounding the principal–agent relationship has not disappeared in the twenty-first century. The timely flow of information is as critical as it has always been.

The case of Enron

The rise and fall of Enron provides some useful insights into how corporate managers pushed the spirit of deregulation and the law to its limits – and beyond. Enron transformed itself from a gas-pipeline company in the 1980s to a mega energy-trading company that bought and sold both gas and electricity in the 1990s. High financial leverage and massive volumes combined to boost the rise of Enron. It sought more and more growth often at the expense of profits. Although profit margins were thin, high volumes and turnover were enough to offset – at least for a while. With the transport of gas being highly regulated and the selling of gas being mainly unregulated, Enron pushed more into the financial field of futures and derivatives trading. The buying and selling of energy futures contracts offered more profit opportunity than the physical side of Enron's business. This suited clients that wanted to trade in contracts but not take delivery. After all, gas prices could move 40 per cent in one year and electricity prices were even more volatile than gas. Unfortunately for Enron, the level of risk-management skill required to successfully deal in derivatives was lacking. When year after year of rolling losses came to the fore, Enron's credit rating nosedived and eventually its line of credit dried up – choking it into submission. When this company fell from grace it became the biggest corporate bankruptcy in American history. As Fox (2003) points out, perhaps it was an overambitious pursuit of profit – namely a stated drive for 15 per cent a year that was the company's undoing? All companies cannot sustain an above-average profit performance for long – Enron was no exception.

On the accounting front, Enron employed several dubious accounting techniques. For example, it employed a mark-to-market accounting technique that treated revenue from long-term contracts as being current. Hence, profits were boosted as though the revenue was received – when in fact it was not. This was a deceitful and misleading practice at best. Massaging the accounts also included unexpected expenses being treated as one-off costs, as 'extraordinary items' or as 'non-recurring' – and so not related to the core activity of the business. This massaging was done in the hope that investors would ignore such costs – as they were portrayed as being random events.

Enron used SPVs or close partnerships with other companies to 'hide' parent company debt, its true financial leverage ratio and other negatives – that is to hold risk. These SPVs were supposed to have a minimum of 3 per cent of their stock held by an independent body – if not that SPV's financial affairs need to be consolidated in Enron's books. Indeed, it found ways of getting around this independence requirement and did hide massive amounts of debt in SPVs and away from its core financial statements.

The SEC did investigate Enron with a view to exposing the severity of related party transactions, that is, pushing and pulling revenues and costs between related parties with the intent of presenting an artificial picture of the company's financial health. The timing of the release of relevant information was also criticized. Why did it take Enron so long to issue profit re-statements or downgrades for the early 1990s?

As a matter of good corporate governance, the board of Enron was not independent but were friends of the executives. The independent watchdog role was therefore compromised and transgressions that should have been discovered (earlier) were not.

A dangerous incentive structure?

As discussed earlier, there is an ongoing heated debate over the importance and morality of corporate executives receiving stock options as a major part of their remuneration package. The rationale for this type of remuneration is that it is 'performance-based' – that is, the higher the company's stock price the more the executive stands to benefit. Normally, a high trigger price on the main stock has to be attained before stock options will accelerate in value – an incentive for company executives to pull levers in order to achieve that high price. Supposedly, there is a strong tie or link between executive strategies and company success. Thus, there are incentives for executives to be energetic and single-minded in pushing the company to greater heights. This is obviously not completely correct as the 'state of the economy' and random events knock the stock price about as well. How do we disentangle state of the economy forces from the success of the CEO? With great difficulty one would say! Perhaps stock option packages are designed to be rewarding when stock prices are on the way up but not penalizing on the way down. Why should CEOs not be made accountable for company failure as well as company success?

What has become evident in recent US corporate history is the dangerous bias for company executives to pump up their own stock price – almost at any cost. Graduates are taught at Ivey League universities that all efforts must be directed at creating shareholder value and an ever increasing stock price. Captains of the Ivey League eventually end up as CEOs in Corporate America and succumb to the temptation of artificially ballooning their own stock price – regardless of fundamentals or ethical standards. Share buy-backs are common in America as they marry the interests of the manager with the investor. Lower capital gains taxes benefit the investor – rather than pay taxes on dividends – and higher stock prices trigger lucrative stock options for the manager. No wonder share buy-backs were popular. However, to the extent that the stock price has been artificially pumped – such behaviour reflects the dark side of self-interest. So what if CEOs make $20 or $100 million from their stock options? Are such sums of money so crucial for company profitability or ordinary stock-holder dividend payouts? First, the fact that an increasing bias towards stock options as remuneration – not just for executives but also many other employees in the company – dilutes the value of stocks held by others. If the stock price roars so do option payouts soar as well – and they must be paid for out of profits. This means less profit for existing stockholders. Such a dilution in value was not well recognized – until recently. Second, to the extent that CEOs artificially raise their company's stock price so is there an inherent danger that it will collapse as true fundamentals eventually become known or as increased pressure for fairer disclosure standards are forced upon CEOs. Biases in the corporate and investor decision making process is what bubbles are made of.

From the discussion we are well aware of the origins of America's corporate governance debacle. The real challenge is how to reform corporate governance standards that are fair, realistic, defined and enforceable.

Regulatory reform and the Sarbanes-Oxley Act

We have discovered some of the major weaknesses and loopholes in America's corporate governance structure. It should not come as a surprise that the new regulatory reforms are aimed at rectifying these weaknesses. In particular, the Sarbanes-Oxley reforms are aimed at improving disclosure requirements, strengthening independent watchdogs, improving the flow of information to shareholders and increasing executive responsibility for the accuracy of the company's accounts and corporate governance in general.

The SEC has introduced tough new laws. For example, auditors are deterred from conducting non-audit work. This is aimed at reducing the conflict of interest between basic auditing and consulting. However, auditors can undertake non-audit work after stepping down as auditor. The definition of what constitutes 'audit work' is a broad concept and so provides leeway and flexibility for the auditor to 'carry on as normal'. Hence, the new law has not totally solved the conflict of interest problem. The SEC has also required key partners in audit firms to be rotated every five years – for the sake of maintaining independence from particular clients.

There is a new watchdog – that of the Company Accounting Oversight Board – under the wing of the SEC that will dictate and oversee auditing standards. From the company's perspective the Board must include a financial expert to chair the audit committee and so the appointment and remuneration of the lead auditor. This person and the committee is to be comprised of non-executives and so their decisions are not to be impaired by company executives.

The Boards of listed companies are to have a major element – indeed a majority – of independent, non-executive directors and such people are to meet at regular intervals without executive directors being present. The non-executives are meant to be independent and not the friends and associates of the existing executive. Executive behaviour is to improve via greater disclosure of share sales – they must be declared quickly. Existing shareholders and the market have the right to know when executive stock options were exercised. Moreover, new laws prohibit executives selling shares when employees are banned from selling. On the issue of timing and speed, there are higher standards of financial disclosure as the accounts are submitted sooner to regulatory authorities. Of critical importance is the requirement of CEOs and CFOs to attest to the validity and accuracy of the accounts – they have to sign off. The use of pro forma accounting is to be curbed. Serious wrongdoing by executives is to be punished by a goal sentence – and regulatory authorities are keen to flag their intention of prosecuting and bringing to justice such wrongdoers.

Not only are auditors and accountants called to higher standards of responsibility but lawyers as well. There is the duty of informing the Board and senior staff of violations of security law – at least as perceived by the lawyers. A stronger version of the proposed law was that lawyers would be required to inform the SEC of security law violations – that is, blow the whistle on clients. They were naturally opposed to this kind of whistle-blowing.

Given that many of the reforms mentioned earlier are aimed at improving executive responsibility and disclosure, the NYSE has insisted on companies publishing corporate governance guidelines that outlines the ways and means by which corporate executives will be held accountable for their actions and so performance. This includes the performance of the Board.

Some commentators acclaim these new reforms as having bite and a vast improvement of the self-regulation framework of the past. However, the resources of the SEC and NYSE to pursue and prosecute are not abundant. It is more likely that only a few prosecutions could be realistically undertaken and won – but nevertheless have a significant signalling impact on other potential executive wrongdoers. Moreover, the investment community would applaud such legal action as a step in the right direction to more meaningful and accurate financial disclosure in the future.

All of this is not to say that self-regulation is dead, or has been abandoned, but rather professional bodies have been jolted into action. Such bodies have responded to America's corporate governance fiasco by tightening standards and requiring greater and more timely disclosure of information. They have also sought to address conflict-of-interest issues. Infinite government regulation is not a substitute for quality self-regulation. Why? Because government resources are limited and have to be provided by someone – namely, the US taxpayer in the main. Regulation is costly as those that pay lawyer's fees will testify. Second, higher 'internal' professional standards are relatively cheaper to enforce – the self-interest of the member coincides with that of the governing body. Third, over-regulation instills fear and so kills initiative. There is balance required between sticks and carrots. The stick of long gaol terms for executive wrongdoers has forced professional bodies into cleaning up their own houses.

Conclusion

As in all post-bubble crashes there is always a lot of headhunting to be undertaken – as investors seek revenge for their lost capital. They seek to blame someone – CEOs, auditors, financial advisers, securities firms, biased media reports, margin lenders, banks, the SEC, the NYSE – to name a few. In the stock crash of 2001–3 there were plenty of culprits to blame – as the excesses of the 1990s were gross. Unfortunately, for the unsuspecting investor there was a combination of powerful forces of self-interest that stampeded the masses headlong into a bubble. It appears that the regulatory environment was weak and only mildly effective. Huge corporate bankruptcies probably could not have been foreseen as disclosure standards did not provide adequate visibility for the ordinary stockholder. An over-liquid financial sector caused investors to be over-optimistic and less cautious than normal.

There were, however, serious inherent biases affecting the decision-making process of Corporate America. The sheer size and sweetness of stock options for CEOs caused stock prices to be inflated and earnings growth to be overestimated. Share buy-backs using company, or even worse borrowed money, further added to the inflationary fuel of higher stock prices. Accounting magic and auditor blindness did the rest. Insider power proved too much of an overwhelming force in delivering short-term non-refutable profit outcomes that stockholders wanted to believe anyway. As the Bible states – broad is the road to hell.

Could the SEC have avoided the expanding bubble and so reduced investor heartache after its collapse? The answer is most likely 'no'. Given the exuberance of investors and the self-fulfilling prophesy of rising stock prices as new waves of investors entered the market no amount of government regulation would have prevented the stock bubble. There were bound to be casualties along the way.

There is an agenda for reform going on in Corporate America – either drastically improve standards of self-regulation or face a litany of government laws aimed at improving the openness and transparency of corporate decision making and profit reporting. Governments must alter the 'incentive structure' that corporations face and make clear the 'rules of the game' in which corporations and investors can make decisions. The new era of regulation is not so much opposed to self-interest or self-regulation but has increased the fear and probability of corporate wrongdoers getting caught and punished.

7　The Federal Reserve

In unchartered waters?

Introduction

As the US economy and stock markets broke new records in the 1990s, there was a curiosity – among policy-makers and economists – as to how to explain this boom within the confines of conventional wisdom. We have already canvassed some of the causes of the stock market bubble. We also examined the origins of the productivity surge in Chapter 5 and we now turn to the role of the Fed steering the economy through these unchartered waters. The irony or dichotomy to be explained is that the financial economy boomed with asset price inflation as its by-product, while the real economy surged and yet goods price inflation was not a by-product. Handling this twin rail dichotomous economy was not an easy task for the Fed.

Old debates in economics came to the fore, such as the disastrous era of the 1970s, whereby stagflation severely reduced economic prosperity and human welfare. Current debates refer to 'speed limits' or constraints on economic growth. Just as heat and light are associated so too are economic growth and inflation – at least in the short run. So why did the US economy grow at 3.6 per cent p.a. in the 1990s compared to 2.8 per cent in the 1980s – and still remain stable? Did it run ahead of potential output? Given the many cited evils of inflation, an overheated economy – running beyond potential output – eventually has to be cooled off. Other *theoretical* constraints on the US economy's economic cruise speed include high current account deficits, a weak currency, declining international competitiveness, high levels of capacity utilization, labour market tightness and the traditional proxy for inflationary heat – the unemployment rate. The Fed scrutinizes a long checklist, not only of the variables mentioned earlier, but also a myriad of other key economic indicators. It is Greenspan's responsibility to monitor any economic imbalances that may develop in the US economy and formulate a monetary policy to shrink such imbalances in line with long-run potential output.

However, the US economy sailed into unchartered waters in the early 1990s – as mentioned earlier the trend in GDP growth did not translate into excessive inflation – causing Greenspan to ponder over why 'old signposts' were fading in relevance. Indeed his 'own' economic paradigm was throwing out the wrong trigger signals to intervene. Indeed, the conduct of monetary policy entered unchartered waters in the 1990s.

Ultimate objectives and trade-offs

The prime mandate or charter of the Fed is to fight inflation. Stimulating output and employment remain important objectives but are overridden by the fear that inflation may wreak havoc with relative prices, distort economic incentives and generate a wasteful diversion of resources into non-productive use. By suppressing inflation and so providing macroeconomic stability, the Fed *indirectly* promotes economic growth and employment. Price stability is the critical prerequisite for long-term investment in human and physical capital and so economic growth. In the Fed's view, low inflation is the path to *sustainable* long-term growth. It is the way, the truth and the life to earthly prosperity. However, if some kind of Phillips curve is to be believed, then the Fed faces the possibility of exploiting an output-inflation trade-off – albeit in the short run. However, there is no evidence to date that Greenspan (2000d) has displayed any desire to tolerate inflation in the quest for any short-term output gain. In his world, real factors drive long-run growth and financial factors only affect growth temporarily.

There are times when the Fed must make choices in the light of known trade-offs. Fighting inflation remains a priority over all other objectives and so the economy may have to be cooled if economic imbalances persist. Deflating the economy via higher interest rates may create *desired* by-products in terms of lower imports, a narrower trade deficit and a stronger US dollar which in turn further suppresses inflation at home. There are also *undesired* by-products in terms of lower investment, bankruptcies, higher unemployment and so lower growth. The Fed often chooses tough measures in the short run in order to achieve maximum benefits for US citizens in the long run.

For the Fed to meet such *ultimate* objectives several policy tools maybe employed. However, such objectives cannot be achieved directly and so *intermediate* targets are employed, such as monetary aggregates or the federal funds rate. Hitting such intermediate targets is achieved by the use of the *policy tools* of legal reserve ratios, the discount rate and open market operations. However, these relationships are not tight. In other words, even hitting intermediate targets is not automatic and the transmission from the buying of bonds (open market operations), to the changing of interest rates, to the change in output or inflation is indirect, may only be weakly transmitted and impact with lags. Even the direct change of the discount rate has mainly an 'announcement effect' rather than a 'decree effect' for the market to follow blindly. Hence, it is more accurate to claim that the Fed has *influence* over the money supply and interest rates rather than complete *control* over such intermediate targets.

The yield curve

A common feature of the yield curve is that it is upward sloping, that is, government securities of the same risk class, but of different maturity and liquidity type, display higher interest rates at the long end of the yield curve than at the short end. The pure expectation hypothesis of the term structure of interest rates claims that lenders require a liquidity premium and borrowers must decide how much of a premium they are prepared to pay. If the slope at the long end of the yield curve moves upward, it could be due to either a higher liquidity premium or expectations of higher short-term rates. Obviously, lenders require compensation for risk, uncertainty and liquidity and so long maturities command higher yields. However, an inverted yield curve – sloping downward – normally reflects a view that a recession approaches. That is, short-term rates are higher than long-term rates – so typical of a credit crunch.

It is obvious that expectations play an important role in determining interest rates – in the line with the famous Fischer effect. If the inflation rate is expected to be higher in the next period, so will interest rates rise to compensate – in order for the real rate to remain constant. Therefore, government policies in general must not raise inflation or inflationary expectations if the administration of the day wants to avoid an interest rate backlash. Although the Fed can *influence* interest rates at the short end of the yield curve, it cannot *control* rates at the long end. Greenspan employs a two-pronged traditional approach to suppressing interest rates at the long end – one, by keeping inflation in check now and second, by encouraging 'sound' government policies with regards to budget deficit reduction and private capital formation. Manipulating or cosmetically altering short-term interest rates is not a panacea for sustainable growth if the long end of the yield curve reacts violently to an inflationary resurgence. In Greenspan's mind there are no short cuts, no free lunches and no artificial expansions. For example, post-September 11 the US administration implemented various platforms of a growth package – including fiscal expansions – that will have longer term repercussions for real interest rates. Greenspan has registered his lack of enthusiasm for such a return to a series of budget deficits in the coming years. He has openly criticized the Bush administration's fiscal strategy and made himself unpopular in the process.

A degree of care is therefore required, the precept that the Fed is 'all powerful' is somewhat misplaced as it adheres to its inflation watchdog role – *it is a facilitator not a creator of growth*. Besides, a realignment of burden between fiscal and monetary policies is the outcome of a democratic process and not the sole discretion of the Fed.

The government environment

As in all markets, the forces of supply and demand determine stock prices. However, such prices are not solely determined by private sector decisions or even determined endogenously. Just as there are uncontrollable external influences impinging on stock prices (unavoidable risk), there is the power and influence of government to contend with. Government policies of all kinds affect relative prices. Although exchange rate, industrial and protection policies have been used in the past by US policy-makers, they are now less favoured than previously. Fiscal policy became popular under the prescription of Keynesian economics – spend and prosper – taken literally by several US administrations. Some economists claim that relative prices are disturbed and the allocation of resources 'distorted'. The issue of 'crowding out' whereby growing government budget deficits 'caused' interest rates to rise attracted serious attention. The threat of higher taxes in the future caused distress among many middle-class Americans. As successive higher budget deficits pushed the national debt towards

$4 trillion, so did public pressure increase to dampen government deficit spending. A striking feature of policy-making in the 1990s is that there was less reliance on use of a fiscal policy and so a heavier burden placed on the use of monetary policy – at least up until September 11.

Any sign of an overheated economy could trigger the Fed to raise interest rates and so correct excessive imbalances. Conversely, a flagging economy would require lower interest rates. Hence, the Fed uses monetary levers to keep the economy at a comfortable cruise speed without igniting inflation or its cousin – inflationary expectations. However, the reduced use of policy levers – partly as a result of greater deregulation – has its cost in terms of less ability by government to steer the US economy. During fine weather the need for policy levers are remote, but during an unanticipated storm – the non-availability of potent policy levers leaves the US economy vulnerable. There is a fierce debate in America over the strategy to stimulate the economy further via tax breaks – the abolition of the double taxation of dividends, lower marginal income tax rates and capital gains taxes. Neo-liberals desire more government spending and tax cuts for low income earners and not tax cuts for the rich.

As this book makes clear, the reliance on a monetary policy, and an interest rate strategy in particular, may not be enough to avert or solve any current or future US financial crisis. Just as in Japan, zero real interest rates and lower taxes did not kick-start their economy and the Nikkei average tested new 'lows' right up until March 2003. Hence, the US economic recovery has been a very stop–start affair since 2001 even in the face of many interest rate cuts. As we will examine in the next chapter – a reliance on lowering interest rates to stimulate economic activity *and* stocks has its flaws.

America's economic cruise speed: what guideposts?

So what forces determine a comfortable economic cruise speed? The neoclassical and monetarist schools of thought argue that 'real factors' such as the size of the capital stock, the work force, preferences for saving and work drive growth. More importantly, it is technological progress and productivity that dictate long-run growth and so cruise speed. So what is left for US government to do? The answer is basically nothing, other than to provide a system of property rights, law and order and macroeconomic stability. Under these conditions the private sector will flourish. And so small government is preferred to big government as resources are released for private investment and market interest rates are left to find their own level. These schools of thought abhor any concept of 'fine-tuning' the economy in order to smooth the fluctuations of the business cycle. If the economy is basically stable and possesses self-healing properties, then the role of the policy-maker is secondary, as time will heal the wounds of a temporarily wayward economy. This view of small government and the ability of markets to allocate resources efficiently is an economic paradigm accepted by Greenspan (2000c).

So, are the fluctuations of a business cycle to be accepted? According to Real Business Cycle (RBC) theory such fluctuations are real and are to be left alone. It is doubtful whether Greenspan is an RBC disciple but he accepts that preferences of consumers, investors and workers are to be respected. High levels of spending may be a function of inter-temporal choice by these groups in response to changes in wages and interest rates. The Fed's track record of intervention under Greenspan's reign (1987) has been one of moderate intervention and certainly not one of fine-tuning. There have been fairly wide tolerances for GDP growth and very high tolerances for rising asset prices. This is a laissez-faire helmsman at work.

What evidence would spur Greenspan to respond to 'excessive swings' in the business cycle? High rates of inflation or even worse accelerating inflation are the prime movers. Where there is heat there is light and so it is with growth and inflation – at least according to a traditional Phillips curve relationship. If the US economy belts along at a rapid clip, the risk of inflation rising is high. If left unchecked, rampant inflation will destroy any civilization via distorted incentives and prices that in turn misallocate resources. Just ask those German people that recall such vivid and horrific memories of the 1920s. Any inflationary outburst, if checked by the Fed by raising interest rates, under normal conditions, will cause an economic contraction and a removal of excess heat. Even though there is a movement away from 'full employment' for a time. Lowering inflationary expectations is the key to returning to a lower interest rate regime in the medium term.

Another prime mover is that of imbalances and constraints in goods and labour markets raising their head. According to the neoclassical paradigm, such indicators as labour market tightness (Greenspan's favourite), mounting wage pressure, rising unit costs, high levels of capacity utilization, etc. may provoke the Fed into action – such as its pre-emptive strike against inflation in 1994. Old guideposts justified the move. Inflationary expectations also qualify as a key catalyst for Fed action, as the original forces of inflation may have subsided but economic agents adjust their expectations adaptively or sluggishly.

Other threats to a comfortable economic cruise speed or a deviation from potential output include a ballooning current account deficit, a loss of international competitiveness, a weak US dollar and an exploding monetary aggregates. The Fed monitors trends in these variables, as well as inflation, in forming its policy strategy. Although current account deficits are not evil per se, they do reflect a degree of demand-side heat in the US economy as US incomes rise causing imports to be sucked in. Given that foreign capital flows or capital account surplus is but the opposite side of the same coin to a current account deficit – foreign goods are purchased with foreign money. It is possible that foreign capital inflows provided Americans with the wherewithal to indulge in 'over-consumption'. A weak US dollar generates inflationary heat via higher import prices and inputs in the production process. A lack of international competitiveness may result from higher wage growth and lower productivity growth than US trading partners. A rapidly growing money supply – beyond 'bands' set by the Fed – can also cause alarm as pent-up (but not yet visible) inflationary heat builds up in the economic system. Even so, the Fed 'watches' money supply growth figures but is wary of drawing any quick conclusions.

In summary, there are theoretical constraints to a rapid economic cruise speed – as imbalances accumulate, akin to uncontrollable vibration of a speeding motor vehicle, necessitates the economy to slow down. The paradox, however, is that the US economy was not plagued by the constraints on growth in the 1990s – or at least they were not binding. In fact, for much of this period the US dollar was strong, productivity growth robust and above its long-run trend, unit labour costs were subdued and inflation benign – generating a virtuous circle of rapid growth and a high cruise speed. Did this high growth–low inflation performance fit a standard macroeconomic model or the conventional paradigm employed by Greenspan? The answer is probably not and so the trigger signals for monetary policy intervention were most likely faulty – based on an old 'high inflation–low growth' paradigm.

Times changed however by 2000 and persisted through 2002. The US dollar was under attack, the Current Account Deficit (CAD) was widening, net capital inflows were shrinking and US stock prices had lost their gloss. Inflation remained low despite the US dollar falling significantly but GDP growth and economic activity collapsed in tandem. Hence, the Fed has been challenged by the threat of recession and deflationary fears since 2000 and has responded via monetary expansion in order to push the US economy closer to it natural cruise speed. This is a tough task considering that some of the 'constraints' – such as the CAD, capital flow shrinkage and a softer US dollar – have got worse since 2000 and not better.

Diagnosis of imbalances

How does the Fed gauge that the economy has deviated from potential output? The Fed monitors several imbalances in the economy that may undermine an economic expansion or detract from long-term sustainable growth. In other words, such imbalances signal that the current growth rate is not sustainable. History tells us that persistent imbalances will 'at some point' lead to inflationary acceleration.

The *first imbalance* comes from the labour market. Some economists point to a Natural Rate of Unemployment (NRU) that acts as a constraint or barrier to growth. It is like hitting a wall or hitting a cruise speed that cannot be 'artificially' improved upon. In the past, full employment meant just that – all those who wanted to work could find jobs. The 1 or 2 per cent of visible unemployment constituted just those that were frictional – just improving their lot in life by switching jobs. Cyclical unemployment may visit from time to time but was not a permanent influence. However, the Friedman-Phelps creation of the NAIRU claims that unemployment will not be 'zero' but a figure that includes structural as well as frictional unemployment. This figure or *estimate* for the United States was around 5.2 per cent in the 1960s, 7.0 per cent in the 1970s, 6.5 per cent in the 1980s and 6.3 per cent for much of the 1990s (Canterbery 2000c). However, in the late 1990s when the actual rate was pressing on 4 per cent so did economists revise their estimates of the NAIRU down to around 5 per cent or less.

If the actual unemployment rate fell below the NAIRU, then it was a warning of impending inflation – even if inflation was not currently visible it would soon appear! Conversely, if the actual rate of unemployment rested above the NAIRU, then it was a sign that inflationary pressures were subsiding. Alas, there is a problem – the NAIRU is an *estimate* and so we do not know with precision what the real figure might be. Perhaps we will never know. Economists such as Galbraith and Thurow question the validity of the whole concept – the NAIRU may not even exist at all! Nevertheless, the Fed considers the NAIRU a useful concept and repeatedly points to deviations from it as cause for concern. Greenspan (1999d) continually refers to high pressure in the labour market as a cause for policy concern and often comments with a degree of disbelief that the actual unemployment rate has sunk to around 4.3 per cent below any previous estimate of the NAIRU and yet inflation remains subdued. This is a paradox that Greenspan and others have not convincingly explained.

Perhaps Greenspan's (1997h) major concern is that of a tight labour market eventually generating higher wage claims and squeezing the profit share of the national income. For example, in October 1997 he states 'The performance of labour markets this year suggests that the economy has been on an unsustainable track. That the market rate of absorption of potential workers since 1994 has not induced a more dramatic increase in employee compensation per hour and price inflation has come as a major surprise to most analysts.' His explanation for worker patience with regard to pay claims is that they have traded low-wage increases for job security. He states 'Another explanation I have offered in the past is that acceleration in technology and capital equipment, in part engendering important changes in the types of facilities with which people work on a day-by-day basis, has also induced a discernable increase in fear of job skill obsolescence and, hence, an increasing willingness to seek job in lieu of wage gains . . . but the force of insecurity maybe fading' (Greenspan 1997h). Again, Greenspan is at a loss to explain why a tight labour has not eventually caused a wage explosion and so shaken profit growth in the corporate sector. A shrinking profit share of national income would in turn inhibit future capital formation. History did not repeat itself in the 1990s.

A *second imbalance* is that of demand exceeding supply or spending exceeding capacity. An old benchmark in policy-making is that an Okun-type output constraint exists whereby output growth equals the sum of productivity growth and labour force growth. In the late 1990s, labour force growth has been around 1 per cent and productivity growth around 2.5 per cent yielding a potential growth rate of 3.5 per cent. For many years, economists believed that the US cruise speed of output growth was 2.5 per cent – constrained mainly by lower productivity growth.

Hence, just as the NAIRU appears to have shifted *left*, so has the Okun rule shifted *up*. In other words, the speed limits of the US economy have been raised and so the Fed should not be trigger happy in responding to apparent signs of tightness in accordance with an old economic paradigm. But why the US enjoyed a higher non-inflationary cruise speed – than in recent history – is a critical question that needs answering. It may be that profitability and a huge surge in capital flows explain a higher than normal growth path – and the productivity miracle alone.

A *third imbalance* is that of imports exceeding exports or persistent deficits on current account. The United States can run such deficits for a long time – being the richest country in the world – but eventually finance markets will censure persistent imbalances. However, the willingness of foreigners to forgo consumption in order to finance US current account deficits is not a given. When unease grows within finance markets concerning the funding of this 'gap' the US dollar normally comes under pressure. Recently, Bergstein (2000) has expressed concern over the growing trade deficit 'The trade and current account deficits both hit an annual rate of 4 per cent of GDP in the last quarter. They are rising sharply. They are clearly into zones where in the past there has been a sharp reaction, including a reaction in the exchange market for the dollar.' While there is no doubting the power of a fall in the US dollar to force a rise in domestic interest rates it is not likely to emanate from a blow-out in the trade deficit. The surge in US imports is mostly a function of foreigners pushing huge amounts of money into the US economy causing a domestic spending spillover into foreign goods. After all, macroeconomic theory predicts that when domestic investment is greater than domestic saving then a trade deficit results. So long as rates of return remain solid in the United States, and so long as foreigners are willing to hold US assets, the financing of this imbalance will not be a problem. Greenspan will not be lured into a monetary tightening on the grounds of a trade deficit blow-out alone. Besides, the United States is doing the world a favour by remaining open to foreign exports at a time when many developing countries are struggling. The United States is expanding its trade deficit on terms favourable to itself and United States consumers are benefiting from low US dollar prices.

It is here that we have discovered the Achilles heel of the post-bubble era. Rates of return collapsed between 2000 and 2002, and not only have capital gains not been available, there have been downright massive capital losses in this era. Given the dramatic fall in US asset prices the desire of foreigners to hold US dollar denominated assets collapsed as well. Therefore, the concern over whether the US current account deficit can be financed without upward pressure on interest rates is well founded in the current era. We know that the US dollar has been under downward pressure for three years since 2000 and such a fall has placed upward pressure on US import prices. Whether any serious inflationary outbreak flows from a falling US dollar depends on whether there are other deflationary forces at work that is in the US economy – such as falling incomes or at least a reduction in the rate of GDP growth. Subdued stock prices and capital losses propagate adverse wealth effects and so dampen both spending and inflation. Greenspan counsels against any policy of scaring off foreign capital. 'Efforts to limit directly or to discourage the inflow of capital from abroad would aggravate the problem of budget deficits by raising real interest rates in the United States and lowering domestic investment towards levels consistent with already low domestic savings. Even limited measures affecting only certain capital flows, such as direct investment, would necessitate larger inflows through other channels, which could only be attracted at higher rates of return or with a weaker dollar' (Sicilia and Cruikshank 2000).

The *fourth imbalance* of usual concern is that of the budget deficit. If government spending exceeds its capacity to raise revenue then aggregate demand is boosted and in the meantime places upward pressure on interest rates. However, with US budgets in surplus for much of the 1990s, Greenspan's monetary management task was thwarted less by upward pressure in long bond yields, that is, the traditional by-product of 'crowding out' was not a pressing issue. With the tragedy of September 11 and the administration's desire for a fiscal package to assist economic recovery the fear of the 'dangers' of persistent budget deficits have re-emerged. There is a delicate trade-off here in the employment of a monetary fiscal policy mix. An 'over-reliance' on fiscal policy generating a rise in long-term bond yields eventually incites a tighter monetary policy response at the short end of the yield curve. The prospect of higher inflation can scare the bond market so profusely that much of the government-led policy stimulus dissipates over the medium term.

Do these imbalances provoke Greenspan into action? The answer is sometimes. They are certainly the excesses he peruses when evaluating a monetary response. He is also concerned about wealth effects from stock market gains generating an imbalance between aggregate demand and supply. Demand running ahead of capacity is his prime concern. Fear of labour market 'tightness' also bothers him as old relationships seem to have faded away. The Fed's model of inflationary dynamics is firmly set in the labour market. Wage growth and cost rises are well upfront of the queue in the Fed's mind. As examined earlier, Greenspan expresses concern over power of *expected* productivity growth to induce people to both buy stocks for capital gains and to consume out of those *unrealized gains* – now. Hence, additional demand pressure flows from the whirlwind bubble and creates supply-side bottlenecks. It follows that the money and asset markets are just as important as the labour market for the Fed to watch.

Hitting targets: what policy mix?

In the 'old economy' environment, the policy-maker would rely traditionally on fiscal and monetary policy to steer the economy, that is, manipulating interest rates, taxes and government spending in order maintain the economy close to potential output or the NAIRU. Given the ill side-effects of continual fine-tuning such as a higher level of interest rates, persistent budget deficits and a skyrocketing national debt in the 1960s and 1970s there was an economic and political backlash by the early 1980s. The Keynesianism policy paradigm was under challenge. Despite burgeoning welfare payments and a deep commitment to defense spending, there was growing unease in middle-class America concerning both their current and future tax liabilities. It was President Reagan who switched policy reliance from fiscal to monetary policy, producing the famous Reaganomics era. Such a policy mix was greeted with great enthusiasm by middle-class America as it promised lower taxes, lower interest rates and the cherished opportunity for capital gain. Other policy instruments, such as protection and exchange rate policies, faded in importance. America had become more open to trade and turned from being the world's leading creditor nation to the world's leading debtor nation by the mid-1980s. But such a commitment to free trade *is a policy* in the special case of the United States. Why? Mainly because the United States stands to gain the most from a more open global village in terms of capital and trade flows. It is the giant US corporations that have increased their exposure to offshore markets during the last fifteen years and this partly explains why the Dow and international NASDAQ stocks roared in the aftermath of the Cold War.

In the new economy environment, the US policy-makers have relied more on research, technology, trade and competition policies to stimulate growth and so cause the economy to move closer to its long-run potential. More openness in the global village spells more monopoly profits for US companies and in turn higher stock prices – at least until the bubble burst. Changes in risk perception and profit disappointment were mainly responsible for the major overall of estimated *P/E* ratios and so stock prices.

As we shall discover in the next chapter, Greenspan and the US economics profession in general, believe that minimal policy intervention is required for the purposes of stabilizing the business cycle and even less for the purposes of stimulating economic growth.

What economic indicators?

Measuring the pulse or heartbeat of the economy is complicated by the fact that statistical data available to the Fed is both 'old' and subject to later revision. Formulating policy is something like looking in the rear-vision mirror, seeing where the economy has been rather than where it is going. Revisions can also be substantial enough to alter interpretation months later. Nevertheless, several key economic indicators provide a rough guide as to the location of the economy on the business cycle. Leading indicators such as new orders for consumer goods, the producer price index, vendor performance, contracts for orders of plant and equipment, housing approvals, housing starts, retail sales, average workweek of production workers, changes in sensitive material prices, an index of stock prices and growth in the money supply are all useful signals employed by the Fed. The aim of using these indicators is to predict changes in real GDP and gain a feel for the heat and tightness that is present in the economy. There are obviously value judgments involved and past experience is drawn upon but such experience is thoroughly tested in this bizarre era of financial history.

However, as discussed earlier, there are several sources of confusion for the Fed concerning the appropriate cruise speed of the US economy. One school of thought is that the Fed has placed too much emphasis on old guideposts and speed limits based on past empirical relationships. Not that the economic paradigm is 'wrong' as such, but that it has been applied too strictly. Another school of thought is that the paradigm itself is wrong and benchmark concepts such as the NAIRU and Okun's law are irrelevant or do not exist.

For example, two key indicators of tightness have diverged in the 1990s. There appears tightness in the labour market, if the official unemployment rate is any guide, but there is not the same degree of tightness, from a historical perspective, with regards to capacity utilization. As can be seen from Figure 7.1, the unemployment rate is the lowest for thirty years – in 1999. From Figure 7.2, the capacity utilization rate in the 1970s broke through 85 per cent twice in the 1970s and was associated with inflationary bouts. Capacity utilization rates in the 1990s were only marginally above the long-run average of 81.7 per cent. Therefore, current capacity constraints do not appear to be serious threats to an inflationary outbreak. Likewise, inflationary heat from the labour market has been subdued – even though it was exceptionally tight for most of the 1990s.

Perhaps a shifting paradigm explains why there are so many puzzles that Greenspan can't explain. For example, there is the query concerning the length and

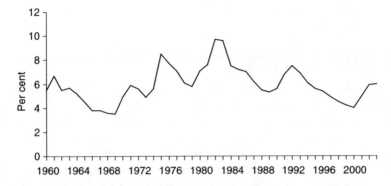

Figure 7.1 Unemployment rate.

Source: Board of Governors of the Federal Reserve System.

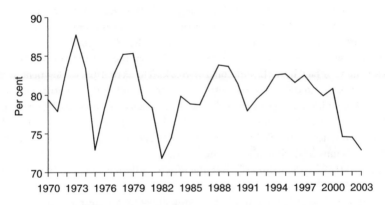

Figure 7.2 Capacity utilization.

maturity of the 1990s boom. It did not reveal the patterns of 'old age' similar to those of past booms. Greenspan has often puzzled over the longevity and freshness of the recent stock and economy boom as it has departed from old signposts. Past 'experience' in formulating monetary policy may count for little in these turbulent unchartered waters of US financial history.

The Keynesian view is that fine-tuning the economy is both possible and prudent, given major advances in computer power and the plethora of statistical information gathered by government agencies. However, there is no evidence to suggest that the Fed gathers statistical information and evaluates key economic indicators for the purpose of *managing* the economy. Rather, it uses such indicators to assess the degree of economic imbalances within the economy and predict future inflationary heat. It does not seek to smooth the business cycle as such, but rather remains alert to inflationary outbreaks that might detract from long-term economic growth. It, therefore, does not seek to fine-tune the economy in any Keynesian sense. The risks of such actions being counter-productive are too great in Greenspan's view.

Critics of the 'Wrong Paradigm'

It is an understatement to say that Greenspan has his critics. For example, Lester Thurow (1996a) rejects the measurement of the official unemployment rate and claims, 'properly calculated, our rate of joblessness is well into double digits'. His estimates of the real unemployment rate are closer to 28 per cent. Given the changed nature of employment in the United States, there is a vast pool of contingent or fringe workers that lack bargaining power and pose no threat to most of the entrenched workforce. More importantly, such workers do not place upward pressure on wage rates and so cannot create wage inflation – they work on the terms and conditions set by their employer. In fact, there is not one labour market but a myriad of segmented markets that are insulated from the pressure of 'outsiders'. Hourly wage and compensation rates in the United States were under pressure from 1978 onwards and continued a downward trend until the mid-1990s. According to Thurow, *real* hourly wages were declining at 1 per cent per year during this era. How can a tight labour market era such as this generate real wage falls? Only in the late 1990s did real hourly wages pick up. It therefore follows that the current estimates of the NAIRU may in fact be well wide off the mark. The actual unemployment rate of 4.3 per cent is far to the left of such estimates. James Galbraith is another economist who has denied for many years the existence or relevance of the NAIRU, or the need to accept that the US economy faces any binding speed limits. In general, these authors cannot accept the Fed's assertion that US labour markets are tight – as there is a large amount of slack – albeit unmeasured.

Thurow (1996b: 186) also criticizes the official inflation rate, claiming that it is biased upward. He points to the Boskin Report, which claims that the CPI may contain an upward bias of 1.0 to 2.6 per cent. After allowing for greater quality improvements and excluding the health care component of the CPI, Thurow claims the over measurement may be closer to 3 per cent. It appears that Thurow has lunged for the trifecta by casting doubt over the mismeasurement of capacity utilization biased by the increased use of outsourcing, the IT revolution gouging more output from less inputs and the increased threat to US producers from developing world producers experiencing excess capacity. In other words, the old signposts of 'slow down' and sacrifice output – may not be as relevant as they once were.

The camp of Blinder, Canterbery, Galbraith and Thurow are critical of the billions of dollars of lost output while the US economy has been kept from realizing its output potential. In their view, there have been many years of waste and lost opportunity. This camp also feels strongly about the biased distribution of income and wealth in America, as blue collar workers are the 'working poor', while white collar professionals enjoy a premium above their worth – acquiring 'unearned income'. When the economy runs hot, it is the working class that are asked to make sacrifices and dampen their wage claims. Vast amounts of wealth accumulated in the hands of the few has created a national policy power base that is reflected in the pursuit of conservative objectives.

In the tradition of 'private wealth and public squalor', this camp believes that America should devote more of its resources to public infrastructure – for both economic and social reasons. There are many examples of public investment supporting private investment albeit with lags – a complementary relationship between the two. Therefore, the United States should run budget deficits to boost long-run growth potential and to rebuild some of America's old public infrastructure. For social reasons, this camp argues that public intervention is necessary to arrest growing income inequality in America. Hence, these economists argue that the US economy should be allowed to grow faster – more in line with its potential.

Canterbery's Vatican paradigm

A recent paradigm developed by Canterbery (2000b) views the conduct of monetary policy from a shared power perspective. In this paradigm certain characters and institutions are identified. Alan Greenspan is the Pope of Wall Street, the Federal Reserve the Vatican, Milton Friedman the High Priest, Wall Street and the Fed the Sacred College of Bonds and Money and the vast army of economists at the Fed are the Monks. In this religion, it is the pursuit of capital gain that is a godly cause and the central pump of the capitalist system. If the Fed raises interest rates – bond prices fall and capital losses result. A rise in rates sends stocks lower and further capital losses result in this market as well. The welfare of bondholders is of paramount importance in this capitalist system that relies heavily on long-term investment for its economic vitality. Likewise, the large US budget deficits required funding and it was America's rich that supplied much of this funding by buying US bonds. Therefore, in this Vatican paradigm, the Fed has a responsibility to bondholders and the bond market not to rock the boat. The prime objective is to maintain a low interest rate structure that produces an environment conducive to trading in bonds and stocks. Canterbery (2000b: 19) queries the Fed's bias in relation to its crusade against goods price inflation over its nonchalance towards asset price inflation. The working poor must make sacrifices and wage inflation is dangerous to the well-being of American society but a burgeoning asset price bubble is to be tolerated on the basis that millions of investors have got it right.

What is also cause for concern is the extent to which the Fed is indeed independent. In this Canterbery paradigm, the Pope listens carefully to the science of the High Priest, the Monks are blindly loyal in their obedience to the religion, the White House is fearful of Wall Street and the bondholders are not greedy individuals but rather patriotic citizens lending money to their government for the service of the community. Power is shared among the wealthy and powerful elite as they share common interests. At the macro level, inflation is the foe of the Fed. At the financial level, inflation is the foe of the bondholder as it devastates capital gains. This common foe of inflation culminates in a marriage of the powerful elite.

The upshot of this Vatican paradigm is the Fed's fear of Wall Street and the Administration's fear of both. If the bond market is unsettled and 'disapproves' of government policy it can censure the government by demanding high interest rates for a time. Public auctions of government securities may be poorly bid. In the mid-1980s the Japanese refused to bid for government bonds for a day or so as they were dissatisfied with low interest rates and a falling US dollar. They went on a 'capital strike'. Such 'blackmail' resulted in domestic interest rates rising. No US administration can afford to upset the bond market. This implies that the Fed keep a close eye on the inflation rate and the money supply and the government keep its own house in order by keeping budget deficits at modest levels. By so doing, interest rates could remain low and the potential for capital gains remain high. Room for policy manoeuvre in this paradigm is limited – as fiscal policy is constrained and a commitment to free trade, handcuffs policy activism towards industry. In short, policy manoeuvrability is severely checked.

The offshoot of this paradigm is that monetary policy has been too restrictive in the United States, based on the notion that the Fed pays 'too much' attention to the bond market. The monetary brakes are therefore applied too easily. This view is embodied in Blinder–Canterbery–Gailbraith–Thurow camp that an 'unfounded obsession' with stabilization over growth has been overdone in recent US financial history.

Reputation and credibility of the Federal Reserve

It is important for the Fed to 'build reputation' and maintain enough credibility to strengthen the effectiveness of monetary policy. There exists an opportunity for the Fed to exploit the short-term trade-off in the Phillips curve by reneging on its commitment to fight inflation. By so doing, output can be raised without any short-term inflationary cost, that is, *after* economic agents have formed their expectations, the Fed has the incentive to expand the money supply and finesse an increase in output. Workers experience a real wage fall and are 'burnt once' but learn from the Fed's bias towards cheating and so raise their own expectations of what inflation will be in the next period. Systematic errors are not made. In the case of the US Fed, the bias towards finessing short-term gains in output is particularly weak. Why? For the simple reason that the long-term cost involves a loss of reputation, permanent damage to policy effectiveness and a loss of face in its fight against inflation. If the Fed is to be 'believed' and credible in the eyes of the public then wringing inflationary expectations out of the business and wage calculus becomes an easier task. Reducing inflation therefore, involves a less painful economic contraction.

There are several ways in which the Fed can build and preserve its long-term reputation. In this quest it seeks to raise levels of openness and transparency by publicly announcing changes to interest rate targets and more importantly *shifts* in monetary policy. Detailing and explaining to the public the rationale of such decisions is aimed at building public confidence. Speeches by the Chairman and others of the FMOC in public forums can assist the fostering of greater public understanding and awareness of how the Fed arrives at its policy strategy. Making available minutes of the last FMOC meeting in a timely manner can also promote transparency in decision making (Greenspan 1999b). In reality, the Fed has embarked upon this 'new classical prescription' for the formulation of monetary policy and the maintenance of its reputation. In the section 'The yield curve', reference is made to Chairman Greenspan's efforts in explaining and justifying the current stance of monetary policy in front of Senate committees on national television.

The caterpillar market and fear of the Fed

When the Fed adopted monetary targeting in the early 1980s a vast army of Fed watchers closely surveyed monthly and weekly figures for hints of a changing wind in monetary policy. If money supply targets were broken on the upside, there was a likelihood of the Fed contacting the money supply via open market operations and indirectly causing a rise in interest rates. Diligent Fed watchers could profit by correctly anticipating the Fed's reaction to money supply bands being broken. Great theory, but not always, as the Fed sometimes gave 'lip service' to such bands being broken and even altered the bands themselves to accommodate or capture the most recent actual trend. Perhaps monetary targeting was a useful tool for the Fed to use when it saw fit and more importantly a smoke screen set up for Fed watchers believing that the strict laws of monetarism were being adhered to. *Unanticipated changes* in monetary policy could then have a maximum impact.

In the 1990s the Fed publicly stated that money supply figures and bands are useful in determining the stance and change of monetary policy but only constitute a part of the big picture. The Fed monitors a whole array of key economic indicators when formulating monetary policy. Targeting inflation is the Fed's prime objective and employing an interest rate strategy is its monetary tool. The debate over whether it employs a Taylor rule is discussed in Chapter 8.

What has not changed over the last forty years, is that the Fed is feared by all market traders and investors alike. Knee jerk reactions by the Fed can wipe off tens of billions of dollars of stock value in just a few days. An incompetent interpretation of the data, a poorly formed strategy or a tenacious cling to an old paradigm by the Fed can cause stock prices to oscillate wildly and/or remain under or overvalued for an excessive amount of time. However, even justified responses by the Fed over concern over macroeconomic stability and persistent imbalances – a deviation from the NAIRU – can wreak stock market havoc. Hence, investors are sensitive to any prospective change in interest rates and more importantly to any change in direction in monetary policy. By being one step ahead of the Fed, the smart investor can set stock positions immediately by anticipating changes in the Fed funds rate or discount rate. The even smarter investor can trade when the 'news' is released or when the announcement is made. If, for example, some professional investors correctly anticipate an interest rate fall or 'factor in' such a fall then stock prices may fall on the day of the announcement. Such Fed watching generates a caterpillar like market – one that humps on anticipation and slumps on facts. Timing is everything when dealing in such a moving caterpillar type market. Inexperienced retail or day traders normally get hurt in the short run by the 'forward-looking' professional traders.

When Alan Greenspan delivers his public speeches and testimonies before Senate committees, he is often questioned about the apparent desire of the FMOC to 'spoil the party', destroy jobs, inflict pain on the poor, its bias against growth and its obsession in fighting inflation. In other words, senators often ask 'why can't we have more growth and why do we live in fear of the Fed pricking the bubble of prosperity?' 'Why can't we reduce the inequality of income in this country?' 'Why do so many Americans live without health insurance?' His responses are normally of a reassuring nature – that indeed the Fed is aware of human suffering, the plight of the working poor, the needs of families and categorically stating that the Fed does not wish to sacrifice output and destroy jobs without cause. However, Greenspan quenches the fire of his critics by claiming his unswerving quest for price stability is *the best way* to solve most of America's deepest economic problems. Cynics often interpret this strategy as support for 'trickle down economics' with the unfortunate emphasis on trickle! However, the Fed's charter is to balance the pursuit of economic objectives and not pursue unbridled growth – that is the domain of a democratically elected administration.

Confessions of a central banker

Alan Blinder (1997: 10), who served as Vice President of the Fed in the mid-1990s, has passed some useful insights into the workings, procedures and mindset of the FMOC. He is particularly critical of the lack of clarity in specifying ultimate targets and formulating monetary policy in a short-termist, ad hoc manner. Even though lags are a persistent curse and data may not be as recent as one would like, these are not excuses for the FMOC members to cling to a 'wait and see' attitude or 'we don't want to get locked in' mentality. According to Blinder (1997: 15), the Fed is ever conscious of the NAIRU but has never formally adopted such a concept as a bench-mark tool in formulating strategy. There is also the issue of how 'captive' the Fed is to the whims and fancies of the finance markets. For example, if the professional traders are concerned with inflation and the effect it has on the long end of the yield curve, then they can demand or 'provoke' the Fed on CNBC to raise interest rates 'or we will do it for you'. This is intimidation at its best! If the community perceives the Fed to be soft on inflation, then there is a great risk of the Fed losing its reputation. It is thus tempted to deliver the outcomes that finance markets demand. Another example in the mid-1980s was the 'capital strike' by Japanese investors in not pur-chasing US bonds. For a couple of days such investors did not bid and so conveyed the message to the US administration that inflation was too high and the US dollar too weak. Market interest rates soon went up in response to this 'strike' and message. Hence, the Fed may influence the short end of the yield curve, but the long end is dominated by market sentiment, which may in turn reverberate back down the yield curve and so force the Fed into action. Nevertheless, the Fed finds itself in a sea of uncertainty and must remain flexible enough to adjust to changing circumstances.

Is the Fed secretive?

Given that billions of dollars of stocks, bonds, securities and currencies can change hands on basis of a shift in Fed thinking on the future course of interest rates – it should not come as a surprise that Greenspan is guarded about what he says and how he says it. Moreover, how policy is formulated, what theoretical foundations are respected, what analytics are employed and what key economic and financial indicators are watched more closely than others is not entirely obvious. Fed watchers believe that they know how the Fed operates but such a belief is more wishful thinking than concrete fact.

In some ways the Fed is open and transparent. After all it does make available the minutes of its FMOC meetings. It seeks to make clear the bias, if any, in monetary policy. It does not wish to spook finance markets with careless words. Greenspan does comment in detail on the state of the economy and he does appear before the Senate and Congress.

On the other hand, the Fed cannot reveal all of its inner workings. To do so would be to give away power and perhaps some effectiveness in the conduct of monetary policy. Some monetary theorists stress the importance of 'surprise' or 'unanticipated' changes in monetary policy that has a maximum impact on the economy. If investors monitored the Fed workings and comments passed by Fed members by the minute then it is likely that finance markets would be far more volatile than what we observe now. Investors would try and predict the effect of every word and every move and possibly misinterpreting what was meant.

Conclusion

Throughout the twentieth century the Fed faced a multitude of challenges in its conduct of monetary policy. In the main, it has been flexible enough to adapt and steer the US economy along a reasonably high non-inflationary growth path. Traditional techniques within a conventional economic paradigm were employed along the way. Old guideposts and constraints on growth were watched closely – such as inflation, persistent current account deficits, international competitiveness, capacity utilization, tight labour markets, consumer sentiment etc. – particularly in the early 1990s. No two business cycles are the same and so the Fed has to weigh up and pass judgment on the weighted economic indicators it has before it. Different circumstantial combinations require different policy responses. It is fair to say that the Fed has sailed into unchartered waters for more than a decade. Puzzles over the relevance of the NAIRU and the fear of labour market tightness, probably caused the Fed to be overcautious in its reactions to the longevity of the US expansion – in the late 1990s. Old speed limits may have been updated as the surge in productivity growth has raised the economic cruise speed of the US economy. Nevertheless, as Greenspan cautions, the uplift in productivity growth has to prove itself above and beyond that of a mere cyclical aberration. It is still too early to light up cigars with $100 notes. On the matter of hidden surplus labour, there needs to be a greater statistical effort by US authorities to capture whatever slack there is in the labour market. However, there is another constraint that is both binding and dangerous. It is the purpose of this book to highlight the dangers of asset price inflation and the responsibility of the Fed to carefully monitor this inflationary twin. Greenspan and the Fed – from hindsight – may have something to answer for here. However, before we burn the Fed at the stake we must consider a wider range of challenges that it faces in conducting monetary policy. This is the task of Chapter 8.

8   Shifting ground beneath the Federal Reserve

Introduction

Formulating and conducting an appropriate US monetary policy over most of the twentieth century was fraught with great difficulty for many reasons. There was a sea of change in terms of the institutional environment, structural changes within, and deregulation of the financial sector and a rapid technological revolution in the latter part of century. Given that the major priority of the Fed is to control inflation, and given the rise of monetarism in economic policy circles in the 1960s and 1970s, monetary targeting was employed. Keeping the lid on inflation implied an adherence to a Constant Money Supply Growth Rule (CGR) in some form. However, the strict relationship between money and output went awry in the 1980s and so prompted a revision of monetary targeting as a monetary policy strategy. The Federal Reserve's fight against inflation was thwarted by the deterioration of old empirical relationships caused by a rapidly changing economic environment in which it operated. Rampant inflation in the 1970s, partly a result of the oil crisis, tested the skill and nerve of the Fed. Executing an appropriate monetary policy was not only complicated by inflation and moving intermediate targets but also by financial innovation and a more open credit market. Thus, deregulation and greater competition had its costs. A less regulated financial sector brought with it greater credit risk, greater leverage and more volatility in prices. It is here that a serious conflict arises between the Fed and stock traders – as they are diametrically opposed. Stock traders want increased volatility in financial markets (in order to create profits) whereas the Fed wants to preserve economic and financial stability. There is a case for arguing that the abandonment of monetary targeting laid the foundation for the escalation of asset prices – as excess liquidity searched for a home. It will also be noted that although stocks were very interest rate sensitive for many years – they were less so in the 1990s. It was rapid money supply growth that fuelled the asset price bubble in these years. This chapter examines some of the challenges faced by the Fed in the recent era.

Deregulation of the financial sector

For many years the US financial sector was compartmentalized, as walls were erected between financial company categories – a legacy of the depression era. The rationale for this segmented framework was to increase the stability of the financial system and the supervisory power of US authorities. In exchange for such regulation and restriction, the profitability of banks was enhanced via such protection and territorial assignment. This was a marriage based on mutual respect and gain, but unfortunately the consumer suffered out in the cold. Interest rates were lower on deposits, and the costs of borrowing higher than would otherwise be, in a deregulated environment. Over time US authorities realized that greater competition in the financial sector was a necessity. With the advent of the Depository Institutions Deregulation and Monetary Control Act (DIDMCA) in 1980 and the Garn-St Germane Amendment in 1982 there was a major transformation of the US financial system. The prohibition of savings and loans, mutual savings banks and credit unions providing checking accounts was lifted and such accounts were allowed to earn interest. Households responded by shifting funds out of non-interest bearing accounts and into NOW accounts (Marquis 1996). Even though the checking accounts of businesses were not eligible to attract a rate of interest, banks 'bent the rules' for close business clients. Both households and firms became more receptive to a variety of financial products that met their liquidity, risk and rate of return requirements. Increased demands for cash management were assisted by the growth of Money Market Mutual Funds (MMMFs) and money market deposit accounts (MMDAs) that lured the savings of small investors. These accounts became popular as a direct result of interest ceilings on savings accounts in the 1970s and of course the rampant inflation of the same period that crushed real interest rates. As firms and households shifted funds out of the banking system, a period of financial disintermediation followed. As deregulation caused funds to shift between monetary aggregates, so did the volatility of such aggregates increase and so further compound the task of conducting an appropriate monetary policy. In this deregulated credit market environment issues of moral hazard arise. Bank managers appreciate the competition in the market place and may succumb to temptation by issuing loans to high-risk marginal borrowers. In the chase for market share in a highly competitive market, bank managers are pressured to lower credit quality and indulge in moral hazard. That is, rely on the Fed's commitment to lender of last resort, deposit insurance or a balanced loan portfolio whereby the reliable clients subsidize the unreliable others. In summary, the move towards deregulation and greater competition was the right move but there were costs associated with the creation of a more open credit market – in terms of risk and exposure.

Financial product innovation

The birth of several financial products has not only reduced the effectiveness of monetary policy but also reduced the effectiveness of the Fed's supervisory and regulatory network. For example, the rise of *securitization* whereby real estate and car loans are 'packaged', turned into marketable parcels on the stock market and/or on-sold to other financial institutions. These assets that were once stored in the portfolios of original lenders are now in a large market, ready for sale and resale. The Collateralized Mortgage Obligations (CMOs) and Real Estate Mortgage Investment Conduits

(REMICs) of the 1970s turned banking and credit into a national not a local set-up (Kaufman 2000). Many 'other' financial institutions entered the home mortgage market and so intensified competition. However, there are several downsides to this securitization trend, such as the increased access of marginal borrowers to what is basically an open credit market. Shopping around lead to eventual loan approval. Converting non-marketable financial assets into marketable commodities raises questions concerning the ability of the market to price these assets and more importantly monitor their trend. The assumption that the market for these financial assets is both liquid and continuous is indeed a giant leap of faith. Asymmetrical information and disturbances in real estate and car markets may shock securitization packages disproportionately, as forward-looking financial investors anticipate the collapse of prices that may result from a sellers' stampede. The valuation of the last marginal sale in real estate means nothing when consumer sentiment changes and sellers scramble for the exit door simultaneously. Hence, the depth of these markets is a concern. More importantly, these 'other assets' are placed under the scrutiny of the market and are visibly sensitive to interest rate changes. Combined with the difficulty in pricing securitized assets, interest rate rises can put holes in financial asset prices – even a free fall as marketability declines sharply. Such a lack of pricing precision adversely impinges on meaningful credit assessment. How are credit risks assessed in such a soft market? There is an uneasy marriage here, between financial institutions that want to push securitized packages (thus lowering credit standards) and desperate, marginal borrowers that want to acquire an asset without much heartburn. For these reasons, the financial markets are more volatile and so more vulnerable to 'corrections' than ever before – as they operate at the margin.

Another innovation in financial markets is the increased use of *derivatives* as a means to hedge against fluctuations in other markets. Well, at least this is the 'risk management' justification of derivative trading but in reality such trading is highly speculative and offensive, rather than defensive, in strategy. The lifeblood of profitable derivative trading is volatility not stability. Professional managers have enjoyed a buoyant environment in recent years as inflation has been low and a willing clientele has queued up to dabble in financial assets. The deregulation of the financial sector and more competition between US financial institutions has pushed more resources into a wide range of financial instruments, including derivatives. From Chapter 1 there is a vast pool of wealth stored in the United States – looking for a 'home' – but not a safe home as in the 1950s. Aggression is common among portfolio managers when sitting on mountains of money – all seeking abnormal rates of return – and so risk-taking is higher and more fierce in this portfolio manager's competitive dynamic game. In fact, professional managers acquire open positions in the hope of beating other less skillful traders and do not just rely on commissions from trading. There is a danger here in that such aggression and chase for market share can cloud professional judgment and lower credit standards. Again, this is an issue of moral hazard whereby each bank manager is pitted against his colleagues and he knows very well that if does not 'sign up' with the potential client then others will. As outlined in Chapter 2 – individual rationality does not necessarily add up to collective rationality amidst abundant liquidity and speculative hype. On the demand side, huge amounts of funds have been pushed towards derivatives trading – attracted by high leverage – and so booming profits when skillfully traded. However, these instruments are also known as 'weapons of mass destruction'.

How does the exponential growth of derivatives trading affect the stability of the financial sector? Most would argue that more volatile markets result. As discussed in Chapter 6 – major accounting weakness comes to the surface – in that derivative exposure or liability does not appear in the balance sheet. For example, Long Term Capital Management (LTCM) had an exposure of more than $1.3 trillion but was not declared or known until the dire stages of financial disaster. Assessing risk exposure in this case was difficult, as accounting practices generated only an opaque view of financial health. Not only was the lack of disclosure of major concern but also the high-risk strategies undertaken by LTCM. The Fed passes the comment 'LTCM indicated that it sought high rates of return primarily by identifying small discrepancies in the prices of different instruments relative to historical norms and then taking highly leveraged positions in those instruments in the exception that market prices would revert to such norms over time. In pursuing its strategy, LTCM took very large positions, some of which were in relatively small and illiquid markets.' (Greenspan 1999). There was a lack of understanding by creditors of LTCM's high-risk strategy preferring to trust in the reputation of this large firm. The collapse of US financial giant shocked the Fed into greater action. They expressed their concern by stating 'In addition, the extraordinary degree of leverage with which LTCM was able to operate has led the federal agencies responsible for the prudential oversight of the fund's creditors and counter-parties to undertake reviews of the practices those firms employed in managing their risks. These reviews have suggested significant weaknesses in their dealings with LTCM and – albeit to a lesser degree – in their dealings with other highly leveraged entities.' (Greenspan 1999). Thus, the Fed has expressed concern over its less than perfect supervisory function, by allowing a financial tornado to develop in this first place.

Another recent example of the dangers of derivative trading comes from East Asia. The ability of Nick Leeson to torpedo his employer – Baring Brothers – is testimony to the silent, but deadly nature of derivatives trading. Once large companies like these 'fail' there is a clamour by regulatory authorities to rescue such companies that are 'too big to fail'. Why? There is a fear that the whole financial sector may 'go under' or at least generate massive disintermediation that chokes real economic activity. But the lender of last resort function and support by government only encourages moral hazard. Portfolio managers in large financial institutions may succumb to temptation and bear high levels of risk in the belief that the US government, and so taxpayer, will bail them out in a crisis. Enron was examined in Chapter 6 and it came to light that the corporate hierarchy was all too willing to take on abundant risk.

The concern over expansive derivative trading centres is on whether market volatility is increased and the business cycle accentuated. To the extent that derivatives trading attracts marginal borrowers with low credit quality and a high propensity for risk this concern is well based. Traders want volatility and there is an inescapable risk associated with unexpected asset price fluctuation. Given that financial institutions wish to generate more turnover and/or greater volatility, and given that credit standards have been compromised in order to achieve such objectives, the vulnerability of the US financial system is high. Heightened financial leverage only complicates the task of conducting an effective monetary policy. This partly explains why the Fed announces to the market shifts in monetary policy stance or current policy biases – so that there is less likelihood of highly leveraged traders being completely caught unawares. The Fed does not want to cause abrupt changes in market sentiment but rather incremental changes in the quest to maintain an orderly market.

Technology and innovation

Even though the Fed had good reason to adhere to money supply growth targets – the implementation of monetary targeting was more difficult than what economic theory predicted. As the payments and check clearance systems became more efficient over time so households and firms transacted more efficiently. Improvements in technology reduced the demand for money and raised the velocity of circulation. The period between 1960 and 1973 witnessed a stable velocity and a predictable demand for M1. However, velocity increased between 1973 and 1980 partly as a result of better cash management practices to counteract the low and/or negative real interest rates of the period. Hence, the demand for money – M1 – fell. From Figure 8.1 it can be seen that the growth rate of M1 was volatile – it ranged between 3 and 9 per cent from 1965 to 1972. Between 1972 and 1974 the growth rate of M1 fell dramatically. As the Fed underestimated the speed of structural changes in the financial sector it *systematically oversupplied money*. Inflation was a by-product of this misinterpretation by the Fed. As Figure 8.1 reveals, the volatility of the growth of M1 increased in volatility as the decades wore on – it became extremely erratic from 1983 onwards. The growth in M1 decelerated sharply in the mid-1990s. Needless to say the erratic nature and unreliability of the M1 renders it a poor monetary indicator in the eyes of the Fed.

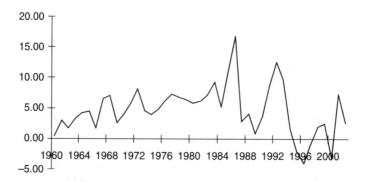

Figure 8.1 Growth rate of M1 (1960–2002).

Source: Board of Governors of the Federal Reserve System.

The period of 1980–2003 revealed a volatile and declining velocity of M1 as the opportunity cost of holding money in checking accounts was lowered by deregulation. Therefore, the demand for M1 became both unstable and unpredictable. During the 1970s, amidst this growing instability of the demand for money there were short-term pressures on the Fed to lower interest rates. No doubt the oil crises of 1974, and again in 1978, placed upward pressure on the price level as well as interest rates in the United States. Monetary targets were presented to Congress and rationalized away when broken. Interest rate targeting became an acceptable policy strategy in the light of the internal and external stresses on the economy in the 1970s.

There was a change in monetary policy strategy in 1983 as the Fed switched to targeting M2 but preferring non-borrowed reserves to borrowed reserves as the interest elasticity on M2 was lower than M1 (Marquis 1996). Such a move came with a cost: interest rates displayed more volatility and eventually caused the abandonment of specified M2 targets. A return to interest rate targeting (the federal funds rate) took place again in the 1980s as M2 displayed volatility (Figure 8.2). In fact, the growth rate of M2 continued to fall from the mid-1980s until 1993. Only after 1993 did this growth rate rise and indeed rise faster than nominal GDP growth. Open market operations were employed using non-borrowed reserves to maintain the federal funds rate near its predetermined target. Hence, the targeting of interest rates became the Fed's prime objective. However, the M2 roared after 1993 and its growth rate averaged 8 per cent in recent years. There is a clear association with the rise in both GDP and stock prices since1993.

From Figure 8.3, the growth rate of M3 decelerated in the 1980s and then accelerated faster than GDP growth in the 1990s. The growth rate of both M2 and M3 were rapid after 1993 – fuelling both economic growth and stock prices. As the Fed states 'The robust expansion of bank credit underlies much of the acceleration in M3 this year. Depository institutions have issued large time deposits and other managed liabilities in volume to help fund the expansion of their loan and securities portfolios.' (Greenspan 2000). This is a confession by the Fed that the 'upper band'

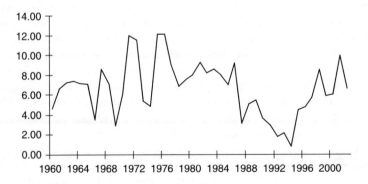

Figure 8.2 Growth rate of M2 (1960–2002).

Source: Board of Governors of the Federal Reserve System.

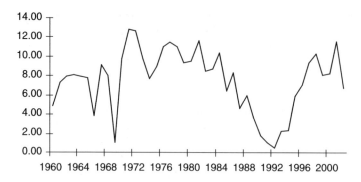

Figure 8.3 Growth rate of M3 (1960–2002).

Source: Board of Governors of the Federal Reserve System.

of money supply growth was indeed fuelling the stock market boom. In fact, from Figures 8.2 and 8.3 the rate of increase of these money supplies – rapid acceleration – was quite staggering. At face value, the stock boom possessed a strong liquidity driven market underlay.

Other forces were at work changing the growth rates of monetary aggregates and so their policy importance. Further innovation in terms of credit cards impacts on the demand for money by providing convenience to the user and reducing the need to have 'on call' cash. The ATM is open twenty-four hours and substitutes for any pre-cautionary demand motive. Hence, the Fed also needs to be wary of such 'miscellaneous forces' that effect the growth rate of monetary aggregates.

The effectiveness of monetary policy

Providing the demand for money is stable, the Fed can alter the supply of money accordingly. In fact, the monetarist doctrine and monetary targeting rests heavily on a stable demand for money function and so constant velocity. From the earlier discussion, the power of the Fed to affect the real economy is severely diminished by unpredictability of money demand, clouding the degree of monetary expansion required. It is also troubled by having to choose the appropriate monetary aggregate. As stated above, the M1 became unstable whereas the M2 *appeared* more reliable in later years but even then had to be abandoned by the mid-1980s. From Figure 8.4, it can be seen that M2 velocity has diverged from historical norms – despite the fact that the opportunity cost of holding M2 fell dramatically between 1989 and 1992 the M2 velocity still rose sharply. Divergence occurred again in 1995–6. Given that the velocity of M2 increased sharply in the 1990s – the implications are two-fold. One, the reliability of this monetary aggregate has diminished in the eyes of the Fed as a monetary tool. Two, the MV = PY relationship is more powerful – as money times velocity implies higher nominal GDP (Price times Income) – and economic activity than just from a spurt of M alone. Stock prices enjoy the ride.

In fact, there are other reasons why the Fed does not have complete steerage power over monetary policy. The relationship between bank reserves and the money supply

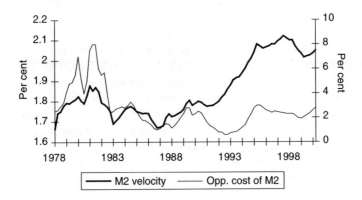

Figure 8.4 M2 velocity and opportunity cost.
Source: Board of Governors of the Federal Reserve System.

is not constant but tends to fluctuate. In other words, there is variation in the elasticity of the money multiplier. Even though the Fed sets minimum reserve requirements for the banking system, the banks themselves may choose to hold excess reserves as a liquidity precaution for any sudden depositor withdrawals. Other leakages from the credit creation process occurs when the non-bank public desires greater liquidity or transfers funds out of the banking system which in turn diminishes the power of the money multiplier. As stated earlier, velocity of circulation is also volatile at times.

Even if the Fed has a clear vision of what economic variables it wishes to target, it cannot hit them directly but only indirectly, by using the tools at its disposal – open market operations, reserve requirements and the discount rate. It resorts to using intermediate targets (monetary aggregates or the federal funds rate) in the quest to hit final targets (output, inflation and unemployment). This chain of command is by no means tight or stable as the transmission of power from monetary tool to final target is plagued by leakages, uncertainties and random shocks. If the economy is being hit by waves of permanent productivity improvement, then the appropriate monetary policy response is to accommodate such waves. However, given that preference shocks affecting allocation decisions towards leisure and savings are temporary the Fed should not intervene.

The effectiveness of monetary policy is also limited by recognition and impact lags. As discussed in the section 'what economic indicators?', the Fed is really looking in the rear vision mirror in terms of old data and passing judgment on the location of the economy in the current business cycle. Key economic indicators are estimates and are often revised months later that may in fact cast doubt or falsify the earlier policy decision. Impact lags are uncertain and only complicate the timing of monetary policy. According to the Monetarist, money is like fire: don't play with it.

If the Fed is overzealous in terms of trying to exploit the output-unemployment trade-off it must confront a credibility problem in the eyes of the public. This dilemma is known as the dynamic inconsistency hypothesis which states that authorities are biased towards the creation of inflation and have an incentive 'to cheat' by expanding the money supply *after* economic agents have formed their expectations. Thus, a one-shot rise in output may be purchased but only at the expense of central bank reputation and a growing awareness by the public (wage earners) that discretionary monetary policy is biased towards inflation. Such distrust between central bank and the public inhibits long-term commitment to capital formation. The solution to potential 'cheating and bias' is to remove discretion from the policy-maker and follow a monetary aggregate growth rule. However, the Fed has already accrued years of credibility and has not yielded to this theoretical temptation of purchasing short-run output growth. Besides, as discussed earlier, the monetary targets have proved unreliable in recent years and so a constant monetary growth rule would be difficult to implement in practice.

Target interest rates or monetary aggregates?

From the earlier discussion it is obvious that monetary targeting fell from grace for a whole host of reasons. Which money supply? The rise and fall of both income and interest velocities rendered money supply changes less potent. Nevertheless, from a theoretical perspective the Fed has a choice between monetary and interest rate targeting. For example, if the real economy is buffeted by real disturbances to aggregate demand, the appropriate monetary policy should focus on anchoring a monetary aggregate. If temporary preference or productivity shocks generate instability in the goods market, then the Fed should target the money supply. However, if productivity shocks are of a permanent nature, then this shock should be accommodated with an increase in the money supply. Conversely, if the real economy is buffeted by transitory velocity shocks, the appropriate monetary policy response is to target interest rates rather than a monetary aggregate. Hence, shocks in the money market (e.g. the instability of money demand) should be met with an interest rate target in order to keep the economy near full employment output.

Targeting the inflation rate via an interest rate strategy is reflected in the Taylor rule. In this model, the Fed funds rate is a function of four factors. The following form illustrates the Taylor model

Fed funds rate = current inflation rate + real interest rate
+ 0.5 (inflationary gap) + 0.5 (output gap)

Hence, the Fed funds rate would rise in response to a rise in the current inflation rate, a rise in the inflationary gap or a rise in the output gap. However, there is a high degree of subjectivity involved as the real interest rate is often assumed to be 2 per cent (its historical average) and the target inflation rate is chosen by the Fed and so may vary according to regimes. Moreover, the weightings of 0.5 and 0.5 are subjective. If the Fed is biased towards fighting inflation the co-efficient of 1 may be chosen for the inflationary gap. There is no evidence that the Fed actually employs a Taylor type model in setting interest rates but Taylor (1998) does provide evidence that this model fits the data quite well from the 1980s and 1990s. Taylor also gives the Fed credit for fighting inflation more efficiently in the 1980s and 1990s than in the 1970s. In his words, there were less 'policy mistakes'. There is no doubt that the Fed has adjusted short-term interest rates in response to inflationary surges but not so obvious when confronted with deviations from potential output.

Just because the shortcomings of monetary targeting are known, we should not jump to the conclusion that interest rate targeting is superior in all circumstances. Even if shocks in the money market are to be avoided, there are ill side-effects of a build-up in monetary liquidity via endogenous money creation generating spillovers into asset markets. In a liquid economy, the demand for money can rise forcing monetary accommodation by the Fed. Waves of endogenous money creation can result from a buoyant economy keeping rates of return above the short-term interest rate – as the Fed honours its commitment to peg the short-term rate. Providing inflation does raise its head or accelerate, this monetary expansion can continue indefinitely. As discussed later in this chapter, there are reasons to believe that manipulating interest rates is not an instant panacea to cure inflation or raise output within a short time frame – the responses may be weak.

There are other channels through which investment and spending are affected. These include the health of bank balance sheets, bank lending policies, the net worth of corporations and expectations of economic agents. In other words, wealth effects out of asset markets may swamp the cost of money effects out of the money market. The former is a stock concept whereas the latter is a flow concept.

Does money affect output?

Most economists accept the monetarist proposition of the neutrality of money in the long run but concede that money may affect output and employment in the short run. Friedman (1968) does not deny that an increase in the money supply may have a real effect on output in the short run, but there are long and variable lags, that make it difficult if not impossible for policy-makers to oversee. In short, monetary expansions are dangerous not only because of inflation but because a mistimed monetary policy elicits further monetary policy responses in the future. Besides, initial rises in output are short-lived and therefore not sustainable. Only improvements in the capital stock, labour force and technological progress drive output growth in the long run. In this monetarist paradigm, the role of the Fed is to oversee a constant growth in the money supply and allow the private sector to flourish. That is, facilitate productivity and efficiency improvements and so underpin profit growth. The theoretical channels through which monetary policy affects output growth is via cash in advance constraints or when prices are set in advance (e.g. contracts). Another explanation from Lucas (1976) is that of the signal extraction problem. Producers are more aware of their own prices – not the general price level – and so are 'fooled' into producing more output, as they believe that relative prices are higher.

Evidence on this money–output relationship is clear but the direction of causation is not. In fact, most empirical evidence supports the money–output relationship as in Figure 8.5. No surprise here. But the direction of causation debate is ongoing. Some researchers, such as King and Plosser (1984) argue that when firms plan to raise

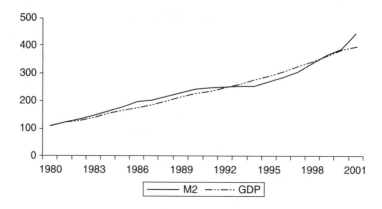

Figure 8.5 United States: growth in GDP and M2, 1983–2002 (1983 = 100).

production levels they increase their money holdings in order to purchase more intermediate goods. Consumers act in a similar manner. Thus, an increase in the demand for money elicits an increase in the money supply. It may well be that money growth precedes output growth but is not the driver of output growth under this scenario. From a Keynesian perspective, the reason why money growth is endogenous is because economic activity raises the demand for money and causes the Fed to increase the money supply accordingly. Here are two perspectives as to why money growth is endogenously determined.

Other economists argue in favour of exogeneity. Research by Friedman and Schwartz (1963) concludes that the direction of causation runs from money to output. Romer and Romer (1994) also find that monetary policy severely affects the real sector of the economy rather than the other way around – as recessions have followed major monetary tightenings. Cook and Hahn (1989) also conclude that Fed open market operations affect interest rates over very short time horizons – an observation not consistent with developments in the real sector.

Channels of the monetary transmission mechanism

There are various schools of thought as to *how* monetary policy affects output or more precisely income. There is not one, but many channels, through which the Monetary Transmission Mechanism (MTM) may operate. What is of policy relevance for the Fed are the unwanted by-products of each channel in terms of inflation, lags and wealth creation. It is not just the flow of income that should concern the Fed but also incremental changes to the stock of wealth. Why? For the basic reason that the potency of monetary policy is reduced in an economy laden with wealth. The net effect of an interest rate rise on consumption is to some extent indeterminate amidst abundant middle class wealth. More importantly, it is the health of corporation and household balance sheets via sizable yet unrealized capital gains that determines the near term impact of higher interest rates on economic activity and inflation.

The huge build-up of paper wealth in the United States is a direct outcome of interest rate targeting.

First, the elasticities approach emphasizes the *interest rate and the exchange rate channel*. The former channel focuses on a change in the interest rate affecting investment and consumer durables, whereas the latter points to a change in the exchange rate affecting exports. From a demand perspective, consumers welcome an environment of low cost or cheap credit and respond accordingly. On the supply side, investors welcome a lower cost of capital as pressure is eased off cash flow and more importantly the gap between rates of return and the lower cost of capital is widened. In the case of the United States, this channel appears to be effective in stimulating aggregate demand. However, the experience of Japan in the 1990s was the opposite; even though the cost of capital 'appeared' cheap by historical standards, rates of return were even lower and so there was little incentive for new investment. The marginal efficiency of investment was less than the interest rate. Real interest rates also 'appeared' cheap, but with fear of a capital loss and with little prospect for any significant asset price inflation there was no great rush for portfolio adjustment towards long-term assets and no great demand for credit. In other words, other factors swamped the power of this transmission channel.

Second, the monetarist view of the MTM focuses more on the *quantity of money and cash balance effects*. A broader monetary transmission mechanism is evident as economic agents adjust their portfolios according to changes in relative prices and marginal utilities. Excess liquidity drives all asset prices higher by disturbing the investor's portfolio. In response, the economic agent finds herself with excess cash and bids up asset prices until all returns are equated (Meltzer 1995). Money has a direct effect on output.

A third view of the MTM is the credit channel, of which one aspect is *bank-lending* whereby the central bank conducts a policy change that affects the deposits of banks and credit creation. The supply of credit is affected and disintermediation sets in. Banks lose their lending confidence and recall loans where possible. This is the *bank balance sheet channel*. Indeed banks become defensive concerning their own profitability and balance sheets at the expense of the corporations and households. Matters are complicated by aysmetric information – demanders of credit are more knowledgable about their own financial positions than banks. A lower interest rate strategy by the Fed may provide windfall gains for banks – as purchasing government bonds during a period of deflation may be the low-risk strategy for balance sheet repair and not incresaing exposure via lending to the private sector.

A variation of this balance sheet channel is that of the *external finance premium* – normally higher than any internal source of financing. As higher interest rates lower the net worth of corporations so does the external finance premium rise (Bernanke and Gertler 1995). Collapsing asset prices damage company balance sheets and adversely affects cash flows. Higher interest rate premiums and restricted access to credit choke off activity. A virulent interaction between damaged bank balance sheets and corporation balance sheets culminates in a downward spiralling credit crunch.

Cautious and low-risk lending policies by banks may assist in repairing bank balance sheets but not in re-stimulating aggregate demand or asset prices. Herein lies the dilemma: weak asset prices generate more non-performing loans, which in turn weaken bank balance sheets which further reduce lending confidence. Income growth collapses, further depressing asset prices. This is financial disintermediation at its worst, whereby the MTM works in reverse and actually contracts the economy due to rational bank behaviour.

Damage to household balance sheets also creates the same kind of contraction in aggregate demand. High transaction costs in fleeing out of assets, and general illiquidity, cause consumers and savers to favour cash. Debt service costs also imply balance sheet repair. Adverse wealth effects inflict serious damage on an economy.

Does money affect stock prices?

An article by Bradford De Long strongly denounces the concept of 'vulgar monetarism' as it relates – and perhaps 'explains' – the run-up in US stocks prices. From Figure 8.6, the correlation appears strong but De Long argues over the choice of 'which' monetary aggregate? The M3 is used in this figure – but why use this in preference to others? This author prefers the monetarist interpretation of US stock markets being strongly underpinned by a liquidity foundation. All stock brokers appreciate the power and surge of monetary liquidity in driving stock prices higher. Unfortunately, economists far less so. There is no other singular variable in the 1990s that explains the stock boom better than does buoyant monetary liquidity. Why did the Fed allow the money supply growth rate to explode? Partly because targeting monetary aggregates had been abandoned (due to volatility) and because interest rate targeting was believed to be effective in steering economic activity – and to a lesser extent asset prices. Quite to the contrary, the money supply growth had more impact on both economic activity and stock prices than did interest rate changes – particularly from the early 1990s onwards. To re-emphasize what was stated earlier – the abandonment of monetary targeting – had its costs in terms of excess liquidity that found its way into assets – and so high asset prices. We shall see later that although interest rate changes strongly affected stocks up until 1990, the impact was far less

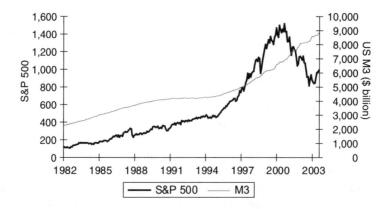

Figure 8.6 Performance of the S&P 500 and the Level of US M3.

after 1990. Vulgar monetarism or not, the fact remains that excess liquidity inflated America's stock price bubble – beyond sustainable limits. We can see from Figure 8.6 that the acceleration in the M3 coincided with the explosion in stock prices. The continuation of M3 growth (a deliberate orchestration by Greenspan) *after* the stock market crash has led to the 30 per cent rebound in stocks in 2003.

In the aftermath of the stock bubble, the Fed resorted to an avalanche of interest rate cuts and the effects on economy and real GDP growth have been rather slow – and the impact modest as of October 2003. However, the Fed has backed up these interest rate cuts with massive expansions in the money supply – the economic system is awash with money and 'cash is trash'. Greenspan has pushed economic agents out of cash and into assets and stock prices have responded handsomely since the 'end' of the Iraqi war. In this 'special era' – lower interest rates have spurred stocks to higher levels in the short term but long-run sustainability stems from persistent growth in the money supply.

Interest rates: how effective on output?

As the section 'Does money affect stock prices?' highlights, there are several monetary transmission channels not just one, and so relying on interest rate changes to curb activity in a deregulated and more open credit market is a dangerous foundation on which to build a monetary policy. Individuals and companies can find ways of ignoring a monetary tightening in an eager, widely diverse credit market that wishes to pump out loans. The cost of capital is not the sole criteria in the business calculus. Hence, other influences such as wealth effects and the behaviour of the financial sector significantly affect liquidity and lending and so may offset any interest rate potency. For example, rates of return may rise faster than interest rates during a boom and so bank lending rises. Conversely, when rates of return fall faster than interest rates during a deflationary recession, bank lending may still collapse. Even though the change in real interest rates may be a better guide to changes in lending and activity, this potency may also be swamped by the availability of credit in a deflationary environment wreaking havoc on all balance sheets – banks, corporations and households alike. And so unexpected movements in wealth, and not changes in the cost of capital, may be more powerful in affecting economic activity in an affluent nation like the United States. The Fed has recently acknowledged the importance of wealth effects on consumer spending as the percentage of household wealth tied up in stocks has accelerated appreciably. Just as in the 1920s, the fortunes and welfare of households are tied to the chariot wheel of the stock market.

What happened to the old-fashioned credit crunch? In the 1960s and 1970s when the local bank manager said 'no' he meant no! Credit was rationed and there were quantity restrictions. Cocktail loans were arranged during times of severe monetary tightness. By implication, a monetary policy that puts the monetary creation process into reverse and contracts the *availability* of credit was effective in crunching both output and inflation in a short time frame – just a matter of months. Yes, economic activity was devastated but the saving grace was that the recession was short-lived – short sharp pain. In this monetary aggregate regime, there was no doubt about the effectiveness of monetary policy – with all its harshness. However, with the advent of the deregulation of the financial sector and the use of interest targeting, the effectiveness of monetary policy withered significantly. The whole structure of interest rates has to ratchet upward far more than under the old monetary aggregate regime to produce the same restraining effect. Why? One reason is that banks can avoid a Fed tightening or discipline by rearranging their asset and liability portfolios. They can also go offshore in search of funds. After all, banks nowadays are margin lenders – it does not matter so much about the level of interest rates – high or low – but the spread they receive from borrowing and lending. In this 'floating market', banks can seek to pass on the Fed's interest rate structure to consumers. This leads to second reason for monetary policy slippage. Bank customers also like to avoid the Fed's discipline by borrowing at higher interest rates and so fulfil what contracts they have outstanding as well as pass on their higher interest rate bill to their own customers. A whole series of elasticities will determine how effective these 'pass on' initiatives will be. US businesses have often complained that when the Fed applies the monetary brakes – it does not appreciate the importance of contracts in propelling economic activity for number of months beyond what was anticipated by the Fed.

In summary, the breaking distance under an interest rate targeting regime is far longer than under a monetary aggregate regime. There are too many avenues for the banks and the non-bank public to avoid monetary discipline in what is basically a large money supermarket. Therefore, the long and variable lags that Friedman spoke of are far more deadly under interest rate targeting and more likely to provoke more Fed responses in the medium term. The consequences for macroeconomic management are serious. Not only can the real economy overheat for a far longer period of time but also abundant liquidity build ups in the economic system that spills over into asset markets. Hence, there can be an odd coexistence whereby interest rates are raised to relatively high levels and yet money supply growth remains buoyant. Under this scenario, higher interest rates may eventually restrain goods price inflation but not soak up enough liquidity to restrain asset price inflation. There are grounds for arguing that the Fed is locked into a monetary policy bias – there are political and social forces at work that oppose an 'excessive or prolonged tightening'. Forward-looking investors know that asset prices will only soften for a short time while the monetary brake is in lock – and that asset prices will soon escalate when the *expectation* of the tightening is over. This belief also constitutes a type of moral hazard, whereby the investor plays upon the Fed's disposition to attack only goods price inflation. Once the goods and labour markets have cooled off, the investor knows that impediments to a recovery in asset prices are almost nil. By contrast, an old-fashioned credit crunch via severe credit contraction reduced asset prices *and* wrung asset price inflationary expectations out of the system. To the extent that the Fed raises interest rates but does not soak up monetary liquidity, the asset markets are left to continue their upward run.

Interest rates: what affect on stocks?

As this book has continuously stated – stock prices are driven by rates of return. That is, earnings per share are the prime fundamental. But as we shall see – interest rate changes are major drivers of stock prices – over the medium term. Siegal (2002) makes the case for the potency of interest rate changes on stock prices with clarity. He cites evidence from 1955 and employs 3, 6, 9 and 12 months lags (Table 8.1). Between 1955 and 2001 there was asymmetric power – as decreases in interest rates possessed far more power in raising stock prices (elasticities were greater) than did interest rate increases in curbing stock price rises. Interest rate rises often dampened enthusiasm to purchase stocks and stock sometimes fell or were flat in the first six months. Conversely, expansionary monetary policy (via interest rate cuts) were very powerful – in the short periods and even more so over twelve months. Perhaps monetary authorities can push on a string!

According to this evidence, the power of interest rate changes to move US stock markets is unquestionable. Even the lagged impacts appear plausible. However, the impact of interest rate cuts appears to have weakened (1990–2003) – as does the asymmetry. This may be a reflection of a highly deregulated era mentioned earlier whereby the price of money was not an insurmountable obstacle to overcome by the investor. Second, the abundance of liquidity (the M2) in the economy could still offset the impact of interest rate changes. Third, the sheer build-up of US wealth makes it difficult for a 'price of money' monetary policy to deflate the huge asset price bubble that had developed in the late 1990s. Liquidity had to be soaked up as well. Fourth, stock prices, and in particular technology stocks, kept rising while interest rates rose in 1999–2000. This occurred in part because the technology craze and related investment was not interest rate sensitive – at least that is what investors

Table 8.1 Interest rates and the stocks

	3 months (%)	6 months (%)	9 months (%)	12 months (%)
1955–2001				
Increases (99)	1.2	2.9	5.9	7.4
Decreases (99)	5.3	9.7	12.4	16.6
Benchmark[a]	3.0	6.1	9.1	12.2
1960–9				
Increases (22)	−1.2	1.2	1.4	2.6
Decreases (17)	3.5	6.1	7.4	8.6
Benchmark[a]	2.2	4.1	6.2	8.4
1970–9				
Increases (29)	−1.9	−1.2	3.7	4.8
Decreases (26)	6.5	11.1	13.8	17.7
Benchmark[a]	1.9	4.3	6.7	9.3
1980–9				
Increases (16)	3.9	4.2	9.1	8.6
Decreases (23)	6.5	12.9	14.9	21.1
Benchmark[a]	4.3	8.8	13.0	16.9
1990–2001[b]				
Increases (14)	3.2	7.1	8.8	13.1
Decreases (25)	4.0	5.4	7.4	10.5
Benchmark[a]	3.4	6.8	10.4	14.4

Notes
a Average of all time periods in selected sample.
b Assumes S&P 500 remains flat for 2002.

Source: Siegal (2002), p. 193.

thought. Fifth, while sales and profits were greatly affected in the short run, investors were not fazed by minor movements in the costs of capital. Besides, foreign capital flows stampeded into the US bond market because interest rates were higher and because of the expectation that capital gains would peak alongside the low in the interest cycle. This kept the US economy liquid – for a time.

Conclusion

The Fed, like many other organizations, has been forced to adapt to change in the economic environment in which it operates. The last thirty years have brought forth many challenges in the formulation and conduct of monetary policy. Volatile monetary aggregates thwarted the pursuit of a monetary targeting strategy. Changing bank and household behaviour also complicated the conduct of monetary policy. A disintermediation trend, as depositors shifted funds out of the banking sector, weakened the credit creation process of the entire banking system. As technology was increasingly applied in the financial sector – as in the economy at large – so old empirical relationships faded. As America became wealthier and as the money growth rate exploded so did an asset price bubble develop. Thus, the old pillars of monetary policy vibrated on this shifting financial soil.

Despite the difficulty in anticipating changes in the financial sector, and even the economy at large, the Fed has been the target of much criticism for its reactive role and slowness in adapting to change. Consequently, the US economy may have suffered losses of welfare as obsolete and unreliable monetary aggregates lost their informational content and so misguided the policy-maker. However, moving away from reliance on monetary aggregates towards interest rate targeting also has weakened the speed at which the Fed can restrain economic activity and inflation. Raising interest rates (putting on the monetary brakes) in a vastly deregulated environment will not automatically restrain the economy within a short time frame. There is a high degree of endogeneity in the monetary creation process that can render a Fed monetary tightening ineffective for a time. More importantly, this brand of monetary policy has contributed to rises in asset values as abundant monetary liquidity has inflated the stock market bubble.

Given the rapid pace of technological progress and financial innovation there is a constant challenge for the Fed to catch up to the modernization of the financial sector. Securitization, the explosion of derivatives trading and increased leverage has exponentially increased the vulnerability of the US financial system to shocks. The existing regulatory network may not be sufficient to ensure the safety and stability of the recently transformed financial sector whereby the old depression era segmentation has faded and multidimensional financial institutions have re-evolved. Even if new legislation is not introduced, the Fed must acknowledge that the financial world beneath its feet has changed dramatically. Not only are there ongoing challenges for excellence in prudential supervision as stated earlier, there are even more formidable challenges for the impact of monetary policy on economic activity – and stock prices. The Fed's recent challenge is dealing with deflation – and the ill side-effects that flow from a burst stock price bubble. We now examine the thoughts and attitudes of Chairman Greenspan to both historical and contemporary challenges in the next chapter.

9 Evaluating the Greenspan years: 1987–2004?

Introduction

The election of a new Fed chairman will take place in 2004. There is already much conjecture over who will be the likely replacement. It may well be that Greenspan re-applies at the age of 76? Nevertheless, there will be much political discussion as to who will be the right person for the job in terms of qualification, specialist expertise, technical skill, respect among peers and political adeptness to name a few. Whoever takes over the helm will have an impressive Greenspan track record to beat and enormous challenges to face – as America crawls out of recession. This chapter outlines some of Greenspan's economic and philosophical background, in the hope that it will shed some light on the way he formulates policy. His views on a whole range of issues impinge on how 'interventionist' or 'active' monetary policy should be in order to ensure economic growth *without* compromising stability. Although the Fed has no clear mandate to 'target' stock market values, it appears as no coincidence to the author that Greenspan intervened, in some way, when the Dow reached record highs in 1994, 1996, 1997 and again 1999. The converse also appears true – that he intervened to support the stock market in 1987, 1998 and 2001 – when investor panic was gaining momentum.

Why he tolerated a prolonged asset price bubble is questioned. His power to move markets and the economy is also surveyed. A re-examination of his respect for traditional economic paradigms provides some useful insights into the way he formulates and conducts monetary policy. There is an attempt to identify what mistakes he made, if any. Finally, an evaluation of the Greenspan era is outlined. This era is a tough one to criticize – as we all acknowledge and respect the dedication and knowledge of the man. If there were errors of judgment it was to be human. If there was a lack of a wise theoretical paradigm upon which to base monetary policy it was because one of 'clear consensus' did not exist – within the confines of conventional wisdom. And, of course, any criticism that is leftover stems directly from the Fed's lack of power to control the ebb and flow of the giant US economy. It is too large and too sophisticated to be 'controlled'. There will always be a business cycle that cannot be harnessed by man – or the Fed. Therefore, some humility in judgment is warranted for this Greenspan era.

Greenspan's background

He was born in 1926 in Manhattan, the son of a stockbroker. He displayed an interest in music early in life but formalized his interest and passion in economics by gaining a Master's degree from NYU in 1950. Although he enrolled in a PhD in the early 1950s, he did not complete one until 1977. A successful career in stockbroking intervened (his own firm) right up until the 1970s where he acquired great acumen for detail, employed forecasting models and could make sense of the generated results for his clients. He gained great knowledge of money and markets in this private sector job.

There was, however, a public side to Greenspan's career. He acted as a policy advisor to President Nixon in the late 1960s. He also accepted a prestigious position as Chairman of the Council of Economic Planning under President Ford – from 1974–7. A Ronald Reagan victory pulled Greenspan back into public life via the National Commission on Social Security. He was partly responsible for introducing tough social security reforms. He improved his knowledge of the US budget process, intergenerational transfers and the critical importance of the saving rate in generating economic growth.

It is worth noting Greenspan's right wing views on many issues – partly shaped by his association with a right wing think tank/discussion group led by Ayn Rand in the 1950s while at NYU. Rand was a critical thinker and social philosopher who preached that capitalism was not only efficient but also moral. Property rights, and indeed civil liberty, were protected under capitalism and free enterprise. Greenspan has never changed his mind on such core issues and consequently is opposed to big government and over-regulation. It fact, he is great believer in self-regulation within the private sector.

It was in 1987 that Greenspan became Chairman of the US Federal Reserve. He had big shoes to fill – as Volcker, it was generally agreed, did a good job in fighting inflation during the Carter years. His reign from 1979–87 was full of merit, particularly as both inflation and interest rates declined after 1980. He had the respect of Wall Street, Main Street and Washington. And so, Greenspan faced an uphill battle to build a reputation of his own and win the respect of various power brokers in the United States. Later in his career he did just that – but first he had to face his baptism of fire – that of Black Monday, 1987 – the 508 point one-day fall in the stock market.

Greenspan's economic philosophy

To understand policy initiatives of the Fed it is more than useful to appreciate the mindset of Greenspan. He is right wing, conservative and neoclassical in his views of economics. He has great faith that markets work, that competition generates efficiency and that preferences of consumers dictate what constitutes economic value. He also believes that asset values are best left and determined by rational economic agents. Such views impinge upon the way in which monetary policy is formulated and conducted, that is, it is not government's role to force its own view of what is and what is not economic value upon its constituents.

On the issue of economic growth, he believes that technological progress is the prime driver, with the saving rate a reasonably close second. With regard to the importance of new knowledge, he acknowledges that ideas are overwhelming physical labour in driving growth in America 'The most important single characteristic of the changes in US technology in recent years is the ever-expanding conceptualization of our gross domestic product. We are witnessing the substitution of ideas for physical matter in the creation of economic value – a shift from hardware to software, as it were' (Sicilia and Cruikshank 2000: 214). For example, a vast variety of businesses have benefited from telecommunications and information technology revolutions – driving unit costs lower.

A low savings rate in the US perplexes Greenspan as it implies less commitment to capital formation, downward pressure of the capital–labour ratio in the future and acts as a constraint on future productivity growth. He states 'The damage from low savings does not show up immediately. It is more insidious. It chips away at the productivity gains we are able to achieve over time; it gradually hampers our competitiveness in international markets; and after a period of years, it results in lower standards of living than we would otherwise enjoy' (Greenspan 1991).

Not only is he concerned with the adverse effects of a low savings rate on future US productive capacity (and so dependence on foreign savings), he is also concerned with funding for retirement. America's social security retirement plans are to some degree unfunded and he uses this fact to push for government budget surpluses – to partly offset the low private savings rate. 'I have testified often before committees of the congress about the corrosive effects that sustained large budget deficits have on the economy and about the way our economic prospects in coming years will hinge on our ability to increase national saving and investment. One factor that argues for running sizable budget surpluses . . . is to set aside resources to meet the retirement needs of today's working population' (Greenspan 1990).

With regards to employing an active fiscal policy he remains adamantly opposed to any attempt to fine-tune the economy. This view is linked to his view on the driving forces of economic growth, namely that real factors drive growth and not the *reshuffling of resources* by government or the stifling of economic incentives. He states

> I believe that we should stop trying to engage in short-term fiscal fine-tuning, which at best we are poor at and at worst is counterproductive. We should try instead to focus on solving longer-term problems, and in that process engage in as little policy as was both economically and politically possible. My view is that we had to slow down the pace of governmental policy actions if we were to restore a level of risk in the system consistent with long-term inflationary growth.
>
> (Sicilia and Cruikshank 2000: 6)

Greenspan is more pointed and forthright with this comment on crowding out – 'The deficit is a corrosive force that already has begun to eat away at the foundations of our economic strength. Financing of private capital investment has been crowded out, and not surprisingly, the United States has experienced a lower level of net investment relative to GDP than any other of the G-7 countries in the last decade.'

(Greenspan 1993). This is a critical issue for Greenspan, as he views capital per worker as being a serious driving force of growth and prosperity. He has been challenged many times before Senate Committees on his view of crowding out – his preference for private over public sector investment. He normally responds by stating that 'evidence' is in his favour, that choice is the centrepiece of a capitalist system and that higher interest rates (via crowding out) only thwarts his monetary policy strategy.

In response to events of September 11 and the US economy slipping into recession since 2001, the US administration has 're-employed' fiscal policy in an attempt to bolster spending and activity. Greenspan has viewed such fiscal expansion with some degree of skepticism. First, because the Fed has aggressively employed an expansionary monetary policy via lower interest rates and providing the economic system with abundant liquidity. Second, the long-term 'corrosive effects' of a fiscal policy in terms of crowding out, future tax rates, biases to economic incentives and the misallocation of resources offset any positive short-term effects. In fact, he presented his strong views to the Congress and the nation in early 2003. He stated his disapproval of growing budget deficits and a lack of fiscal discipline in the following manner

> I am concerned that, should the enforcement mechanisms governing the budget process not be restored, the resulting lack of clear direction and constructive goals would allow the inbuilt political bias in favor of growing budget deficits to again become entrenched. We are all too aware that government spending programs and tax preferences can be easy to initiate or expand but extraordinarily difficult to trim or shut down once constituencies develop that have a stake in maintaining the status quo.
>
> (Greenspan 1997d)

One of Greenspan's major concerns with a lack of budget discipline over the near term is that the United States is going through a 'demographic lull' and an aging population will pressure the public purse for years to come. It is a tall order for productivity and immigration to offset these growing and largely unfunded liabilities. Otherwise, tax rates and revenues may have to rise in the future to cover the prospect of increasing government expenditures for many years to come. This is why Greenspan favours a comprehensive set of budget scenarios being presented to the American public and why he favours government accrural-based accounting over cash-based accounting. This accounting change would provide greater illumination of future, intergenerational liabilities.

In summary, Greenspan believes that the private sector, together with a competitive drive, provides the best opportunity to create sustainable long-term prosperity. His job is to create a low inflation-low interest rate environment in which investors can make long-term decisions bounded by a limited amount of uncertainty.

Greenspan and the markets

As Greenspan's credibility as a policy-maker increased in the early 1990s so did fear spread throughout the professional investor community about what he could say that could significantly shift asset values – and within minutes. Professional investors would listen carefully to any hint that the *direction* of interest rates would change sometime soon. They also knew that interest rate hikes and falls tended to be in clusters or a series. Which one would be the last in the series – signalling a 'permanent' change in the direction of monetary policy – for the medium term at least. Professional traders were alert to signals of 'turning points' or major policy reversals that would provide green or red light for investing. The Fed would signal a 'bias' in future monetary policy – or state that it is currently 'neutral'. Investors would often wait for Greenspan's testimonies and not take large positions in the market for fear of a clear shift in the future direction of monetary policy. Or they would wait in the hope that Greenspan would say nothing and so remove the shadow overhanging traders in the finance markets.

A degree of caution is required when interpreting Greenspan-speak as 'bad news' maybe good news for the market and 'good news' may in fact turn out to be bad news. This resembles the Goldilocks economy referred to earlier – 'not too hot and not too cold'. Bond traders want bad news concerning the economy to translate into lower inflationary heat and so lower interest rates. Hence, capital gains on bonds would rise. And stock prices would normally rise with a lag – as the future level of interest rates – remain low. Therefore, the inexperienced investor needs to be careful when assessing the impact of Greenspan's words on the markets. Too much good news concerning growth, capacity utilization, retail sales, consumer spending on durable goods, etc. may provoke a rise in interest rates and so scare off bond investors. Equity buyers must then decide on whether to ignore rumblings in the bond market and so buy stocks. The perversity of this goldilocks economy is that real bad, recessionary news or past data gloom may imply lower interest rates in the near term and so a surge on Wall Street via a calm bond market. After all, Wall Street is more concerned with the future not the past.

Some examples of hints or signals that would influence traders are references made by Greenspan to current or future inflationary heat, demand persistently outstripping supply, wage pressures, labour market tightness, job creation, the unemployment rate, growth being too rapid, gross imbalances or the onset of deflationary forces. Any hint that inflation is subsiding would spell a prospect for interest rates to fall and so a signal to buy stocks. However, such hints could be seen in a negative light – that of imbalances being unsustainable and excess demand pressuring limited resources. Hence the risk that long-term interest rates would rise. Of course, the famous phrase that investors jumped on was that of 'irrational exuberance' uttered by Greenspan. While some signals are clear others are not, perhaps for the reason that Greenspan speaks in the hypothetical and in the abstract. It is therefore very easy for the investor to misinterpret.

What are some examples of Greenspan's words moving the market? First, we shall examine those periods when, somewhat coincidentally, the Dow was at or near all time highs. The chairman had a habit of moving against investor enthusiasm in 1994, 1996 and 1997 – all record highs in US stocks – by raising interest rates or jawboning the market down.

The famous utterance of stock markets displaying 'irrational exuberance' was delivered in a speech entitled 'The Challenges of Central Banking in a Democratic

Society' on Thursday 5 December 1996. Not only did he use this phrase but also used the word 'bubble', although mostly in reference to Japan. Investors read this as Greenspan's way of telling them that stocks were overvalued in his view. And perhaps speculation was rife, generating values that were not sustainable in the long term. These words scared the market, causing it to see-saw on Friday but closing down and losing 3 per cent by the end of the next week. The damage overseas was more vicious as Friday in Asia and Europe are normally down days anyway – for fear of the US markets collapsing on the weekend. These markets lost 2 and 3 per cent on their Friday immediately after Greenspan's speech. Perhaps Greenspan wanted to warn the markets of danger and maybe he was doing investors a favour? Rumour has it that he warned Wall Street power brokers earlier that week of his stern view that stocks were overvalued and that these brokers should counsel their clients. According to theory, this is a cheap way of cooling off asset prices and inflationary heat by 'jaw-boning' – that is, scaring markets to cool off without having to raise interest rates.

On another occasion, the 8 October 1997, Greenspan took the opportunity to talk the market down. In early October, the stock markets had been humming along spurred on by robust economic data. For example, the Dow rose 61 points on the Monday and 78 points on the Tuesday to sit at 8,178 points. The recent Dow high of 8,260 was hit in early August. The stage was set for Greenspan to throw some cold water on investor enthusiasm. On Wednesday, he made some points very clear concerning labour market tightness – the likely near term rise in wage growth and hence inflation. His basic thrust was that labour was willing, for the time being, to temper higher wage claims in exchange for greater job security. In his view this 'treaty' could not last. He states

> To be sure, there is little evidence of wage acceleration. To believe, however, that wage pressures will not intensify as the group of people who are not working, but would like to, rapidly diminishes, strains credibility. The law of supply and demand has not been repealed. If labor demand continues to out-pace sustainable increases in supply, the question is surely when, not whether, labor costs will escalate more rapidly.
>
> (Greenspan 1997d)

Greenspan's basic message to the markets was that inflation was on the horizon and he may well have to act. In the same speech he felt compelled to warn investors again about overvaluation and the remoteness of stocks rising in the near term by anywhere near the magnitudes of the last two years. He stated 'Aside from the question of whether stock prices will rise or fall, it clearly would be unrealistic to look for a continuation of stock market gains of anything like the magnitude of those recorded in the past couple of years.' (Greenspan 1997d).

Although this 'warning' was not stating anything new, as the investment community knew that stocks were running hot and were near all-time highs, there was an element of realism and urgency in the warning. The markets did not like the strength or tone of what Greenspan had to say in his statement. The Dow retreated a 120 points the next few days or around 1.5 per cent. The bond market did not like the tone either and bond yields rose – this time there was flow on effect to home mortgages – and now much of middle-class America felt what Greenspan had said!

If we go back to 1994 we witness a similar desire by Greenspan to cool-off expectations and stock prices. When the Dow hit 4,000 points in 1994 Greenspan responded swiftly by raising interest rates. Giving him the benefit of the doubt, his target was a lower *goods price* inflation rate but he was not disappointed that *asset prices* would fall as well.

A similar picture develops when we examine Greenspan's fear of financial contagion in late February 1999. His concern was that financial disturbances and failure overseas could be transmitted to the United States quickly and traumatically. Shaky foreign economies could soak up would-be capital headed for the United States and so cause foreign capital inflows to subside. This in turn would impact on the US dollar and so spur imported inflation – prompting higher domestic interest rates. The other channel by which interest rates may rise is via a shrinking pool of domestic savings. Greenspan (1999e) stated his concern 'Foreigners presumably will not want to raise indefinitely the share of their portfolios in claims on the United States. Should the sustainability of the buildup of our foreign indebtedness come into question, the exchange value of the dollar may well decline, imparting pressures on prices in the United States.'

Any inflation hike or interest rate scare was bound to unnerve investors whether the origins were financial contagion or not. Greenspan's fear was realized soon after. The Dow fell 250 points within three days or 2.6 per cent. The experienced investor knew from previous confrontations with Greenspan that it was always wise to run – for simple reason that your fellow investor would most likely run anyway – and you had to run faster than him to the exit gate. A sliding US dollar has become a real concern for US policy-makers – as foreigners have displayed their reluctance to hold the US dollar in the face of a widening current account deficit. The Iraqi crisis added greater uncertainty to the business calculus.

From this section we have a clear picture that Greenspan's views on the state and dynamism of the US economy will move markets quickly but what we have not told you is that the effects normally fade within a few days. *Jawboning has its limits.* Only if Greenspan's words alter perceptions of risk permanently – will the investment community take heed and adjust their asset allocations. For example, when investors perceive that turning points in interest rate cycles are near or that a productivity surge is sustainable – they shift their perceptions of risk and alter asset allocations accordingly. From the historical record, there are times when Greenspan has moved markets – in a lasting manner – from expressing his views on the US economy. Most times, however, his view is acknowledged within the gambit of many views and market participants conduct their own analysis and act accordingly.

The earlier discussion assumes that the Fed wields *absolute* power. There are those that remain grossly skeptical of the Fed's power to decree what the level and structure interest rates will be. For example,

> The Fed cannot move interest rates, because its open-market operations occur in the federal funds market, a tiny, artificial marketplace by comparison with the total market for short-term debt securities. The Fed's domain is comparable to

a child's sandbox stuck in one corner of the football field. Consequently, the Fed cannot move interest rates through brut force, the buying and selling of treasury securities. Its influence over interest rates stems directly from the perception that it can move rates, much as the Wizard of Oz's influence over the Munchkins grew from their belief in this power.

(Ely 1996)

This skepticism highlights the point that the Fed may *influence* interest rates at the short end of the yield curve but not *control* them. Perhaps why the Fed appears so effective is because of its credibility, its authority and its ability to bluff the investment community into believing that the interest rates they set are indeed 'official' – and will stick.

Sifting wheat from the chaff

Listening to Greenspan and watching the Fed is almost a sport in America. Trying to second-guess the most powerful man in the world is both fun and profitable – that is, if one can interpret what he *means* from what he *says*. Herein lies the problem, as 'Greenspan talk' is full of double negatives – is guarded, hypothetical, abstract and conservative. He deliberately speaks from a historical and theoretical background concerning the economy but will not state categorically where the United States is on the business cycle, or whether growth is too rapid compared to potential output or whether inflation is too high or whether asset values are excessive, etc. He is more cautious with what words he uses – often preferring 'in all probability', 'most likely', 'on balance', 'possibly' – in order not to signal to markets that the Fed has superior, secretive knowledge concerning the economy and its future. He does not wish to give 'advice' to investors that later on may turn out to be erroneous.

He is also very careful with regard to his comments on interest rates. He knows that any loose word or phrase concerning the future course of interest rates could send the finance markets into a frenzy. He also knows that professional traders will hear what they want to hear and so it is essential that he says what he means or not say it at all! This is why we observe that Greenspan will deliberately avoid any discussion of interest rates if at all possible. Only when he decides that markets should be informed would he send a 'clear' message , at least by his own standards. It is here that shifts in monetary policy stance are made clear and that the expectation is created that a series of interest rates changes will be made over the coming months. Again, according to theory, Greenspan does not want to surprise or shock the markets unnecessarily.

What is also worth noting is that most of the power of Greenspan to move markets comes from within his Humphrey-Hawkins testimonies. Occasionally, he may use his addresses at universities and other public forums to gain some media attention and so impact but this is not the norm. His carefully designed speeches in front of the Senate and Congress committees are his forum for analyzing the most recent trends in the economy and to respond to questions during question time. It is in this forum that Greenspan addresses issues that are close to his heart and the more time he devotes to them the more we should listen. Hints to interest rate policy often flow from these topics. He recently shared his heart concerning the danger of US budget deficits in March 2003 – but was careful in stating that 'these views are my own and are not necessarily shared by my colleagues at the Federal Reserve'.

Power to move the economy?

How much of a contribution did Greenspan make to the many years of US prosperity under his reign as chairman of the Fed? I believe that the jury is out on this one. Neoclassical economists, including Greenspan, do not believe that government policies drive long-term growth. Such policies may aid macroeconomic stability in the short run and so create a stable setting for certainty in decision-making – particularly capital formation in the long run. His basic paradigm of 'growth via low inflation' is very much a conservative view of the growth theory – the private sector will invest and create new knowledge in the calm sea of certainty. The size of the government should be kept small so as to not stifle economic incentives. It then follows that Greenspan or the Fed does not possess any power to create long-run growth. Most economists believe that the ebb and flow of the money supply does not stimulate any lasting growth nor does the manipulation of interest rates. There may be short-term *real* effects on output and employment and such stimulii may assist in kick-starting the economy – but not in maintaining any long-term growth momentum. Despite what theory has to say, the Fed did create an environment in which growth could flourish and the Fed did remain 'alert' to clear and present dangers concerning 'threats' to growth. It maintained levels of real interest rates that were conducive to growth. The Fed also managed the US banking system well – in that credit could flow smoothly to credit worthy customers. A healthy financial intermediation function – by the banks – was a major supervisory watchdog role cherished by the Fed.

In summary, Greenspan has the power to move financial markets around for a time but not so much the real economy. Perhaps, it is more accurate to say that the Fed has the power to move the economy closer to full employment or full potential. That is, to restore the economy's actual cruise speed closer to its natural potential. We discussed such concepts as Okun's law and the NAIRU in the previous chapters.

Mistakes in the Greenspan era?

In his early days of office, in mid-1987, he raised the discount rate by half a point. This may have been a premature and hasty move given that the economy was already cooling off. This move was also not welcomed by an already nervous stock market. It fell by 508 points or 22 per cent of its value on Black Monday – the 19 October. Although the driving forces of collapse were manifold, the signal sent out by Greenspan to the markets was of possible more interest rate hikes. This signal changed risk perceptions and investors wanted out. After Black Monday, Greenspan reacted rather promptly by lowering the discount rate from 7.5 to 6 per cent. Although a swift policy reversal was warranted, the question remains whether Greenspan was cleaning up his own mess, that is, raising interest rates only to lower them five weeks later. It would be unfair to 'blame' Greenspan for the sudden collapse in investor sentiment but no doubt he learnt the hard way that he did have power to alter risk perceptions and all too quickly at that. After all, the growth rate of the money supply lost its momentum in that era.

A persistent theme in Greenspan's thinking is that a financial crisis should not be allowed to damage the real economy and therefore the Fed should stand ready to provide liquidity to the limit of calming investor nerves. He made this point clear

> Early on Tuesday morning, 20 October, we issued a statement indicating that the Federal Reserve stood ready to provide liquidity to the economy and financial markets. In support of that policy, we maintained a highly visible presence through open market operations, arranging system repurchase agreements each day from 19–30 October. These were substantial in amount and were frequently arranged at an earlier time than usual, underscoring our intent to keep markets liquid.
>
> (Greenspan 1988b)

Greenspan's view of the causes of the 1987 stock market crash focused on portfolio insurance, program trading and a breakdown in the effectiveness of arbitrage trading. What began as technical plays in a falling market ended up as psychological panic in a collapsing market. Professional traders placed program sell orders if certain levels were breached. They were breached and waves of selling were triggered. The exchanges were overloaded with orders far beyond the limits of technical capacity and such a jam caused investors to panic in an effort to get out. Normally, arbitragers would be at work to close the gap between current and future prices but they too panicked and followed the trend down. Greenspan believed that an interaction of technology and human nature accentuated the collapse. 'On October 19th and immediately thereafter, one could observe the interaction between technology and human nature quite clearly: the news of sharply falling stock prices, communicated instantly to a sensitive investment community, triggered an avalanche of sell orders on both futures and stock exchanges' (Greenspan 1988c).

Despite such a horrendous collapse in stock markets Greenspan (1988b) still maintained his philosophic stance that markets are efficient and do self-correct. 'We must carefully distinguish those problems that are self-correcting, or can be addressed within an existing regulatory frameworks, from those that will require more fundamental, perhaps legislative, solutions.' He adamantly favours self-regulation over government regulation – 'As a general principle, it is in the self-interest of the exchanges and associations of market makers to protect and enhance the integrity of their markets. They also have superior knowledge of their own markets. Thus, we should rely where possible on the private organizations to correct the problems that were evident last October.' (Greenspan 1988a).

Thus, during this crisis Greenspan offered support via lower interest rates but he did not seek heavy-handed intervention over the way stock exchanges conducted their business. It should also be noted that Greenspan was concerned, *as always*, with the possible damage that collapsing stock values would inflict on the real economy. As it turned out the damage was minor – probably because the economic system remained liquid for months after the 1987 crash.

In 1994, I was in the United States happily watching CNBC and hoping for a good investment year. I was sadly disappointed of course as this was the year that Greenspan embarked on his pre-emptive strike against inflation – or as some say the 'old enemy'. According to his economic paradigm there were flashing signals of imbalances, excess demand heat and tight labour markets that all spelt an acceleration of inflation – that was underway but somewhat opaque. There were many angry critics of his strategy of attacking an enemy that was not a 'clear and present danger'. His defense was that it was easier to wrench inflationary expectations out of the system now than to wait for inflation to accelerate and so pay a higher demand management costs later. His critics pointed to lost output and jobs, hurting workingclass America and to falling equity and bond prices hurting middle-class America – these were the visible current costs of his engagement with the invisible and perhaps phantom enemy. Greenspan's response was that inflation did not accelerate in 1994 or 1995 and so his policy tightening was justified. Others counteract this claim by saying that inflation was not a problem anyway – in 1994 or 1995 – and so the Fed was on a self-indulgent wild goose chase. The jury is out on this one and perhaps we shall never know. Perhaps the eighteen months of lost output and financial market weakness was a price worth paying for greater certainty and a more stable economy over the longer term. After all, the growth stint from 1995 through 2000 was impressive.

There is, however, a lesson that Greenspan may have learnt here and that is the neat and well-loved paradigm that he claims to be conventional, neoclassical theory of growth and stabilization may have shifted beneath his feet. He knows that the US economy has an economic cruise speed or a level of potential output that according to history is around 3 per cent. Any growth rate beyond that 'speed' will generate inflation and the greater the speed the faster will inflation accelerate. It is the Fed's role to ensure that speed limits are not broken for any length of time as the inflationary cost will only escalate. It is here that Greenspan based his pre-emptive strike against inflation in 1994. Unfortunately, the paradigm may have shifted as the United States experienced higher than trend growth in the late 1990s and did not suffer inflationary outbtreaks! Likewise, in the labour market the unemployment rate fell as low as 4 per cent in the 1990s and there was no wage explosion. In other words, extreme labour market tightness nor 'excess' demand caused inflation – anything like past experiences. Therefore, Greenspan learnt that relying too much on old empirical relationships to be time-consistent, and indeed too much reliance on the neoclassical paradigm, may not be effective on every occasion – or in the current 'unchartered waters'. The US economy broke old cruise speeds without igniting inflationary chaos – a fact that Greenspan is still trying to explain to this day. He is now more cautious about predicting *when* inflation will raise its head. Finding a new paradigm that can explain America's high growth speed and therefore low levels of monetary policy intervention is now a challenging issue.

A pressing question relates to Greenspan's tolerance of asset price bubbles during his reign as chairman of the Fed. Why did he just ignore them? Why did he not act aggressively enough to deflate them? Were the spillovers of effects on the real economy going to be minimal? We have seen in Chapters 7 and 8 that he has quite clear and strong views as to how they develop, why they persist and why the valuing of assets is best left in the hands of the private sector. Greenspan states

> Most of the variations (in degrees of confidence) are the result of the sheer diffi-culty in making judgments and, therefore, commitments about, and to, the future. On occasion, this very difficulty leads to less-disciplined evaluations, which foster price volatility and, in some cases, what we term market bubbles – that is, asset values inflated more on the expectation that others will pay higher prices than on a knowledgeable judgment of true value.
>
> (Sicilia and Cruikshank 2000: 197)

Has human nature changed over history? Have human beings discovered a different set of rules for valuing assets? Are they driven by a different psychology? Greenspan answers 'no'. He states

> There is one important caveat to the notion that we live in a new economy, and that is human psychology. The same enthusiasms and fears that gripped our forebears are, in every way, visible in the generations now actively participating in the American economy. Human actions are always rooted in a forecast of the consequences of those actions. When the future becomes sufficiently clouded, people eschew those actions and disengage from previous commitments. To be sure, the degree of risk aversion differs from person to person, but judging the way prices behave in today's markets, compared with those of a century ago, one is hard pressed to find significant differences. The way we evaluate asset and the way changes in those values affect our economy do not appear to be coming out of a set of rules that is different from the one that governed that governed the actions of our forebears.
>
> (Sicilia and Cruikshank 2000: 41)

In short, he argues that volatility in asset prices is not a new phenomenon that we should puzzle over. Human nature has not changed.

Greenspan's two flagships

There are two key flagships of Greenspan's economic rationale. One is the fervent belief in the current US productivity miracle. The other is the linchpin importance of consumer confidence. All economic activity can be traced back to the health, wealth and optimism of the consumer. All investment and saving is aimed at future consumption. It then follows that any sustainable revival in US private sector invest-ment spending must ride on the back of healthy, if not rising, consumption levels. Greenspan is all too aware that a consumer without confidence will collapse and shrink back into a shell – causing economic stagnation and eventual contraction if left to wallow in despair. Consumer expectations are influenced by a number of variables – some of which can be fortified by the government. Hence, Greenspan is circumspect and guarded as to what he states in public and how he phrases it. He knows that the media will pounce on any loose word or pessimistic view. This is why he often uses an understatement – such as 'the economy is going through a soft spot' – to portray a situation that is rather more serious like a 'recession'. He does not wish to alarm consumers or create an unnecessary air of pessimism. He knows that the current 'soft spot' in economic activity is chugging along on the sail of consumer doggedness.

The persistent rise in US productivity is often referred to by Greenspan as the saving grace and rear guard of the US recovery. Even though stock prices have softened, adverse wealth effects kicked in and several types of investment have collapsed – the foundation of the real economy (productivity growth) has not faltered. He notes that productivity growth in 2001–2 was even better than in the 1990s – 'During the recent downturn, however, productivity held up comparatively well, a performance that makes last year's surge all the more impressive. Indeed, productivity rose at an average annual rate of nearly 3 per cent over the past two years, faster than the average pace of increase during the late 1990s.' (Greenspan 2003).

We need to be careful in proclaiming the virtues of productivity growth. Businesses may operate more efficiently by shedding labour and extracting more output from a shrinking work force but there are negatives to consider. First, this 'type' of productivity gain is not necessarily sustainable – shedding labour has its costs in terms of losing experienced workers and re-training new workers in the future – when economic expansion recovers. Second, there are limits as to how much labour can be shed in relation to organizational structure and capital stock. Too many layoffs may actually be counterproductive over the medium term – even though visible cost reductions accrue in the short-term. Third, the best 'type' of productivity gain is based on both rising output and employment levels. That is, expanding employment numbers in the face of rising aggregate demand. This is particularly relevant to the US economy in 2004–5 – as cost cutting and labour shedding has probably reached its limits – and now improving labour productivity is required amidst an expanding work force and aggregate demand. This is the true test of real productivity gains affecting human welfare. We want job creation not job destruction despite what the productivity statistics tell us.

Flexibility: Greenspan's hallmark

There have been many trials and tribulations during Greenspan's reign. The crash of 1987, the recession of 1991, the Asian crisis of 1997, the bubble years of 1999–2000, the implosion of stock prices in 2001–2 and the collapse in economic activity that ensued. He is one of the few Fed Chairmen who has faced both asset price inflation *and* deflation in one reign. Deflation, both of asset and goods prices, is a relatively new phenomenon and Greenspan has admitted himself before senate hearings in May 2003 that persistent deflation constitutes uncharted waters for the Fed. There is no relying on past experience to finesse solutions.

Another dimension of the chairman's job is to consider more closely geopolitical events, other nation's monetary policies and the cohesion and symmetry of the world's recovery. He knows that both Japan and Germany are languishing under deflationary clouds and signs of economic revival are weak. He also knows that his analysis and decisions on both the level of interest rates and the timing of those changes have an enormous impact on the rest of the world. As the global village has shrunk so has the power of the Fed chairman increased. The stock markets of major economies are strongly linked to the health of the US stock market.

Perhaps, in previous discussions we have revealed Greenspan's loose affection for any one economic paradigm or model. He displays all the hallmarks of being an eclectic – one who gleans wisdom from a whole host of data – and evaluates the different results generated by different models. He uses a plethora of data to evaluate inflationary heat – not just one.

With regards policy initiatives there are distinct pluses from his analytical framework. First, he acknowledges that low interest rates, of themselves, may not be enough to maintain the gradual lift in economic momentum. The price of money may not be enough to illicit a response in long-term investment. As the old saying goes on the effectiveness of monetary policy – 'you can't push on a string'. People can't be made to borrow money. Other forms of the monetary transmission mechanism need to be considered – such as corporate net worth, spreads between corporate and government bond yields and the availability of credit in general. Greenspan is aware that the US system needs to be kept as liquid as possible and he has done so since September 11.

A key insight of Greenspan is that he has expressed willingness to buy long dated government securities in an attempt 'to tame' the long end of the yield curve. Even if his efforts to drive down interest rates at the short end of the yield curve 'fail' to encourage the long end to come down as well – he is willing to act. The long end sometimes, as in 2002, believed that the aggressive monetary and fiscal policies in train would result in inflationary pressure in the medium term. Such a belief was mis-founded and long-term interest rates actually eased late in 2002 and 2003. Nevertheless, Greenspan has revealed his flexibility and willingness to conduct a monetary policy that will be effective in the first stage – and that is keeping both short- and long-term interest rates relatively low. He is also aware of the beneficial flow-on effects to corporate debt ratings of this two-pronged monetary strategy.

One reason why this approach is so ingenious is that most analysts think that interest rates can't conceivably go any lower in the United States What would the recent interest rate cut from 1.0 to 0.75 per cent achieve anyway? Perhaps a fall all the way down to 0.5 per cent may have significant real effects? However, market analysts often talk about further cuts below the current 1 per cent as a sign of panic by the Fed. After all, we have witnessed Japan use the interest rate tool until it cannot use it any more – and the real effects on the economy failed to eventuate. Greenspan does not wish to over-depend on the interest rate tool as he knows the limits are being reached. Nominal rates can't go negative. True, real interest rates could be pushed negative by a combination of lower nominal rates and 'allowing' a mild rise in the inflation rate. This still remains a viable option for the Fed but not lower nominal rates alone. Although Greenspan publicly states that the level of the US dollar is the concern of the administration, he knows that monetary policy will affect expectations of asset prices and capital flows. Any further aggressive interest rate cutting and the US dollar may be sold off further.

This leads to another insight into Greenspan's tactics with regard to the effectiveness of monetary policy. He teases the finance markets with the possibility of an interest rate cut, knowing that a fully anticipated cut will have little impact whereas the opposite is true when the finance markets doubt an interest rate cut but Greenspan delivers one. This is standard text-book theory, *unanticipated* shocks have more effect on economy activity and the markets than does an anticipated shock. This is not to say that he attempts to beat or fool the markets – he does not. But he will time his announcements, biases in policy settings and rate cuts when he thinks maximum impact will be achieved.

Another example of flexibility in policy-making is when Greenspan uses the principle of *insurance*. In mid-2002 when the stock markets tumbled and US economic data revealed signs of extreme weakness there was much pressure on the Fed to cut rates further and soon. Although Greenspan's long-term view was that the economy was on track for recovery there were reasons for concern and even doubt – that the economy may be headed for a double dip recession. His fundamental view was that enormous stimulus was already in the pipeline and so we just had to wait – more cuts may turn out to be over-kill and more inflationary heat later on. Besides, the long end of the yield curve wouldn't like it. He gave in and did cut rates further based on the notion of taking out insurance. What would it cost to lower interest rates anyway? Even then, the costs of getting it wrong would be low. Would a spike in inflation be an immediate threat? Probably not with sizable excess capacity and idle labour. Corporations lacked pricing power and were undertaking massive cost-cutting operations and so immediate price pressure was not likely. Perhaps, the casualty was the slide in the US dollar but then again there is some credibility to the view that a lower dollar was desirable. From hindsight, Greenspan's use of insurance worked well. He has also stated his willingness to employ this principle of insurance in 2003 if need be.

In summary, Greenspan's flexible approach to formulating and executing monetary policy has been commendable. He has been *solutions* and not *constraints* orientated. He has not been tied to one economic paradigm even though he probably has been confined to neo/new classical schools of thought.

Conclusion

This chapter surveyed some of the highlights of Greenspan's achievements as prime policy-maker in the United States from 1987 till 2003. There were many victories during his reign and only a handful of failures – if I could be so bold. Whether his tolerance of asset price bubbles taints his stewardship record in the future remains to be seen. What is fair to say is that his knowledge of economics and finance has been of a high standard and his use of an economics paradigm on which to formulate monetary policy has been sound – at least within the confines of traditional wisdom. He has favoured caution over flair and insurance over risk-taking and yet he has acted swiftly and decisively during times of crisis. He maybe not as conservative as what his testimonies portray. During the 1987 and the September 11 crises he opened the discount window widely and made sure that markets understood his resolve that abundant liquidity would be provided to the financial sector. He also sought to soothe the nerves of markets during the Asian crisis in 1997–8. America experienced eight years of solid economic growth *with* stability and part of that triumph can be attributed to Greenspan's helmsmanship. What remains in doubt is the bursting of the stock price bubble and the potential of the subsequent asset price deflation to overhang and suffocate the real economy for years after the collapse. It is here, fighting deflation, that Greenspan may have his finest hour. He has displayed a substantial degree of wisdom and courage in forming a strategy to re-float America's economy. He will most likely triumph once again.

10 The great asset price bubble of 1929

Introduction

Rarely does an economic crisis scar the minds of people for life, but the Great Depression is the exception. Many years after the event, even when many ordinary people had become millionaires, they remained frugal in their lifestyles. Fear of another depression burnt the importance of thrift into their mindsets. Given the magnitude of the disaster, and its long aftermath, it should not come as a surprise that governments introduced regulatory changes in the 1930s that were aimed at reducing speculative tendencies within the economic and investment arenas. The financial sector was a major target, as it significantly fuelled the boom of the 1920s, as was the stock broking fraternity that fostered 'buying on margin'. Nevertheless, it was the individual speculator's greed that drove the quest for quick capital gains, rather than medium term dividends, and so the speculator could accept a major slice of the blame for the economic and social crisis that ensued. What were causes of the Great Depression? How important were speculative forces in this crash? What lessons have we learnt? Could history repeat itself? This chapter examines these questions in the light of the recent boom in US stocks prices. Of particular interest is the degree to which speculative forces overshadowed real economy-wide forces in driving the crash of 1929.

Seeds of the bust in the 1920s

There were economic developments in the 1920s that may have spurred the rise of the stock market later in the decade. The economic power of the United States was given a boost post First World War as Europe was still recovering from the ravages of that war. There was a race to lift inventory levels and so a boom developed in 1920–1. The domestic economy was also undergoing a transformation, as an industrial organization revolution saw US companies develop new management techniques, generate economies of scale and scope and benefit from innovation as science was applied more to industrial problems. Such a transformation is analogous to the 'peace dividend' spoken of after the end of the Cold War in the 1990s. Hence, real factors or better economic fundamentals may have laid the foundations for the improved economic performance of US companies in terms of earnings and dividends throughout the 1920s. Higher productivity could then explain the 'real bubble' in stocks from early 1927 until October 1929.

Structural changes in the world economy were underway as a result of the dislocation of war. New producers, and therefore competitors, contributed to obsolescence in some industrial countries and more importantly caused a misalignment of exchange rates. New parities had to be found. Europe held comparatively small gold reserves and so any disruption to old world trading patterns was going to place stress on 'old equilibrium' exchange rates. The environment was ripe for a series of competitive devaluations.

Major shifts were taking place in US industry. General Motors challenged Ford as the industry's leader and such stocks were seen as 'frontier stocks' – offering much 'blue sky'. Utility stocks were in favour, as they promised lucrative returns from consolidation and economies of scale. RCA emerged as a 'growth industry' stock in radio and so provided an example of how new technology stimulated investor imagination and the possibility of enormous future dividends. Hence, this era possessed the 'high-tech' growth stocks that are so common in the frenzied markets of the late 1990s. Unfortunately, rampant expectations ran far ahead of what dividends were even likely to eventuate and so profit disappointment was inevitable. This was particularly true for the high-flying 'new economy' stocks of the era.

Even though domestic industry was enmeshed in a technological and innovation push there were nevertheless growing pains and instability in the real sector that threatened to derail the industrial boom. Problems of overcapacity and overbuilding were the downside of the real sector's speed in the fast lane. Market saturation set speed limits on industrial expansion and sales. A continuing boom in consumption was constrained by a lopsided distribution of income. Overcapacity in industry was linked to market penetration limits, which in turn was constrained by the fault line in the distribution of income. Companies that wished to break this barrier or fault line were venturing into waters of high-risk credit buyers of dubious credit quality that were bound to default during hard times.

If it is not a fundamental productivity-driven boom driving the stock market boom in the 1920s then would a speculative bubble provide a better explanation of such euphoric stock prices? In other words, was this an economic or a financial crisis? There is much empirical support for the view that the stock market boom, bust and subsequent depression were all of a *financial* nature. The underlying forces generating such a financial crisis were easy access to credit, high leverage ratios, speculative mania, 'vested interests' pumping the market up like a balloon and rapid changes in risk perception to name a few.

However there are several reasons for caution in this 'fundamentals versus bubble based' stock market boom. First, the additional wealth created by the productivity boom of the postwar era indirectly contributed to additional liquidity in the economic system – a 'problem' of growing prosperity, that is, where to place the surplus? Second, as pointed out by Blanchard and Watson (1982), there was a risk assessment issue, as the fundamentals of individual stocks, old economy versus new economy or significant shifts within specific industries, posed analytical problems for the would-be investor. Third, a subtle distinction may help reconcile this 'either/or' debate in that the early stages of the boom, or economic recovery in 1927, may have been legitimately based on fundamentals but was quickly subsumed by large and not-so-large speculators seeking quick-fire profits. Moreover, if government authorities had not 'mismanaged' both the stock market collapse and the economy later on – then the healthy strides made by US industry may have continued into the 1930s, that is, a smooth trend line of growth and consumption and not a bumpy ride of plenty or famine.

Damage to the real economy

From Figure 10.1, the massive drop in the Dow can be seen. From the peak in 1929 to the trough in 1932 the fall was around 85 per cent. The duration of the collapse was over four years and it was not until 1934 that both the Dow and the economy partially recovered. Even so, the rest of the 1930s were not spectacular and it was not until the next war boom conditions that prosperity returned.

Given the major scramble out of stocks and into cash, one might expect that other more productive and physical assets such as real estate would be given a boost. After all, payments for land and building were not 'on call' as in margin calls for stocks. Such loans were more long-term in nature and so would not suffer from a credit squeeze? However, this line of reasoning proved false, as real estate assets along with financial assets tumbled albeit with a lag. Rates and taxes still had to be paid, pressuring the cash flow of real estate owners and this combined with the recalling of loans by banks brought more sellers to the market. Again, falling asset prices damaged bank balance sheets stimulating more loan recalls and further straining cash flows which in turn damaged asset prices. In short, this vicious circle of contraction in the real estate market caused many banks to fail. Bank failure was more a result of collapsing real estate prices and non-performing loans than of non-performing loans from stockbrokers or speculators in stocks. Such a contraction was partly a result of a contracting money supply – as can be seen from Table 10.1. Hence, the rolling financial wave of disaster spread over the whole economy and devastated all asset prices in its wake. Non-discriminating contagion was at work.

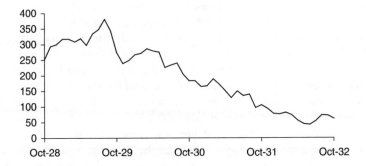

Figure 10.1 Level of Dow (Oct 1928–32).

Source: Board of Governors of the Federal Reserve System.

Table 10.1 Key economic and financial variables

	Unemployment	Inflation	Money supply	Real interest rates
1929	3.2	—		5.9
1930	8.9	−2.6	−4.0	3.6
1931	16.3	−10.1	−6.6	2.6
1932	24.1	−9.3	−12.5	2.7
1933	25.2	−2.2	−5.7	1.7
1934	22.0	7.4	+10.0	1.0
1935	20.3	0.9	+18.7	0.8
1936	17.0	0.2	+14.2	0.8
1937	14.3	4.2	+4.4	0.9

Source: Mankiw (1999).

Undoubtedly the distinguishing feature of the Great Depression was the huge instability of the financial sector that transmitted reverberations into the real sector of the economy. Everyone's daily life was affected. Output and employment collapsed sharply in a short time frame as can be seen from Table 10.1.

Causes of the 1929 crash and depression

It is important to distinguish between the forces that caused the stock market crash from those driving forces, which caused the slump in economic activity for over five years. It is also important to appreciate those forces that were triggers from those that were part of the propagation mechanism(s). In other words, distinguishing between causes and symptoms – and between exogenous and endogenous – driving forces of the crash. Even though 'direction of causation' issues have not been resolved, there are several interesting theoretical twists that may shed some light on these matters.

The Keynesian view

The Keynesian view centres on a collapse in aggregate demand. The money supply fell in response to lower levels of demand and economic activity, and so represents an endogenous view of monetary creation process. It is true that spending collapsed, but why? One reason given is the housing boom of the 1920s, and so overbuilding, that caused a building recession as the stock of the nation's housing became excessive. Slowing migration in the 1930s probably compounded this slack demand for housing. Another explanation for collapsing demand is the adverse wealth effect that devastated stock prices and so worker–consumer balance sheets. Lower wealth and greater uncertainty restricted spending. Higher real interest rates dampened spending and so interest rate sensitive expenditure suffered immediately. Moreover, higher unemployment rates and the fear of job loss forced consumption lower. In this view, it was the collapse in aggregate demand that caused or initiated the depression. As Christine Romer (1993) points out, consumer–worker expectations of *future* income was an important factor that caused lower spending *now*. Fear drove abstinence, further job insecurity and rising unemployment triggered a drastic revision of near term spending plans – 'awaiting information about the future'. In fact, Christine Romer (1993) claims that 'domestic shocks related to the stock market crash were crucial in the first year of the Depression, while monetary shocks were important in later years'. What then caused spending to collapse? The stock market crash itself – working through the above channels? Where were the self-correcting forces of the market? Some economists claim that prices and wages were not flexible prior to 1930 and so a fall in aggregate demand had real effects on the economy. Moreover, the Pigou effect could not be relied upon – where falling prices causing a rise in real money balances making people 'feel more wealthy' – was more than offset by pessimism, deflation and the devastating interaction of debt and inflation.

On the financial front, the health of banks had deteriorated because of the quality of assets held and the growing percentage of non-performing loans as households and businesses struggled to meet repayment schedules. Bank lending slumped under the weight of falling asset prices (a cumulative momentum) and the potential of the private sector to spend vastly slashed as banks either closed their doors or restricted lending. Investment spending was hit hard. Hence, the circular flow of income had collapsed or shrunk, in true Keynesian style. Once the downward spiral had begun, it possessed a life of its own.

Did government policies smooth or exacerbate the collapse of private sector spending? The economic orthodoxy of the day was to balance the government budget. Even amidst a severe economic contraction there was a desire by the government of the day to raise taxes and lower government spending in order to balance the budget. Unfortunately, this strategy is akin to a dog chasing its own tail. The downward spiral of output and employment is a self-fulfilling prophesy in some circumstances, particularly amidst falling asset prices, as further uncertainty sets in and destroys current horizon spending. Unfortunately, the Fed raised interest rates in 1931 as part of a strategy to stem capital outflow and defend the US dollar. The Fed also failed to raise the nominal money supply in face of a declining real money supply caused by falling prices.

The earlier discussion highlights the workings of the propagation mechanism of the Depression but what force(s) triggered the 1929 crash from a Keynesian perspective? Uncertainty, a change in risk perception concerning expected earnings and eventually investor pessimism sent the market into a tailspin. Animal spirits were at work.

The Galbraith–Kindleberger view

A second view, and still Keynesian in perspective, is that of Galbraith's notion of the role of 'vested interests' in euphoria and mania. As Galbraith (1998) stated 'the vested interests in euphoria [that] leads men and women, individuals and institutions to believe that all will be better, that they are meant to be richer and to dismiss the notion as intellectually deficient what is in conflict with that conviction.' The 'vested interests' he speaks of includes corporations that seek fresh capital, stockbroker's prosperity based on trading volume, large speculators and company promoters pushing new issues and the potential capital gains available. Although a craze or mania helps explain the upward momentum in stock prices it was indeed easy credit that fuelled this mania. Kindleberger holds a similar view that easy access to credit was the major culprit of the ballooning asset price bubble, citing the rise in call money from $6.4 billion at the end of December 1928 to $8.5 in early October 1929 (Kindleberger 1978). A down payment of 10 per cent for buying stocks was common. Moreover, the rationing of credit amidst the crisis, and the paralysis of the credit system after the crisis, choked any possibility of financial or economic recovery. His view is based on that of Minsky, that the financial system is fragile and the credit system inherently unstable.

A variation of this second view is that of Minsky's model of debt structures, leverage and bank credit. During the boom there is an expansion of bank credit, including personal credit, and economic agents take advantage of high leverage ratios in this 'one-way street' and indulge in the purchase of speculative assets. Credit from outside the banking system joins in on the lending craze and the associated rising wave of asset prices. Not only is credit creation the domain of the banking sector but also non-banks and other institutions providing personal credit. The wave eventually breaks through a 'displacement' or shock that hits the economic system. In the aftermath, loans are recalled and credit is rationed – accentuating the fall in asset prices. Just as the boom feeds on itself so does the crash – *a negative feedback mechanism* – that possesses a momentum of its own. Such a scenario is similar to that of the chronology of the depression era.

However, this view of easy credit causing the Great Depression has been challenged by White (1990). From Figure 10.2 there is an obvious close association between the extension of credit (broker's loans) and rising stock prices. However, the claim that broker's loans drove the stock boom is no more than an assumption. In his view, the demand for new issues and the insatiable hunger of the public for stocks generated an increase in the supply of stocks and credit. Kindleberger stresses the point that broker's loans went down from $1.64 billion at the end of 1928

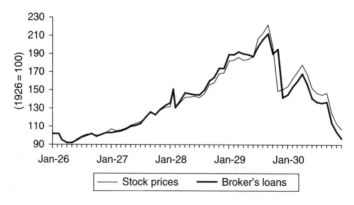

Figure 10.2 Stock prices and broker's loans.

Source: White (1990).

to $1.1 billion by 4 October 1929. Call loans from outside banks went up from $2 billion at the end of 1926 to $3.88 billion in late 1928 to $6.64 billion by 4 October 1929 (Kindleberger 1978). There was not only an overall rise in credit supply but also a change in its source, indicating that demand was strong for stocks and credit even though the Federal Reserve had raised its discount rate and New York banks were tightening up. More hot money flowed from outside banks and into the provision of call money. The rise in broker's call rates in early 1929 should have dampened the enthusiasm of investors to buy stock on margin but did not. In his view, the *independent nature* of the stock market bubble forced changes in financial markets and the supply of credit. However, Kindleberger makes the point that the *threat* of the stock market closing for a few days – or even worse indefinitely – triggered a capital flight of call money by out-of-town banks (Kindleberger 1978).

In this view, the trigger mechanism for the stock market crash was the withdrawal of easy credit, first witnessed by the rise in the discount rate and second by rises in call rates signalling tighter credit conditions in the future. Even though more expensive credit was not enough to dampen speculator enthusiasm in early stages – the shrinkage of supply, burgeoning margin calls and excessive leverage colluded together to eventually squeeze investors into submission.

The monetarist view

A third view of why the Great Depression took place is based on money and monetary policy. This is essentially the view of Milton Friedman, espousing the fact that the money supply did indeed shrink by 28 per cent between 1929 and 1933. This fall was due to a combination of factors; bank behaviour in response to their own balance sheets being suffocated, waves of bank failures and the fault of the Federal Reserve not acting quickly enough to restore liquidity to the economic system. Monetary liquidity was a major cause of the boom of the 1920s as it was a cause of the bust after 1929. A shrinkage in bank reserves caused 'high-powered money' to lose its potency – and even work in reverse. Friedman and Schwartz (1963) argue that waves of monetary contractions after 1929 generated a plethora of bank failures, which in turn reduced the money multiplier and the money stock. In this paradigm, a lack of monetary creation was the major propagation mechanism of the prolonged depression.

A corollary of this view is that the Fed reacted to the outflow of gold and so raised interest rates in order to defend the exchange rate under the gold standard regime of the time. Even though there was a choice between devaluation and deflation, the Fed in this era choose deflation by raising the discount rate from 3.5 to 5 per cent. There was a contagion effect as European countries were forced to raise interest rates as well. Hence the Fed policy commitment to the gold standard came with a cost: *the spreading of deflation worldwide.* Lower international income and confidence spelt lower exports for all, including the United States. Foreign governments faced with a choice between further deflation or devaluation eventually were forced to forsake the former and choose the latter.

However, the raising of interest rates by the Fed was also targeted at cooling off the stock market bubble and its speculative heat. The interest rate rises were significant but nevertheless modest. Perhaps the Fed aimed for a soft landing. It is true that *real interest rates* did rise appreciably in 1928 – from around 5.5 to 9.5 per cent. Technically, 'money was tight' but the Fed was not in supreme control of the money creation process – despite its confidence. Investors could not only access broker's loans but also out-of-town banks provided funding for margin calls and so offset the tightening of liquidity by the Fed in short term. In fact, the rising interest rate environment before the 1929 crash orchestrated by the Fed only caused investors to circumvent formal channels and caused some banks to oblige such credit demand in what was still a lucrative capital gain environment. As outlined in Chapter 5, rising interest rates are not always a cure for an overheated economy. Higher rates of return and credit availability may offset any higher cost of capital. Out-of-town banks were willing to rely more heavily on the more 'expensive' borrowed than non-borrowed reserves in response to credit demand driven by the stock market boom.

However, after 1929 there was a flight to quality by banks and people driven by fear and uncertainty. Banks appeared liquid and the Fed misinterpreted such liquidity as potentially dangerous – not realizing of course that banks gave priority to repairing their own balance sheets and not lending. Moreover, the Fed was fearful of lower interest rates accentuating the already visible outflow of gold and so tightened credit conditions and raised interest rates to support the US dollar. From hindsight, this policy was the tail (external balance) wagging the dog (internal balance).

Research undertaken by Temin (1993) criticized this monetarist explanation. He claimed that consumption deviated from 'trend' and so *caused* the fall in the money supply. In this Keynesian view, consumption depends mainly on income but leaves open the question as to why income fell and what adverse wealth effects were at work? On the issue of causation from spending to money, the interest rate should fall if a reduction in spending precedes the decline in the money supply. In fact, nominal interest rates did fall and not rise. On the issue of the falling nominal money supply Temin (1993) points to his evidence of *real* money balances actually rising for much of the period. But the swamping effects of debt-deflation more than offset this *apparent* rise in the real money supply.

Another source of criticism is over the Friedman and Schwartz (1963) view of *exogenous* monetary contraction causing output declines with lags. There is an implicit assumption that the demand for money is stable. However, Field (1984) claims that hyper-intensive stock trading increased the demand for money in the face of a declining money supply in 1928–9. Such forces pressured real interest rates higher and crunched economic activity. Therefore, the monetary creation process contained some *endogeneity* according to this view and so reinforces the view of White that a speculative demand for money drove both the credit and stock market booms.

An undeniable fact remains however, that is, a contracting money supply was *associated* with the collapse of the real economy and a dramatic rise in the money supply was associated with GNP rising by 10 per cent each year between 1933 and 1937. Such an increase in the money supply had an external origin – the inflow of gold into the United States went unsterilized by the Roosevelt administration. Meanwhile, a failed and bitter artist was making his mark in European politics, causing people and money to flee the continent.

The trigger of the crash, according to the monetarist, was the Fed tightening and the contracting money supply. Banks in the Federal Reserve system were instructed to severely restrict credit for would-be stock market investors as stocks were 'overvalued'.

Financial sector disintermediation and balance sheets

The ways in which damaged balance sheets of households, corporations and banks interacted and caused a slump in spending was discussed in Chapter 7. Access to credit is limited when balance sheets are depressed by lower asset values and when the prospect of falling asset prices remains. Banks do not wish to lend money as they are uncertain of which lenders remain both liquid and solvent and so capable of loan repayment. Bernanke (1983) highlights the importance of company net worth when accessing bank credit. A shock to bank net worth also results in disintermediation. The gathering of costly information acts as a stumbling block to the efficient alloca-tion of capital. Insiders (company directors and accountants) have a greater appreci-ation of the company's financial position and cash flow than outsiders (creditors and stock investors) and so external funding is higher the greater the difference in 'knowl-edge'. Hence, the 'external finance premium' skyrocketed during 1929. It was only the very large companies that were able to access bank credit and the credit crunch fell disproportionately on small businesses. Capital markets never operate perfectly, but the great deflation of the depression era interacted with contractual debt com-mitments to suffocate household balance sheets and so consumption. The dominos began to fall. Over 9,000 banks closed their doors and/or were suspended between 1929 and 1932.

It is worthwhile to note the nature of American banking at the time; it was frag-mented, small and undiversified, that implied it was exposed to regional shocks within the economy. For example, agricultural clients who suffered from drought or poor harvests could place an enormous amount of stress on local banks that in turn affected other banks. Bank runs therefore could easily spread. Given that out-of-town banks assisted in the fuelling of the stock boom they were exposed to the 1929 Wall Street crash. Banks that lacked portfolio diversification were hit from both sides – agricultural shocks and the deflationary fire originating from the stock market.

The trigger of the stock market crash in this view was the collapse in bank lending and the extension of credit. Lenders who were previously content with high lending premiums (after all, that is what attracted them in the first place) that 'offset' higher than normal risk all of a sudden became nervous by investor panic. An avalanche of margin calls crushed asset values and caused non-performing loans to escalate. Creditors panicked and fled.

Goods price deflation

There is a fourth view of the crash and that is deflation interacting with debt and real interest rates. In this view, falling prices inhibit current borrowing, as forward-looking producers believe that sales and profits will be lower in the future and that the burden of debt repayment will be higher in terms of deflated dollars. This stagnation is caused by the belief of *expected* deflation. A second channel of contraction is that of *existing* commitments – paying off debt is far more difficult amidst falling prices – and of course job loss. Deflation causes national income to fall via higher *current* real interest rates and investment plans are deferred indefinitely. Another explanation of how national income might fall in response to deflation is based on the redistribution of income from debtors to creditors as the latter group is likely to have a lower spending propensity. The value of debt repayment is raised via deflation as debtors are forced to pay the creditor in higher valued dollars. Therefore, debtors contract their own spending for two reasons. Hence, the collapse of national income and employment may be largely attributable to falling prices and their effects on investment confidence and real interest rates. There is evidence supporting the view that deflation between 1929 and 1932 was largely *unanticipated* (Hamilton 1986). Further fall in prices *surprised* both producers and consumers causing past decisions to be poor ones. Paying back debt in a deflationary environment was a real short-term burden that acted as a constraint on immediate spending plans of all groups in the community.

Asset price deflation

A fifth view requires examination of asset price deflation. The views mentioned earlier are focused on the goods, labour and money markets. Each accounts for part of the story. However, the almost forgotten leviathan of the Great Depression is across the board asset price bubble of the 1920s. The huge upward momentum created a 'whirlpool effect' whereby butchers, bakers and hairdressers were caught up in the investment (speculative) craze. Utilizing one's own income and wealth to buy assets was legitimate but to be highly leveraged by borrowing from financial institutions was to enter a whole new world of risk. When asset prices collapsed, the overcommitted investor was placed in a severe squeeze in gathering sufficient funds to meet medium term repayments or even worse immediate margin calls. But there was an irony in the crash of 1929. Who actually was taking the risk? To paraphrase Keynes (1936) 'If you borrow a $100 from a bank and cannot repay ... then you have a problem. If you borrow a $1,000,000 from a bank and cannot repay then the bank has a problem!' He quite rightly pointed to a critical threshold, which once broken, meant that the balance sheets of banks would be severely dented. Financial disintermediation results as banks loose their confidence to lend, lack liquidity, call in loans and seek to avoid any kind of risk.

How did this burst-of asset price bubble damage the real economy? First, 'stored wealth' was shaken, if not destroyed, and so the wealth effect inhibited all kinds of spending. Second, investment in capital goods, factories, equipment, etc. stalled. Third, banks as intermediaries aborted their function and so lending shrunk. Fourth, damaged private sector balance sheets inhibited borrowing potential and so consumption. Fifth, the arduous task of repayment of borrowed capital locked into low value assets that could not be sold without incurring huge capital losses acted as a drag on spending.

To appreciate the mystery of the causes of both the 1929 stock market collapse and the Great Depression requires the appreciation of the importance of asset levels and just not income flows – and so wealth effects and not just income effects. Economic activity, jobs, income flows were devastated after 'stored wealth' dissipated or evaporated in financial assets and then later in physical or productive assets.

What were the triggers?

If the Galbraith–Kindleberger view is to be believed, then any disturbance or shock to investor expectations is sufficient to puncture a bubble. Some of the possible triggers of the crash of 1929 were the introduction of the Smoot-Hawley Tariff, the rise in the *real* interest rate orchestrated by the Federal Reserve, the earlier decline of the London stock market and tighter margin lending conditions to name a few. Even though identifying the triggers of panic has never been settled, the compression of rates of return by rising interest rates and higher rates on margin lending weighed heavily on asset prices. Out-of-town banks and fearful lenders withdrew their provision of call money and so contributed further to the panic of squeezed investor-borrowers. The fact, that the Fed raised the discount rate on several occasions before the crisis tightened lending conditions. European countries followed the lead of the Fed and raised interest rates as well, creating an environment of lower activity and beggar thy neighbour tariff initiatives by the United States. Hence, the international repercussions of the United States raising both interest rates and tariffs elicited retaliation by other countries and dampened world activity. It is more likely that a combination of adverse factors built up over time – that in turn caused an abrupt change in investor expectations. Bubbles may burst for any number of reasons and the size of the deflation is inversely related to the magnitude of the overvaluation of stock prices in the first place. If the crash did not take place in 1929 it would have been soon after – for the sheer fact that speculators had pushed asset values to absurd and *unsustainable* levels that could never have delivered dividends in line with expectations.

What lessons have we learnt?

Markets normally function well and on most occasions there is a degree of rationality. However, the 1929 crash revealed several weaknesses in the financial and regulatory systems of the United States. We have learnt that the conduct and timing of monetary policy is crucial to the economic well-being of a nation. If the Federal Reserve in 1928 had raised interest rates faster, and tightened the availability of credit more quickly, the crash of 1929 may have been more akin to a soft landing. If the response of the Fed after the stock market crash had been more accommodating in terms of liquidity there would have been less of a credit squeeze, less pressure on call rates to rise and so less selling pressure on stocks. Thus, the bubble may have shrunk more slowly and deflated without major implications for the real sector of the economy. Allegations of policy mistakes abound as the Fed went the 'wrong-way' and did not pump the real money supply enough – much to the detriment of asset prices and aggregate demand. From this policy debacle came the realization that the economic system needs a 'lender of last resort'. The Fed learnt this lesson and has sought to reassure markets in timely ways that additional liquidity would be provided to asset markets in distress when there was a real risk of spillovers into the real economy. The crash of 1987 was a prime example, and even the Asian crisis of 1997, whereby monetary policy was deliberately loosened in order to reassure investors.

Alas, the control that the Fed had over the credit creation process was incomplete and so lacked the firepower to subdue the flames of speculation. Greater regulatory control by the Fed over the US financial system has been an indirect result of the 1929 crash. Critical deficiencies in stock exchange regulations were also exposed. Overgenerous lending margins by brokers were seen as a major fuel of the crisis and such margins were raised to 50 per cent in the 1930s. Even so, the desire of investors to speculate and employ high gearing ratios was not confined to the 1920s. High leverage and a lack of appreciation of risk have been perennial biases in stock markets throughout recorded history. Just as investment trusts of the 1920s wielded price-making power so did mutual funds achieve similar power in the 1960s. The dangers of margin lending, privately and on mass, have not been learnt well. Instability in the credit creation process has plagued, and will plague, economic systems for a long time to come.

Could history repeat itself?

Mankind claimed that the Titanic was unsinkable. As the Almighty pointed out, great calamities are not always the artistry of man. And so any claim made by man that the Dow is unsinkable should send shudders down our spines. It is interesting to note that man's attitude to severe crises has always been one of conquest and opti-mism. Faith in the SEC and the Fed has created an air of reassurance in the minds of many people that economic catastrophes, like the Great Depression, will never occur again. Such reassurance is partly based on he power of a set of comprehensive regula-tions by government authorities that can control the 'unbridled optimism' of the risk-loving investor for quick capital gains. Besides, the Fed has monetary tools avail-able to fine-tune the economy or create a soft landing for the economy. Any financial excesses can be modified in a relatively short time frame. Moreover, the experience gained by the Fed and the economics profession in general, ensures that any great economic calamity would either not be allowed to eventuate or foreseen so that the appropriate corrective would be undertaken swiftly. This is the faith of mankind in mankind. Governments can save us . . . even from ourselves!

Quite aside from governance problems, the excesses of the financial system and everlasting greed of the people will always pose a continual danger to financial stabil-ity. Perhaps the extremes of Great Depression will never be seen in the developed world again but a severe and painful correction that damages the welfare and liveli-hood of ordinary people remains a possibility. Why? Governments may choose to let those investors who embraced abnormal levels of risk 'pay for their own sin' by allow-ing substantial market corrections without intervention. An alternative, and more serious scenario, is that the lender of last resort function may fail . . . at least in the short run. There is always the temptation to print money and/or monetize the national debt. Or the coordination of international central banks to agree on a combined and comprehensive strategy to rescue collapsing asset prices may not be reached or at least take time to package together. In short, severe market corrections may develop into crises and so cause living standards to decline significantly for a time. An event similar to the Great Depression is not likely but the likelihood of a Great Recession is still with us.

Conclusion

There is no doubt that the 1929 crash was the result of a speculative bubble. The origins of the crisis were financial and not economic in nature. In fact, the real sector and production side of the economy deteriorated *after* signs of financial stress. Easy credit and loose margin lending by stockbrokers fuelled the prior boom. Additional credit from outside banks, and a reallocation of funds away from productive investment and into speculative financial assets fed the hunger of speculators for more leverage. This switch of funds from one corner of the economy to the other was probably more important than the stance of monetary policy or the growth rate of the money supply. This compositional change in the source and direction of credit proved deadly. Vested interests also fuelled the boom by promoting 'overtrading' and new issues of stock. Unsuspecting and unsophisticated investors only complicated and accentuated the rising wave of asset prices.

The real sector suffered after the collapse of the stock market via balance sheet destruction of households, corporations and banks. Severe stress in the financial sector spread to the real sector via lending shyness and the recalling of loans. An old-fashioned credit crunch depressed asset prices further. Financial sector disintermediation suffocated any real sector recovery for many years and as banks placed priority on repairing their own balance sheets first. The crisis fed on itself as collapsing asset prices reduced the demand for credit by the private sector and physical investment. Even though the symptoms of the Great Depression were more visible in the goods and labour markets, as idleness set in, the origins were in the asset and money markets. Unfortunately, the Fed did not have enough expertise at the time in dealing with a financial bubble of this type or magnitude and so misread monetary and credit signals and overcommitted to the gold standard. Policy mistakes were made and devastating deflation was tolerated for fear of excess liquidity building up in the financial system causing interest rates to fall and igniting another round of speculation. Such a fear by the Fed was grossly unfounded as people indulged in a 'flight to quality', taking precaution against future illiquidity. What we have learnt from the era of the 1930s is that deflation can be just as devastating in destroying real economic activity as that of inflation.

11 Lessons from Japan's financial crisis

Introduction

Just as rampant speculation in assets, excess liquidity and high financial leverage ratios generated the US stock bubble of 1929 so too did similar forces drive up stock and real estate prices in Japan in the mid-1980s. Asset prices became unsustainable and eventually collapsed – suffocating the real economy in its path. The huge fall in the Dow of 89 per cent by 1932 can be compared to the 80 per cent fall in the Nikkei by 2003. Interlocking relationships between Japanese companies only complicated the downward spiral of asset prices and economic activity. Japan experienced serious unemployment problems for the first time since the Second World War. In fact, the implosion of asset and money markets sent shock waves throughout the labour and goods markets albeit with lags. A loss of confidence in the financial sector spread throughout the real economy via lending contraction and an aversion to risk. Japan's policy response was first one of wait and delay, then astonishment as 'flagship' bankruptcies mounted. The intermittent application of traditional monetary and fiscal initiatives failed to offset a prolonged collapse in aggregate demand. Such *traditional* strategies failed to stimulate economic recovery. Relying on the old strategy of the US locomotive to pull Japan out of recession via export-led growth no longer proved to be effective. This chapter outlines the root causes of Japan's prolonged recession and why policy responses have failed to date. It also examines why the stock market imploded year after year. And what of the Japanese Model? Is it not relevant anymore? What of Krugman's ideas – are they that radical? There are also lessons for the rest of Asia.

Japan's old growth strategy

It is a matter of historical record that Japan's economic performance after the Second World War was nothing short of magnificent. Its growth strategy was based on first mover advantage, tapping a wealthy US consumer market, industrial organization and efficiency, reverse engineering, a tightly knit cross-holding of companies, government guidance by Ministry of Trade and Industry (MITI) and the Bank of Japan (BOJ), easy access to directed credit and a vast pool of saving to name a few. Convoy Japan moved in unison as industries and sectors were targeted for growth and given all kinds of government support, including long-term cheap credit, to expand and capture market share. The export sector was the lead ship in this convoy to prosperity and high income elastic goods were given priority. Manufacturing excellence – to a world standard – was achieved in only a few years. The prime growth strategy was to hitch a ride on the US market – its high income level and its potential to grow after the Second World War. Even if the United States went into recession all Japan had to do was to wait a few months and it knew that the US recovery would be robust and swift. It could then free ride on a world recovery. In a bouyant and reliable export environment there was little need for an active monetary and fiscal policy by Japanese authorities during times of recession – as they were *always* short-lived. This over-dependence on export success had its drawbacks as the non-traded goods lagged behind in efficiency and other nations threatened to erode market share in many standardized products.

So what of the Japanese Model? Roubini (1999) outlines some of the key characteristics of this model:

- An economic and social system valuing social cohesion and collective goals over individualistic pursuit of welfare.
- An economic system based on limited market competition and oligopolistic market structures – rather than free market competition.
- Strong amount of government regulation, intervention and direction in most markets.
- A protectionist trade regime, favouring exports over imports and restrictions towards Foreign Direct Investment (FDI) policies.
- System of life-time job security.
- Implicit/explicit systems of social insurance to adrress risk-averse behaviour by households and firms.
- Keiretsu corporate organizational structures.
- Process 'innovation' model not 'product innovation'.
- Educational system based on traditional values rather than promoting innovation and creativity.

This is a fair overview of how Japan organized itself into an economic power. There are several points worth emphasizing. In this convoy approach to economic development the BOJ, and the Ministry of Finance (MOF) in particular, controlled the channeling of resources (cheap credit) into industries and sectors that possessed both long-term growth and export potential. In their view, market share *now* spelt profits *later*. Through consensus building – between government and industry – Japan could move forward. More importantly, the government ordained above normal profits in many industries by assigning selling rights, implicit franchises, segmenting markets and turning a blind eye to price rigging and to private distributional agreements. Those companies that complied with national (MOF) objectives were blessed with security, guaranteed clients and protected profits. Those that did not conform were denied privileges, including access to cheap credit. In short, Japan employed a large-scale industrial policy to orchestrate development and avoid, according to their view, unnecessary overlap and competition.

Weaknesses and seeds of destruction

Some economists argue that the Japanese model was a major reason for its success. Fewer economists believe this now. Strategies that assisted Japan recover in the early years after the war – as a developing country – are not as potent now as Japan achieved developed country status. Moreover, what were seemingly 'strengths' in this model now appear as 'weaknesses'.

For example, the over-dependence on banks as a source of credit, and the manipulation of them by government policy, came home to roost in the 1990s. Poorly developed capital markets pushed Japanese companies towards an over-reliance on banks for investment capital. When banks contracted credit – the alternatives were not plentiful and indeed those companies (and banks as well) that sought offshore lines of credit suffered under the 'Japan Premium'. Second, the avoidance of competition and the allocation of resources by the MOF only inhibited the potency of market signals. This largely explains why the non-traded goods sector was, and still is, grossly innefficient. Third, the tightness of interlocking relationships in the corporate sector and with the banks exacerbated the domino effect when many within the 'family' fell on hard times. Stresses and strains were felt throughout the whole network. Fourth, the cross-subsidization culture of winners supporting losers, Convoy Japan pulling together consensus for the national good and stiff protection for politically powerful lobby groups kept much of Japan from modernizing towards world standards. Fifth, an over-reliance on exports and the dogged protection of domestic industries from foreign 'threats' was a lopsided policy that was bound to fail in the end.

A mercantalist policy can be effective for a time but eventually the United States will demand an abandonment of a Japan's free-rider policy. Unfortunately, financial and investment excellence was not achieved – as Japan squandered many years of export profits on overpriced American assets, poor stock market investments and ill-concieved 'white elephant' projects at home. A very poor financial investment record has overshadowed its manufacturing and export success. On the social side, Japan acted as a family by indulging in the cross subsidization of industries and support for the non-traded goods sector. In this way everyone gains access to prosperity as the wealth is spread throughout the community. However, the downside of this 'family approach' was innefficiency in sheltered industries and a domino effect of bankruptcy pressure – when the economy endured many consecutive years of recession.

Macroeconomic challenges

Many of the current challenges facing the US policy-maker have confronted the Japanese policy-maker for years. These post-bubble challenges are quite typical after an era of excesses.

- Sluggish and intermittment GDP growth
- Asset price deflation
- Goods price deflation
- Financial sector fragilty

- Financial sector disintermediation
- Weak investor and consumer confidence.

Deflation, and the expectation of further deflation, has suffocated the real economy and caused the banks to be timid and hestitant with regards to lending and investment. Ironically, Japan needs inflation and the authorities need to specify a target rate for inflation and credibly hit it. This cannot be achieved without a firm resolution of the banking crisis.

Policy levers

As discussed earlier, the interwoveness of Japan's corporate and financial sector should not be underestimated. Both stock prices and land values impinge directly on the financial sector's health and its ability to lend. When stock and land values are rising the financial sector is flush with funds and actively seeks to lend. When stock and land values are falling the opposite is true – the financial sector contracts its lending out of fear and compression of their capital adequacy ratios. Such fear is based on rising nonperforming loans and the threat of more to come, as well as a shrinking capital base that fails to conform to international standards. In the past, the MOF could manipulate asset prices (land inflation) and so push on a lever to push prices up and down at will (Hayes 2000). It did so by its control over a whole array of land and inheritance taxes. It should be obvious as to why Japan could not refloat via this lever in the 1990s – overwhelming deflationary pressure in real estate could not be overcome – and so aggregate demand could not be controlled by the government.

In theory at least, the BOJ could also inject liquidity into the system with the objective of raising asset prices and so spur a chain reaction through the tight relationships between land, stock prices and in turn bank lending. Hence, the MOF and the BOJ could wipe out past credit mistakes by using this asset price lever. Those companies in tight financial situations and highly leveraged would be 'saved' by the next wave of asset price inflation orchestrated by government authorities. Land as collateral was at the heart of bank lending policy. Asset backing was favoured over cash flow. An underdeveloped capital market pushed corporate Japan to excessively rely on banks and so indirectly government guidance schemes. At the heart of government strategy was the dependence on land values as collateral for lending. Asset values, and not necessarily short-term corporate profits, drove the whole credit cycle.

The other major policy lever is that government authorities exert *some* control over the Yen. The movement in this variable affects all price levels in Japan. A low Yen causes Japanese goods and assets to appear cheap in foreign eyes. However, Japan has been xenophobic for much of its life. It has devised a myriad of schemes and laws to keep Japanese assets in the hands of nationals. A strong Yen acts as a deterent to foreigners to buy Japanese goods and assets. If authorities are concerned about *deflation*, then a lower Yen should be favoured as higher import prices will raise the domestic price level and create a degree of pricing power for Corporate Japan. Foreign buyers of domestic assets should push these prices higher as well. A revaluation of the Yen, and reflation that it brings, should not however, be seen as a substitute for structural reform.

Therefore, Japan has three policy levers to reflate with: taxes (land and inheritance), money supply expansion and the Yen. The other sub-levers of income tax cuts and low nominal interest rates are possible avenues of revival but have not been effective to date. However, a key external force of revival is that of US demand, and world demand in general, that will stimulate export growth and industrial production. Greater efficiencies in production, combined with technological progress, can lower unit costs and so increase international competitiveness – despite Yen appreciation.

Why the asset price bubble?

Japan's huge escalation in asset prices in the 1980s was due to a combination of forces such as high debt–equity ratio, cross-ownership of financial and real assets by Japanese companies, accumulated trade surpluses, money supply creation by the BOJ, speculation in stocks and real estate and a financial system that over-lent for private sector speculation. Thirty years of current account surpluses also generated a huge pool of liquidity – a build-up that fuelled the asset price boom. Japan endured a prolonged recession, failed to deal with the root causes of its own economic problems and basically wallowed amidst policy failure. Two key curses, associated with deflation, suffocated any potential economic recovery: the debt overhang (non-performing loans) experienced by many Japanese finance companies and the asset price overhang (non-performing assets) experienced by investors in general. The Tokyo stock market has languished for years – falling to a low of 7,780 in 2003 after reaching 39,000 in the late 1980s – as can be seen from Figure 11.1. Commercial real estate prices in the late 1990s returned to their 1985 levels. Such adverse wealth effects severely dented consumer and business expenditure, depressing sales, income and employment.

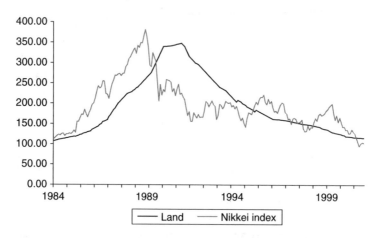

Figure 11.1 Land prices versus Nikkei index (base year: 1984=100).

Source: Ministry of Land, Infrastructure and Transport and BOJ.

Gross overvaluation in asset markets sent shocks waves throughout the entire economy for many years after the visible epicentre of 1990. Investment and money multipliers have worked in reverse, *accentuating* contraction throughout the entire economy. However, the stock and real estate markets were *pumped* by both the money market (abundant liquidity) and the financial sector (loose lending). Hence, the origins of Japan's bubble were attributable to the interaction of these three markets.

What can be seen from Figure 11.1 is that the Nikkei average − as of the first quarter 2003 − has given back all of its gains over the last twenty years. Stock price levels fell back to those set in 1983. The fall from the peak of 39,000 points in 1988 to the recent low in 2003 of 7,780 is a staggering 80 per cent − comparable to the fall in commercial real estate. Although this is an extreme comparison of a high and a low − a comparison from the average in 1992 of 20,000 points to the average ten years later in 2002 of 10,000 points is still a huge 50 per cent fall. This is asset price deflation at its worst. It is no wonder that Japan's real economy and its national balance sheet suffered under such extreme deflationary weight. However, there remains a glimmer of hope for Japan's economic revival in late 2003 as the Nikkei has rallied from its low of 7,780 to above 11,000 points − for a time. Stock prices have been supported by a increase in GDP growth and more importantly foreign buying into Japan's situation and cyclical stocks. The prospects of world recovery raises buying interest in Japan's cyclical and export type stocks. As discussed earlier, a rising stock market will underpin the vitality of the financial sector − if it is sustainable and robust enough. In some ways the Yen can be viewed as a proxy for world recovery and so explains why foreign investors demand Yen-based securities. They seek a double layered capital gain via rising Nikkei stock values and a rising Yen − as in 2003.

Financial not economic constraints

What appears to be an economic crisis in Japan is in fact a financial crisis. Stagnating economic indicators are but symptoms of more deep-seated financial problems. Japan has lost its financial pulse and heartbeat, akin to blood slowly circulating the body. Japan's financial sector faces declining profits, a high percentage of non-performing loans, damaged balance sheets and a gross unwillingness to undertake risk. A lack of credit is suffocating the real sector. Financial *disintermediation* is taking place, as the financial sector accepts deposits but reluctantly and cautiously on-lends to its customers. It is here that a banking liquidity trap has been forged. Interest rates instigated by the BOJ have furnished the financial sector with windfall gains via bond holdings − gains that have taken priority over extending credit in what is still a deflationary environment in the late 1990s and early 2000s. Hayakawa and Maeda (2000) highlight this point '... An unpredictable phoenomenon has occurred within the interbank market: while the Bank of Japan has adopted the exceptional zero interest rate policy', funds supplied by the Bank are not maintained as bank reserves, but are being accumulated as on-hand funds of tanshi companies (money market broker-cum-dealers).' As a result, the monetary transmission mechanism has been damaged or lost its signal; in short, Japan has fallen into a Keynesian-type liquidity trap. The

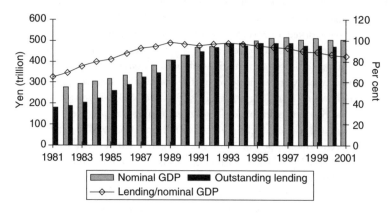

Figure 11.2 Trend in lending and nominal GDP (1981–2001).

Source: Bank of Japan (2004).

most formidale challenge facing Japan is how to overcome the bank's hoarding of funds. Figure 11.2 reveals the collapse in lending in absolute terms and as a percentage of GDP.

Although banks are unwilling to lend – so too are customers unwilling to borrow. It therefore follows that there are several constraints to any significant *supply-side restoration* of bank lending in Japan. First, raising low levels of capitalization may be addressed by operating profits. Here again, government attention to address inadequate capitalization levels is at loggerheads with its desire for banks to undertake more lending. Second, the banks are encouraged by government to use operating profits to write off bad debts and so reduce the abnormally high levels of non-performing loans. However, this strategy has the damaging side effect of reducing lending in the near term, creating further doubt over outstanding loans as spending and asset prices remain soft. Third, while risks in lending to corporate Japan are still perceived to be high, there is great reluctance by the banks to risk exposure to higher levels of non-performing loans. The core issue here is one of non-performing assets and not just non-performing loans. This dilemma may not be so much a credit crunch than a credit stalemate. Lenders are under no compulsion to borrow when rates of return are low and even below the level of real interest rates – as deflation clouds the business calculus.

Japan's asset price bubble: liquidity roots?

There is no doubt that *excess liquidity* in the Japanese system drove asset prices higher across the board – a case of too much money chasing too few assets. A monetarist interpretation of this bubble revolves around the excess liquidity that built up in the Japanese economy in the mid-1980s. According to Meltzer (1995), the BOJ deliberately pumped up the money supply in order to lower the value of the Yen against the US dollar, in accordance with an agreement that was reached at the Plaza Accord in 1985. A second interpretation is the *loose lending policy* view, which points to inadequate risk management and an over-reliance on asset backing rather than cash flow by Japanese banks. A lack of surveillance of high financial gearing ratios employed by the private sector accentuated the boom in asset prices. The cross-holdings of shares between companies (ziabatsu) also clouded prudential judgement. A third interpretation of Japan's bubble is that of *poor prudential supervision* whereby moral hazard and overambitious lending policies were partly government backed via a government safety net that 'secured all'. Government regulation and protection from competition, mergers, takeovers and bankruptcy cocooned the whole banking system from market discipline. A 'convoy approach' was employed, whereby healthy banks would cross-subsidize or pull along weaker and even non-viable banks. A fourth interpretation is the vast build-up of *export related wealth* in Japan that was looking for an investment home. Many Japanese investors shied away from overseas investment partly because of exchange rate risk and partly because of unfamiliarity with overseas investment opportunities. Japanese banks were among the biggest in the world by the 1980s and Japan gained the nickname of super-creditor.

From that stated earlier there are a multitude of interpretations as to why the bubble expanded to such a size, vast amounts of credit were used for speculative purposes that pushed up asset prices to heights that could not possibly yield long-run, or even normal rates of return. In other words, price–earnings ratio reached heights that were unsustainable. What was not foreseen amidst the hype of the bubble was not only the size of the implosion to come, but also the extent to which Japan would suffocate itself from the devastation of *asset price deflation*. Japan entered unchartered waters in the 1990s, a test of the skill and finesse of the BOJ and MOF as well as Japan Inc, in responding to a crisis embracing a new set of challenges.

What of the export growth strategy?

For many years Japan relied upon export-led growth – particularly to the United States – and so it would always wait for the locomotive of US recovery to pull it out of recession. During the 1990s, Japan's export growth was around 3 per cent annually, but still nowhere near enough to cover or offset the severe damage inflicted by asset price deflation of between 50 and 80 per cent throughout the whole of the 1990s. Such deflation suffocated domestic investment and to a lesser extent consumption spending in Japan. Although current account surpluses, as a percentage of GDP, averaged more than 2.5 per cent of GDP in the 1990s – they were not powerful enough to subdue deflationary forces.

So why was such a powerful export response not enough to pull a deflationary Japan out of a prolonged recession. First, the sheer size of wealth destruction in the aftermath of the bubble would require many years of liquidity injection via export growth to offset. Even a 3 per cent current account surplus, along with export expansion, could take more than fifteen years to cover a 50 per cent collapse in asset prices. Repairing Japan's national balance sheet would take time. Second, reliance on the US markets has lost some of its locomotive power as the US economy has shrunk in percentage terms in the total world economy. Third, this one-pronged strategy was bound to be inadequate with only mild support from monetary and fiscal stimuli for most of the 1990s. We shall examine why monetary and fiscal policies failed to stimulate Japan's economy below.

Monetary policy failure

How did the Japanese government seek to reflate its flagging economy in the 1990s? An 'expansionary' monetary policy was part of the recovery strategy, that included lowering interest rates, to exceptionally low levels of around 0.25 per cent in 2000 from a decade high of 7 per cent in 1990 (Figure 11.3). However, the deterioration of the economy and the threat of a triple dip recession in 1998–9 caused the BOJ to commit to a 'zero interest policy' – in real terms. We now examine why a series of interest rate cuts failed.

On the demand side of the fence, business and consumer confidence was low, rates of return from business enterprises under severe downward pressure and so the demand for credit remained weak. Although bank lending grew at a rate of 11 per cent from 1985 to 1989, it drastically shrunk – even into negative territory by the mid-1990s. As can be seen from Figure 11.2 the massive and decisive decline in credit and lending from the early 1990s can largely explain the equally sharp decline in asset prices (with lags) in the early 1990s (from Figure 11.1). Hence, an apparent monetary 'expansion' via a low interest rate policy was not enough to offset the deflationary effects of sluggish money supply growth. This failure was particularly evident in 1997–9 as Hayakawa and Maeda (2000) state 'the relationship between the growth in money and the economy in the past two years looks different from what orthodox economic theory tells us. That is, money growth accelerated in 1998 while the economy was in recession and yet money growth decelerated in 1999 as the economy picked up.' Traditional empirical relationships seem to have gone astray.

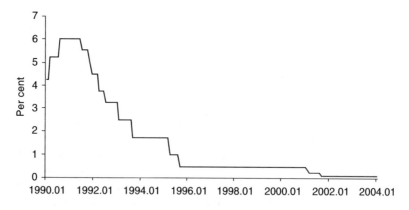

Figure 11.3 Bank of Japan cash rate (1990–2003).

Monetary transmission mechanism: clogged pipes?

Japan seems to have suffered from the 'clogged pipe' syndrome whereby monetary stimulii have not translated into economic activity. There is not one, but many channels, through which the Monetary Transmission Mechanism (MTM) may operate.

The monetarist view of the MTM focuses more on the *quantity of money and cash balance effects*. A broader monetary transmission mechanism is evident as economic agents adjust their portfolios according to changes in relative prices and marginal utilities. Excess liquidity in the 1980s drove all asset prices higher in Japan.

The elasticities approach emphasizes the *interest rate and the exchange rate channel*. The former channel focuses on a change in the interest rate affecting investment and consumer durables, whereas the latter points to a change in the exchange rate affecting exports. Japan has witnessed a strong responsiveness in the latter channel but not the former. From a demand perspective, while the cost of capital 'appeared' cheap by historical standards, rates of return were even lower and so there was little incentive for new investment, that is, the MEI $< r$. Real interest rates also 'appeared' cheap and even negative, but with fear of a capital loss and with little prospect for any significant asset price inflation there was no great rush for portfolio adjustment towards long-term assets and no great demand for credit.

A third view of the MTM is the credit channel. One focus is on the *bank-lending channel* whereby the central bank conducts a policy change that affects the deposits of banks and credit creation. However, in Japan's case, the lower interest rate strategy of the BOJ has provided windfall gains for the bank holdings of bonds and a risk-free rate of return at that. This has curtailed the extension of bank credit and so exposure to more risk could be avoided.

Another focus is on the *bank balance sheet channel*, as bank 'health' affects confidence and its own lending policies. Given the massive need to recapitalize Japan's banks and the squeeze on bank profitability, there was a move towards a credit crunch, partly as a result of risk-aversion, information aysmmetry and continued asset price deflation. Given the size of non-performing loans in Japan (15 per cent of GDP) and the questionable quality of assets supporting these loans, it is difficult to discern credit worthy from non-credit worthy customers, due to aysmmetric information. Moreover, capital adequacy ratios have taken a hit from weak and falling equity values, as unrealized profits could normally be counted as bank capital. This crucial link with equity prices has proved troublesome for the vitality of Japan's banking sector, as a *Nikkei* below 15,000 points has generally been regarded as a critical danger level for the whole of Japan's financial sector. The trading range of the Nikkei at around 11,000–12,000 points in mid-2004 – although up from 7,800 lows of 2003 – is still a threat to the stability of Japan's banking system.

Another debilitating influence of the banking sector's behaviour on the real economy is its desire to rebuild and repair its own balance sheet by exploiting the privilege it has with the Japanese authorities. Official cuts in prime interest rates benefit banks in that lending margins can be maintained or widened and so operating profits can be increased, allowing write-offs of further bad debts. Banks could also invest in safe government securities and so reap a profitable margin without taking lending risks and thus insulate themselves from exposure to possible company bankruptcies.

The legacy of such bank behaviour is that the volume of bank lending may not increase, the real economy may not be given a boost. Short-term interest rates fell from 7 per cent in 1990 to 0.5 per cent in 1997 and yet bank lending grew by only 1.5 per cent a year during this period. In the early 2000s interest rates fell to 0.25 per cent. Cautious and low-risk lending policies by banks may have assisted in repairing bank balance sheets but not in re-stimulating aggregate demand or asset prices. Herein lies the dilemma: weak asset prices generate more non-performing loans, which in turn weaken bank balance sheets which further reduce lending confidence. Income growth collapses, further depressing asset prices. This is financial disintermediation at its worst, whereby the MTM works in reverse and actually contracts the economy due to rational bank behaviour.

Damage to household balance sheets creates the same kind of contraction in aggregate demand. Fear of high transaction costs in retreating out of assets, and general illiquidity, cause consumers and savers to favour cash. Debt service costs also imply balance sheet repair. What is often forgotten in explaining the potency of the MTM is the damage done to private sector balance sheets. Adverse wealth effects, debt servicing amidst sluggish sales and balance sheet repair impact on expectations and spending. The demand for credit contracts in response.

Japan displays all of the hallmarks of a breakdown in the credit channel of the MTM, which more than offsets any theoretical benefits from the elasticity or interest rate channel. In short, the collapse of rates of return, caused in largely by asset price deflation, is faster than the collapse in the price of credit. Hence, the MEI shrinks to a point whereby both the demand and supply of credit contract to almost stagnation between borrower and lender.

Fiscal policy failure

Fiscal policy was another major alternative to stimulate economic recovery, attempting numerous public work programs and increasing government expenditure to boost aggregate demand. There were a series of attempted piecemeal fiscal rejuvenations in the 1990s including a \$120 billion package in mid-1998. While such a fiscal impetus was theoretically well founded, the end results were disappointing. Why? Because many projects had little long-run economic value, multipliers were weak, tax cuts were presumed to be temporary, private sector balance sheets were still damaged and many economic agents feared there was worse to come in terms of asset price deflation. Japan's demographics point to an aging population (mindful of retirement) and with their security under threat and unemployment rising there was a definite drag on the willingness to spend. Continual downward pressure on asset prices, further weakened the balance sheets of banks and in turn compromised lending for productive investment. Despite the fact that interest rates are still extremely low in 1999, the rates of return from real estate, business and stocks are also very low and fragile.

There was also a policy mistake made in the mid-1990s, a premature attempt to employ a fiscal contraction (raising taxes) in the belief that a sustainable recovery was underway. From hindsight this policy initiative was unwarranted and only delayed

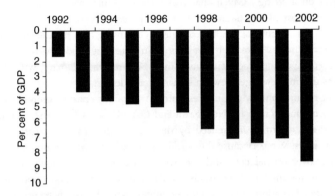

Figure 11.4 Japan's budget deficit: 1992–2002.

Source: OECD (2003).

any potential recovery. In fact, there is some evidence to suggest that Japan's under-lying structural budget 'deficits' were in fact budget 'surpluses' for the early part of the 1990s.

Despite the problems associated with the use of a fiscal policy – the authorities did attempt to refloat the economy – as can be seen from Figure 11.4. The budget deficit as a percentage of GDP ballooned from 1.75 per cent in 1992 to 8.5 per cent in 2002. These are quite staggering figures. However, these raw budget deficit figures should be treated with a degree of caution as they are not adjusted for the cycle. The aver-age cyclically adjusted budget deficit as a percentage of GDP in the 1990s was less than 2 per cent, in effect, a very weak contribution to aggregate demand stimulus. Even recently, the cyclically adjusted figures are probably only half that of the raw figures.

There are good reasons to believe that Japan's policy-led expansions have reached their limits. From a monetary policy perspective, interest rates hit historical lows, even negative in real terms and so there appears little room left for policy impetus. A policy constraint exits in that the BOJ can only force the overnight rate to near zero – not below. Driving real interest rates lower entails raising the inflation rate – a difficult task amidst asset price deflation, industry and financial sector restructuring and the fear of job loss. Hence, suppressing the nominal or the real interest rate lower appears remote in the immediate term. Besides, any BOJ move to improve liquidity is soaked up by the *financial sectors' liquidity trap*. Balance sheet repair, combined with risk-aversion, remain the financial sector's primary objective. Monetary initiatives, via the expansion of the *money base*, have failed because the financial sector has obstructed the expansion of the *money supply*.

Japan's monetary policy failed to stimulate demand and output as financial sector disintermediation further depressed asset prices, ballooned non-performing loans and caused consumption and investment spending to be weak. On the demand side, economic agents cannot be forced to borrow and so monetary policy can be likened to 'pushing on a string'. Given that real rates of return have been either soft or declining for most of the decade why would potential investors wish to borrow? Banks defend their cautious lending policies by claiming that the demand for credit has collapsed whereas potential investors claim they are credit worthy customers being refused funds for productive investment. There is a stalemate, with declining asset prices driving a wedge between borrower and lender.

The over-reliance on low real interest rates to stimulate consumption is also debatable. Research undertaken by Nagagawa and Oshima (2000) suggest that Japanese consumer/savers are more influenced by the income than the substitution effect of low interest rates. Why? Because the percentage of safety assets (liquid assets) in their portfolios is over 60 per cent and the dependence on credit is low. Japan's aging population is inclined to save harder under this scenario. The opposite is true for the United Kingdom and the United States, whereby the percentage of safety assets is low and willingness to use credit far higher than in Japan. Hence, the substitution effect dominates the income effect and so lower real interest rates stimulate consumption.

The use of an expansionary fiscal policy also has its limits, as Japan's public debt as a percentage of GDP is around 200 per cent – the highest among OECD countries. Conservatism and balanced budget philosophies act as a constraint on a series of budget deficits being employed as they contribute to further long-term indebtedness and future tax rises. What has become evident in the money market, is the rise in interest rates at the long end of the yield curve in response to the cumulative effects of Japan's budget deficits on the national debt in the 1990s. Japan's demographics also interact with the budget deficit and the national debt. Japan's aging population generates a long-term liability for government that will impinge on the government budget over the medium term.

With regards to the effectiveness of Japan's fiscal policy, there is the question of whether tax cuts are potent in raising private consumption. Consumer–savers must believe that tax cuts are permanent, raising permanent income. It may be that future productivity gains from structural reforms may persuade consumers to lift consumption levels. Nevertheless, consumption responses from tax cuts to date have been muted. Another major reason why a fiscal policy has not been effective is because the size of the *apparent* stimulus – after adusting for the cycle – has been modest.

Export-led growth also has its limits as large surpluses with the United States incur Congressional concern and retaliatory measures. There will be some point in time when the United States' current account deficit as a percentage of GDP is considered to be 'excessive' and market censure will lower the US dollar and raise the Yen.

Krugman's insight

How is Japan to get out of its liquidity trap? That is, how to persuade investors and consumers to prefer spending over saving – and assets over cash? Krugman (1998) argues for a massive printing of money in order to push economic agents out of cash and into assets for fear of 'missing out' as asset prices rise. Not only should current monetary policy be expansionary, but future monetary policy as well, for the BOJ needs to credibly commit to sustained (asset price) inflation well into the future, that is, set an inflation rate target and employ whatever tools the BOJ has at its disposal to that target. Some economists argue for a 2.5 per cent target. It is raising inflationary expectations that is the key to Japan's economic recovery, not just a cut in the cost of capital via lower interest rates. Abundant liquidity rather than cheap money should be the intermediate target of monetary policy. By expanding the money supply growth rate to at least 2.5 times that of the GDP growth rate and by driving *real* interest rates negative; to −2.5 per cent then there should be less incentive to save and more to spend.

Krugman (1998) appreciates that the 'cost' of such negative real interest rates will probably cause the Yen to depreciate further, but in his view this would place upward pressure on inflation and inflationary expectations. Production, exports and asset prices should benefit from such depreciation. However, there is considerable fear in the Asian region that such Yen depreciation will cause China to devalue its own currency and trigger a round of competitive devaluations around the region. Any prospect of other Asian nations dragging themselves out of the current crisis via an 'export-led recovery' would diminish. Therefore, Krugman's panacea of printing money in Japan does contain an element of risk, not from a rapid rise in inflation but from regional instability.

But does Krugman's recommendation address the root cause(s) of the crisis? Yes, in that Japan has a demand-side, not a supply-side problem, and because investor and consumer confidence has sunk very low. In many ways Japan 'over-saved' in the 1970s and early 1980s, 'over-invested' in the late 1980s and then 'over-saved' in the 1990s to compensate for lost wealth and poor investment decisions – albeit at lower levels of income and amidst sluggish growth. A typical paradox of thrift scenario whereby what is rational and productive for the individual is not for the economy as a whole. Yet the answer to Krugman maybe 'no', as this is no ordinary deflationary spiral in the Keynesian tradition, but a downward asset price spiral that debilitates corporate and financial sector balance sheets and not just income and spending flows. The Krugman recommendation has merit in that any boost to aggregate demand that raises rates of return to business activity must raise asset prices. While this is an *indirect* and possibly slow method of recovery, a more *direct* method of asset price support may be required.

Japan's policy response: why so ineffective?

The first mistake was to allow the economy to lose its dynamism. An economy that grinds to a halt and loses its confidence requires enormous energy to restart. Central to any recovery strategy is to engineer a 'jump start' for the economy in order to restore lost dynamism. Policy reactions were left 'too long,' imposing severe costs in terms of foregone income flow and allowing asset price deflation to destroy balance sheets to the point of illiquid firms becoming insolvent.

Asset price deflation affects all sectors of the economy and cannot be confined to asset markets alone. The appropriate response, at some point, is to reflate asset prices and re-stimulate the virtuous circle of income flow. Japan's second mistake was not to arrest the viciousness of non-performing assets souring non-performing loans, as weak asset markets placed stress on an already weak financial sector. Japan's mistake was to address wounds in the financial sector rather than wounds in the asset market.

A third mistake was an incremental, piecemeal approach to refloat the Japanese economy. Government spending initiatives, combined with low multipliers were not enough to kick-start the economy. Many stimulus packages were announced and yet the impact on economic activity was low. Given the massive decline in wealth and asset prices, a more aggressive and comprehensive policy stimulus is required – a big bang approach to restart the economy is required by the BOJ.

A fourth mistake was to rely on a supply-side strategy to overcome an excess supply-side problem. Fiscal stimuli were aimed at public works spending and a public sector revival. The objective of raising productive capacity was ill-founded and misdirected as many of these projects contained little short-run productive value.

A fifth mistake was the strategy of over-reliance on cheap money, a low interest rate monetary policy to jump-start the economy once it had stalled. This strategy met with blatant failure. Other channels of the MTM, money supply growth and liquidity are crucial to economic revival, a lesson that Japan is only beginning to learn. Post financial crisis, the objective is to raise asset prices via monetary creation and credit expansion.

Lessons from Japan's financial crisis

Much of Japan's economic misery in the 1990s, and failure to recover, can be traced back to the asset price bubble of the 1980s and to the macroeconomic mismanagement that followed. There were two dark economic clouds that dwelt over Japan for much of the 1990s – *an asset price hangover and a debt hangover*. Collapsed asset prices spelt massive deflation and damaged corporate-sector balance sheets that in turn translated into economic stagnation in the real sector. Although the origins of Japan's excess liquidity were somewhat different from those of East Asia, the consequences of excess liquidity were, and are, basically the same: asset prices boomed and eventually burst, causing major reverberations in all sectors of the economy. Of key interest to the rest of Asia is how Japan's financial sector reacted to prolonged asset price deflation in terms of managing non-performing loans and extending further credit in a high risk corporate environment. Second, how the Japanese government sought to assist the bewildered financial sector suffering damaged balance sheets and a loss of confidence. Third, how effective Japan's traditional policy strikes were in reviving spending flows against a backdrop of spiralling deflation. Asia can learn 'what not to do' from Japan's financial nightmare.

A multi-pronged approach to recovery

Given the complexity of Japan's problems, there is a need for a simultaneous and comprehensive policy effort to stimulate economic activity. While supply-side reforms are necessary, there is an even greater need to revitalize domestic demand.

First, the BOJ needs to become more aggressive with a big bang philosophy towards money supply creation. Extra liquidity holds the key for raising both asset prices and rates of return. Economic agents need to be simultaneously pushed out of cash via the threat of *future* inflation and the threat of a lower Yen.

Second, raising consumption and durable good demand impacts on rates of return. Raising profitability via an income stimulus is preferable to depressing an already minuscule cost of capital as a higher MEI (Marginal Efficiency of Investment) will provoke more investment. Hence, the multiplier-accelerator interaction may be invigorated by an aggregate demand side stimulus. In this strategy, a bias should exist towards permanent tax cuts, rather than government spending, aimed at restoring private consumption.

Third, priority needs to be given to the restoration of private sector balance sheets over financial institution balance sheets. Raising asset prices will indirectly reduce the severity of non-performing loan problem suffocating financial sector vitality.

Fourth, public confidence in the financial sector must be maintained. Therefore, public funds must be made available for deposit insurance and for the re-capitalization of the financial sector.

Fifth, government policy attention must focus on the excess supply of real estate with the objective of either supporting real estate prices or clearing excess stock or both. Failure to arrest asset price deflation will drag the financial sector into a deeper malaise and the stock market with it. Stimulus to residential housing construction holds the key to raising consumption demand.

Sixth, measures aimed at improving financial sector efficiency are likely to yield long-term results. There is no doubt that foreign competition and take-over bids will make Japan's financial sector more efficient and generate lower costs. However, this supply-side initiative may generate adverse effects on capitalization and lending that pose significant short-term transitional problems.

Flow on effects from Krugman's solution

To the extent that the Krugmanite solution is appropriate, if implemented, the Asian region may be blessed by several benefits. First, a lower Yen may stimulate domestic demand in Japan and exports abroad, reviving Japan's income growth. Expected inflation becomes the motivating force to spend. Such a revival in income growth should encourage more imports from the rest of Asia. Second, the Asian component of the financial sector's non-performing loan problem should become less of a problem under a lower Yen. Third, the prospect of a lower Yen should also push Japanese investors offshore into 'cheap' Asian assets. This could result in the second wave of FDI flowing to Asia based on a strong current Yen but an expected weaker forward rate. Fourth, excess liquidity may cause Japan to export lower interest rates around the world via a stronger US bond market. Downward pressure on the Yen may assist in the current export of capital and purchase of US bonds. Buoyant world activity is a prerequisite for an early Asian recovery.

However, there are negatives of a lower Yen. Competitive pressure is placed on various Asian exporters, together with adverse valuation effects on US dollar denominated foreign debt. A devaluation by China may trigger further devaluations by South-East Asian exporters of labour intensive goods. To the extent that a lower Yen implies a stronger US dollar, there is pressure on Asia's foreign debt to rise.

An appropriate policy response

Even though Japan's economy is languishing under two heavy debt and asset price overhangs, there is still a real opportunity to reflate economic activity by aggressive demand-side stimuli. Recent supply-side initiatives have failed to solve what is basically an excess supply-side problem. A 'Big Bang' approach is required, not only in the financial sector, but in the real sector also, boosting aggregate demand. Such a package should have several prongs and be implemented simultaneously, maximizing cumulative momentum. However, the Japanese policy-maker must be mindful of raising deflated asset prices, directly, if possible.

Hence, a vibrant expansionary Japan may raise demand for East Asia goods and cause FDI around Asia to rebound and a recessed, yet liquid, Japan may cause United States and European recoveries to be sustained via lower world interest rates.

Lessons from Japan's stagnation

A key lesson from Japan's experience is the destructive power of asset price deflation that may hound an economy for years after the initial collapse. Damaged corporate and financial sector balance sheets cause spending flows to shrink as debt repayment retains priority over new spending on consumer durables and investment. Adverse wealth effects send contractionary propagation waves through the economic system for years. Therefore, a demand-side stimulus to offset private sector strangulation is required to avoid the two poisonous debt and asset price overhangs.

Indecision by policy-makers is also costly in terms of greater balance sheet damage and its spreading effects to the rest of the economy via reverse multipliers. Waiting for the natural 'self-correcting forces' of the market may be a fruitless wait in that changes in inflation rates, wage rates and profit rates may not be enough in terms of *flows* to offset the massive damage inflicted on the *stock* of wealth. A 50 per cent fall in asset prices cannot be healed by an incremental yearly decline in prices and wages – unless a wait of ten years is acceptable. East Asian policy-makers need to respond quickly and decisively in terms of restoring asset values – albeit not to former levels.

Restoring financial sector health is a major priority as lending flows hold the key to increased economic activity post crisis, and indeed the indirect key to supporting sagging asset values. However, the financial sector should be prevented from repairing its own balance sheets at the expense of the corporate sector and the community in general. Bank stockholders should bear some of the burden of recovery.

Conclusion

Asset price bubbles are the privilege of wealthy nations and Japan had its turn just as Holland, Britain and the United States had done so at their peak. It should come as no surprise that a mercantilistic Japan fell victim of its own success. Accumulating wealth has its costs in terms of asset price inflation and underwriting speculative fever. Unlike previous recessions that were inventory and overcapacity related, this great recession of the 1990s stemmed from Japan's overheated asset market. Expenditure *flows* contracted in response to collapsing asset price *levels*. Financial sector disintermediation compounded the softness in aggregate spending by constricting lending flows. A vicious circle of debt-deflation suffocated corporate, household and financial sector balance sheets. Such a virulent interaction posed an enormous policy dilemma for Japan's policy-makers, that is, how to kick-start the economy once dynamism was lost. A lethargic and sick economy plagued Japan for most of the 1990s and alas even into the twenty-first century. East Asia could learn well from Japan's corporate sector and policy mistakes. Chapter 12 examines how East Asia can turn a crisis into an opportunity by learning from Japan's financial sector malaise and its own governance mistakes.

12 The Asian bubble and crisis

Introduction

In previous chapters the driving forces of stock market bubbles were examined. In the case of East Asia, the origins of stock market euphoria shared common threads with the experience of Japan, the bubble of 1929 and the US bubble of the late 1990s. Excess liquidity and loose lending policies destabilized these three regions by ballooning both stock and real estate prices to peaks that could not be sustained – leaving a wake of bankruptcies and bad debt – in the deflationary aftermath. Balance sheets of corporations and individuals were severely dented – if not permanently damaged. Spending flows were severely restricted as a consequence and these economies went into a tailspin. What shocked Asian investors was the suddenness of the crisis – as it came like a thief in the night.

This chapter seeks to finesse some of the commonalities between these four stock market bubbles. Each displayed a 'real' foundation or an initial phase of economic expansion based on solid productivity growth and a build-up of human capital. What began as a *boom* based on real fundamentals ended up being a *bubble* based on speculative euphoria. Somewhere amidst the economic boom investors became over-optimistic and overconfident and so fell into speculative activity and hubris. We discover that both the origins and aftermaths of these bubbles are remarkably similar. However, US policy-makers and citizens hope that the US post-bubble recovery is not similar to that of Japan – plagued by non-performing loans and a financial sector that lost its confidence.

Some commonalities

Export success and the acquisition of hard currency were the major driving forces of East Asia's economic rise and consequent stock market bubble – as was the case in Japan twenty years earlier. Abundant liquidity also drove East Asian stock markets as central banks, in the main, were able to expand the money supply without any major adverse consequences in terms of goods price inflation. However, abundant liquidity did propagate asset price inflation. East Asia may have fallen victim of its own success, in that export success, accumulated wealth and high savings rates generated both a huge asset price bubble and an overheated economy. Just as in Japan in the mid-1980s, asset prices were bloated by strong export growth and an accelerating money supply (prompted by the Plaza Accord) so did such a build-up of financial forces operate in East Asia in the early 1990s.

Relative prices were also affected. This biased investment decisions and the allocation of long-term capital towards quick-fire capital gain. A casino mentality gradually subdued rational business calculus undertaken by private investors in 'normal circumstances'. The financial sector compounded the upswing of the economic boom by indulging in loose lending policies that focused on asset backing, rather than cash flows, thus adding to the liquidity fire. Thus, speculative activity possessed a life of its own.

Debt-deflationary spirals were common to all cases. As the financial sector overindulged in its lending to both real estate and stocks so did the probability of a higher percentage of non-performing loans result. As asset prices collapsed so debt repayment become highly squeezed. Highly geared and over-indebted corporations pressed heavily on overextended banks that soon indulged in disintermediation and the hoarding of money. Banks lost confidence as to who was and who was not a good credit risk.

There were also causes that were not common. The United States did not enjoy any sizable amounts of export created wealth in either 1929 or 1999. Whereas both Japan and East Asia were dependent on export created wealth for much of the last century. Bubbles in the United States and East Asian asset prices were partly fed by the inflow of foreign capital whereas in Japan's case it did not. After all, it had its own freshly earned capital to play with. Another devastating force in the aftermath of the East Asian bubble was that of the debt–deflation–devaluation spiral – capital flight exacerbated already weak currencies causing foreign debt in local currencies to double. Japan and the United States did not suffer from this vicious circle of contraction – unless the decline of the US dollar from 83 Euro to 124 Euro holds greater contractionary pressure than is currently visible. Potential deflation in the United States is a major worry to international investors. Such investors witnessed the carnage caused by collapsing asset prices in East Asia and then collapsing currencies.

This chapter examines the major causes of East Asia's crisis with particular reference to financial factors generating an asset price bubble in stocks and real estate. Speculation and greed played major roles in the craze.

Financial origins of the bubble

Just as excess monetary liquidity was the prime engine that drove Japan's asset price bubble, so too did this same force drive East Asia's bubble in real estate and stocks. In true monetarist tradition, it was 'too much money chasing too few assets'. Liquidity was abundant for many reasons. Excess demand for assets was driven by the monetary authorities' failure to completely sterilize capital inflows, adequately supervise their financial systems' foreign borrowing programmes, monitor the credit boom, censure high corporate sector leverage ratios and the printing of money before the outbreak of the crisis. The sheer magnitude of capital inflows implied that complete sterilization was not possible. There was also an ongoing reform process in many East Asian nations that fostered ambitious lending programmes by their financial sectors. Increased deregulation and openness heightened the desperation by bank managers to 'place funds' in a very liquid and competitive environment. A huge credit boom followed that fed on itself. Unfortunately, a complicating factor arose when some Asian economies faced adverse economic signals and the central banks yielded to macroeconomic temptation by printing money to 'buy time' for the defense of the currency, meet debt obligations and even avoid the collapse of the entire financial sector.

The quest for rapid economic development caused 'temporary blindness' among monetary authorities regarding monetary and credit laxity. Liquidity became the means to increase the *speed* of economic development at a pace incommensurate with the formation of human capital and productivity levels. In summary, the origins of excess liquidity rest with vibrant export sectors that reassured foreign investors that economic take-off was well underway, and so profits were available from re-exports to mature economy markets and growing domestic demand. Foreign investment complemented trade profits in creating liquidity, as did the opening of the financial sector that borrowed from abroad.

An examination of Thailand's case is particularly revealing from the point of view of conducting a monetary policy in a 'fixed' exchange rate environment. Massive capital inflows compromised the independence of monetary policy. There are two key and separate layers of analysis. The first layer is the *pre-crisis environment* for the conduct of monetary policy. By targeting the exchange rate, the Thai authorities lost partial control of both interest rates and the money supply. When Thai interest rates were 300–400 basis points above those of the United States, there were pull factors causing Thai businesses to want to borrow abroad, as there were push factors causing foreign investors to want to invest in Thailand – at both relatively high and seemingly safe rates. Was this a marriage made in heaven or hell? It appears that it was the latter. Why? If such capital inflows went unsterilized, then a build-up of liquidity would result as the central bank issued baht in exchange for foreign currency. Such liquidity filtered throughout the whole financial sector. If capital flows were sterilized, in an effort to stabilize the baht, then domestic interest rates and the interest rate premium over US rates would widen – therefore further driving domestic investors offshore. Thus, there was a dynamic inconsistency inherent in the conduct of monetary policy pre-crisis. Higher interest rates attracted another wave of foreign capital flow which only added to excess liquidity. However, post-crisis the dynamic worked in reverse. Capital outflows triggered higher interest rates in East Asia which in turn compressed the MEI, depressed expectations, lowered demand and with it, asset prices. Thailand's credit crunch had two prongs: high interest rates and contracting liquidity. Such a tight monetary policy only accelerated short-term capital outflows by compounding repayment difficulties and slaughtering expected rates of return. The baht did not stabilize under this monetary strategy in the early months after the crisis – despite the theoretical appeal that it would.

Much of this monetary policy dilemma rests in the nature of the foreign funds that flowed into Thailand as well as the response of the Central Bank of Thailand to such flows. While the first wave of foreign capital to invade Thailand was long-term (FDI) in nature, the second wave of the 1990s was portfolio and short-term in nature. This capital was debt, not equity, and was willing to leave when higher interest rates threatened to destroy asset prices and the ability to repay.

Corporate sector leverage before the crisis

Given that East Asian economies were both buoyant and liquid, there was every incentive for corporations to exploit a rampant rise in economic activity via the use of high financial leverage. As Table 12.1 shows, Japan's corporations indulged in high debt–equity ratios in the mid-1980s – a precursor to its huge asset price bubble. Other Asian nations applied a similar strategy a few years later, singularly rational for corporations, but collectively disastrous for the nation.

It is worth noting that Japan's debt–equity ratios fell in the aftermath of Japan's asset price bubble. Korea and Thailand's debt–equity ratios were relatively high by mature economy standards, before the crash, whereas that of Malaysia was far lower. Taiwan's debt–equity ratio actually fell before the crisis and so was less exposed to a corporate profit collapse. Both Korea and Thailand appeared exposed, according to these data, as did Japan in the late 1980s. High leverage ratios are a great servant but a tyrannical master. As corporate profits dried up, Asian companies faced the domino effects of inability to meet debt obligations, a financial credit squeeze, and a reduced cash flow that further choked corporate sector balance sheet health.

The roller-coaster of speculation

In an environment of excess liquidity, there was plenty of fuel for speculation on asset prices. Easy access to credit combined with aggressive financial sector lending policies caused price–earnings ratios to skyrocket along with real estate prices. Internal speculation would trigger interest rate rises eventually, as the central bank would react to preserve its own reputation. Canterbery (1999) provides insight and warning on the self-fulfilling nature of a speculative bubble 'pure speculation takes over whereby players buy for resale rather than income'. It is the belief that asset prices will rise that spurs even the ordinary working-class citizen to purchase assets irrespective of expected income flows. Such 'irrational exuberance' flies in the face of the rational expectations view of economic fundamentals driving asset prices. A rise in the interest rate or even an expected rise may be enough to cause the bubble to collapse. There is

Table 12.1 Debt–equity leverage

	1986	1988	1990	1992	1994	1995	Average
Japan	69.2	60.8	56.1	56.1	52.8	50.4	57.5
Korea	73.8	64.5	65.2	71.9	67.9	67.1	67.5
Malaysia	25.4	28.7	25.6	27.0	30.4	36.1	29.5
Taiwan	40.5	37.0	31.9	33.1	30.2	28.2	33.1
Thailand	45.1	35.7	28.9	46.8	47.4	52.1	42.5

Source: Alles *et al.* (1998).

some evidence of rising interest rates in Asia (even before the crash) generating fear and anxiety among asset holders. Moreover, the interaction between the (more liberalized) financial sector and the casino mentality of 'investors' proved to be a very potent mixture in driving asset prices to unsustainable limits in terms of cash flow and realistic rates of return (profits). In short, asset bubbles are inherently unsustainable but also may be pricked by government-led interest rate rises.

Crony capitalism and accelerated development

Given the success of Japan and the respect for the 'Japanese Model', many East Asian nations favoured active government intervention in order to accelerate economic development. Three implicit government guarantees were employed, in the hope of accentuating development. The first involved pegging the exchange rate to the US dollar. There were no doubt very good reasons why some Asian nations pegged their exchange rate to the US dollar. Benefits included the appropriation of 'US Federal Reserve credibility', stability for decision-making on trade and investment and most importantly the attraction of capital inflows for very large and ambitious development plans. There was an implicit guarantee to the foreign investor, by government, that exchange risk would be absorbed by the central bank and domestic citizens. Foreign investors interpreted such a guarantee as the host government's commitment to sound economic management, and 'promise to pay' in US dollar, in time of crisis. Such an open cheque was drawn upon in 1997.

A second type of implicit guarantee given by the government was for large development projects, both public and private. Foreign capital required reassurance that such projects met with government commitment and legitimacy. From hindsight, the 'close relationship' between government and business backfired in that 'crony capitalism' eventually failed to satisfy foreign investor demands for openness and transparency in decision making.

A third type of implicit guarantee involved closeness of governments to the financial sector via shareholdings by government officials, government deposits and the lender of last resort facility available from the central bank. Depositors seemed reassured by government association.

From the point of view of macroeconomic stabilization, several mistakes and failures were evident. First, financial sectors were fragile and most governments failed to adequately supervise such an important sector of economy in terms of money creation, foreign borrowing, domestic lending polices and bank capitalization. Second, there was a significant delay in raising interest rates and tightening liquidity when it was blatantly obvious that asset price inflation was escalating. Such an asset price bubble was ballooning in the very early 1990s (even though goods inflation was modest) and yet most Asian central banks were reluctant to cool off an already overheated property market. Third, when it became obvious that the whole financial sector was at risk in 1997, by way of increasing non-performing loans, deteriorating balance sheets and softening asset prices, the central bank increased domestic liquidity via money creation. Such a rescue effort was knowingly undertaken despite all of the ill side-effects of increased domestic liquidity (e.g. Thailand, Indonesia). However, such an excess liquidity response to a collapsing financial system should be seen in the light of a choice of two evils – an exchange rate collapse or a collapse of the whole financial sector.

Financial sector failure: the fading heartbeat

It was not only the corporate sector that employed a high leverage strategy to secure high profitability, but the financial sector did the same as well. Heavy reliance on banks and finance companies, rather than bond markets, was a distinct characteristic of Asian financial markets. Such a structure created a bias in favour of short, rather than, long-term borrowing. A mismatch arose when financial institutions borrowed short offshore in US dollars and lent long in domestic currency (e.g. Thailand). The corporate sector in Indonesia followed a similar strategy. To make matters worse, when the crisis broke, a lack of clear, enforceable bankruptcy procedures complicated the effective collection of debt.

The size of the non-performing loans' problem became apparent in 1998 and as Table 12.2 reveals there was no significant improvement in official estimates by September 1999. Perhaps this was because the unofficial size of this non-performing loans' problem was far higher than official estimates. In terms of the fiscal costs of restructuring, the estimates for Indonesia and Thailand appear to be the highest.

Erosion of competitiveness

Several East Asian nations witnessed their competitiveness erode in the 1990s. Several forces were at work. First, by pegging to the US dollar, several Asian currencies rose on the back of a rising US dollar and so became 'overvalued' in comparison to other trade competitors. Second, large capital inflows placed upward pressure on non-traded goods prices and so the 'internal' real exchange rate became overvalued. Third, inflation and wage costs in particular, in many Asian countries displayed an upward trend above those of trading partners. Fourth, China with its low level of the real exchange rate and wage levels in particular posed a competitive threat to the South East Asian region. Fifth, the appreciation of the US dollar and the depreciation

Table 12.2 Non-performing loan ratios and fiscal costs of restructuring

	Official estimate, end of 1998	*Official estimate, September 1999*	*Unofficial estimate, peak level*	*Fiscal costs of restructuring as share of GDP*
Indonesia	—	—	60–85	58
Korea	7.6	6.6	20–30	16
Malaysia	18.9	17.8	20–30	16
Philippines	11.0	13.4	15–25	—
Thailand	45.0	44.7	50–70	32

Source: Asian Development Bank (2000).

of the Yen in the mid-1990s caused much consternation and currency realignment in the region. Increased competition from Japan posed a threat, as did the shrinkage of capital flows from Japan to the rest of Asia. Thus, Asian currencies were placed under downward pressure. Given a decline in competitiveness, there should have been no surprise that several Asian nations experienced an export collapse in 1996, at least in growth terms. That is of note is the severity with which Thailand's exports crashed and the rapid export recovery of both China and the Philippines.

Foreign forces

Many Asian policy-makers have voiced their views on foreign currency speculators. In the early days of the crisis, much of the blame was placed at the feet of *foreign speculators* that sought to extract large profits from the forward sale of some Asian currencies. Quick profits were no doubt the objective. But the question remains as to whether such external speculation triggered the crisis or whether it signalled the deterioration of a deeper set of economic and financial fundamentals. Forward-looking, rational economic agents obviously were perturbed by national policies, declining corporate profitability, an export collapse and unsustainable asset prices. It appears that the foreign currency speculators sought the exit door before other (more long-term investors) made their way to the same exit. Blame, therefore, is in the eye of the beholder.

Worldwide fund managers could also share some of the blame. In the early 1990s when rates of return were low in Europe, and extremely low in Japan, there was a push of funds to the Asian region with a kind of self-fulfilling optimism. Developing Asian markets seemed ripe for the picking, and with vast amounts of world liquidity there was ample room for fund managers to diversify their portfolios. As more Asian nations liberalized their financial sectors and economies in general, so did foreign fund managers increase their portfolio investment. What also should be noted is that the international financial system is in need of an improved architecture, as international capital flows have become extremely volatile. The continual search for higher rates of return combined with increased international capital mobility has increased the vulnerability of developing Asia to an international financial business cycle.

It is also possible to allocate blame towards the *US Federal Reserve* and its 'pre-emptive strike' against 'inflation' in the United States in 1994. The US Federal Reserve raised US interest rates which caused industrial activity to decline and created a worldwide economic slowdown, with a lag, in 1995. Other factors affecting demand included the possibility of market saturation, rising protectionism and depressed demand from Japan. Such downward pressure on aggregate demand further compounded Asia's export slowdown. Moreover, upward pressure on Asian interest rates further squeezed profit margins in the region.

Pre-crisis contagion effects were still being felt, as the ongoing recession in Japan only exacerbated Asia's export slowdown as intra-regional links amplified Japan's economic and financial contraction. Conversely, China's expansion and growing share of world exports sent warning signals to policy-makers and investors alike around Asia that competition in labour-intensive exports was not a temporary phenomenon.

In summary, there is some credibility to the view that Asia's crisis was partially externally driven, as international forces were at work in destabilizing the region.

Excess liquidity revisited

Just as Japan accumulated much wealth from its industrialization drive, and export drive in particular, so too did East Asia capture super profits from exporting to the West. Much of these profits were ploughed back into the export drive in the early years of development but later on were channelled towards conspicuous consumption and speculation on asset prices. More precisely, export earnings in US dollars encouraged foreign capital inflow that provided a base for further monetary expansion.

Given that East Asia enjoyed superlative export success, it earned and accumulated valuable foreign exchange, and so liquidity, for development goals. In a sense, it was such liquidity that fuelled domestic inflation rates, asset price speculation and raised development expectations beyond current productivity constraints. Export success, also contributed indirectly to a speculative boom in assets via the provision of national 'balance sheet' credibility upon which foreign funds could be attracted. The foreigner believed that he would be repaid.

A massive flood of foreign capital in Thailand, Indonesia and Korea also fuelled abundant liquidity – much of which *could not be sterilized* by the central banks. Many foreign investors were lured by an impressive track record and readiness to indulge in consumption as East Asian citizens acquired more discretionary income. Although foreign investment took on many forms, much of it was short term and 'hot' in nature. Such foreign funds further fuelled domestic liquidity and significantly contributed to a credit boom that in turn fuelled higher asset prices and created 'false wealth' in corportate balance sheets. This raises the whole question as to why East Asia borrowed so much when domestic savings rates were already high by world standards.

Why did the bubble burst?

Was the crisis predicted? A key prediction of Krugman (1994) was that East Asian growth would eventually slow down as a result of diminishing returns to factor accumulation. The emphasis is on slow down not a sudden crash. As Krugman himself admits, his prediction was not of a sudden collapse in growth. Therefore, this model is inappropriate in explaining the crisis in terms of a collapsing MPK or productivity. However, there were signs of a corporate profit slow down in East Asia in the mid-1990s as over-investment and idle capacity squeezed profit margins. Hence, it appears more likely that East Asia suffered from a *profitability* rather than a *productivity* slow down. There were signs in East Asian stock markets in 1996 that stocks were grossly overvalued as *P/E* ratios were extremely high.

In summary, it was export success and the associated attraction of foreign capital (in a short time frame) that sowed the seeds of East Asia's crisis via the impact on monetary liquidity.

What kind of crisis was this? At face value it was an *economic crisis*. However, it is difficult to accept that real factors, such as capital and labour accumulation, suddenly turned sour or that diminishing returns caused economies to collapse in 1997. After all, the solid foundations of growth – that of human capital, productivity levels, education, receptiveness to knowledge flows and a hard work ethic were not disappearing. Moreover, economic fundamentals in general, such as inflation rates, current account deficits, size of government and budget deficits were not, by and large, at alarming levels. The exceptions, however, were Thailand and Malaysia, especially as they breached the magical 8 per cent of GDP – an alleged benchmark signal that concerns finance markets.

A second view is that of a *currency crisis*. Large depreciations of 40 per cent or more were common. Such depreciations created widespread havoc in terms of foreign debt repayment, acquiring inputs denominated in US dollars, as well as disrupting trade and foreign investor certainty. In many cases, East Asian authorities sought to defend their currencies against overwhelming capital outflows and short-selling by drawing upon foreign exchange reserves. This was a costly defense for Korea, Thailand, Malaysia and Indonesia that failed by mid-1997. Taiwan, Hong Kong and Singapore weathered the storms of currency attack, partly due to stronger underlying fundamentals, greater commitment by authorities and sizable foreign exchange reserves. But why did capital exit with such mass force and speed? External speculation was commonly blamed, as opportunities arose to slay the Asian water buffalo caught in the mud. This mud was a large percentage of short term to total debt falling due within months – and visibly so.

There was doubt as to whether domestic businesses and investors could pay off this short-term debt in the face of increasing softness in asset prices, declining corporate profitability and collapsing export values. George Soros smelt blood, and so he and other speculators short-sold some East Asian currencies in mid-1997. However, this view is not totally 'external' in nature, as rational forward-looking agents critically assess economic, financial and government fundamentals and so are *reactive in response*.

A third view of the East Asian crisis is that of a *debt crisis*. Not only was there over-borrowing by the domestic private sector but also over-lending by many mutli-national companies. There were two critical mismatches. The first mismatch was the short-term nature of such foreign capital flows, and yet the long-term nature of the domestic assets held – there was always a risk that debt servicing would pose a problem. This type of strategy has to be soundly based on expected rates of return *and* cash flow being substantially greater than the cost of capital in order to compensate for any unforeseen risk. Unfortunately for East Asian borrowers, these risks were real and eventuated in the form of deteriorating financial fundamentals. The second mismatch was the overwhelming bias of foreign debt in US dollar, and yet much of the revenue driven by such debt was in local currency. Such a bias was compounded by the rise in the US dollar against many currencies in 1996 and 1997 creating both unrealized, but sizable, capital losses along with the difficulty in debt servicing. Moreover, devaluation and high foreign debt worked interactively in destroying corporate balance sheets and instigating a vicious circle of economic contraction.

A fourth view is that of a *financial crisis*, whereby the financial sectors of many East Asian countries were too loose in their lending policies, prudential supervision was weak, accounting and audit standards were below international standards, capital adequacy was low and an overemphasis placed on asset backing rather than the cash flow of lenders. Excess liquidity was generated not only by the financial systems, but also by the central banks and global funds searching for higher than normal returns in East Asia. The sheer flood of foreign capital, in such a short time frame, made it exceptionally difficult for profitable opportunities to be both found and realized. Price–earnings ratios hit both unprecedented and unsustainable highs. Lending officers in the financial sector were under enormous pressure to discern between good and bad credit risks, as asymmetrical information in favour of the borrower clouded prudent financial judgement. In this competitive lending environment, the financial sector undertook enormous credit risks in early 1990s for fear of losing market share and smug in the belief that implicit government backing would save major financial institutions in times of trouble. This is known as a moral hazard problem, as lending in East Asia was premised on the idea that 'heads, the bank wins; tails, the taxpayer loses' to quote the Krugman insight. Such a belief generated a false sense of security and caused lending policies to be reckless.

Hence, East Asia's financial system, in general, was seen as being fragile. But this begs the question – would such a 'fragile' financial sector have been able to grow in sophistication and perform satisfactorily under less of a flood of foreign money? Financial collapse may have been more of a case of too much capital, too quick, too soon and too footloose.

A fifth view is that of a *liberalization crisis*. Montes (1998) sees this crisis as occurring by the twin liberalization of the domestic financial sector and the capital account of the balance of payments. Such a free trade in money has its costs in terms of foreign speculators desiring high and quick returns in exchange for short-term loans oiling development aspirations. Some economists claim that such liberalization led to over-borrowing, over-investment and overcapacity as well as mis-investment. But why was financial openness such a problem for many East Asian nations? A major reason was the lack of appreciation by domestic investors of potential exchange rate risk – as domestic financial intermediaries 'had borrowed on their behalf' offshore. Even so, these same intermediaries lacked any fear of exchange rate risk by the unhedged nature of their foreign borrowing. Furthermore, such massive capital inflows placed great pressure on domestic companies to generate high rates of return in order to meet debt service. Skepticism was echoed by Greenspan (1997a), 'In retrospect, it is clear that more money flowed into these economies than could be profitably employed at modest risk.' Rate of return disappointment was bound to set in eventually. Moreover, savings rates in East Asia appeared high by world standards in the late 1980s and 1990s and so the 'need' for additional capital was questionable.

Given the suddenness of the crisis, it appears unlikely that any visible deterioration of economic fundamentals were the precipitating force. Financial rather than real factors have greater explanatory power in shedding light on the speed and fury with which the crisis broke. Moreover, the complexion of the crisis was virulently interactive, in that a vicious spiral of debt–liquidity–leverage–currency–deflation spilt over into the real sector of the economy. Just as East Asia's economic boom possessed a financial origin, so did its economic collapse.

The Asian crisis: why so sudden?

Many economists were puzzled by the suddenness, speed and lack of warning that was associated with the Asian crisis. The economics profession did what it does best – it looked backwards towards theory – with a degree of disappointment. First generation models by Krugman (1979) and Flood and Garber (1984) focussed on the crisis as being a by-product of fiscal laxity. Cumulative and persistent budget deficits needed to be financed, and governments were tempted to use seignorage as a weapon. A fixed exchange rate could not endure under such circumstances, as foreign investors withdrew funds and diminished the host nation's foreign exchange reserves.

Moreover, rational economic agents would foresee the host nation's foreign exchange reserves declining to a critical level, and so via a speculative attack, *cause* this level to be struck. As noted earlier, fiscal laxity (*in any visible form*) was not observable in these Asian nations in the 1990s and so these models appear to lack applicability to the Asian crisis.

Second generation models by Obstfeld (1994) viewed a crisis as being the result of a conflict between maintaining a fixed exchange rate and either the pursuit of domestic expansion or monetary laxity. These models have a 'macroeconomic temptation' foundation whereby the government may choose employment creation over exchange rate stability. While this view does not strictly fit the East Asian experience, in that money creation was not a prime motive, there is enough evidence to state that East Asia was awash with money – due to capital inflows and so there was a special type of monetary laxity, partly of an external origin. There was also a strong pro-growth rather than pro-stabilization bias that was bound to eventually pressure the exchange rate.

Third-generation models concentrate on moral hazard via implicit government guarantees to the financial sector that 'underwrites' a lending and investment boom. Krugman (1998) claims, in Asia's case, this was a 'hidden investment subsidy' and Corsetti *et al.* (1998) claim that it represented a 'hidden government budget deficit' as banks possessed unfunded liabilities. Beneath the surface it was governments that underwrote a huge lending boom – to the private sector.

The financial sector (and investors) felt comforted by the thought that governments would bail them out if the investment boom faltered and non-performing loans became troublesome.

A variation of this implicit guarantee view is that of Canterbery's 'casino economy' view whereby governments grant privilege to the rich in society via tax breaks and investment incentives. In the case of the United States, the Reagan supply-side initiatives were in essence a huge wealth stimulus to the American rich. As Canterbery (1993) states 'During the Reagan years the entrepeneur's share of national income declined drastically even as the rentier's (unearned) income share has soared. All of the increase in disposable income during the 1980s is more than accounted for by the rise in the share of interest income, while the shares of labor and other income sources declined.' Hence, real capital formation took a back-seat while enormous speculative profits were made – America moved away from making goods to making fast money. It was the lopsided distribution of income that compounded the speculative craze and so contributed to the speculative bubble that burst in 1987. The relevance of this 'speculative bias' in the United States for East Asia is that the desire to make fast money transcends national boundaries – with dire consequences for the real economy – sooner or later. The granting of privilege, by government, to the small wealthy business class of East Asia acted as a funnel that caused a diversion from productive activities.

Another strand of the third-generation models is based on financial fragility and Diamond and Dybvig (1983) view bank runs. In these models there can be a sudden exit of funds from the financial sector resulting from a herd mentality and panic. Investors may panic because they fear other investors are panicking and withdrawing funds. This self-fulfilling prophesy scenario is capable of explaining the speed and suddenness of the Asian crisis. There is a clear distinction between liquidity and solvency of a financial system and indeed a nation. In these models, the financial system is somewhat exposed and vulnerable to a funds withdrawal as it borrows short and lends long. Any panic that demands immediate payment causes long-term investments to be liquidated at fire-sale prices. There is no doubt that with the onset of collapsing asset prices around Asia in 1997, there was enormous pressure placed on the liquidity of the financial system.

There is a growing movement towards the creation of fourth-generation models led by Krugman (1998). This embryonic model is based on the health of private or corporate balance sheets that is adversely affected by a currency depreciation. Amidst a contractionary or deflationary period, it is declining sales, higher interest costs and a depreciating currency that squeeze a firm's profitability but more importantly suffocate its balance sheet. The firm's ability to lend is drastically reduced, even if its willingness remains. In short, it is capital inflows that inflate the health of a firm's balance sheet, and capital outflows have the opposite effect. Such capital inflows combined with high corporate sector leverage create a potent investment boom that interacts positively with a firm's balance sheet. However, this expansion strategy is high-risk in nature, as panic and capital outflows can impose cumulative deflationary effects on the private economy and the financial sector.

Of all of the generation models, the most promising in explaining Asia's crisis is the fourth-generation profitability variety. A key reason for such optimism is that this generation is mainly financial and not economic in nature. It also embraces the concept of an open and not a closed economy. Nevertheless, fragments of other generation models also have some plausibility. The theoretical search continues for an explanation that adequately comes to grips with the suddenness of the crisis, the ferocity of impact on the real sector of the economy and the lack of anticipation of its occurrence.

Stock market performances: post bubble

The growth experience of East Asia was *different* to the path worn by most modern day mature economies – as exports as a percentage of GDP was exceptionally high. Many of these developing nations of East Asia experienced robust growth from the 1970s onwards and attracted much foreign investment. As financial sectors and stock exchanges matured so did a more conducive environment emerge for more trading and speculation. While US stock markets boomed and the US economy sucked in more imports so did East Asian stock markets perform well. A roaring NASDAQ lifted tech-related issues throughout East Asia. Japan's stock market was also roaring along in the 1980s and many Japanese corporations invested heavily throughout East Asia – supporting investor confidence. Several East Asian stock markets outperformed those in mature economies as investors extrapolated past super performances and (over) anticipated near term prospects. Hence, many East Asian stock markets suffered from excessive exuberance as stock values could not be justified by real fundamentals. To a large extent the flood of foreign money ballooned already high *P/E* ratios.

There is another distinction in the growth experience that is worth noting. The nations of South East Asia, as per the Flying Geese paradigm, are less industrialized and possess lower productivity levels than their northern counterparts. Hence, nations such as Thailand, Malaysia, Indonesia and the Philippines are more prone to monetary and financial disturbances than say Taiwan (with low foreign debt levels), Singapore (with a highly educated work force), Hong Kong (with strong trade links with mature economies) or Japan (engineering excellence). The exception being that of Korea that overindulged in acquiring foreign debt and so left itself vulnerable to a collapse in export sales and world determined prices. Such North-East Asian economies could fall back on higher levels of human capital and higher product ladder goods in time of crisis. The export of sophisticated manufactured goods will always find a market or at least so the argument goes.

Conversely, most of the South-East Asian nations rely more heavily on foreign know-how and capital and so are more susceptible to exchange rate fluctuations, credit crunches and foreign capital flight. We observe that stock markets have responded, and possibly overreacted, to both the deterioration of economic and financial fundamentals in their respective economies. What seems typical of the post-bubble years is that those East Asian nations that enjoyed the most explosive bubbles also endured the most painful and drawn out economic recoveries. Stock values suffered accordingly. We shall see that those countries that relied heavily on foreign funds during the boom took a while to recover – as confidence remained a critical factor.

If we examine the stock market performance of Thailand and Indonesia we can see the massive collapse in 1998 (Figure 12.1). The impact of the mid-1997 crisis was felt by mid-1998 as foreign capital flight became severe, debt burdens became alarming and currencies had still not stabilized. All asset prices, including stocks were pummeled as EPS prospects collapsed in response to weak economic activity, higher interest rates and fleeing foreign capital.

Despite the huge fall in stock prices in 1998, there was a rally in both countries in 1999 – mainly because of the euphoria in US stock prices. However, such a rally proved to be false dawn as the same excesses of early 1990s were still being worked off and as the United States went into recession post-2000. However, a remarkable rally – probably based on catch-up growth – occurred in 2002–3. Thailand's rally was quite staggering.

The Korean economy and stock market took a large hit during the crisis because of interaction between foreign debt and the Won (Figure 12.2). Foreign investors got nervous and fled until the exchange rate stabilized. A sizable rally in stock prices

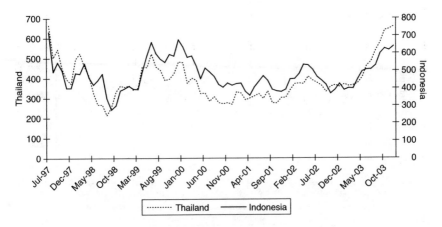

Figure 12.1 Comparative stock market performance: Thailand and Indonesia.
Source: Thailand and Indonesian Stock Exchanges.

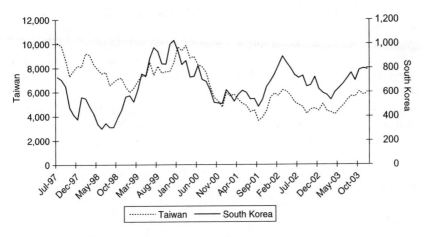

Figure 12.2 Comparative stock market performance: Taiwan and South Korea.
Source: Taiwan and South Korean Stock Exchanges.

occurred in 1999 only to relapse in 2000 as the US markets softened. As the US economy recovers so will Korean stock prices for reasons of financial confidence and manufactured export penetration into the US market. Note that the financial wounds of the crisis were less onerous on Korea than Thailand. Taiwan stocks were not as prone to the Asian crisis as say Korea, Thailand or Indonesia. Although stock prices softened during this period they did not crash. However, a lack lustre performance followed the crash of the NASDAQ in the United States between 2000 and 2003.

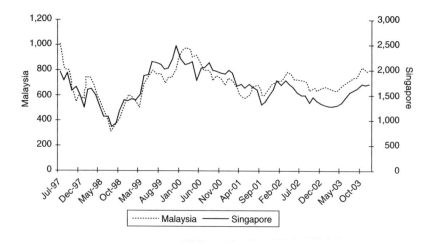

Figure 12.3 Comparative stock market performance: Malaysia and Singapore.

The Sinagaporean economy suffered in fits and starts (Figure 12.3). Contagion effects were at work during the Asian crisis and regional banks were hard pressed for a time. Singaporean stocks floundered with the region in 1998 only to recover quite well in 1999. Again, the softening of US stock prices from 2000 onwards placed pressure on export oriented stocks as well as a climbing exchange rate against the US dollar. Higher incomes and more export competition from the region is thwarting any significant rally in stock prices. Structural problems persist. Malaysia's post-bubble recovery has been slow but sure and stock prices have reflected such an improved economic outlook. Abundant resources have helped. Higher commodity prices provide support for the stock market in the near term. Like all Asian nations that are 'developing' their immediate future depends on the gaint US economy maintaining a head of steam into 2005–6.

Conclusion

East Asia learnt the hard way that an extended boom sows the seeds of the next downturn. There were similarities with Japan's bubble – super-profits from exports, high corporate financial leverage, loose lending policies and monetary accommodation that fuelled asset price speculation. There were also similarities with the US experience in that several waves of foreign capital inflow and hot money drove up the exchange rate, overinflated asset prices and created an air of investor exuberence. Excess liquidity and credit creation were *common* causes of asset price bubbles in all three regions in question – the United States, Japan and most of East Asia in general – even though the origins of excess liquidity differed.

Despite the fact that financial variables had turned soft there was also a degree of concern over economic fundamentals turning sour. Foreign speculators seized on an export downturn in the region, rising current account deficits and uncertainty over the sizable amounts of the short-term foreign debt that was coming due. There was an air of inevitability of rising interest rates to 'protect' the exchange rate and so raise domestic savings levels. A once virtuous circle of prosperity turned into a vicious circle of poverty as asset prices tumbled and a stampede for the foreign exchange gate resulted.

Even though a deterioration of economic fundamentals were part of the crisis story these were overshadowed by several virulent financial factors. A flood of foreign capital caused fragile financial systems to become excessively liquid. A credit boom coexisted with lax supervisory standards and a poor appreciation of the risk-return trade-off sowed the seeds for disaster as non-performing loans escalated. Too much money chased too few assets, that in the end resulted in an imploding bubble that left weak balance sheets and even persistent loss reports. A vicious downward spiral of spending further complicated the prospects of a profit revival in the corporate sector.

Amidst the crisis there was a great deal of panic both within the government and private sectors as to how to respond to crashing currencies and aggressive capital flight. Banks were facing insolvency. Some East Asian nations called in the IMF. Malaysia went in alone. A period of economic austerity followed as the growth rate of the money supplies contracted and interest rates soared. We know from history that these economies and their stock markets bounced. Korea, Taiwan, Hong Kong and Singapore recovered quite strongly shortly after the crisis whereas Thailand and Indonesia were slow to recover.

13 US stock markets

Where from here?

Introduction

We have explored the causes of the extended stock market boom of the 1990s and also the driving forces of the bust from 2000–3. The US economy floundered for more than two years and the stock market with it. This is an unusual and prolonged downturn as the US economy normally rebounds quickly from a recession – and the stock market even more rapidly. As this book has explained, the post-bubble era is no 'ordinary' recession as asset markets, capital spending and balance sheets have been severely dented – despite the liquidity-driven re-floating of asset prices in 2003/4. It may be argued that the excesses of the 1990s are still to be worked off. The excesses of the 1990s are still to be worked off. Such excesses represent a serious obstacle to an investment revival, as fresh additions to the capital stock are essential for the next phase of the recovery – without it there will continue to be excess reliance on the consumer, and to a lesser extent, government spending. Perhaps the sluggish revival in private sector investment and a worn out consumer has prompted the US administration to favour a weaker US dollar in the hope that increased exports will assist in the recovery process? A shrinking current account deficit would also be a welcome by-product of a lower dollar.

While the US stock market languished for two years since 2000, the opposite is true of the US bond market. Bond prices roared – portraying a very pessimistic outlook for economic performance over the medium term. Bond yields hit a forty-five-year low and global investors sought the 'safe haven' of the US bond market while world stock markets have been weak and volatile. However, as the US dollar continues to slide as of early 2004 there is growing anxiety by bond investors to search for high yielding offshore bonds in order to avoid further US dollar weakness. It is here that Greenspan has a problem – lowering interest rates further will more than likely undermine the US dollar – and perhaps the US bond market as well. Why should foreigners support US private and public consumption via their holding of US bonds when yields are low, with little prospect of further capital gain and a weakening US dollar that further erodes their capital holdings? Such fear was evident when the US dollar fell to a low of 128 Euro and to around 105 Yen in early 2004.

This chapter examines the arguments for and against a revival in US stock prices. By so doing it also focuses on the health and stability of the real economy. Nevertheless, just as in Japan's post-bubble experience, the role of financial variables, and balance sheet damage in particular, is scrutinized. Geopolitical influences are also canvassed as they impinge on the growth prospects of US multinationals. As the reader is already aware, a vibrant and revitalized US stock market – as for most of 2003–4 – will transmit confidence signals to the rest of the world's stock markets. The converse is also true, as world stock markets are unlikely to recover while US stock markets remain weak – unless there is strong substitution effect out of US assets and into Yen and Euro denominated assets. Could a lethargic US recovery been seen in the same light as Japan's limp-wristed fake recovery? Full of promise but lacking in substance?

From one bubble to another?

Between 2000 and March 2003 investors fled from one bubble (stocks) into another (bonds). Such a switch generated much volatility – and sizable capital gains and losses along the way. Fear and uncertainty pushed investors into risk-free securities and away from stocks. Such a switch was in response to excessive price–earnings ratio, profit disappointment, weak corporate governance, recessionary fears and September 11, the Iraqi conflict and finally of widespread talk and fear of deflation. However, just as the stampede into stocks lacked rationality so too did the rush into bonds. Bond yields hit forty-five-year lows and still investors clamoured to hold bonds when the expectation of capital appreciation was well-nigh nil. The bubble did burst in July/August 2003 when bond prices collapsed and yields rose appreciably within a few weeks.

And what of the property bubble? Unlike the Great Depression, investors also sought the safe haven of property (and not just bonds) – residential real estate has continued to boom – both before and after the collapse of the stock bubble. Residential housing prices continue to appreciate and residential construction is still soaring – after many years of underlying growth. US authorities must be careful that they do not oversee a fourth bubble in property a fourth bubble in property in order to offset the vibrations in the stock and foreign exchange markets.

Global investors have also fled from the US dollar bubble and into Euros, Yen and other high yielding currencies. Investors act like wild herds roaming the earth, seeking higher rates of return – partly as a result of cunning business calculus and partly because of fear – for not obeying a herd mentality is to miss out. Greenspan has had to balance the two expanding bubbles of bonds and property against the two deflating bubbles of stocks and the dollar – or a mixture thereof. Perhaps this is his strategy of insurance being revealed once again?

What of currency instability?

There is an important currency issue to address before we embark on the prospect of a stock market revival. Recent currency 'misalignments' will count for much as investors reorient their global portfolio according to relative growth, interest rate and rate of return prospects. History teaches us that whenever the US dollar is weak and is aggressively sold off so the price of gold tends to rise – and this is exactly what happened in early 2004 – gold sold for around $425 an ounce. Not only have the 'other' major currencies such as the Euro and Yen soared on the back of dollar weakness but also high yielding currencies such as the Canadian dollar, the

Australian dollar, the New Zealand dollar and the South African Rand. It then becomes a question of whether massive currency realignments are more a function of investors wanting to get out of the US dollar or wanting to get into other currencies that are strong and more attractive in the short term. In 2002–4 there is no clear indication that the European economy is unambiguously stronger than the US economy or European companies more profitable than their US counterparts. This portrays the image of global investors preferring to rid themselves of US dollars and flee into other foreign assets and currencies – a case of US dollar weakness and not Euro strength. In this era, both economies are relatively weak and it becomes a question of investors deciding on relative weakness rather than relative strength.

One key reason for the persistent sell-off in the US dollar is the prolonged and extended eight-year boom in the United States that lured many investors into stocking US dollars as a reserve asset. Not only was the US dollar held and stored for investment purposes but for trade purposes as well. Given the long time span of foreign US dollar accumulation there is now a perceived desire to unwind such long-term positions – portfolio readjustment. Second, rate of return disappointment from major US corporations and poor investments overhanging future cash flows caused foreign investors to reduce their holdings of US dollar stocks. A third reason for the sell-off is the US administration's apparent nonchalance towards the 'strong dollar' policy. It has not publicly committed to a strong dollar either explicitly or implicitly. It is true, however, that President Bush at the G8 summit in France did utter words of support for a 'strong dollar' but without much justification or rationale. Foreign exchange markets normally tend to look at capital flows and fundamentals and not listen to the soothing words of politicians. Fourth, the widening current account deficit is unnerving to many investors as it has to be financed by foreigners who may not wish to support US consumption at a time of low interest rates. Fifth, to the extent the US authorities have pumped the money supply faster than their OECD counterparts the 'excess supply' of dollars finds its way into foreign exchange markets and so lowers its price.

We should appreciate that currency realignments play a major role in determining which stock markets of the world will rise (or fall) faster than others. Massive capital flows from one major economic block to another generates a self-fulfilling strategy of driving up asset prices in the recipient region. This is one reason why Japanese stocks have rallied aggressively in 2003–4 as global investors are attracted by future Yen strength over the US dollar.

The liberation of Iraq

Regardless of the politics involved over the invasion of Iraq, global investors expressed their fears of economic, physical and financial damage to both the United States and world economies. How long would the war last? What would the war cost? How would it be paid for? Would there be long-term disruption to Iraq's oil supplies? Would Iraq's future oil sales be sufficient to fund its rebuilding program? How would the price of oil behave both during the war and after? What US companies would profit from the war?

The answer to these questions is mainly positive from a US and free world perspective. The war proper only lasted a few weeks and not months – and Sadam Hussein himself was captured. Pre war, the estimated cost was around $75 billion, was funded by the United States and was not greeted as being too 'excessive' by investors – even though extended guerrilla warfare has pushed all costs higher. At least the major cost became known and so unbounded uncertainty largely removed. Alas, the liberation period after the direct conflict has dragged on and will waste further resources – but not enough to alter investor sentiment. The price of oil did soar during the midst of the war to around $36. Postwar, the trading range for oil was between the high 20s and $40 a barrel more recently in 2004 – a surprise to some analysts. Analysts are divided on the near-term price of oil – as geopolitical events and Iraq's failure to reach high production levels creates an air of uncertainty. The prospect of world recovery also provides support. On the other hand, once uncertainty subsides the old trading range of below $30 a barrel may emerge.

As far as US companies gaining business from the war itself and profiting from the reconstruction of Iraq – the answer is most likely yes. Time will tell. Just as America bore the brunt of war funding it will enjoy the fruits of victory – as US multi-nationals win large contracts in the rebuilding phase, that is, unless France can find a way of appointing itself as the postwar reconstruction co-ordinator without prewar contribution? Perhaps the billions spent on the war can be recouped via a lower price of oil for many years to come as Iraq steams ahead to full production capacity – albeit with delay? Such increased oil revenue opens up even more opportunities for American companies as world demand picks up for consumption goods initially and capital goods eventually. On the issue of dividing the 'spoils' of victory – US construction companies should do well.

As far as the finance markets are concerned the war went about as well as it could. It was short, the price of oil came off its highs, oil fields were not destroyed and a substantial slice of uncertainty was lifted from the valuation calculus. However, as of mid-2004 the price of oil has surged to 13 year highs and the war in Iraq still lingers on – causing a degree of uncertainty to return to the valuation calculus. Inflationary fears are on the rise. The saving grace for world stock markets is the on-going low interest rate strategy of the Fed that has more than compensated for high gas prices at the pump.

Geopolitical forces

For many years the languishing Japanese economy acted as a drag on global recovery. Japan's modest growth rate was pumped along by exports and less so by domestic demand. Export opportunities to Japan were thwarted by sluggish growth and recessionary fears. Deflation, of both asset and goods prices, suffocated any prospect of economic revival. Deflation more importantly destroyed financial, corporate and household balance sheets and choking domestic spending as a result. How can US stock markets produce a sustained rally in the face of Japan's financial turmoil? The answer rests with the ability and will of Japanese authorities to deal with the financial sector's malaise and the non-performing loan problems. Perhaps the sun is rising in the land of the rising sun? The Nikkei has rallied substantially in 2003 – from a low of 7,750 points in early 2003 to over 12,000 points in early 2004. This rally was in no small way a by-product of a stronger Yen – a mutually reinforcing relationship – whereby investors chose to switch and substitute into Yen denominated assets. Japan's stock markets may rally further even if US stock markets tread water as global investors believe that a revival in Japanese corporate rates of return will continue.

Germany's economy has been in poor shape. The reunification costs have far exceeded the vision of the early 1990s. The marriage of the high income, high productivity West with the low income, low productivity East was fraught with major transition difficulties. Just as in Japan, the prospect of deflation still looms. Although the Bundesbank, and more recently the Euro Central Bank, is fighting the old enemy of inflation there is now a growing belief that a collapse into deflation will have catastrophic consequences for any prospect for a recovery in Germany or Europe. In fact, the sluggishness of Europe's central bank to lower interest rates was noticed by Greenspan and the US administration. There were two choices – either lower interest rates and follow the US lead or face a steeply rising Euro. A higher Euro was the choice and so a constraint on export growth. Several major economies such as France and Italy are still struggling to generate sustainable growth. The UK economy performed solidly, well supported by a real estate boom, and outperformed a gloomy Europe by early 2004.

Even though most East Asian economies rallied after the 1997–8 crisis the impact of SARS has dampened growth prospects for 2003–4. All forms of travel have the potential to spread the disease and so airlines, hotels and tourist destinations have been hit hard. Within Asian countries there is a great reluctance to travel to work, shops, leisure places, restaurants and public places in general. Some people prefer a more homely existence in such a high-risk environment. Hence, the effects on consumption are still working through the system. Not only will retailers be affected but eventually the banks as well. Given the pervasive fear that SARS has instilled into Asian consumers it may take quite a while for confidence to return – even after the actual death of SARS. In fact, lower economic activity can only spell lower GDP growth and less profits for some Asian companies. Moreover, US companies have declared the possibility of SARS damaging their bottom line – as significant percentages of their sales originate from the Asian region.

We know that stock markets are forward-looking and valuations are often based on an *expected* earnings–profit ratio and not just past earnings. Hence, as economic growth prospects picked up in the United States so too did they in Europe, Japan and the rest of Asia – causing company profit forecasts to be revised upwards. By mid-2004 there are signs of economic revival and a world recovery as commodity prices, and metal prices in particular, have roared. Some have touted the Yen as a barometer for world recovery. In fact, China has surged ahead in 2003–4 causing quite a boom in commodity and energy prices – acting as the engine room of world growth. A lower $US has indirectly spurred commodity and energy prices along with world demand for final goods. Perhaps low US interest rates and a low $US are the linchpins of a broad based world economic recovery?

Synchronization and integrated markets

It is well known by investors that prices for all commodities, stocks and money are determined in US markets. It is here that many players trade in deep markets and price outcomes are by and large driven by the forces of supply and demand – and so by volume. Other nations, and their markets, 'follow' the US lead. This is to say that major stock markets are correlated in movement – or are co-integrated. The correlation is not one but in the case of European exchanges quite close to one. In the case of Asian markets they are quite sensitive to changes in the technology laden NASDAQ, metal and semiconductor prices set in the United States. Deviations can and do take place from US closing prices but the deviations – percentage changes – are relatively small and often return to the US closing prices *before* the US markets open the next day. This was particularly true in the post Cold War era up until the 1990s. This era created an air of investor fear – particularly over the weekends – and investors preferred US denominated assets over any other. The United States was seen as a safe haven storage centre during the height of the Cold War. And it was not just the bond market where investors parked their funds but in stocks also – in preference to European stocks or bonds.

Even today, European stock markets keep a close eye daily on the US futures market – with a closer watch on Friday morning. Any hint of a sell-off in US stocks on Friday and the European markets hedge their bets by selling in anticipation of a lousy Monday morning. Even if there is only some doubt on Fridays – the Europeans will often close their positions in Europe and remain neutral for the weekend. Since the end of the Cold War, investors in the United States also tend to exit stocks on Friday and switch to the safe haven of bond market for the weekend. Or if there is extreme caution, bypass the bond market and sit in money market accounts. After all, who knows what kind of war or terrorist crisis might occur over the weekend? Besides, why not accumulate interest safely on the weekend without taking a risk? We know that investors shun uncertainty and nowadays post September 11 there is always the threat of terrorism severely disrupting a region or an economy.

What may be true of percentage changes in world stock markets – following the US lead – is not true of levels. European and Asian stock markets can underperform for several years due to a whole host of domestic factors including interest rate structures, inflation rates, productivity, capital flows, dollar strength, etc. There are stock cycles – the United States versus the rest – whereby global investors substitute out of US markets and into other prospective markets – driven in part by currency realignments. Therefore, previously underperforming markets can catchup and register annual percentage gains above that of their US counterpart.

In the current period of 2004 the safe haven status of US stocks and bonds – relative to the rest of the world – has lost some of its 'safety' because of the slide in the US dollar. Although world stock markets move in tandem with US stock markets they do not move in perfect unison. Global investors are sensitive to relative interest rates, rates of return and exchange rate fluctuations. Just as major stock markets do not move in unison (at least in percentage terms) neither do major economies. As discussed earlier, Japan has been trapped in recession for many years and Germany experienced a serious downturn itself – while the US economy roared along for eight straight years. This lack of synchronization of major economy growth rates has been a key driving force of US stock prices. However, as the OECD converges on a more common growth rate so will global investors substitute out of US assets and diversify into other major economy stock markets. Hence, US stock markets may only provide a general lead for other stock markets to follow.

Given that world stock markets move in tandem and are partially integrated, it then follows that policy coordination – both monetary and fiscal – by the G8 nations becomes essential. How can interest rates differ widely between nations and regions? How can the availability of credit be loose in some regions and not others? How can money supply growth be explosive in some regions and not others? How can one region indulge in an expansionary fiscal policy and another major region 'watch' – or remain fiscal policy neutral? There are significant implications for exports, inflation and the respective current account deficits of these nations.

If a world recovery is to take place then we can do without 'beggar thy neighbour' devaluation strategies or free riders exploiting the policy expansion of others. Perhaps the US economy has pulled along world economic growth for long enough and now the time has come for a more synchronized world expansion? A more broad based expansion will favour higher stock prices in other major countries such as Japan, China, Korea, Australia, South Africa and Europe.

Why the US stock rally?

Post the Iraqi War the US stock market rallied immediately. It is even more precise to say that it rallied on the expectation that the war was won and all but over and also on the belief that Iraqi oil supplies were not severely disrupted. The Dow rallied from a pre war low of around 7,350 to 10,400 points by mid-2004 – a rise of more than 30 per cent – in just 10 months. Despite these rallies being very impressive one has to acknowledge that extreme pessimism and doom was factored into the US stock markets prewar, that is, in all probability the markets were extremely oversold. Hence, a rapid and persistent comeback in US stock indices should not come as a surprise.

Another key factor in driving the postwar rally was the solid results from the first quarter reporting season. Many US companies 'beat the street' estimates and revealed some optimism about near-term future profits. Investors liked what they heard and aggressively bought stocks. Even the strength of the 'buy recommendations' was visible in that investors bought on 'temporary' dips and pullbacks and so displayed their renewed hunger to own stocks. The months of April and May witnessed very strong and aggressive buying (mainly by institutions) of big name stocks and another wave of buying later in the year. Both second and third quarter earnings results were good and the S&P held its ground from the euphoria earlier in the year. However, eager investors purchased stocks in advance of these results and felt justified in holding them. Bidding up stock prices from here is based on the possibility of *accelerated* earnings growth and not just a high level of satisfactory earnings. This expectation of an acceleration in earnings was largely justified as stocks enjoyed a good rally in the 1st quarter of 2004 and corporate earnings growth was solid.

The importance of the sizable US dollar fall should not be forgotten. There is an empirical issue here as to whether US stocks rise with a rising dollar and fall with a falling dollar? In theory, a foreigner wishes to purchase a US stock when the market is weak and desires a weak US dollar as well – in the hope that she will acquire a double layered gain – after both stocks and the dollar rises. The converse also appears true – the foreigner should sell when both US stocks and the US dollar are on highs. In 2001–2 there appears some evidence that US stock markets and the US dollar collapsed together. Foreigners wanted to get out of US dollar denominated assets as they feared a stampede would rob them of existing profits. However, during the months of March–May 2003 the US dollar continued to collapse and yet the US stock markets rallied strongly. Perhaps US residents felt more confident in buying US stocks than foreigners and were justified a few weeks later as the US dollar rallied against the Euro dollar – from 119 to around 109 by mid-2003. Earnings reports also encouraged the finance markets. However, a second wave of dollar selling in late 2003 and early 2004 – to 128 Euro and 105 Yen – made would-be investors in US assets very nervous and acted as a brake on the rise in US stock prices. The question remains as to how well US stocks can perform in a weak dollar environment?

What of a dollar collapse from here? A fall to 100 Yen and to 132 Euro will make many foreign investors nervous and create selling pressure on many US stocks – but not necessarily the exporters or global hunters. This is the substitution effect spoken of earlier – global investors may reorientate their portfolios towards Europe and Asia – holding less of a percentage in US stocks. This does not necessarily imply that US stock prices will collapse amidst this substitution effect but that other stock markets will rise faster and catchup to US stock levels and valuations. It should also be noted that in this scenario of global recovery it is unlikely that US stock prices will weaken in any substantial manner (the dollar not withstanding) as foreign economies and stock markets rally. As the world economic recovery becomes more synchronised so the US economy stands to gain.

The powerful policy stimulus

The Fed has long embarked on an expansionary monetary policy in order to create a cheap credit environment and so stimulate economy activity. As discussed earlier, the Fed funds rate has reached historic lows and yet the recovery in private sector investment has been tentative. Sales of interest-sensitive consumer durables did pick up but that was very much a function of aggressive marketing strategies and motor vehicle manufacturers seeking to clear existing stock immediately after September 11. Households took advantage of low and declining mortgage interest rates to refinance their homes. Extra liquidity could be easily tapped in a rising market and used to purchase home-related items and/or general consumption goods. There are also other channels through which lower interest rates have been effective – by reducing net interest payments made by US corporations to banks and by reducing the spread between corporate bond and government bond yields. Before Greenspan's aggressive interest rate cuts corporate bond yields were dangerously high – partly because investors demanded a higher premium for risk and were also worried about unfunded superannuation liabilities of several big US corporations. Hence, the cost of raising capital was excessively high in 2000–1. No wonder US corporations were unwilling to undertake major investments. Not only were expected rates of return poor and not 'visible' but the cost of raising funds in the post-bubble era was also prohibitive.

Although the effects, mentioned earlier of lower interest rates were quite significant for consumption, the response of private sector investment remained sluggish. Growth theory highlights the importance of modern, fresh vintage capital and high capital–labour ratio that drives medium term growth. The longer additions to the capital stock are delayed the less potent that stock becomes. Technological progress drives long-run growth but even that is often embodied in capital goods in some way. Analysts often point to past economic recoveries and to the central role played by a revival in capital goods spending – for the multiplier effects and chain reaction sent throughout the economy. *Why should this recovery be any different?* In fact, a subdued pick-up in private sector investment is the achilles heal of any potential economic recovery in the United States. The immediate future does not look bright either as excess capacity remains high in manufacturing and job destruction is rampant. Why should corporations invest in new capacity when existing capacity is plentiful and quite capable of quenching any sizable rise in final good demand?

Moreover, the supply-side excesses of the 1990s included both over-investment and mis-investment – in that too much money was placed in so-called investment areas that were never going to yield rates of return in line with expectations – if at all. Large portions of investment – particularly during the technology and telecommunications craze – were nothing short of wasted. Ambitions were over zealous and/or obscelence set in quickly. Projects soon became lemons. How does such mis-investment affect US corporations today? It has shaken their confidence, their balance sheet, their angry shareholders and their ability to borrow from banks. CFOs of major companies have become tight fisted as a result of the bubble era. Not only will the excesses of past take time to work off but also finding new, profitable investment opportunities in a challenging economic environment become more difficult – a legacy of mal-investment. There is the added cumulative constraint of major companies waiting for other major companies to flag intent to outlay more on investment – a game of 'wait and see' before becoming more aggressive on the capital outlay front. Such pessimism and delay was mainly confined to the 2000–2 era but as corporate-government bond yields have narrowed and stock prices risen, so too have US corporations become less hesitant concerning future commitments.

On the fiscal front, the US administration passed an aggressive lower tax and pro-spending bill through Congress. The main features of this Economic Growth and Tax Reform Reconciliation Act are as follows:

- Lower marginal income tax rates
- Child tax credit
- Married joint return relief
- Accelerated depreciation

- Increased expensing for small business
- Capital gain rate reduction for individuals
- Lower taxes of dividends.

The major objective of this 'Economic Growth' package is to reduce taxes and increase the potential to spend. It is both pro-consumer and pro-business. For example, lower marginal tax brackets fell from 15, 28, 31, 36 and 39.6 per cent to 10, 15, 25 and 33 per cent. Those eligible for the 10 per cent threshold have been given additional leeway with increased limits. Those with families were given higher allowances under the child credit scheme and the money was paid to them swiftly. Married people filing joint returns were granted higher thresholds and other benefits. For investors, the reduction the capital gains tax rates from the existing 20 and 10 per cent to 15 and 5 per cent respectively will encourage the buying and selling of more stocks. Likewise, the abolition of the double taxation of dividends is long overdue and will encourage a 'buy and hold' strategy towards stocks. However, some eligibility rules apply to holding periods. Not only are these initiatives valid now but most extend for much of the remaining decade and so can be considered semi 'permanent'. The business community gained relief through accelerated depreciation allowances mainly aimed at 2003–5 period – reducing inventory levels now in order that new durable goods orders would rise. The size of this stimulus must not be underestimated – it is huge by any modern day standard. However, as stated many times in this book – taking monetary and fiscal action to remedy income and spending *flows* may not be enough to offset serious damage to asset price *levels*. Moreover, *over- and mis-investment* can take many years to wear off before new investment springs to life – as past *over-capacity* still hangs over the reviving economy. Hence, economic revival may take longer than normal after a crash of an asset price bubble than a common excess inventory and demand flow slump.

Could the US post-bubble era be compared to that of Japan in the early 1990s? The answer is in some ways yes. As asset prices fell in Japan so did capital spending shrink for most years between 1991 and 2003. Private sector investment languished, as did construction spending that got caught in the down draught of the collapse in commercial real estate and the residential housing market. Consumption remained subdued for most of this period without collapsing. At least the sale of non-durables (daily items) held up while the sale of consumer durables remained patchy. Consumption was never going to be able to cover for the massive declines in investment spending. Japan attempted several fiscal stimuli but these also failed – both wasted and misdirected public investment and tax cuts that failed for reasons of fear. Hence, government spending did not offset the collapse in private investment either. As discussed earlier, exports did make a contribution to Japan staying afloat and current account surpluses with the United States were most welcome. Again, export success and current account surpluses were not enough to counteract the massive contraction in investment spending. Such is the devastation of asset price deflation. Modest changes in flows could not offset the huge damage in levels. The United States was in a similar position in 2003 – it too faces little prospect of an investment revival – and so additional reliance on consumption, government spending/tax cuts – and now under the unofficial 'weak dollar policy' a revival of export growth. It is here that we should note that Japan's export growth and healthy current account surplus were not enough to engineer an economic revival. So how can the United States expect the next boom to be underpinned by a weak dollar? We are left with the dilemma from history – how can there be a recovery without a significant rise in investment? We shall now examine the pros and cons of a continued US recovery into 2005–6.

The US economic recovery: where from here?

We have outlined the massive policy stimuli given to the US economy in terms of exceptionally low interest rates, money supply acceleration, tax cuts and a lower US dollar – all of which should raise the GDP growth rate over the medium term. By how much and for how long is the question? If these policy initiatives are short-lived or lack impact then GDP growth for the next five years may still be below that of the boom era (4 per cent) of the 1990s – at around 3 per cent. We know from earlier work that EPS growth is very much dependent on GDP growth. In 2004, 'looking forward' (apologies to Squark Box) investors are looking to justify a 7–8 per cent rise in EPS which implies a GDP growth of rate 4–5 per cent in the near term. Over the medium term – say five years – both growth rates should roughly converge. There are no free lunches here. As we discussed earlier, the very, very low Fed funds rate is putting a fairly safe *floor* on stock valuations in 2004 but the *ceiling* on stock valuations is determined by the *acceleration* in EPS justified by an *acceleration* in GDP growth. If sales and economic activity do not continue to rise through 2005–6 – the upswing of the cycle – then EPS will stagnate and so stock valuations will have to be revised downward. There are reasons to be cautious concerning a 'prolonged' recovery as there are forces at work that may choke a fledgling revival.

Reasons for caution
- Pricing power of US companies
- Capacity utilization
- Sluggish labour market
- Structural weakness – manufacturing
- Growing current account deficits
- Growing budget deficits
- Long end of yield curve
- Deflationary aftermath
- Earnings acceleration – limited?

All of these reasons for caution focus directly or indirectly on profitability. US markets have already priced in a recovery and next year's profit growth. Any hint that corporate profits will decelerate will also trigger a significant sell-off. America's structural imbalances may come home to roost and tap the over-optimistic investor on the shoulder. Massive monetary and fiscal expansion now implies contraction at some future time.

Reasons for optimism

- World recovery – synchronization
- Japan's revival?
- A weaker dollar
- Real estate boom
- China's explosion
- Lower world interest rates
- Fiscal expansions.

The quick actions of the Fed and its aggressiveness in pump priming the economy has been effective to date. Renshaw (1995) reminds us of the historical evidence in the US – that a positive real growth in the money supply and a budget deficit of 3.5% or more of GDP – are both highly related to a rise in stocks – in the pre 1990 era. Thus, the twin prong attack of monetary and fiscal policies have proved effective in the past. The current era should prove no different. After all, Greenspan made it clear around the debacle of September 11 that he would push people out of cash into assets. And that he did! The whole thrust of this book is that 'money matters' and post-bubble we are witnessing another wave of liquidity revitalizing the economy in tandem with real forces. Balance sheet damage and the threat of asset price deflation requires the Fed's aggression. All of this is good news for the US economy but that does not imply that 'bargains' exist in US stocks in 2004–5. Why? Because the stock markets are forward-looking and have extrapolated and factored in much of the good news. So, be careful!

Lessons from the movie: Wall Street

We should not listen to Gordon Gecko – greed is bad, greed is wrong and greed does not work! Greed traps our own ego and causes us to bend our trading rules and to abolish previously set limits. Greed causes us never to be satisfied regardless of our percentage gain. Greed causes us to become irrational and expedient when we should be calculating and exact. Greed biases us towards short-term and not long-term gain. We become too impatient too quickly. This book favours trading and riding various parts of the business cycle – with a balanced portfolio – and with patience. One does not have to 'buy and hold' forever, there are times when switching between asset classes is both wise and prudent. Therefore, 'Lou' out of 'Wall Street' – the fundamental and patient investor – has something to offer us here.

Conclusion

When evaluating the likelihood of a recovery in the US economy are there reasons to be optimistic? Consumption levels and consumer confidence have doggedly hung in there during some fairly uncertain times and in some ways defied the trend of a 'normal' recession. Although consumption was adversely affected by stock price declines – it has been positively supported by low interest rates, easy credit and easy home refinancing. Hence, the ongoing building boom is stimulating consumption on a broad front. The Bush administration initiatives on the fiscal front have been aggressive, substantial and effective in maintaining consumer spending and confidence. However, the impact on investment spending has been minor as of late 2003. A lower US dollar will assist export growth, and probably for some time to come as well, and so shrink the size of the current account deficit as a percentage of GDP.

Nevertheless, looking forward, there are also reasons to be pessimistic concerning any sustainable economic recovery in the United States. For example, China remains a threat to all manufacturing sectors throughout the world and not just the United States. Hence, the erosion of jobs in US manufacturing will be the norm for years to come. The recovery so far is jobless – companies have laid off workers in the quest for productivity. Creating jobs for the unskilled in America remains a great challenge for the policy-maker. There is also no reason to assume that China and Japan will continue to buy US bonds and so indirectly support US consumption and budget deficits. A weak dollar will eventually lead Chinese and Japanese investors to demand higher interest rates in the United States and this can only choke off an ongoing recovery in America. Although government forecasts for budget deficits over the next few years are optimistic – these should be viewed with skepticism – deficits may persist for years if GDP growth does not persist above a 3.5 per cent clip over those same years. More government and current account deficits may force interest rates higher despite Greenspan's efforts at the short end of the yield curve.

When evaluating the likelihood of a recovery in US stock prices we need to remind ourselves of *new trend line* debate highlighted earlier. If US stock *P/E* ratios have to revert to their long-run average of 14.5 then the S&P may have to retreat to 800 points or the Dow to 7,000 points. If so, this reversion to the long-run mean would entail huge capital losses for some and bankruptcies across the board. The real economy would collapse into recession. An adjustment of this magnitude is not likely. The reason is that this old trend line and mean is probably obsolete and a 'new' more recent trend line has appeared. An increase in productivity offers a partial explanation. The incentive biases covered in Chapter 1 provides some of the rest. Given that the excesses of the boom era have been mostly tamed it seems likely that a correction in *P/E* ratios should fall between the historic highs of 35 and long-term average of 14.5. A higher and established plateau of productivity growth combined with the recent massive tax incentives should underpin high *P/E* ratios and thus valuations – probably in the low-20s. Higher valuations may be justified with sustained GDP growth above 3.5 per cent and with the ten-year bond hovering around 4.5 per cent. Lower stock valuations and *P/E* ratios will stem from lower GDP growth and the possible rise in the ten-year bond to 5.5 per cent in 2004–5.

Perhaps we should respect what history teaches us and not pay *P/E* ratios of thirty or more for the S&P and conversely buy when this same ratio is around 15. This book has warned of the likelihood of mean reversion of EPS and *P/E* ratios based on historical evidence. There are channels and corridors to be respected – even though they may expand and contract over time due to technological waves and government policies. We now appear to be at the upper end of this corridor or band as large tax cuts have favoured financial investment. Therefore, the 'new' trend line for US *P/E* ratios could be around 20 but a retracement to the low teens is ever possible as it is still within the 'new' long-term trading range.

However, as the world recovery picks up ahead of steam then US corporations should do well as the OECD growth train becomes more synchronized with a self-fulfilling momentum. If so, the US stock markets – and the Dow multinationals in particular – should perform well in the light of increased world income. If the world recovery flounders and the structural weaknesses in the US economy are exposed (e.g. current account and budget deficits) then US stock prices will remain at the bottom end of the trading corridor. The optimal outcome for global investors is a synchronized world economic recovery and relative exchange rate stability – whereby economic momentum and demand is more evenly shared among the major world economies.

On a personal note, the investor needs to heed the lessons of diversification and corridor trading. It pays to diversify and that includes not only stocks but also real estate, bonds, gold, foreign stocks and a minor share in cash. US stocks will not always be a 'one-way street'. Second, while past *P/E* ratios may only serve as a loose guide, they do contain predictive content. It is not wise to pay and keep paying *P/E* ratios of thirty five and above for any length of time. It does pay to take profits from time to time and be content. When stocks rally 25 per cent or more within a short time frame – months – it is often wise to realize those gains within the confines of tax constraints and be satisfied. As stated before it also pays to keep an eye on your age – the closer you approach your retirement age so should your portfolio become more conservative and defensive in nature. If your retirement funds are disproportionately tied to the stock market at a mature age then you should improve your financial knowledge and monitor managed fund performance more closely – as well as the markets. The alternative is to seek greater diversification in your portfolio – stocks and other assets. Above all, watch out for the scissors – that of rising interest rates and decelerating profit growth that cuts and squeezes investors out of stocks and into bonds. Looking forward, the rise or fall of US stocks in 2005–6 will be determined by the relative acceleration of corporate earnings and interest rates – with the former rising faster than the latter if stocks are to rise. This also implies that GDP growth has to remain solid, the dollar not fall through the floor and the price of oil to retreat from $40 a barrel to the low 30s. Therefore, listening to Greenspan or the next 'span' at the Fed is an essential exercise in any investor's walk down Wall Street – even though terrorists and external threats may cloud the walk along the way.

Bibliography

Alles, L., Chang, R. and Koundiya, R. (1998), 'Debt finnacing by industrial firms in the Pacific Basion: an empirical study', Institute of International Competitiveness, *Discussion Paper Series*, 97: 07.

Asian Development Bank (2000), 'Asian Development Outlook 2000', Manila: Oxford University Press, p. 25.

Baker, D. (2000), 'Double bubble: the implications of the over valuation of the stock market and the Dollar', *Center for Economic Policy Research*, June, Washington, pp. 1–19.

Bank of Japan (2004), *Statistics and Other Key Statistics*, www.boj.or.jp/en/

Barsky, R. and De Long, J. (1990), 'Bull and bear markets in the twentieth century', *Journal of Economic History*, Vol: 50, pp. 265–81.

Bell, C. (2000), 'Web considerations for busy financial executives', *Solomon Software Company*.

Bergstein, F. (2000), 'White House Conference on New Economy', http://www.usembassy. state.gov/columbia/wwwhwhne.html, p. 17.

Bernanke, A. (1983), 'Non-monetary effects of the financial crisis in the propagation of the Great Depression', *American Economic Review*, Vol: 73, June, pp. 237–76.

Bernanke, B. and Gertler, M. (1995), 'Inside the black box: the credit channel of monetary policy transmission', *Journal of Economic Perspectives*, Vol: 9, pp. 27–48.

Berndt, E. and Morrison, C. (1995), 'High tech capital formation and economic performance in US manufacturing industries: an exploratory analysis', *Journal of Econometrics*, Vol: 65, pp. 177–82.

Blanchard, O. J. and Watson, M. W. (1982), 'Bubbles, rational expectations, and financial - markets', in *Crises in the Economic and Financial Structure*, D.C. Heath and Co, Lexington.

Blinder, A. (1997), 'What central bankers could learn from academics – and vice versa', *Journal of Economic Perspectives*, Vol: 11, p. 10, 15.

Bluestone, B. and Harrison, B. (1997), 'Can't we grow faster?', *The American Prospect Online*, http://www.prospect/archives/35/35, Vol: 8, No. 34, p. 2.

Brooks, J. (1999), *The Go-Go Years*, John Wiley and Sons, NY: p. 136.

Brynjolfsonn, E. and Hitt, L. (1993), 'Is information spending productive? new evidence and new results', *The Proceedings of the 14th International Conference on Information Systems*, Orlando, Florida, December 5–8, p. 51.

Buffet, W. and Cunningham, L. (1997), *The Essays of Warren Buffet: Lessons For Corporate America*, The Cunningham Group, New York, p. 205.

Canterbery, E. R. (1991), 'An evolutionary model of technical change with markup pricing', in *The Megacorp and Macrodynamics*, (William Milburg, Ed.), M.E. Sharpe:Armont, New York: pp. 87–100.

Canterbery, R. (1993), 'Reagonomics, saving and the casino effect', in *The Economics of Saving*, (James Gapinski Ed.), Kluwer Academic Publishers, Boston: p. 153–75, 169.

Canterbery, R. (1999), 'Irrational exuberance and rational speculative bubbles', *Journal of International Trade*, Vol: 13, p. 29; 1–33.

Canterbery, R. (2000a), *Wall Street Capitalism*, World Scientific Publishers, Covent Garden, London: p. 69.

Canterbery, R. (2000b), *Wall Street Capitalism*, World Scientific Publishers, Singapore: p. 19, 41, 195.

Cook, T. and Hahn, T. (1989), 'The Effect of Changes in the Federal Funds Rate Target on Market Interest Rates in the 1970's', *Journal of Monetary Economics*, 24 (November): 331–51.

Cooper, R. and Madden, G. (2004), 'Rational Expectations of ICT Investment', in Cooper, R. and Madden, G. (eds) *Frontiers of Broadband, Electronic and Mobile Commerce, Contributions to Economics Series, Physica-Verlag*, Heidelberg, pp. 267–84.

Corsetti, G., Presenti, P. and Roubini, N. (1998), 'What Caused the Asian Currency and Financial Crisis?', http://nroubini@stern.nyu.edu

Cunningham, L. (2002), *Outsmarting the Smart Money*, McGraw-Hill, NewYork, p. 140, 155.

David, P. (1990), 'The Dynamo and the Computer: An Historical Perspective on the Modern Productivity Paradox', *American Economic Review*, Vol: 80(2), pp. 351–61.

Diamond, D. and Dybvig, P. (1983), 'Bank runs, liquidity, and deposit insurance', *Journal of Political Economy*, Vol: 91, pp. 401–19.

Ely, B. (1996), A Hark Look at the Fed's Wizard of Oz, American Banker, February 15.

Fama, E. and French, K. (1988), 'Permanent and temporary components of stock prices', *Journal of Political Economy*, April, Vol: 22, pp. 3–25.

Fama, E. and French, K. (1992), 'The cross section of expected returns', *Journal of Finance*, Vol: 47, pp. 427–66.

Feldstein, M. (2003), 'Why is productivity growing faster?, *Journal of Policy Modeling*, North Holland, Vol: 25, pp. 445–51.

Field, A. (1984), 'Asset exchanges and the transactions demand for money, 1919–29', *American Economic Review*, March, Vol: 74, pp. 43–59.

Flood, R. and Garber, P. M. (1984), 'Collapsing exchange rate regimes: some linear examples', *Journal of International Economics*, Vol: 17, pp. 1–17.

Fox, L. (2003), *Enron*, John Wiley and Sons, New Jersey.

Friedman, M. (1953), 'The case for flexible exchange rates', in *Essays in Positive Economics*, University of Chicago Press, Chicago.

Friedman, M. (1968), 'The role of monetary policy', *American Economic Review*, March, Vol: 58, pp. 1–17.

Friedman, M. and Schwartz, A. (1963), *A Monetary History of the United States, 1867–1960*, Princeton University Press, Princeton.

Galbraith, J. K. (1998), *The Great Crash 1929*, Houghton Mifflin Company, Boston.

Gapinski, J. (1992), *Macroeconomic Theory: Statics, Dynamics and Policy*, McGraw-Hill, New York.

Gapinski, J. (1999), *Economic Growth in the Asia Pacific Region*, St. Martin's Press, New York.

Gecko, G. (1988), *Wall Street*, CBS FOX.

Greenspan, A. (1988a), 'US Federal Reserve, Greenspan's testimony', *US Senate Committee on Banking Housing and Urban Affairs*, March 31.

Greenspan, A. (1988b), 'US Federal Reserve, Greenspan's testimony', *US Senate Committee on Banking Housing and Urban Affairs*, March 31.

Greenspan, A. (1988c), 'US Federal Reserve, Greenspan's testimony', *US Senate Committee on Banking, Housing and Urban Affairs*, February 2.

Greenspan, A. (1990), 'US Federal Reserve, Greenspan's testimony', *US Senate's Committee on Finance*, February 27.

Greenspan, A. (1991), 'US Federal Reserve, Greenspan's testimony', *US Senate's Committee on Finance*, May 16.

Greenspan, A. (1993), 'US Federal Reserve, Greenspan's testimony', *US Senate's Committee on Finance*, March 24.

Greenspan, A. (1996), 'Humphrey-Hawkins report', *Federal Reserve Board*, December 16, p. 3.

Greenspan, A. (1997a), 'Monetary policy report to the congress', *Board of Governors of the Federal Reserve System*, p. 2.

Greenspan, A. (1997b), 'Budget of the US government', *US Economic Report of the President*, (2000), p. 103.

Greenspan, A. (1997c), 'Congressional testimony', http://www.commdocs.house.gov/committees/bank, p. 9.

Greenspan, A. (1997d), 'Federal Reserve, Greenspan's testimony', *U.S. House of Representative's Committee on the Budget*, October 8.

Greenspan, A. (1997e), 'Humphrey-Hawkins report', *Federal Reserve Board*, February 26, p. 3.

Greenspan, A. (1997f), 'Humphrey-Hawkins report', *Federal Reserve Board*, July 23, p. 6.

Greenspan, A. (1997g), 'Humphrey-Hawkins report', *Board of Governors of the Federal Reserve System*, July 22, p. 3–4, 5.

Greenspan, A. (1997h), 'US Federal Reserve, Greenspan's testimony,' *US House of Representatives Committee on the Budget*, October 8.

Greenspan, A. (1999a), 'Monetary policy report to the congress', *Board of Governors of the Federal Reserve System*, July 22, pp. 19–21.

Greenspan, A. (1999b), 'Humphrey-Hawkins report', *Board of Governors of the Federal Reserve System*, February 23, p. 7.

Greenspan, A. (1999c), 'Humphrey-Hawkins report', *Federal Reserve Board*, July 23, p. 6.

Greenspan, A. (1999d), 'Humphrey-Hawkins report', *The Federal Reserve Board*, February 23, p. 1.

Greenspan, A. (1999e), 'US Federal Reserve, Greenspan's testimony', *U.S. Senate Committee on Banking, Housing and Urban Affairs*, February 23.

Greenspan, A. (2000a), 'Humphrey-Hawkins report', *Board of Governors of the Federal Reserve System*, p. 3.

Greenspan, A. (2000b), 'Monetary policy report', *Board of Governors of the Federal Reserve System*, p. 23.

Greenspan, A. (2000c), 'Humphrey-Hawkins report', *Federal Reserve Board*, February 17, p. 4.

Greenspan, A. (2000d), 'Humphrey-Hawkins report', *The Federal Reserve Board*, July 20, p. 5.

Greenspan, A. (2000e), 'Humphrey-Hawkins report', *Board of Governors of the Federal Reserve Board*, July, p. 2.

Greenspan, A. (2003), 'Humphrey-Hawkins report', *Federal Reserve Board*, February 11, pp. 1–3.

Griliches, Z. (1988), 'Productivity puzzles and R and D: another non-explanation', *Journal of Economic Perspectives*, pp. 9–21; 43–69.

Grossman, G. and Helpman, E. (1991), 'Trade, knowledge spillovers and growth', *European Economic Review*, Vol: 35, pp. 517–26.

Hall, R. (1988), 'The relation between price and marginal cost in U.S. industry', *Journal of Political Economy*, Vol: 96, pp. 921–45.

Hall, R. (2000), 'The stock market and capital accumulation', *National Bureau of Economic Research*, May 12.

Hamilton, J. (1986), 'On testing for speculative price bubbles', *International Economic Review*, Vol: 27, pp. 545–52.

Hayakawa, H. and Maeda, E. (2000), 'Understanding Japan's financial and economic developments since Autumn 1997', *Working Paper Series*, Research and Statistics Department, Bank of Japan.

Hayes, D. (2000), 'Japan's big bang: the deregulation and revitalisation of the japanese economy', Tuttle Publishing, Boston.

Ibbotson, R. G. and Sinquefield, R. A. (2002), *The Stocks, Bonds, Bills and Inflation Yearbook 2002*, Chicago.

Johnson, H. (1976), 'Destabilizing speculation: a general equilibrium approach', *Journal of Political Economy*, Vol: 84, p. 101.

Jorgenson, D. (1988), 'Productivity and postwar US economic growth', *Journal of Economic Perspectives*, Vol: 2, No. 4, pp. 23–41.

Jorgenson, D. and Stiroh, K. (1995), 'Computers and growth', *Economics of Innovation and New Technology*, Vol: 3, pp. 295–316.

Jorgenson, D., Mun, S. and Stiroh K. (2003), 'Lessons from the US growth resurgence', *Journal of Policy Modeling*, North Holland, Vol: 25, pp. 453–70.

Kaufman, H. (2000), *On Money and Markets*, McGraw Hill, NY: p. 54.

Keynes, J. (1936), *The General Theory of Employment, Interest and Money*, Harcourt, Brace and World, New York.

Kindleberger, C. (1978), *Manias, Panics and Crashes: A History of Financial Crises*, Basic Books, New York: p. 61, 132.

King, R. and Plosser, C. (1984), 'Money, credit and prices in a real business cycle', *American Economic Review*, 64 (June): pp. 363–8.

King, R. and Rebelo, S. (1990), 'Public policy and economic growth: developing neoclassical implications', *Journal of Political Economy*, Vol: 98, pp. 127–49.

Kopczuk, W. and Saez, E. (2004), 'Top wealth share in the United States, 1916–2000: evidence from Estate Tax Returns', http://www.Elsa.Berkley.edu/^saez/estateshort/pd

Krugman, P. (1994), 'The myth of Asia's miracle', *Foreign Affairs*, Vol: 73, pp. 62–78.

Krugman, P. (1996), 'Stay on their backs', *New York Times Magazine*, February 4, p. 3.

Krugman, P. (1998), 'Japan's Trap', http://web.mit.edu/krugman/www/jpage.html.

Krugman, P. (1999), 'Its baaack: Japan's slump and the return of the liquidity trap', http://web.mit.edu/krugman/www/jpage.html

Lo, A. and MacKinlay, C. (1988), 'Stock markets do not follow random walks', *Review of Financial Studies*, Spring.

Lucas, R. (1976), 'Econometric policy evaluation: a critique', *Carnegie-Rochester Conference Series on Public Policy*, Vol: 1, pp. 19–46.

Lucas, R. (1988), 'On the mechanics of economic development', *Journal of Monetary Economics*, Vol: 22, pp. 3–42.

Lucas, R. (1989), 'Why doesn't capital flow from rich to poor countries?' *American Economic Review*, Vol: 80, pp. 92–8.

Lucas, R. (1993), 'In making a miracle', in *Econometrica*, Vol: 61, 251–72.

Malkiel, B. (1999), *A Random Walk Down Wall Street*, W.W. Norton and Co, NY.

Mankiw, G. (2003), *Macroeconomics, Worth Publishers*, New York, pp. 296–7.

Marquis, M. (1996), *Monetary Theory and Policy*, West Publishing Company, St Paul, MN: p. 29, 60.

Meltzer, A. (1995), 'Monetary, credit and (other) transmission processes: a monetarist perspective', *Journal of Economic Perspectives*, Vol: 9, pp. 49–72.

Miller, P. and Schmitz, J. (1996), 'Breaking down the barriers to technological progress', *Federal Reserve of Minneapolis*, Annual Report Essay, p. 7.

Minsky, H. (1986), *Stabilizing an Unstable Economy*, Yale University Press, New Haven.

Montes, M. F. (1998), *The Currency Crisis in South East Asia*, Singapore: Institute of South East Asian Studies (ISEAS).

Nakagawa, S. and Oshima, K. (2000), 'Does a decrease in the real interest rate actually stimulate personal consumption?' *Working Paper Series*, Research and Statistics Department, Bank of Japan.

Obstefeld, M. (1994), 'The logic of currency crises', *Cashiers Economiques et Monetaires* (Bank De Fance, Paris) Vol: 2, pp. 369–450.

Oliner, S. and Sichel, D. (1994), 'Computers and output growth revisited: how big is the puzzle?' *Brookings Papers on Economic Activity*, Vol: 2, pp. 273–334.

Oliner, S. and Sichel, D. (2000), 'The resurgence of growth in the late 1990s: is information technology the story', *Board of Governors of the Federal Reserve System*, May.

Olson, M. (1988), 'The productivity slowdown, the oil shocks, and the real cycle', *Journal of Economic Perspectives*, Vol: 2, No. 4, pp. 43–69.

Organization of Economic Development, *OECD Economic Outlook*, various issues, Paris.

Pack, H. (1994), 'Endogenous growth theory: intellectual appeal and empirical shortcomings', *Journal of Economic Perspectives*, Vol: 8, pp. 55–72.

Plosser, C. (1989), 'Understanding real business cycles', *Journal of Economic Perspectives*, Vol: 3, 51–77.

Poterba, J. and Summers, L. (1988) 'Mean reversion in stock prices: evidence and implications', *Journal of Financial Economics*, No. 22, pp. 27–59.

Rebelo, S. (1991), 'Long run policy analysis and long run growth', *Journal of Political Economy*, Vol: 99, pp. 500–21.

Renshaw, E. (1995), 'The stock market's reaction to monetary and fiscal policy', Essay 11S, http://www.albany.edu./^renshaw/stk/stk11S, pp. 1–4.

Ribstein, L. E. (2002), 'Market vs. regulatory responses to corporate fraud: a critique of the Sarbanes-Oxley Act of 2002', *Illinois Law and Economics Working Paper Series* No. LE02–008. p. 5.

Roach, S. (1987), 'America's white-collar productivity dilemma', *Manufacturing Engineering*, August, p. 104.

Roggoff, (1996), 'The purchasing power parity puzzle', *Journal of Economic Literature*, Vol: 36, pp. 647–68.

Romer, C. (1993), 'The Nation in Depression', *Journal of Economic Perspectives*, Vol: 7, pp. 19–39.

Romer, C. and Romer, D. (1994), 'Does monetary policy matter? a new test in the spirit of Friedman and Shwartz', *NBER Macroeconomics Annual*, Vol: 4: pp. 121–70.

Romer, P. (1991), 'Endogenous technological change', *Journal of Political Economy*, Vol: 98, pp. 71–102.

Roubini, N. (1996), 'Japan's Economics Crisis', http://stern.nyu.edu.globalmacro

Roubini, N. (2000), 'Productivity growth, its slowdown in the 1973–90 period and its resurgence in the 1990s: truth or statistical fluke?' *Productivity Growth in the 1990s*, http://www.stern.nyu.edu

Schiller, R. (2000), *Exuberance*, Scribe Publications, Melbourne.

Sergerstrom, P. (1991), 'Innovation, imitation, and economic growth', *Journal of Political Economy*, Vol: 99, pp. 808–27.

Shiller, R. (1999), *Irrational Exuberance*, Princeton University Press, Princeton.

Shleifer, A. and Summers, L. (1990) 'The noise trader approach to finance', *Journal of Economic Perspectives*, Vol: 4, pp. 19–33.

Sicilia, B. and Cruikshank, J. (2000), *The Greenspan Effect*, McGraw-Hill Publishers, New York: pp. 6, 41, 197, 214.

Siegal, D. (1997), 'The impact of computers on manufacturing productivity growth: a multi-causes approach', *Review of Economics and Statistics,* Feburary, Vol: 79 (1), pp. 68–78.

Siegal, J. (2000), *Stocks for the Long Run*, Barnes and Noble, May.

Siegal, J. (2002), *Stocks for the Long Run*, 3rd Edition, McGraw-Hill, New York.

Sicilia, B. and Cruikshank. (2000), *The Greenspan Effect*, McGraw-Hill Publishers, New York.

Smithers, A. and Wright, D. (2000), *Valuing Wall Street*, McGraw-Hill.

Solow, R. (1957), 'Technical Change and the Aggregate Production Function', *Review of Economic Statistics*, Vol: 39, pp. 312–20.

Stiglitz, J. (2002), *The Roaring Nineties*, The Atlantic, W.W. Norton and Co, NY.

Taylor, J. (1998), 'An historical analysis of monetary rules', *NBER Working Paper 6768*, Cambridge, MA.

Taylor, J. (1998), 'Review', *Federal Reserve Board of St. Louis*, November.

Temin, P. (1993), 'Transmission of the Great Depression', *Journal of Economic Perspectives*, Vol: 7 (2), pp. 87–102.

Thurow, L. (1992), *Head to Head*, Warner Books, New York.

Thurow, L. (1996a), 'The crusade that's killing prosperity', *The American Online Prospect*, March–April, p. 1.

Thurow, L. (1996b), *The Future of Capitalism*, Nicholas Brealey Publishing, London, pp. 186, 221, 301.

Tobin, J. (1978), 'A proposal for international monetary reform', *Eastern Economic Journal*, Vol: 4, pp. 13–25.

Western, D. L. (2000), *East Asia: Growth, Crisis and Recovery*, World Scientific Publishers, Singapore.

White, E. N. (1990), 'The stock market boom and crash of 1929 revisited', *Journal of Economic Perspectives*, Vol: 4 (2), pp. 67–84.

Index

International Journal of the Economics of Business

EDITOR
Eleanor J. Morgan, *University of Bath, UK*

NORTH AMERICAN EDITOR
H.E. Frech III, *University of California, USA*

The *International Journal of the Economics of Business* presents original research in economics that is clearly applicable to business and related public policy problems or issues. The *International Journal of the Economics of Business* publishers papers relating to three main spheres: **the organisation** - to analyse and aid decision-making and the internal organisation of the business; **the industry** - to analyse how businesses interact and evolve within and across industries; and **the external environment** - to show how public policy, technological developments and other outside forces affect business behaviour.

This journal is also available online.
Please connect to www.tandf.co.uk/online.html for further information.

To request a sample copy please visit: **www.tandf.co.uk/journals**

SUBSCRIPTION RATES
2004 – Volume 11 (3 issues)
Print ISSN 1357-1516 Online ISSN 1466-1829
Institutional rate: US$506; £315 (includes free online access)
Personal rate: US$128; £80 (print only)
A preferential rate is available to accredited individual members of the Society for Business Economists, the International Society for New Institutional Economics (ISNIE) and also to the Industrial Organization Society and EUNIP. Please contact the publisher for details.

Please contact Customer Services at either:
Taylor & Francis Ltd, Rankine Road, Basingstoke, Hants RG24 8PR, UK
Tel: +44 (0)1256 813002 **Fax:** +44 (0)1256 330245 **Email:** enquiry@tandf.co.uk **Website:** www.tandf.co.uk

Taylor & Francis Inc, 325 Chestnut Street, 8th Floor, Philadelphia, PA 19106, USA
Tel: +1 215 6258900 **Fax:** +1 215 6258914 **Email:** info@taylorandfrancis.com **Website:** www.taylorandfrancis.com